Hosea Stout

Hosea Stout
Lawman, Legislator, Mormon Defender

STEPHEN L. PRINCE

UTAH STATE UNIVERSITY PRESS
Logan

© 2016 by the University Press of Colorado

Published by Utah State University Press
An imprint of University Press of Colorado
5589 Arapahoe Avenue, Suite 206C
Boulder, Colorado 80303

 The University Press of Colorado is a proud member of
The Association of American University Presses.

The University Press of Colorado is a cooperative publishing enterprise supported, in part, by Adams State College, Colorado State University, Fort Lewis College, Metropolitan State College of Denver, Regis University, University of Colorado, University of Northern Colorado, Utah State University, and Western State College of Colorado.

All rights reserved
First paperback edition 2016

ISBN: 978-1-60732-476-8 (cloth)
ISBN: 978-1-60732-477-5 (e-book)
ISBN: 978-1-60732-640-3 (paperback)

Library of Congress Cataloging-in-Publication Data

Names: Prince, Stephen L.
Title: Hosea Stout : lawman, legislator, Mormon defender / Stephen Prince.
Description: Logan : Utah State University Press, 2016 | Includes bibliographical references.
Identifiers: LCCN 2015033645 | ISBN 9781607324768 (cloth) | ISBN 9781607324775 (ebook) | ISBN 9781607326403 (paperback)
Subjects: LCSH: Stout, Hosea, 1810–1889. | Mormon pioneers—Utah—Biography. | Frontier and pioneer life—Utah. | Mormons—Utah—Biography. | Legislators—Utah—Biography. | Peace officers—Illinois—Nauvoo—Biography. | Mormon Church—History—19th century. | Utah—History—19th century. | Nauvoo (Ill.)—History—19th century.
Classification: LCC F826.S76 P75 2016 | DDC 979.2/02092—dc23
LC record available at http://lccn.loc.gov/2015033645

The University Press of Colorado gratefully acknowledges the generous support of the Charles Redd Center for Western Studies at Brigham Young University toward the publication of this book.

Front cover photograph of Hosea Stout, ca. 1860, by Edward Martin. Back cover photograph of Hosea Stout, ca. 1852, photographer unknown. Photographs courtesy the Utah State Historical Society.

Contents

List of Illustrations   *vii*
Preface   *ix*

Introduction   3
1. Shaker Education   7
2. Reunion and Abandonment   17
3. Quakers and Methodists   29
4. Introduction to Mormonism   45
5. Fight and Flight   55
6. Refuge in Illinois   71
7. Rising through the Ranks   83
8. Policing Nauvoo   105
9. The Trek across Iowa   121
10. Winter Quarters   135
11. The Pinnacle of Violence   149
12. Crossing the Plains   161
13. Attorney and Legislator   173
14. Mission to China   197
15. Lawyer and Legislator   223
16. Reformation and Winds of War   243
17. Resisting the Feds   265
18. The Attorney of the Mormon Church   279
19. The Cotton Mission   301
20. Last Hurrah   325

Epilogue   *343*
Appendix   *347*
Bibliography   *353*
About the Author   *369*
Index   *371*

Illustrations

1.1.	Pleasant Hill Community	10
2.1.	Area of the Early Years of Hosea Stout, map	26
3.1.	Charles C. Rich (1809–1883). Rich was an LDS Church Apostle, and Rich County in the Bear Lake region near the Utah/Idaho border was named after him.	37
7.1.	A Portrait of Hosea Stout, 1845, by Robert Campbell	84
12.1.	Route of Hosea Stout from Nauvoo to the Valley of the Great Salt Lake, map	162
13.1.	Early Utah Settlements, map	174
13.2.	Hosea Stout, ca. 1852	175
13.3.	Seth M. Blair (1819–1875). A prominent attorney in territorial Utah, Blair was US District Attorney from 1850 to 1854 and, with Hosea Stout and James Ferguson, cofounded *The Mountaineer*.	185
13.4.	Hosea Stout residence located on Second East, just south of Brigham Street (South Temple). Hosea rushed to complete the house in 1853 before leaving on his mission to China and returned to find strangers living there, his wife and infant son dead, and his family scattered.	191
14.1.	Louisa Taylor Stout (1819–1853). Second wife of Hosea and mother of eight of his children. Four of her children died in infancy or early childhood.	201
14.2.	Family of Hosea and Louisa Stout	203
15.1.	Alvira Wilson Stout, (1834–1910), 1898. Sixth wife of Hosea and mother of eleven of his children. She outlived her husband by twenty-one years.	227
15.2.	Family of Hosea and Alvira Stout	228
16.1.	James Ferguson (1828–1863). With Seth M. Blair and Hosea Stout, Ferguson co-founded *The Mountaineer*.	248

16.2.	Utah Territorial Militia (The Nauvoo Legion). Hosea Stout was an officer in the Nauvoo Legion in Nauvoo and was judge advocate in Utah.	254
17.1.	Daniel H. Wells, co-defendant of Hosea's in the 1872 Richard Yates murder trial.	268
17.2.	Brigham Young	269
18.1.	Hosea Stout, ca. 1860	281
19.1.	Allen Joseph Stout (1815–1899). Hosea Stout's younger brother.	302
19.2.	Hosea Stout, ca. 1870	303
20.1.	Hosea Stout, ca. 1855	327

Preface

I first became acquainted with the historical man Hosea Stout while doing research for my book, *Gathering in Harmony*. I became fascinated with Stout, whose journal was of great interest to me due to his marriage to a sister of one of my direct ancestors, resulting in many entries that were of great use to me in my previous writing. As I delved into the subject, I found Hosea Stout to be complicated, controversial, and surprisingly important in early Utah and Mormon history. Even more surprising was the lack of a true biography (the one existing biography, *Hosea Stout: Utah's Pioneer Statesman*, by his great-grandson Wayne Stout, is for the most part a rewording of Hosea's journal).

Hosea Stout, before his diary was published, was a relatively obscure figure in Mormon history. "His name turned up consistently in Mormon annals," wrote Dale L. Morgan in his review of the published diary, "but none of the standard biographical works contained a notice of him, and what manner of person he was, few could have guessed." Morgan hit the nail on the head, for reasons I will detail after a brief summary of Stout's personal writings.

Stout was baptized into the Church of Jesus Christ of Latter-day Saints in 1838 in Missouri. In 1845 he wrote a brief autobiography for the Eleventh Quorum of Seventies in Nauvoo and nearly two years later wrote another, shorter autobiography covering his earliest years. The two autobiographies were edited by his great-grandson Reed Stout and were published in serial form in the *Utah Historical Quarterly* in 1962. Peter DeLafosse of the University of Utah Press asked me to re-edit the autobiographies, to which I agreed, in the process correcting some very minor mistakes in the previous editing while adding about thirty footnotes. In 2009, the Press reprinted in paperback Stout's journal, *On the Mormon Frontier*, originally edited by Juanita Brooks and published by the Press in 1964 and first reprinted in 1982. Peter believed that the journal, the autobiographies, and a biography, taken together, would complement and strengthen each other.

Some might consider the monumental two-volume *On the Mormon Frontier* the last word on the subject of Hosea Stout. If so, they would be greatly uninformed concerning Stout's life, the role he played in Mormon and Utah history, and how much of his history is not contained in his journal. His journal commences in October 1844 and, with the exception of very brief entries in 1860–1861 and 1869, basically concludes with his entry on Christmas Day 1859. Given that Stout was very active in Utah legal and governmental affairs until a few years before his death in 1889, it is quite obvious that much of his history is untouched by his journal. In addition, his journal, while particularly heavy in details of early Utah political history, presents at best only an outline of his own life.

Stout's first major responsibility in the Mormon Church was serving in 1841 as clerk of the Nauvoo, Illinois, High Council, an ecclesiastical governing body. While still serving in that capacity, he was chosen to be the "recorder," or clerk, of the fledgling Nauvoo Legion, the Latter-day Saints' militia, and so he penned all written records of the legion's early organizational meetings. He rose in the ranks and was promoted to acting brigadier general following the assassinations of Joseph and Hyrum Smith. Shortly afterward he was made captain of police at Nauvoo, guarding church leaders and the city from a threatening mob of anti-Mormons, and in that position he directed the first crossings of the Mississippi River during the exodus from Nauvoo in February 1846. He subsequently also headed police work at Winter Quarters, Nebraska, where the Mormon camp temporarily settled on its way west.

Arriving in Utah in 1848, Stout acted as Brigham Young's attorney and became the first attorney general when Utah was organized as a territory. He was a member of the Utah Territorial Legislature, from 1856 to 1857 was speaker of its House of Representatives, was a regent for the University of Deseret, and served as the judge advocate of the Nauvoo Legion in Utah. Brigham Young frequently counseled with him, relied on his advice, and called on his services to defend the interests of the church, to the point that the *New York Times*, while reporting his appointment as interim United States Attorney for Utah, labeled him "the attorney of the Mormon Church." Primarily through legal and political maneuvering, in which Stout played a central role, the Mormons for decades held off non-Mormon and federal efforts to destroy polygamy and undermine the religion and thereby bought valuable time to settle Utah, construct a government, build an economy, and establish a firm foothold from which the church ultimately prospered. He was particularly influential as an attorney during the occupation of Utah in the late 1850s by the US Army, fighting for the interests of the church against some antagonistic federal judges.

In 1862, President Abraham Lincoln appointed Stout US Attorney for the Territory of Utah. Also in 1862, Brigham Young sent him to southern Utah as a member of the Cotton Mission in which several hundred members were called to go south to colonize the Virgin River Basin and to grow cotton. There he served as St. George's first city attorney as well as president of the St. George High Council. In 1867 he returned to Salt Lake City where he promptly became the city attorney; and in 1881 he capped his career by being elected (at the age of seventy-one) to a final two-year term in the Utah House of Representatives.

Despite his published journal, little attention has been given in the past to Hosea Stout. *On the Mormon Frontier* is widely quoted and is viewed by historians as an important glimpse of Mormon and Utah history, presenting far greater detail on many things than is otherwise available, but many of these same historians know precious little of the author himself. Though he was controversial due to his sharp temper and a number of self-admitted violent actions, he also was a devoted follower and defender of the faith who contributed to the church's kingdom through persistence, reliability, and self-taught legal acumen.

Hosea Stout

Introduction

It was the middle of winter 1846 when the Mormons in Nauvoo, Illinois, began the exodus from their beloved city. The weather in early February was exceptionally mild as the evacuation commenced under the direction of captain of police Hosea Stout. The first wagons rolled out of Nauvoo on February 4; the exiles were ferried across the Mississippi River to Iowa around the clock on a makeshift fleet of vessels including flat boats, old lighters and skiffs and set up camp seven miles inland at Sugar Creek. They were greeted in Iowa by increasingly cold, wet and bitter weather. By the time Mormon leader Brigham Young arrived on the Iowa side on February 15, the mud was so deep that his teams had to be yoked double to pull the wagons up the hill to the Sugar Creek camp.

On February 24 the temperature dropped to twelve degrees below zero, and by the next day the Mississippi River had frozen over. Many wagons that had lined up at the river front waiting to be ferried to Iowa seized the opportunity and scurried across the ice. Within a few days, however, the temperature moderated, melting the frozen river and creating ice floes that complicated the crossing. Nevertheless, more than three thousand evacuated Nauvoo during the month.

Brigham Young held councils almost nightly at Sugar Creek to make plans for orderly travel of the refugees across Iowa. With an eye on security and fearing that enemies might cross the Mississippi River to attack the refugees, Young organized a guard, headed by Hosea Stout, with instructions to encircle the camp and to allow no one to leave after dark without an officially signed permit.[1] Stout also placed a guard at the bridge to the council tent where leaders met.

Among those in camp who possessed considerable knowledge of Iowa was Bishop George Miller,[2] who in 1840 had scouted the Des Moines River on assignment from Joseph Smith.[3] Miller actively participated in councils making travel plans, but he was a strong-willed man who, in the words of fellow traveler Reddick Allred, kept "showing his bullheadedness."[4] Frustrated with repeated delays and changes in plans, Miller became increasingly critical of Brigham Young; conversely, Young viewed Miller as unmanageable and at one point during the trip threatened to expel him from the church for "disobedience."[5]

Despite his contention with Young and others, Miller was astonished one night when Howard Egan, formerly a member of the Nauvoo police as well as one of Joseph Smith's bodyguards, informed him that "orders had been issued by Hosea Stout to all the sentinels" to kill Miller and throw him into the creek if he tried to cross the bridge that led to the council tent. That sent Miller into a rage, and he immediately approached the tent when the sentinel on the bridge challenged him. Identifying himself as the one who was to be killed and thrown into the creek, Miller preemptively took the sentinel by the arms and threw him to the floor of the bridge.

After entering the council tent, Miller demanded of Brigham Young to know what orders had been given the guards. Young pled ignorance but summoned Stout and some of the guards to try to resolve the issue. Stout admitted to saying, "Let all those who pass the bridge to council go unmolested, except Bishop Miller; kill him and throw him over the bridge." He claimed, however, that it was said "by way of a joke," and he assumed that it had been understood as such since he "had spoken at his usual tone of voice, and in a public way." For their part, the guards "did not know whether Stout had been joking or not," but "were inclined to think he was joking," mainly because "it seemed to them a very strange order."[6]

It was a very strange order indeed, particularly among a people united in purpose and direction, but it is notable that the guards, with full knowledge of Stout and his reputation, were not certain it was a joke. Hosea Stout—called Hosey by his friends—was a complex man who had a tender side with genuine love for his family and an enduring love for his religion, but at the same time he was an imposing figure with a sharp temper, ready at all times to rebuke through force. Hawkins Taylor, sheriff of Lee County, Iowa, referred to him as a "great tall man."[7] A daguerreotype made of Stout in 1851 revealed, in the words of historian Dale Morgan, a "personal intensity verging upon fanaticism, his toughness of fiber, the male impact of his being."[8] A passport issued to Stout in 1852 described his appearance in mostly unremarkable terms—sound face and forehead, common nose, dented chin, large mouth, black hair, dark complexion—with the exception of his eyes, which were deeply set and so dark that they were listed on the passport not as brown but as black.[9] They also were crossed, and while the weak eye seemed unfocused, even looking past the object of Stout's attention, his strong, penetrating eye gave the immediate impression that it could pierce one's soul. One glance at him was enough to tell that this was a man who had to be taken very seriously.

Notes

1. Brooks, *On the Mormon Frontier*, 124.
2. George Miller was chosen to succeed Edward Partridge as the second General Bishop of the Church of Jesus Christ of Latter-day Saints on January 19, 1841, and henceforth was typically addressed as Bishop George Miller. See *Historical Record* 7:480; also *Contributor*, August 1885, vol. 6 no. 11.
3. *The Latter-day Saints Millennial Star* (London), 1:231–33.
4. Reddick N. Allred, "Journal," MS 18174, Historical Department of the Church of Jesus Christ of Latter-day Saints (hereafter known as Church History Library).
5. Smith, Smith, and Edwards, eds., *The History of the Reorganized Church of Jesus Christ of Latter-Day Saints* 2:791; Mills, "De Tal Palo Tal Astilla," *Historical Society of Southern California Annual Publications* 10:23. Throughout this book the word Church is capitalized when used as a shortened version of and in reference to the Church of Jesus Christ of Latter-day Saints.
6. Mills, "De Tal Palo Tal Astilla."
7. Hallwas and Launius, *Cultures in Conflict: A Documentary History of the Mormon War in Illinois*, 54.
8. Morgan, "A Western Diary," *American West* 2, no. 2:46.
9. United States Passport issued to Hosea Stout in 1852, "Hosea Stout Papers," Utah State Historical Society. Stout obtained the passport after having been called in August 1852 to serve on a mission in China.

1
Shaker Education

Hosea Stout's father, Joseph, was a third-generation Quaker whose grandfather, Peter Stout, was so devout that he was known simply as "Peter the Quaker."[1] Joseph's parents, Samuel and Rachel, also were firmly entrenched in the religion, but one day after his twenty-second birthday, on July 18, 1795, Joseph was disowned by the Quakers for his activity in fighting Creek and Cherokee Indians with an east Tennessee militia.[2] He soon returned to his native North Carolina to live with his aunt, Pleasant Smith, and while there he fell in love with his first cousin, Pleasant's eighteen-year-old daughter Anna. As the relationship progressed, the mother was placed in a quandary because she, as a Quaker, could not sanction or even attend the wedding of her daughter to a non-Quaker, and Joseph, having been disowned, was no longer a member of the faith.

Under the circumstances, Joseph and Anna decided to elope, marrying on November 3, 1798.[3] As a consequence, Anna also was disowned by the religion. Following their elopement, Joseph and Anna returned and were received by her mother, but the relationship was strained. Disowned by their religion, no longer welcome at home and undoubtedly poor, the young couple looked westward, across the Blue Ridge Mountains to east Tennessee.

Returning to his former environs was an obvious move for Joseph, since at least six of his siblings resided there.[4] Moreover, Tennessee was granted statehood on June 1, 1796, as the threat of Indian warfare steadily disappeared and the number of free inhabitants exceeded sixty thousand, the minimum population that was considered essential to becoming a state.[5] By 1798 various cessations of Indian land had been negotiated, resulting in large tracts of fresh and often fertile land becoming available for settlement. Between 1790 and 1800, Tennessee's growth rate exceeded that of the nation, as each successive Indian treaty opened up a new frontier. During that period the population in the state tripled, from 35,691 to 105,602, as emigrants from the Atlantic states sought to take advantage of the cheap land, fertile soil, and milder climate that Tennessee offered.[6] Yet its rapid population growth scarcely compared with that of the neighboring state of Kentucky, which was growing three times faster than Tennessee as settlers streamed through the Cumberland Gap into the region known as the Bluegrass.

Much of the land in Kentucky was similar to Tennessee, dominated by great deciduous forests dotted with majestic evergreens. Along the rivers in Kentucky there were great stands of canebrake—the only bamboo native to the United States—sometimes two to three miles wide and one hundred miles long, but the region that generated the most superlatives was the famed Bluegrass. Though it is actually green, when seen from a distance in the spring, its bluish-purple grass buds can, in large fields, give it a rich blue tinge.

Early pioneers found bluegrass growing on Kentucky's rich limestone soil, and traders began asking for the seed of the "blue grass from Kentucky." Felix Walker, who later became a US Congressman from North Carolina, wrote in 1775 of "the pleasing and rapturous appearance of the plains of Kentucky . . . covered with clover in full bloom, the woods abounding with wild game—turkeys so numerous that it might be said they appeared but one flock."[7] In 1802, when French botanist Francois-Andre Michaux made a scientific expedition through the region, its population already was as great as seven of the original states of the union, though Kentucky didn't gain statehood—as a commonwealth—until June 1, 1792.[8] Indeed, so many settled in the young state from other regions that Michaux noted, "perhaps there cannot be found ten individuals twenty-five years of age, who were born there."[9]

While in Tennessee, Joseph and Anna had five children—Rebecca, Sarah, Samuel (who died at a very young age), and twins Mary and Margaret.[10] A few months after the birth of the twins, Joseph and Anna Stout joined the migration through the Cumberland Gap to Kentucky, settling in Madison County, where they had a daughter, Anna, and a son, Daniel, who like his brother Samuel died when he was very young.[11] They then moved to neighboring Mercer County, in the heart of the Bluegrass Region of Kentucky about five miles from the Shaker village of Pleasant Hill, where on September 18, 1810, their son Hosea was born.

Though widely considered to be an American institution, Shakerism actually began in England in 1747 as the outcome of a Quaker revival. Ann Lee (whose name was shortened from Lees when she settled in America) was an illiterate blacksmith's daughter from the slums of Manchester who at the age of twenty-two joined an obscure group of dissident Quakers. Members of the group were very animated in their religious expressions; a British newspaper reporter who attended a service in 1758—the year

Ann Lee joined the group—was so taken by the group's vigorous physical gyrations that he derisively called them "Shaking Quakers," from which the name Shakers derived.

Though Ann Lee married and had four children, each child died in infancy and her marriage to a heavy-handed, crude blacksmith was very unhappy. She walked the floors at night in an agony of remorse and became convinced that her miserable station in life was due to divine judgments on her sexual desires. She began to proclaim that "cohabitation of the sexes" was a cardinal sin and espoused a belief in celibacy.[12]

Mother Ann, as she became known after she assumed leadership of the sect, immigrated to America in 1774, settling in New York. Despite some defections after her death in 1784, the Society of Believers, as they called themselves, gained momentum and thrived in upstate New York and New England. Seeking to expand westward, on New Year's Day 1805 three strangely dressed Shaker men set out on a journey from Mt. Lebanon, New York, to southern Ohio and Kentucky.

The missionaries encountered their first success in Warren County, Ohio. Later that year, three farmers in Mercer County, Kentucky were converted; one of them, Elisha Thomas, subsequently donated 140 acres to the Believers near a creek known as Shawnee Run, a land replete with fertile soil, abundant fresh water, virgin timber, stone, and clay. Over the next several years another four thousand acres of some of the finest land in Mercer County were donated, on a rolling plateau high above the deeply slashed gorge of the palisades along the Kentucky River, providing the location for the village of Pleasant Hill.[13]

At the very moment the Pleasant Hill community began to succeed, Kentucky became deeply involved in the War of 1812.[14] Kentuckians jumped into the conflict with great zeal but with little appreciation of the financial strain that the war would place upon the commonwealth.[15] The war initially spurred economic prosperity in Kentucky, but by 1814, as the war began to wind down, financial difficulties threatened many with ruin. So it was with Joseph Stout, who about a year after the birth of their daughter Cynthia "had bad luck, from sickness and other misfortunes, which quite discouraged him; and induced him to put his children out."[16]

The Shaker practice of celibacy precluded growth through procreation; therefore they could expand their numbers only through conversion or adoption. Though the recruitment of orphans did not commence until 1833, the Shakers at Pleasant Hill were very willing to take in children when the opportunity presented itself.[17] Having been disowned by their former Quaker religion, Joseph and Anna were not alarmed when their oldest daughter, sixteen-year-old Rebecca, joined the Shaker community in 1814, evidently of her own free will; of the other children (Sarah, Margaret, Mary, Hosea, and Cynthia) Hosea later recorded, "The

Figure 1.1. Pleasant Hill Community. Photo courtesy of Pleasant Hill Shaker Village.

Shakers, finding he was inclined to let them go, came and influenced him to let them have them, to go to school, accordingly all his children were taken by them."[18]

Children entering Pleasant Hill were divided immediately by sexes, so Hosea was separated from his sisters and placed with a family of boys of his own age in one of the four communal "families." Contact with his sisters would have been minimal, since boys attended morning and evening devotional services, went to school and worked only with other boys and while eating sat in silence at tables separate from girls. Indeed, when Cynthia, the youngest of Hosea's sisters, died in 1815 at the age of three after a year at Pleasant Hill, Hosea saw "the funeral concourse of people marching to her burial" but evidently did not take part.[19]

From the start, children new to Pleasant Hill were drilled in the principles of Society discipline. Each day began very early—four o'clock in the summer and five in the winter—and every activity during the day was planned with precision. This was a shock to Hosea, who later wrote, "I had been, previous to this, allowed to run almost at large, to go where I pleased and make as much noise as I saw proper, which was not allowable with those who were disciplined and brought under the rigor of their rules."[20]

Paramount in Society discipline was the confession of sins, the opportunities for which were plentiful. Children were "not allowed to fight and quarrel nor have any disputation among themselves. In playing they were not allowed to make much noise, nor go only on certain prescribed premises." Transgression of any rule was a sin that had to be confessed. Not long after his arrival at Pleasant Hill, certainly before his fifth birthday, Hosea was summoned to the house of John Shain, the superintendent of the large class of boys to which Hosea belonged. Shain asked him if it was time for the confession of his sins, to which an embarrassed Hosea answered that he did not know. The child's reluctance was overcome when Shain changed the interrogative into a command, and Hosea confessed for the first time in what became a nightly ritual:

> From this time I had, as also all the rest of the boys, to confess our sins every night, so strict were we taught to confess the truth and tell all that we had done, that was wrong, that I have known sometimes to get up out of their beds and confess things which they had forgotten: not daring to let it go till the next night for fear they might die and the "Bad man" would get them. We would scroupulously tell all we had said or done through the day that was not according to the rules laid down, though it might cause us to get a severe reprimand and sometimes a moderate flogging.[21]

The subjects of discipline and punishment were prevalent in Stout's writings of his experiences at Pleasant Hill. The usual methods of punishment, he wrote, were whipping, being kept indoors during play time, and, worst of all, being placed "under the floor in a little dark hole dug out for the purpose of putting roots &c in to keep them from the frost." The "little dark hole" was a root cellar, but it was terrifying by any name, especially with other scare tactics thrown in:

> While there, if this did not humble us enough, they would frighten us with horid stories about the "Bad man" coming and catching us. I have been almost scared out of my wits while in this dark and dreary place and would make any kind of a promise they would demand to be liberated and so would almost all the rest.[22]

Despite the punishments and threats that he had to endure, Hosea had nothing but praise for Shaker approach to discipline as he reflected three decades later upon his years at Pleasant Hill. "The rules were necessary to keep a large company of boys in proper subordination," he pronounced and also stated, "I consider the regulations good and well adapted to keep a large number of boys in subjection." More importantly, and perhaps contemplating his own early family life, he wrote:

> I have often thought if fathers and those who have the charge of families would adopt some of their rules and mode of dicipline, it would be a great improvement to their peace and social happiness. Thus having good order and quietude instead of a continual scene of disobedience, bickering, strife, quarrelling, contradicting each other, bad language, backbiting and the like, and an eternal routine of ill manners, bad conduct &c. the example allways set by the parents or guardian.[23]

High standards were set in all facets of daily life at Pleasant Hill. As Hosea grew older he was placed with a larger class of boys whose ages ranged from about eight to sixteen. In addition to play and school, where he learned to spell and read "tollerably well," each day included work, specifically braiding straw for hats. "It was astonishing to see the work we done," he wrote. Though kept busy, it was never to excess: "The times for our lessons, our brading and our play, was judiciously arrainged, not kept at either long enough to weary us." The children were also taught good manners, repeatedly using phrases such as "If you would be so kind," "I thank you kindly" and "You are kindly welcome."[24]

Notably missing in the Shaker community, however, was the promotion of children's love for their parents; in fact, quite the opposite was true. Hosea's mother made occasional visits to Pleasant Hill, bringing with her not only an infant son, Allen Joseph,[25] but also apples and small gifts for her children. On one occasion she asked Hosea to go outdoors with her for a private moment where she encouraged him "to be a good boy," but the loving request presented him with a dilemma:

> I reluctantly went out with her and was in a hurry to go in again, least the other boys might think I loved her, for we were taught to spurn the idea of paternal affection. I did not yet realize the kind hand of maternal affection that was want to administer to me but deprived of the privelege only in this clandestine way.[26]

Teaching children *not* to love their parents might seem radical, but the caretakers were obligated to make the children "future and dedicated Shakers," and it was in the best interest of the Society to keep them from returning to their family. Nevertheless, when Hosea's eighteen-year-old sister Sarah desired to return home in 1817, she was not prevented from doing so. It was an entirely different matter, however, when it came to Hosea.

A few months shy of his fourth birthday when he entered Pleasant Hill, Hosea grew to consider the Shaker community, not his father's house, to be his home. And thus on August 21, 1818, when he heard from other boys that "Old Jo. Stout" (as he and his friends called his father) was coming to visit, Hosea, sensing his father's intentions, ran and hid, only to be returned by Anthony Dunlavy, who had charge of Hosea's group of boys.[27]

Joseph Stout requested to be allowed to take his son home for one week, saying that Hosea's mother was very anxious to see him. Dunlavy, however, concluded that Stout was disingenuous in his appeal and would not consent. Following a prolonged conversation with Dunlavy, Stout tried to persuade his son to go but to no avail.

That was enough for Joseph Stout, who decided to take matters into his own hands—quite literally—by picking up Hosea, setting him on his shoulders and walking off. "I screamed and cried as loud as I could," Hosea later wrote, "and tried to get away but, in vain." Many were aroused by the noise: the Sisters, the most earnest and vociferous of whom were Hosea's own sisters, echoed his cries while the men, who easily could have stopped him, offered no resistance, "it being contrary to their faith."[28]

Joseph Stout lingered to mollify his daughters by vowing that he would return Hosea to the Shaker community the following Sabbath, but they remained unconvinced and at length Joseph picked up his son and walked away. Hosea was terrified, for the Shakers at Pleasant Hill taught children in their charge that the "worldlings" had nothing to eat and that running away would lead to starvation. He therefore took notice of the surroundings as he traveled with his father through the countryside, harboring the plan of escaping at the first chance, but his hopes were crushed as they entered a deep forest:

> At length we passed through a low bottom of sugar maple where the dark gloom which overshadowed me, caused such a lonesome and solitary feeling as I viewed this dark, cool, damp, wildering maze, as I sat on his shoulder and the cobwebs drawing over my face that I gave up the last and my lingering ferlorn hope of escape for I was affraid to pass alone through this trackless, and dismal forest.[29]

Joseph reassured his son that he would have plenty to eat, but Hosea trusted more in the Shakers than in his father. Joseph also promised that Hosea would be returned to Pleasant Hill the next Sunday, but the pledge failed to calm the child, who was "almost in despair and began to weep and wail" due to his unhappy fate, fully convinced that he wouldn't live that long anyway.[30]

Notes

1. Teague, *Cane Creek: Mother of Meetings*, 36.
2. Disownment in Quaker society is the involuntary termination of membership in a meeting (congregation) due to acts that are contrary to established discipline. Reasons for disownment have changed over time, often reflecting contemporary societal mores. http://trilogy.brynmawr.edu/speccoll/quakersandslavery/resources/glossary.php
3. Stout, *The Autobiography of Hosea Stout*, 1.
4. Ibid., 2. According to Quaker records, Joseph's siblings Mary, Rachel, David, Jacob, and Isaac were members of Lost Creek Monthly Meeting in Jefferson County, Tennessee.
5. Finger, *Tennessee Frontiers*, 149.
6. *Tennessee Blue Book*, 370.
7. Ranck, *Boonesborough, Its Founding, Pioneer Struggles, Indian Experiences, Transylvania Days and Revolutionary Annals*, appendix G.
8. Other commonwealths are Massachusetts, Virginia, and Pennsylvania.
9. Michaux, *Travels to the Westward of the Allegany Mountains*, 70.
10. Stout, *Autobiography*, 2. According to Hosea Stout family records at www.familysearch.org, the dates of birth were: Rebecca, May 20, 1798; Sarah, October 29, 1799; Samuel, 1802; twins Margaret and Mary, November 23, 1804.
11. Ibid. Anna was born December 22, 1806; Daniel was born in about 1808.

12. Houchens, "Shakertown at Pleasant Hill, Kentucky," 264.
13. Ibid., 269.
14. Ibid., 12.
15. Hammack, *Kentucky and the Second American Revolution: The War of 1812*, 27–28.
16. Stout, *Autobiography*, 2. Cynthia was born April 12, 1812.
17. Ibid., 62–63.
18. Ibid. The children taken, excluding Rebecca who already was with the Shakers at Pleasant Hill, were Sarah, Margaret, Mary, Hosea, and Cynthia. Hosea's two brothers, Samuel and Daniel, had died previously.
19. Ibid.
20. Ibid.
21. Ibid., 3. In his autobiography, Stout frequently used the term "bad man," obviously alluding to the "devil," as well as the term "bad place," which Stout identified as "hell."
22. Ibid.
23. Ibid., 5–6.
24. Ibid.
25. Allen Joseph Stout (who Hosea sometimes called Joseph Allen) was born December 5, 1815, in Danville, Kentucky. The first time Hosea saw his brother was on one of his mother's visits to Pleasant Hill.
26. Stout, *Autobiography*, 6.
27. Anthony Dunlavy III, born in Virginia in 1772, was one of four children of Anthony Dunlavy II and Hannah White to join the Shakers; of the other three siblings (Daniel, Rebecca, and John), his brother John wrote "*The Manifesto or a Declaration of the Doctrine and Practice of the Church of Christ*," a very important and lengthy statement of Shaker beliefs.
28. Stout, *Autobiography*, 6. Of Hosea's five sisters, Rebecca and twins Margaret and Mary were still at Pleasant Hill; Cynthia died in 1815 and Sarah returned to her parents in 1817.
29. Ibid.
30. Ibid., 7.

2
Reunion and Abandonment

Joseph Stout was a poor man who supported his family by tending Robert Reagan's gristmill on Shawnee Run, about five miles from Pleasant Hill. His family lived in a single room adjoining the mill, a dramatic change for Hosea, who was accustomed to the shared yet spacious living quarters at Pleasant Hill. The joy of reunification with his family was further diminished by Hosea's lingering fear of starvation and death, and he "felt more like a condemned criminal than a son just returning to the sweet embraces of an affectionate and doating mother."[1]

Shortly after arriving home, Hosea went with his three-year-old brother Allen to a milldam adjacent to the gristmill, into which he threw a number of stones, thereby inflicting some damage. Suddenly he was conscience stricken, supposing to have transgressed, and resolved to confess when he returned to Pleasant Hill. That afternoon his father took the entire family fishing at a nearby creek, which Hosea thought was "a most flagrant violation of the law of God," even though many of the Shaker brethren participated in the sport.[2] Once again he determined to confess all the next Sunday at Pleasant Hill, but when the Sabbath arrived and he was still at home, Hosea knew that he had been tricked. Within hours, however, his perception of the deception changed radically:

> After we returned home several of our neighbours came in to see me. All with one accord endeavoured to turn me against the Shakers . . . I became now convinced that they were my friends and were kind to me and would not kill me nor starve me to death as I had been taught. I began to think the Shakers had taught me wrong and first gave up the idea of confessing my sins any more and in a few hours more was entirely converted over to the ways of the world and at dark was perfectly turned against the Shakers and would have abhorred the idea of going back any more.[3]

Hosea immediately was transformed. Out of the reach of Shaker discipline, with nothing to confess and no boys to tell on him, a floodgate of freedom was opened for him and he drifted quickly in a different direction from Pleasant Hill. With no fears of reprisal or of the "Bad-Man" and having only to keep his misdeeds from his parents, he "soon was well initiated into all the rude mischief which the white, black, and yellow customers of a large mill and and distillery could bring forth and went forth and acted in all cases perfectly free and uncounsciensce-bound."[4] His mother, who had assumed responsibility for his education, gave him lessons to study whenever he was "caught in mischief," which was nearly every day.[5]

During the winter of 1818–1819, a few months after Hosea left Pleasant Hill, his uncle Ephraim Stout came from Missouri to visit siblings in Ohio, Kentucky, and Tennessee. He was said to be "a large man of commanding presence. His early education had been neglected, so that he could not be said to have much book knowledge; but his practical knowledge of the world was extensive, and his ability to judge the qualities of men almost complete."[6] A true frontiersman in the mold of Daniel Boone, who was said to have been an occasional companion, Ephraim consistently displayed a desire to live on the frontier and to that end in 1801 became one of the first settlers in Wayne County, Missouri, where he had a Spanish land grant.[7] In 1805 he became the first white settler in Iron County, where he built a cabin on a creek that would bear the Stout surname, in an area that for at least the next two decades was very sparsely populated.[8]

While in Kentucky, Ephraim persuaded Joseph to go to Clinton County, Ohio to be with their brother Isaac. Accordingly, in the spring of 1819, Joseph prepared to move his family, stopping first for about a week at the edge of Pleasant Hill, where Hosea's sisters as well as his former playmates tried to convince him to return to Pleasant Hill; however, he had drifted so far away in the months since he returned home that he now "scorned the idea of being called a Shaker boy."[9]

The journey north to Clinton County took the family through Lexington, Kentucky and Cincinnati, Ohio—at the time the two largest towns west of the Appalachian Mountains.[10] Their arrival in Adams Township, about three miles west of the Clinton County seat, Wilmington, seemed more like a homecoming than an uprooting: at Isaac's home, Joseph's family was greeted with such joy and excitement that some wept, some laughed, and some undoubtedly did both. The only shock for Hosea was the first sight of his uncle Isaac, who seemed to be nearly an exact image of his old Shaker tutor Anthony Dunlavy.[11]

The resemblance of Isaac Stout and Anthony Dunlavy notwithstanding, there was no mistaking that this was a Quaker, not a Shaker community. A great migration of southern Quakers to Ohio began in

1800, primarily due to the desire of friends to move away from the environment of slavery, especially in North Carolina. Rather than moving on to all parts of the "frontier," as did other migrants, they tended to congregate near friends or family.[12] The Stout family was typical in this respect. John Stout, a first cousin of Joseph and Isaac from Cane Creek, North Carolina, was the first Stout to settle in Union Township, adjacent to Adams Township, arriving with his family on Todd's Fork November 4, 1804, and followed in the next two years by his brothers Charles and David, also from Cane Creek. Then, in 1808, Isaac moved with his family to Clinton County from Tennessee.

Seemingly omnipresent in the vicinity, the Quakers would have an important long-term influence on Hosea, but that had to wait, for his first order of business was becoming acquainted with his cousins and new playmates, Isaac's youngest sons Isaac Jr. and Isaiah. After about a month, however, Joseph rented a farm about a mile south of Isaac's and introduced an unenthusiastic Hosea to a new order of business, namely preparing the ground for the spring crop:

> My situation was now materially changed, being separated from my two cousins society, I was put to work, picking up and burning brush. This was fine sport for me at first, but I soon found that it was work, which I did not relish quite so well as playing with my cousins: but when I would not pick brush fast enough to suit my father, he would apply one to my back, as a prompter for me to put away childish things.
>
> When summer came I was put to pulling weeds: but as soon as I was left alone would stop and go to play, which seldom failed to bring down the prompter on me when my father came: it done good however, about as long as it was in opperation, for he was no sooner gone than I was to play again.
>
> One day, being impatient at my indolence and me arguing that I was not used to work; after giving me a severe flogging, [my father] put a chain around my neck and started away, swearing that he would "usen" me.
>
> I supposed he was going to hang me forthwith and began to beg most lustily and promise to do better: but he went on paying no attention to me and took me out in the corn field, to a green beach tree and tied me to a long "swinging limb" and there set me to pulling up the weeds which were "in the reach of my cable tow" and went away. As soon as he was gone and I saw he had no notion of hanging me, I laid down in the shade and went to sleep soundly. The next thing I knew he had me

by the chain using a beach limb as usual, swearing it was more trouble to make me work than my neck was worth.

The above is a fair specimen of my industry for several years.[13]

It is evident that Joseph was extremely strict with Hosea and that their relationship was strained. Not only was Hosea punished readily for slacking off, but his assignment was solitary, and many times he wished he were back among the Shakers (who had a sizeable community a few miles away at Union Village in neighboring Warren County), both for the company of other boys and the anticipation of a lighter work load. Realizing that he would not go back, however, he dreamed of revenge and comforted himself with the knowledge that some day he would be "big enough" to treat his father as his father had treated him.[14]

In the meantime, Hosea practiced his revenge on his four-year-old brother Allen. On the occasion that their mother would allow Allen to go into the fields, Hosea gave orders but "the little fellow" would not know what to do:

> If he went with me I was sure to beat him shamefully and if he refused to go [I] would whip him for that the first oppertunity. If I chanced to mark him, I told him what to say when questioned which he never failed to do but once and was not then believed but I learned him better than to ever tell again.
>
> Notwithstanding my tyranny and ill treatment, he always loved, feard and obeyed me and was kind and docile, ever ready to take my advice and instructions, which made me repent of my abuse to him and [I] would resolve to do so no more, which would last till he done something to displease me.[15]

Hosea had learned well from his father. According to his own admission, he never failed to set Allen "at something he could not do and on his failure would most unmercifully beat and whip him and then make him promise not to tell on me, swearing if he did I would kill him the next time I got him out."[16] It was the first but definitely not the last time that Hosea threatened to kill someone, no matter how vain the threat.

A few months after moving to Ohio, in January 1820, Joseph and Anna had a baby girl, Lydia, their fourth child living at home;[17] directly after the birth Anna became severely ill and was bedridden until spring. Then in the fall, Hosea had a bad case of the mumps and was joined in his misery by Allen. In the spring of 1822 a final child, Elizabeth, was born. That summer, Joseph and Anna received a letter from their daughter Mary, who expressed a desire to leave Pleasant Hill. Joseph was apprehensive, having received a similar letter from daughters Mary and Anna the previous year only to be disappointed when at the last moment they were induced to remain at Pleasant Hill, but this time Mary already had left the Shakers and was living with Daniel Burfett, an old family friend. As Mary and her father prepared to leave for Ohio, Anna joined them, and a few months later Margaret also returned home. Suddenly Joseph and Anna had eight children living under their roof.

To support his large family, Joseph moved from one job to another, working mostly in the field. During his first five years in Ohio, he successively had a sugar maple orchard, raised corn and wheat, had a large crop of flax, raised pumpkin, squash, beans, and melons in the summer and then turnips and parsnips in the fall, planted castor beans and finally grew cabbage. In the spring of 1823, after returning from Kentucky with his daughter Margaret, he tried to supplement his farming income by buying a flock of geese to harvest their down, but by summer they had become so annoying and troublesome to one of his neighbors that Joseph sold the flock before effecting much in the "feathered kingdom," as Hosea later described the venture.[18]

Sometime during that period, a man by the name of William Stout (no relation) came to town.[19] A weaver by trade, Bill courted Joseph's daughter Margaret and obtained his consent to marry her. A marriage was not forthcoming, however, as Bill ran off to Lebanon, Ohio, not only with Margaret but also her sister Mary. At first Joseph decided just to let them go but soon was driven into a fury by friends who persuaded him to pursue his daughters.

Joseph set off after the trio, with thirteen-year-old Hosea in tow for the purpose, as Hosea later learned, of assisting in killing Bill.[20] The confrontation turned out non-violent, and the girls concluded that they had acted imprudently. To defuse the situation, on June 6 Bill married Margaret and the next day Joseph, Hosea and Mary began the twenty-mile journey home.

Halfway home and very tired, they encountered a man who was taking two barrels of "cider oil," a concentrated derivative of hard cider, to sell in Wilmington.[21] The bumpy road caused the cider to "foment," so the owner drew out some and replaced it with water, surmising it would calm the eruptive liquid. The result was most memorable for Hosea:

> At length it became so bad that he commenced drawing it out and we all went to drinking at a round rate. This was fine times for me and made the road easy. It was the first I

ever tasted and pleased me well. Not knowing its power I drank deep, and long before I got home was under full sail beyond the bounds of cares and sorrow. Everything seemed to rejoice.[22]

The good times did not last long, however. Shortly after the return from Lebanon, the four youngest children—Hosea, Allen, Lydia, and Elizabeth—came down with rubella, at the time called French measles (now known as German measles).[23] Though very ill, all four recovered only to succumb to rubeola, the highly contagious measles (then known as spotted measles). Father Joseph did not escape this disease and nearly died; Elizabeth, the youngest, was not so lucky and, though briefly showing signs of recovery, suffered a relapse and passed away. But the heaviest blow came in the fall when mother Anna was stricken with consumption (tuberculosis); her condition deteriorated and before spring she was confined to her bed. Though they may not have known it at the time, it was the beginning of the end of their family as a unit.

After helping his father plant a large crop of cabbage in the spring of 1824, Hosea was farmed out as a laborer to Job Cooley, who lived a few hundred yards away; after a month he moved even farther away to work and live with Benjamin Howell. Though Howell's farm was little more than a mile from home, Hosea for the first time was totally separated from his younger siblings Allen and Lydia. Overcome by homesickness, for several days Hosea could do nothing but cry and think of his family. His work in the field, hoeing corn, was difficult and distasteful to him and did nothing to diminish his inner pain. Relief of a sort was forthcoming, however, when he received word that his mother, whose health was declining steadily, wanted to see him. His return was the beginning of a prolonged stay at home, for his report of mistreatment by Howell was sufficient to convince Joseph that his son should not remain with someone whom Hosea considered a "mean, narrow contracted, and dishonest man and totally unfit to bring up a boy."[24]

Being home was bittersweet at best, for his mother had weakened significantly and continued to deteriorate until she died on July 28. For Hosea personally and the family in general the loss was devastating:

> By her death I lost the only unwavering friend that I had and our family was now left like a ship without a rudder to be the sport of misfortune and I severely felt and realized her loss, and now when deprived of her, could begin to see my own ingrattitude and disobedince to her, and when too late would gladly have served her.

> The rest of the family now remained together a short time but did not go into any arraingements to live but all seemed lossed and knew not what to do, for our helm was gone.
>
> The loss of my mother was a misfortune which reached my heart and caused me deep and lasting trouble, which I feel to this day when I ponder on her tenderness and goodness to me.[25]

Gone was the greatest stabilizing influence for Hosea, and since he and his father had a negative synergy, Joseph determined that it was best not to have Hosea at home. Hosea's statement that Benjamin Howell was "totally unfit to bring up a boy" was a clear inference that the fourteen-year-old had been sent to Howell for that purpose, and it was no surprise, particularly in a time of family grief after his mother's death, that in short order he was sent to live elsewhere.

Fortunately for Hosea, the result this time was much happier. He first mowed and packed hay for twelve and a half cents a day for John Fallis, "an old rich Quaker," working with others in the field and enjoying himself, and then went to live with Fallis's son-in-law Eli Harvey. It was likely the most positive experience of Hosea's young life:

> He was the best man I ever lived with, good, kind, and obliging. [He] would exact all that I could do and no more and was a good judge of the amount of work a boy should do. I soon found that he only wanted the fair thing and would not be satisfied without it He never misused, never repremanded or seemed to be dissatisfied with out I was to blame and I soon loved, obeyed, and respectd him and, what was still more strange I worked well and became interested in his welfare a thing before unknown to me.
>
> Eli was also a Quaker . . . Here I enjoyed myself better than I ever had done before and felt that I was in a way to learn to be some account
>
> Hitherto I did not think I was doing well and had nothing to encourage me, but now, full of hopes and bright expectations I assumed new life and determined to be worth something.[26]

The blissful summer faded away, however, and with the onset of cold weather Hosea returned home to an inactive existence of "despondency and gloom." The moody, slothful teenager became too much for his father to bear, and before long Joseph decided to send Hosea away once again, this time to Wilmington to learn a trade since in winter there was no work for a boy in the fields. It was a move that marked the beginning of the end of Hosea's age of innocence.

Isaiah Morris, in his eighth year as clerk of the Supreme Court in Clinton County, became Hosea's new keeper. Though popular and influential with others, Morris was scarcely a mentor to his young charge and Hosea was little more than a servant, given menial tasks such as making fires and feeding horses, never allowed to eat until the master family had finished and then only to pick through the leftovers. No trade was taught, no tutoring was given, and Hosea realized that he "was doomed to serve for a season."

What Hosea didn't realize was how quickly and how much his life would change. Upon his arrival in Wilmington, Hosea was given an order by Morris not to loiter in the city after nightfall, as was the custom with other boys, which suited him perfectly since, by his own admission, he "had been thus far raised in a civil Quaker settlement and was in fact an uncommon civil boy, for the simple reason that [he] had never yet had the opportunity to learn anything else." Presented the opportunity, however, Hosea changed in a heartbeat.

Sent by members of Morris's family to help calm some raucous boys in the days before the presidential election of 1824, Hosea joined instead and, lacking any degree of self-control, commenced to become the loudest of the pack.[27] He found the "lively rude and good natured town boys" far preferable to his "old civil Quaker comrades" and anticipated the "great joy to be had in their society." He did not anticipate, however, the cost of membership, as he discovered that "they always made a country boy fight before they would acknowledge him as a regular playmate."

Hosea was disinclined to participate in the requisite fisticuffs, even when cursed and called a coward for not doing so. A former neighbor, Elihu Millikin, took the lead in aggravating Hosea and at length put him "in the proper mood for the case in hand." Elihu began sparring with Hosea while boys, anxious to see a fight, pushed him into the developing fray. Almost in desperation Hosea jumped on Elihu, knocked him down and gave him three severe kicks to the small of the back, instantly disabling the aggressor.

It was an epiphany for Hosea who, for the first time, realized the reward of physical force and now "was ready for any kind of a fight and perfectly regardless of the consequences." All the boys save Elihu hailed him as a "first rate fellow," and even he fell into line after "three or four more severe whippings." But Hosea's notoriety was achieved at a stiff price as his life whirled out of control:

> With all my civil Quaker habits and the disgust with which I first looked on the behavior of these boys I was soon one of the worst in town and in fact many became ashamed of me and often reproved me who I once thought so reckless and wild.
>
> We would meet together late at night and wander in droves stoning houses and abusing the more civil part of [the] community and particularly if we had any thing against a man we were shore to do him a displeasure.[28]

In the midst of his downward spiral, Hosea was filled with joy and gratification as he visited his brother Allen and the three sisters—Mary, Anna, and Lydia—who remained at home. A second visit not many weeks later, however, ended tragically for Hosea. As he approached his father's house he made loud noises, hoping to surprise and perhaps scare family members when they came to investigate the disturbance; to his surprise, all remained quiet inside, so he instead investigated and discovered the house was deserted. He had been abandoned. "I found myself in this lonely desolate place of my former joys," he later wrote. "All gone far away and I here alone whereas I had anticipated so much satisfaction at this moment. But O, my people are gone."

Hosea surmised (correctly) that his father had taken the family fifty-five miles south to Cincinnati, as on occasion he had hinted, but it was unthinkable that he would go without at least notifying his son. In effect, Hosea had been orphaned and could do nothing but weep bitterly:

> It seemed that I was the most forsaken being on earth and now doomed to eternal loneliness and sorrow and I must mourn out the remainder of my day. It seemed that I could hear the weak plaintiff voice of my departed mother admonishing me to do better and would look in the house but alas she was gone and I truly alone and where is the family.[29]

While the account, written more than twenty years after the fact, is undeniably overly sentimental, it is clear that fourteen-year-old Hosea truly was alone: his mother was dead, the rest of his family had left town without him, and Isaiah Morris provided him a bed to sleep in and leftover scraps to eat but little else. Hosea was responsible for buying his own clothes (which he badly needed but couldn't afford) and had no opportunity to go to school. Knowing that Morris intended him only to be a servant, he resolved to be slothful and therein realized a great aptitude for laziness. His life was at a crossroad and, lacking guidance, he definitely was headed in the wrong direction.

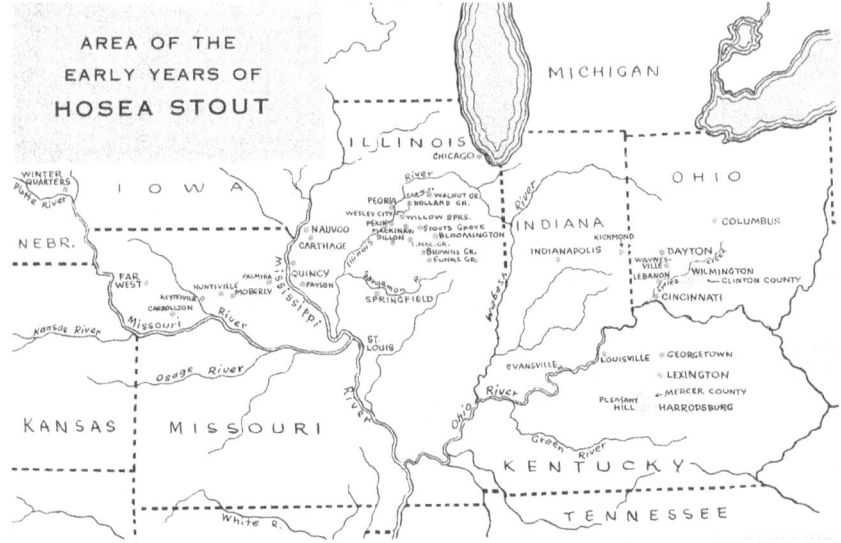

*Figure 2.1. Area of the Early Years of Hosea Stout.
Courtesy of Utah Historical Quarterly.*

Notes

1. Hosea Stout, *Autobiography*, 7; Allen Joseph Stout, "Autobiography." Allen specifically wrote that his father was poor while Hosea gave the location of the gristmill.
2. Clark and Ham, *Pleasant Hill and Its Shakers*, 61.
3. Stout, *Autobiography*, 7–8.
4. Ibid. Early nineteenth century gristmill owners in the western frontier areas of the United States, especially Kentucky, often built a distillery next to the mill to produce whiskey from the grain (especially corn) they ground. Though only eight years old at the time, it would seem from his description that Hosea imbibed the alcoholic beverage.
5. Ibid.
6. Hasbrouck, *History of McLean County, Illinois*, 567.
7. Conrad, *Encyclopedia of the History of Missouri* 6:410. According to E. Duis in *The Good Old Times in McLean County, Illinois*, 217–18, "Ephraim Stout was a great hunter, greater than Nimrod, or Esau, or Daniel Boone, indeed the latter had been a companion to Ephraim, and many were the stories told by him of their adventures together." If true, Boone and Stout likely met in Missouri, where Boone retired in 1795.
8. Conrad, *Encyclopedia*, 3:386–87.
9. Stout, *Autobiography*, 8.
10. US Bureau of the Census, 1820. In 1820, Lexington had a population of 5,279 and Cincinnati 9,642. They were the 34th and 14th largest cities in the United States at the time.

11. Stout, *Autobiography*, 8.
12. Snarr, *Claiming Our Past: Quakers in Southwest Ohio and Eastern Tennessee*, 3, 5.
13. Stout, *Autobiography*, 9–10
14. Ibid.
15. Ibid.
16. Ibid.
17. Sarah, Hosea, Allen, and Lydia were at home, while daughters Mary, Anna, Margaret, and Rebecca remained at Pleasant Hill.
18. Stout, *Autobiography*, 11–12.
19. In the journal of Hosea's brother Allen, he is referred to as "William McStout, an infamous rascal." See "Journal of Allen Joseph Stout," M270.1 S889s 1889, Church History Library.
20. Stout, *Autobiography*, 13.
21. Applejack or "cider oil" as it was once known, is made in the colder climates simply by allowing fermented or hard cider to freeze and removing the ice, thereby increasing the alcohol content of the remaining liquid.
22. Stout, *Autobiography*, 13.
23. In the early nineteenth century rubella was thought to be halfway between measles and scarlet fever. French scientists made important contributions to the study of the disease, leading to the name French measles, but since German scientists did most of the work, the disease later became known as the German measles.
24. Stout, *Autobiography*, 14–15.
25. Ibid.
26. Ibid., 16.
27. Andrew Jackson had 41.3 percent of the popular vote and 99 electoral votes compared to 30.9 percent of the popular vote and 84 electoral votes for John Quincy Adams; William Harris Crawford had 41 electoral votes and Henry Clay 37. As no candidate received more than 50 percent of the electoral votes, under the provisions of the twelfth amendment to the constitution, the House of Representatives voted to decide the election and selected Adams.
28. Hosea Stout, *Autobiography*, 18.
29. Ibid., 19–20.

3
Quakers and Methodists

The New Year 1825 found Hosea Stout stuck in a virtual quagmire. He waited expectantly but in vain for his father to return from Cincinnati and retrieve him, unaware that Joseph gradually dispersed his family as he continued heading south along the Ohio and Mississippi rivers.[1] He became increasingly disenchanted with his treatment by Isaiah Morris and shunned work as much as possible but would not leave because it seemed "sacred" to him that his father had enjoined him to stay there; and he resolved to amend his ways to do better but found he had no self-control in the company of other boys.

Concerning the latter, Hosea's situation was perhaps more quicksand than quagmire, for with the passing of days he sank steadily lower. He spent most of the summer loitering around town and in the surrounding country and admitted, "with other like truants I evidently grew worse every day."[2] To help stabilize his life, Hosea considered organized religion in the form of Methodism. He later wrote, "Upon the whole in all my wild career, I was uncommonly wrought on about religion when my mind could be brought to reflection, and had any of the religious part of [the] community undertaken it would soon have brought me to the 'anxious seat' to get religion, but who would have thought so of me?"

Certainly not Hosea's cousins, who witnessed his tirade directed at a neighbor boy during a visit in which he "gave a full specimen of [his] 'manner of speech' which perfectly astonished them." The cousins reported the outburst to their father (Hosea's uncle Isaac Stout) who placed the blame on Morris for allowing Hosea to run "uncontrolled and untaught." Isaac, who was a personal friend of Morris, asked that Hosea be released into his care, a request that Morris was loath to deny. It was a measure of salvation for Hosea, who upon later reflection found great irony in the situation:

Thus by doing evil, good came for my outrageous bad language and habits served to awaken my uncle to a sense of duty and thus delivered me from such a place which nothing else could for Eli Harvey had been to see me to go and live with him again a thing most desireable to me, but Morris objected and I undertook to run away which he found out and persuaded me not to do notwithstanding he so readily yielded to my uncle.[3]

Freed in December 1825 from his yearlong servitude with Morris, Hosea was back in a community of Quakers and was delighted both to be "at once delivered from all bad company" as well as to have the "society of [his] cousins to play with." His good fortune continued, again with irony, when while staying with his thirty-four-year-old cousin Jesse Stout he lacerated his foot and, disabled from work, was taught to write by Jesse's younger brother Isaac. Tutoring in arithmetic followed, and Hosea began to focus his thoughts and intentions upon having an education.

Hosea's transformation continued when, in April 1826, he went for a second time to live with Eli Harvey. "I now felt perfectly restored and redeemed from all trouble for I had often thought and sighed for the privilege of again living with him," Hosea later reminisced. Though only seven years Hosea's senior, Harvey displayed uncommon wisdom in dealing with the troubled youth. It was obvious to Hosea that while living in Wilmington he "had contracted indolent habits," but Harvey was a perfect mentor, "well calculated to cure without any harsh words or bad feelings."

Hosea was put to work in the field, but tasks that had been distasteful when meted out by others, such as by his former custodian Benjamin Howell, suddenly seemed pleasant. "When the time came I was put to ploughing," wrote Hosea. "This suited me well. I was delighted with a farmers occupation and can say that I worked hard this summer." Harvey paid a fair wage yet unilaterally decided that Hosea needed more. In addition to increasing wages, he purchased a badly needed new suit for Hosea that "made a fine tall appearance," in sharp contrast to a hand-me-down suit previously given him by Isaiah Morris—a large man—that completely dwarfed the pubescent youth.

Eli Harvey was a strict adherent to his religion, and Hosea gladly followed along, typically going to Quaker meetings twice a week. "I mostly went civilly and willingly conformed to all the sober habits of a Quaker life," he recorded. Returning to Wilmington during the summer, he found that he no longer had a desire to join with his old mates and admitted, "I was now fairly a Quaker in my heart and intended some day, when I learnt how, to join their society."

Hosea was reasonably successful in living a Quaker life, though he was severely tested while studying at Eli Harvey's school. Harvey was a good schoolmaster who assisted Hosea in his studies, helping him to make great strides in his handwriting and arithmetic. But when school resumed in winter 1827, after months of work in the fields, Hosea was confronted by a nemesis and learned a valuable lesson on human nature, albeit the hard way.

Samuel Savage, a profane and disagreeable fellow student (according to Hosea), was a non-Quaker in Harvey's mostly Quaker school. Ever ready to pick a fight, Savage at length commenced abusing Hosea in hopes of creating a sparring companion and victim. With his schoolmates unanimously supporting and egging him on, Hosea finally gave in and administered "a most unmerciful beating over the head" to Savage that accomplished exactly the opposite of the desired result:

> Eli [Harvey] soon came out and gave me a severe reprimand for my "Town boy capers" and threatened to dismiss me from school. The schollars [schoolmates] unanimously turned against me and sympathized for Samuel Savage calling me fighter. I now found I had done a thankless job for it was as much to accommodate them as to gratify my own feelings. The fact was they did not really want any one whiped [sic] and while saying so did not expect to see it done . . .
>
> I learned that it was not good policy to do fighting for people who had not courage or a disposition to do it for themselves and it proved a useful lessen to me in after life and caused me to begin to observe the inconstancy and ingratitude of mankind and no doubt it has prevented me from falling into worse difficulties by trying to help those who will not help themselves. For if you ever do you may depend on being forsaken in times of trouble.[4]

Already abandoned by his father, Hosea became even more forlorn upon receipt of news that his sister Mary had died due to consumption and once again was filled with grief and sorrow.[5] Despite continuing hardship and anguish, he resolved to better himself through education. Though destitute and still having to provide clothing for himself, he refused to cease his studies to go to work until the last day of school, by which time he "was literally flying in rags with both knees out bare." With the arrival of summer he worked first for Eli Harvey for twenty-five cents a day, then for Ezekiel Hornaday for four dollars a month and finally was persuaded by a one dollar a month raise to work for Eli's cousin Jesse

Harvey who, in Hosea's eyes, turned out to be "a mean narrow contracted little soured man." As was the case a few years prior in the employ of Isaiah Morris, Hosea became dissatisfied and tried to do as little as possible to please his master, who in turn refused to pay Hosea all he was due.

In 1828 Hosea continued his education, going to the school of George Carter while once again living with Eli Harvey, whom he assisted in the late-summer harvest. Though he made steady progress in his studies, acquiring a reasonable knowledge of grammar, it was readily apparent that in general he was going nowhere. His life took a dramatic turn, however, when second-cousin Stephen Stout asked Hosea to accompany him in a move to Illinois.[6] For Hosea it was an offer too good to refuse and he readily accepted upon the condition that his sister Margaret (whom he called Peggy) come along.[7]

Prior to the move, Hosea first sold items that he could not take, settled some outstanding accounts at Todd's Fork and then visited Eli Harvey and his family. Upon hearing that Hosea was going to Mackinaw, Eli assumed that he would end up working at the infamous lead mines (though they in reality were 180 miles north of his destination), where "the fame of profanity . . . was proverbial," certainly unfit for a good Quaker and perhaps the ruin of Hosea. It was the last time Hosea ever saw Eli, though his influence on Hosea was so great that two decades later and half a continent removed he would name a son Eli Harvey Stout.

The three Stout cousins set out on the National Road on September 9, 1828, nine days before Hosea's eighteenth birthday. The idea of a "national road" to facilitate travel from Baltimore to St. Louis dated back to the 1740s, though actual work did not commence until 1811. The route chosen was as direct as possible, with the result that across western Ohio and Indiana engineers had to contend with broad swamps and wet meadows, some of which were miles wide.[8] Moreover, funding and therefore construction was sporadic, and by the time the Stouts began their journey in 1828, according to Hosea, almost "all the road from Richmond to Indiana was uncommonly bad."[9] In the midst of the construction, the road, though relatively level, "was now full of logs and trees felled across the road and lay there while we had to zigzag from side to side of the road across the State through a disagreeable mud all the way."

The beech and maple forest of central Ohio and Indiana gradually opened to a wet grassy prairie west of the Wabash River, which formed the boundary of southern Indiana and Illinois. Hosea was truly astounded by the sight:

> After crossing the Wabash river we soon came to the grand prairie which I had heard so much talk about and it was truly a

grand scenery to me for I gazed upon the boundless ocean of meadow before me, which seemed to meet the horizon on all sides except an ocasional grove which presented a dark line in the distance, with unmingled delight.

It was the first time that my eyes ever beheld such a wide expanse. Just before me I thought I beheld a beautiful elevation some twenty feet high like a wave and to that I pushed forward to have a more wide and extended view from its sumit of the wide spred prairie but I traveled hard for [a] long time still looking forward to the high grounds before me untill weary and fatigued I looked back and saw another elevation behind me which explained the matter for I did not know how to look upon a prairie and my eyes had decieved me for the country was a beautiful level.

I gazed with admiration and delight upon the beautiful scenery before me as I journeyed along, untill my eyes pained me and my head ached which was in consequence of not being accustomed to such an extended view, I suppose.[10]

The open prairie was a stark contrast to the gently rolling topography, dominated by the hardwood forests, of the areas of Kentucky and Ohio where he spent his youth. The ease of travel most definitely was facilitated by the open expanse, though hours on the road without timber or water created a parched traveler:

> This was my initiation into a prairie life in recieving which I partook of both the good and the bad in a measure, for I was allmost suffocated with heat and drouth when I got through and eagerly plunged into the first brook I came to, with the cattle and all drank together of a putrid stagnant stream and better watter I thought I never drank, but not with standing all this I was highly pleased with a prairie country from that day forth until now.[11]

The otherwise open prairie was punctuated with groves of trees that appeared to Hosea "like islands in the midst of the ocean." Rather than trying to establish themselves on the extensive prairie lands, early settlers partially cleared these wooded lands along rivers and creeks where they congregated in settlements. After about sixteen days of travel, Hosea, Margaret, and Stephen arrived at one of these, named Stout's Grove after their uncle Ephraim, the grove's first settler in the fall of 1825—eight years prior to the founding of Chicago.[12]

Stout's Grove was a well-timbered area in central Illinois, in McLean County, about twelve miles northeast of Bloomington on the Mackinaw River.[13] Approximately one to four miles wide and five or six miles long, Hosea described it as "a most beautiful and delightful place, with good timber and prairie well calculated for farming." Impressed with the beauty of this new countryside, Hosea wrote: "From the most elevated parts of the prairie near this grove you have an extended view of the wide spread prairies before you bespotted with beautiful groves of timber so well calculated to captivate the feelings of a new comer."

Though Ephraim Stout is credited with being the first settler in Stout's Grove, he was accompanied by several family members at the very least, including his eighty-four-year-old mother, Rachel, most likely his spinster sister Margaret (who constantly attended her mother), and nephews Amasa and Mathew Stout.[14] Ephraim's brother Samuel and nephew John Stout were the first settlers of Little Mackinaw Township, about seven miles west of Stout's Grove, where a sister also settled.[15] Close by, in Brown's Grove, were Ephraim's brother David and nephew Samuel Stout, who settled in 1826.[16] Thus, by the time he arrived in 1828, Hosea was surrounded by at least three uncles, two aunts, his grandmother Stout and about seventy cousins.

A few days after his arrival in Illinois, Hosea traveled on foot twenty miles west to see his sister Anna and brother Allen for the first time in five years, visiting and introducing himself to cousins along the way. While becoming lost on the journey, Hosea had the good fortune of running into John Stout, a cousin whom he had never previously met. "Big John," as he was called, directed Hosea properly and a happy reunion with his siblings took place, though Allen, who was a few months shy of his ninth birthday at the time of the separation, did not recognize his older brother.

Hosea returned to Stout's Grove with Anna in tow. Shortly thereafter he witnessed the marriage of his cousin Amasa Stout, who had lived with their uncle Ephraim for ten years and got a closer look at Quaker life and customs than ever before. Though he felt "perfectly at home" with the Quakers in Ohio, he was taken by the rustic manners of those in Illinois as well as the beautiful countryside. "All these things together made me unusually well contented and I according wrote to Ohio to inform my relations there how well I was suited," he later wrote. He also was astonished when his cousin Ephraim hired him for a month for ten dollars, twice as much as he ever had received in Ohio. "Business was carried on here very differently from any way I had been accustomed to in Ohio for instead of being up and out at work at daylight driving and pushing everything we never went to work untill after late breakfast and then no hurry and would stop along time before night," he noted, and though he felt restless, wanting to hurry as in Ohio, he gladly accepted pay for the time that he felt he had idled away.

As the year 1828 came to a close, Hosea's sister Margaret, always weak, became ill with consumption (tuberculosis) and traveled with Anna to Dillon's Settlement for treatment, picking up Allen on the return trip to live with their cousin Ephraim. The medical treatment was of no avail, however, and Margaret succumbed a few months later, on February 28, 1829, becoming one of the first to be buried in Stout's Grove.

Despite the loss of his sister, Hosea seemed upbeat and continued to improve himself educationally, studying during the winter at a school started by his cousin Jesse Stout, who had recently moved to Illinois from Clinton County, Ohio. He was "as Quakerish as ever" in his feelings and gladly attended Sunday meetings at cousin Ephraim Stout's home, being punctual as an example to his fellow youth. As the "fame and the novelty" of the meetings began to spread, however, dissension began to divide the small community.

The elder Ephraim Stout's original intention was to make Stout's Grove a Quaker settlement and to that end gathered Quaker friends and relatives from far and near.[17] His goal was not realized, however, as Squire Robb, a Cumberland Presbyterian, and other non-Quakers soon settled in the grove.[18] The fervor of the Quaker meetings seemed to arouse feelings among the other religious groups, particularly after the Quakers "manifested a narrow, bigoted feeling towards all the rest" (at least in Hosea's eyes), and by spring 1829 Methodists and Cumberland Presbyterians living in and around Stout's Grove began to hold their own meetings.

Her Quaker upbringing notwithstanding and though she was living with her uncle Ephraim, Hosea's sister Anna became a Methodist and succeeded in having Hosea and Allen accompany her to the church meetings, though Hosea confessed to having "no religious motive in going what ever." This was all too much for both uncle and cousin Ephraim, who began to insult and slander the Methodists, which in turn put Hosea in the position of feeling the necessity to defend the religion. Cousin Ephraim thereupon upped the ante by informing Hosea (and likely his siblings) that they would no longer be welcome in his house if they attended any but Quaker meetings, though he would not end his friendship.

Hosea initially took Ephraim's pronouncement in stride, but upon second thought he became incensed with the religious directive. Hard feelings—"a prejudice," in Hosea's words—arose between him and father and son Ephraim, the beginning of a family rift. For the time being, however, James Watson, with whom Hosea was living, advised Hosea simply to avoid the conflict by staying away from the two Ephraims, advice that was wisely heeded, temporarily putting the matter to rest.

The family divide continued to widen, however, when following a brief armistice Hosea and his cousin Ephraim had a falling out, whereupon Hosea took Allen away to live with him at the Watson's. For uncle Ephraim, whom Hosea described as a "wise and cunning old smooth toungued 'Snake in the grass,'" it was the last straw. Ephraim, who was a County Commissioner, in revenge reported Allen to be an orphan and applied to the Commissioner's Court to appoint a guardian in order to remove him from Hosea's control. This unleashed emotions in Hosea that would prove to be a watershed event in his life:

> When I learned this my wrath almost arose beyond endurance however no accident happened and so when I learned the law on the subject I made an agreement with Mr. Watson, who was willing to have Allen bound to him and then we went to the man who had been appointed his [Allen's] guardian and had him bound to Watson. Thus we thwarted my uncle's plans, for he intended to have him away from there. We were now all well satisfied now and here it rested for the present.[19]

Though the matter rested, Hosea detested both his uncle and cousin Ephraim, though his other uncles, David and Samuel, remained neutral and friendly. Hosea, in the meantime, attended a Methodist camp meeting in Dillon's Settlement and, caught up in the emotion of the moment, "struggled and prayed and contended for religion, a change of heart, to pass from death unto life." While he received neither an answer nor a confirmation, he consented to join the Methodists on a trial basis for six months, as was their custom, while confessing that any conviction he had was a "contrivance of mind" and not of heart.

Joining with the Methodists gave ample reason for his uncle and cousin Ephraim to gossip about Hosea, an opportunity that they did not let pass. Hard feelings in the family were exacerbated even further later in the year with the arrival of Hosea's father from Ohio, with daughters Sarah and Lydia, bringing together the six remaining members of the family. Joseph did not want his son Allen to be bound to anyone and blamed his brother Ephraim for the predicament. He managed to have "the indentures taken and Allen released" and took Allen, Sarah, and Lydia to live with him at Little Mackinaw, but at the cost of estranging himself from the rest of the family, particularly his brothers.

For his part, Hosea, while continuing to live with the Watsons, attended another camp meeting in Bloomington and became, "a regular Methodist." Religion continued to be very important to him, though by spring 1830, in great need of new clothes, his focus switched to finding

Figure 3.1. Charles C. Rich (1809–1883). Rich was an LDS Church Apostle, and Rich County in the Bear Lake region near the Utah/Idaho border was named after him.

better employment than Watson could offer. In the summer he heard of an opportunity at a new saw mill on Ten Mile Creek, about fifteen miles up the Illinois River from Pekin, and set out to explore it only to take the wrong fork and become lost.[20] After wandering until it was nearly dark he happened upon a man plowing his field who, considering the lateness of the hour, invited Hosea to stay the night. This was Hosea's introduction to Morris Phelps and, subsequently, to his two neighbors, Charles C. Rich and Sanford Porter.[21]

After reaching his destination the following day and liking neither the work nor the environment, Hosea returned to take up Phelps on a work offer for ten dollars a month. While working for Phelps, Hosea attended a meeting in Pleasant Grove, headed by Neil Johnson, brother of Archibald Johnson whose school Hosea attended in 1829, for the purpose of forming a Temperance Society. Drinking to excess was no temptation for Hosea, and he joined the society with the expectation that he would never again "taste another drop of ardent spirits," though he confessed to dreaming that night "a man handed me a bottle of whiskey and I drank deep."

Hosea was mocked somewhat by Phelps and his neighbors for deciding to quit something he never did, but nevertheless he didn't touch a drop of hard spirits until he went to work at a mill some time later that Jonas Hittle of Mackinaw was building on the Mackinaw River. Hittle furnished whiskey for his men every morning, which Hosea at first resisted but then allowed an exception for health reasons (it was considered necessary to drink whiskey when working in the water at the mill). His fellow workers "shouted applause" when he gave in, and Hosea, seeing no harm in drinking at his own discretion, quit the society and "never troubled [himself] any more about the Temperance cause."

Not long thereafter, Hosea was beset by a fever and severe sickness that made him weak and feeble. He undoubtedly was suffering from mosquito-borne malaria or "ague," which was very common in Illinois as late as the 1840s.[22] His sister Anna was summoned to attend him, which she did faithfully, though the illness was unrelenting, with fever, chills, and violent shakes (commonly known locally as the "Illinois Shakes"), followed by relatively normal days and then total relapse.[23] Hosea was effectively disabled for months. "Having a chill and fever every day I became so stupid that I would not move from the fire when my clothes would scorch till they would smoke," he wrote. "It is incredible what a stupifying effect that fell disease will have on anyone. I was at several different places while here this winter and experienced and tasted the very dregs of adversity for some places I was not welcome and I knew it and could not get away and who knows the disagreeable feeling to be in such a condition but those who have experienced it."

The fever and chills were constant for Hosea during the winter of 1830–1831, one of the most severe in the history of Illinois, with snow depths of four feet and drifts as high as twenty feet.[24] It was a time of great hardship for the early settlers, who relied greatly in the winter on gathering Indian corn, most of which was still in the fields buried by snow. For Hosea, however, to his "full enjoyment" the cold of winter had a cooling effect on his fever.

Still debilitated by the fever and unable to work throughout the first half of the new-year, Hosea attended the school of Lyman Porter (who had succeeded Archibald Johnson). Such was the state of education in

Frontier Illinois that following sporadic and relatively limited studies, including a summer under the tutelage of Mr. Porter, Hosea considered his education to be finished, though it "only consisted in a knowledge of Reading, Writing, Arithmetic, English Grammar, Geography and a tolerable insite of Logic." Indeed, of his first teacher at Stout's Grove Hosea wrote, "[Archibald] Johnson was no very good schollar and when I left of[f] going to him was as good a schollar as he was."

In his education he found hope, even after a serious medical relapse in the winter that rendered him delirious for three days, by which time his neighbors had given him up for dead. Unable to work in the field and destitute of clothing (though with fourteen dollars in his pocket from the sale of a colt), Hosea concluded, upon the advice of friends, that he was better suited for a business that would spare his health, and teaching fit the mold perfectly. After all, as Hosea recounted, Archibald Johnson "was too lazy to enjoy good health and would lay in bed till school time in the summer which made him look sickly and pale," yet was well suited to teach.

And so Hosea set out in spring 1832 in hopes of being able to raise a school, traveling first twelve miles north to Walnut Grove but finding that all were too busily engaged in planting crops to worry about educating their children. He then journeyed to Dillon's Settlement to see his sisters Anna and Lydia (their father had departed with their brother Allen the previous summer and had no contact with the family for about six years). While there he once again tried to stir up interest in a school but failed. Confused and discouraged, Hosea was on the verge of giving up:

> I felt like I was totally abandoned to eternal disappointment, poverty and disgrace. Nothing but dark forebodings in view I retired to the broad prairie and sat down and wept bitterly and there alone and aloud mourned my hard fortune for a long time I felt that my life was only the sport of misfortune and sorrow After giving vent to my feelings I determined to leave entirely the land of my acquaintance and bad misfortunes and throw myself in the midst of strangers and see if a change of fortune would follow Knowing it could not well be worse. But where to go I knew not.[25]

Discouraged and feeling that he was an abject failure, Hosea penned a letter to his sister Anna, which he left with Lydia with instructions that nobody else see it lest he feel totally disgraced:

April the 5th, 1832

Dear Sister,

This is to let you know the situation I am in at present. I have tried to get a school in this settlement but failed and what I am going do now I do not know it appears that misfortune comes at me at every attempt to make an honest living, and as to dishonesty I want to have but little to do with it. I hope that Heaven may direct me in the way I should go. I am resolved to live respectible or not at all. I am now in the prairie not knowing where to go and I hope you will not be disheartened if I leave the country for if I stay hear I can make nothing. I will go whearever I think I can do the best and write you a letter as quick as I stop; if I stay here I am compassed [surrounded] with sickness and poverty and I do not see how much worse I can be off any where else if I labour sickness is sure to follow if I try any other way I am attended disappointment which is worse than sickness. What shall I do? a poor off cast without a friend to assist me or even to communicate my troubles to. may the Lord guide my steps in the rite way and despose of me as he thinks best. if I knew what to do gladly I would quit my pen a go and do it quickly. When I shall see you I can not tell but I want you to do the best you can the day may come when prosperity may be in my favour when I may live and enjoy myself better than I do no more at present but remaining your friend and affectionate brother.

Hosea Stout[26]

Down but not out while harboring a glimmer of hope, Hosea journeyed to Pekin to see Robert McClure, with whom he had lived the previous winter, with the intention of heading south to procure seed corn to sell for the spring planting. Disappointed in finding that McClure already had left, Hosea instead headed north in hope of achieving some of his desired prosperity, perhaps through the formation of a school. Though discouraged from going further north by William Holland, a traveling companion and founder of Holland's Grove adjacent to Peoria Lake, and despite lingering illness, Hosea trudged on to Crow Creek, a small Illinois River tributary, and then on to the Ox Bow Prairie, both in Putnam County.

So named from the lines of surrounding timber that, with a little imagination, resembled the shape of an ox bow that settlers used on their draft animals, the Ox Bow Prairie was a rich tract of land five miles long and a mile or two wide about ten miles south of Hennepin. With the encouragement of William Burt, who had known Hosea at Stout's Grove, and two other men, Hosea presented his case to Asahel Hannum and others in the settlement and succeeded in creating a small school that was attended by up to forty children, some of whom came great distances and boarded with nearby farmers.[27] It was perhaps the greatest success of Hosea's life thus far.

The school was suspended after just a few months by the outbreak of the Black Hawk War. In the Treaty of 1804, Sauk and Fox Indians ceded to the United States nearly all of their land in Michigan Territory (present day Wisconsin) south of the Wisconsin River as well as most of Illinois. Black Hawk, a proud Sauk warrior, claimed the treaty to be invalid and in 1832 demanded that white men evacuate recently ceded lands, resulting in a series of conflicts in Illinois. Many, including Abraham Lincoln, answered Governor John Reynolds' call for volunteers to defend their home, but when an inexperienced group from Tazewell County led by Major Isaiah Stillman was routed by a much smaller band of Sauks at the Battle of Stillman's Run on May 12, 1832, nearly all business was suspended, and on May 21 Hosea joined the 40th Regiment, Illinois Militia, commanded by Colonel John Strawn.[28]

For the first time in many months, Hosea was in full health and, despite initial misgivings concerning what effect the horrors of war would have on him, found that he was well suited to be a soldier and "only desired to march to meet the enemy." Hosea considered his military service a patriotic duty and looked down upon those who were too terrified to stand guard or who were ready to abandon the fort for their own safety. As would be proved in the future, he felt that he had the character to confront conflict, though his regiment was mustered out of service at Hennepin on June 18, a scant twenty-nine days after being formed and it is unclear whether he was involved in any skirmishes while in service.[29]

The war ended in August after the Battle of Bad Axe in Wisconsin, after which Hosea went back to the Ox Bow to run another school for a term of three months. Things definitely were looking up after his school was out and he returned to Stout's Grove "in good circumstances and tolerable plenty of money and uncommon good health." Thereafter he set out for Dillon's Settlement to see his sisters Anna and Lydia, having had no contact with them since the previous spring, but he was greeted with news that shocked and dismayed him: Not only had Anna married a widower with five children, but, perhaps worse, he was a Mormon!

Just a few months into its third year of existence, the Mormon Church already was well on its way to gaining a reputation in Illinois (and elsewhere) that led the author of the nineteenth century *History of McLean County* to write, "In 1817 regulators disposed of a band of horse-thieves that infested the territory. The Mormon indignities finally awoke the same spirit."[30] Hosea's knee-jerk reaction to Anna's marriage was to leave his sister forever since he "considered it a disgrace beyond endurance to be any way connected with the mormons." He had heard stories of the "gold Bible" and of the "fortifying" of Jackson County, Missouri, and had no reason to disbelieve the "universal slang then going about them." However, upon meeting Anna's husband, Benjamin Jones, he quickly altered his view and, as a consequence, the direction of his life—both figuratively and literally—in a way he never could have imagined.

Notes

1. Following the death of his wife in 1824, Joseph Stout acted quickly to remove from himself the burden of his children who remained at home (Mary, Lydia, Allen, and Anna). His first stop was Cincinnati, where Mary met and married Nicholas Jameson. After a few weeks, Joseph moved on with Allen and Anna for Little Rock, Arkansas, while leaving Lydia in the care of Mary. Joseph stopped short of his goal of Little Rock and eventually joined his brother Ephraim in Missouri and followed him to Tazewell County, Illinois, where he deposited Anna and Allen as he traveled about for two years, finally returning to Ohio. See "Journal of Allen Joseph Stout."
2. Stout, *Autobiography*, 21.
3. Stout, *Autobiography*, 22–23.
4. Ibid., 24.
5. Hosea evidently was unaware at the time that his oldest sister, Rebecca, had died more than a year prior at Pleasant Hill, also due to consumption.
6. Stephen Stout was born in North Carolina September 29, 1802. His grandfather Charles Stout was a younger brother of Hosea's grandfather Samuel.
7. Hosea was being very protective of his sister, and for good reason. Her husband Bill abandoned her in early 1824 in Kentucky while she was pregnant. Her son Samuel, born in October of that year, died at the age of two in 1826. In poor health and scarcely able to walk, shortly thereafter she was reunited with her sister Mary, who also was very ill, and she remained with her until Mary's death about two months later. When spring arrived, still weak she returned to Ohio.
8. Karl Raitz, ed., *The National Road*, 58.
9. Richmond, through which the National Road passed, is in Indiana, less than two miles from the Ohio/Indiana state line. Hosea's phrase should have been written "from Richmond *through* Indiana." Raitz, *The National Road*, 336.
10. Stout, *Autobiography*, 26–27.
11. Ibid.
12. Ephraim Stout and his son Ephraim were 2 of 133 taxpayers listed on the Northern Illinois 1825 Tax List, which included Chicago. See http://genealogytrails.com/ill/1825taxlistnorth.html. Chicago was organized on August 12, 1833, with a population of about two hundred.
13. Peck, "A Gazetteer of Illinois," in *Three Parts: Containing a General View of the State, A General View of Each County, and a Particular Description of Each Town, Settlement, Stream, Prairie, Bottom, Bluff, etc.; Alphabetically Arranged*, 299.

McLean County was created when Tazewell County was divided in 1830.
14. Allensworth, ed. *Historical Encyclopedia of Illinois and History of Tazewell County*, 697.
15. Ibid., 814. In his autobiography, Hosea mentions staying with a cousin, Samuel Whiten in Little Mackinaw; Mary Stout, Hosea's aunt, was married to Gilbert Whittin and was most likely the mother of Samuel Whiten (Whittin). This is likely the sister who lived in Little Mackinaw.
16. Hasbrouck, *The History of McLean County, Illinois*, 567.
17. Duis, *Good Old Times*, 218
18. Cumberland Presbyterians separated from the Presbyterian Church in 1802 in southern Kentucky and Tennessee for the purpose of licensing and ordaining men who could not meet the educational qualifications established by the old Presbytery.
19. Stout, *Autobiography*, 37. Binding out pauper apprentices was a widespread practice in early America in which poor, illegitimate, orphaned, abandoned, or abused children were raised to adulthood in a legal condition of indentured servitude. Most of these children were without resources and often without advocates. Local officials undertook the responsibility for putting such children in family situations where the child was expected to work, while the master provided education and basic living needs.
20. Ten Mile Creek in Tazewell County rises in the Great prairie near Putnam County and enters Peoria Lake five miles above Peoria. Pekin, the county seat of Tazewell County, is situated on the east side of the Illinois River about ten miles south of Peoria. See Peck, "A Gazetteer of Illinois," 267, 301.
21. Phelps, "Autobiography," MS 21298, Church History Library, 15.
22. Jensen, *Illinois: A History*, 12.
23. From *History of Tazewell County*, 331–32, "One of the greatest obstacles, and one which wielded a very potent influence in retarding the early settlement of this county, was the 'chills and fever,' or the 'ague,' or the 'Illinois shakes,' as it was variously styled. This disease was a terror to new comers. In the fall of the year everybody was afflicted with it. It was no respecter of persons; everyone shook with it, and it was in every person's system. They all looked pale and yellow as though they were frostbitten. It was not contagious, but was a kind of miasma that floated around in the atmosphere and was absorbed into the system. It continued to be absorbed from day to day, and week to week, until the whole body corporate became charged with it as with electricity, and then the shock came, and the shock was a regular shake, with a fixed beginning and an ending, coming on each day, or each alternate day, with a regularity that was surprising. After the shake came the fever, and this 'last estate was worse than the first'. It was a burning hot fever and lasted for hours. When you had the chill you couldn't get warm, and when you had the fever you couldn't get cool . . . You felt languid, stupid and sore, and was down in the mouth and heel and partially raveled out, so to speak."
24. Allensworth, ed., *Historical Encyclopedia of Illinois and History of Tazewell County*, 888.

25. Stout, *Autobiography*, 45.
26. Stout, "Hosea Stout Papers," Mss B53, Utah State Historical Society. Stout repeated this letter, with improved spelling and punctuation and minor changes in wording, in Stout, *Autobiography*, 45–46.
27. Duis, *Good Old Times*, 217.
28. Ellsworth, *Records of the Olden Time; or Fifty Years on the Prairies*, 124; Burt and Hawthorne, *Past and Present of Marshall and Putnam Counties, Illinois*, 23.
29. Ibid. As Hosea later found, his service of twenty-nine days was one day short of the requisite thirty necessary for a Black Hawk War pension—letter of R. M. Young, April 21, 1854, Hosea Stout Papers, Utah State Historical Society.
30. Hasbrouck, *The History of McLean County, Illinois*, 106.

4
Introduction to Mormonism

Morris Phelps was far from perfect in the eyes of Hosea Stout. Though he had enjoyed making fence rails for Phelps in spring 1830 and considered him to be "a tolerably good man" though "very austeer and grouty at times," Hosea was understandably upset when Phelps tried to leave town without giving him proper remuneration for his work. In the winter of that year, Anna Stout arranged a meeting to collect the amount due her brother (Hosea being too ill to fend for himself), but on the appointed day Phelps failed to show; Hosea later learned that Phelps planned to move away without paying him and probably would have succeeded were it not for the intercession of Phelps's friend and neighbor Sanford Porter, who collected and gave the money to Anna. Though this episode left him very critical of Phelps, it was also Phelps who set in motion a chain of events (if unintentionally so) that would be life altering for Hosea.

A few months after selling his property in Tazewell County and moving to Chicago in late 1830, Phelps returned to his former home for a visit and while there received a letter from a relative in Ohio regarding a new church:

> She wrote concerning a new Book called the Book of Mormon that it was translated from writings on plates. Said to be done by the gift and power of the Holy Ghost and the plates were of pure gold found by the direction of an angel in New York State. Several families had mooved on to captain Morles [Isaac Morley's] farm and had comensed a new Chirch and this was all don under the directions of a Prophet. Verry respectable men and women had joined their Chirch such as Isaac Morley and Edward Patridge [Partridge] and they have all things common amongst them. Several of their preachers will soon leave for the west. Perhaps you may see some of them.[1]

45

DOI: 10.7330/9781607324775.c004

The prophet mentioned in the letter was Joseph Smith, who organized the Church of Jesus Christ of Latter-day Saints—quickly nicknamed "Mormon" due to the *Book of Mormon*. Subsequent to the books' publication, Joseph Smith and his brother Hyrum, along with four other men, met at Fayette, Seneca County, New York on April 6, 1830, to formally organize the new religion, which initially was named *The Church of Christ*.[2] The organization was the culmination of visions and visitations experienced by Joseph Smith over a period of about ten years that called him to restore the true Christian religion. That Isaac Morley and Edward Partridge, both of whom Phelps knew and respected from his years growing up in Lake County, Ohio, were members of the church gave it instant credibility in Phelps's eyes. Full of excitement, the next day Phelps read from the letter to Charles Rich and later to Sanford Porter concerning the *Book of Mormon*, both of whom showed great interest.[3]

Phelps returned home to Chicago in early July and had just completed a letter of inquiry regarding the new faith when he noticed two men "passing through the field on foot in traveling costume, knapsack and valise on their back." They were traveling with Phelps's acquaintance James Emmett, who asked Phelps if he had seen what was called the *Book of Mormon*. "No sir, only heard of it by a letter," Phelps replied, whereupon Emmett identified the two travelers, Lyman Wight and John Corrill, as Mormon preachers and asked if they could preach in Phelps home, to which he consented.[4]

Wight and Corrill were among twenty-eight men instructed in a revelation proclaimed by Joseph Smith a month prior, on June 7, to travel two-by-two from Kirtland, Ohio to Missouri, preaching by the way.[5] They, along with John Murdock and Hyrum Smith (brother of Joseph), journeyed from Kirtland to Detroit by lake steamer on June 14 and undoubtedly traveled the Chicago Road, the major thoroughfare from Detroit to Chicago.[6] Though a network of roads had allowed migrants to settle most of southern Illinois, there was only one road from Chicago to the south, mostly paralleling the Illinois River to Peoria where it split into three highways, one of which tracked by the eastern bank of the river into Tazewell County.[7] Armed with a letter of introduction from Phelps to Sanford Porter, Wight and Corrill took that fork and not only met but baptized Porter in August before continuing on to Missouri; Porter in turn baptized Phelps the same month.[8]

Charles Rich and Sanford Porter were Morris Phelps's only neighbors when Phelps settled in sparsely populated Tazewell in 1830, and Rich also was taught by the missionaries prior to their departure, who presented him with a copy of the *Book of Mormon* which he "read and advocated." He was not baptized at the time but was anxious to learn more about the new religion. The opportunity to do so came in March

1832 when two more missionaries, George Hinkle and Daniel Cathcart, appeared and preached in Rich's neighborhood. On the first day of April, Rich, his parents, and his sister Minerva were baptized. Also baptized that day was Benjamin Jones; about eight months later, on November 29, Jones and Anna Stout were married in a ceremony performed by Rich.[9]

Hosea Stout visited the newlyweds, who were living on Farm Creek near Peoria. He was pleasantly impressed with Jones upon introduction, though the name "Mormon" carried with it "stigma and disgrace" that weighed upon Stout's feelings as he tried to "put on a cheerful and happy countenance." Despite his curiosity, the subject of religion was not mentioned in conversations with Jones.

Such was not the case when Stout was reacquainted with Charles Rich, whom upon their first meeting he had determined to be "an uncommon civil steady, honest young man but [who] made no pretentions to religion." Stout and Rich spent several days together, discussing religion the entire time. Stout later recorded:

> Suffice it to say that we passed over the grounds of our different belief, refering our opinions wherever we differed to the Bible.
> It is not necessary to mention our investigation which resulted in all cases in the loss of my position while he always sustained his on the fairest possible terms.
> The perplexity which this threw me into can only be realized by those who has been through the same thing with the same anticipations before them that I had. I saw plainly that my positions were wrong and did also verily believe Mormonism to be correct.[10]

Though Stout didn't fit the hereditary profile of the typical early Mormon convert—a good majority of whom (including Charles Rich, Sanford Porter, Morris Phelps, James Emmett, and Benjamin Jones) were of New England ancestry stretching back at least five generations—his religious background, particularly the years as a Shaker at Pleasant Hill, may well have prepared him to readily accept the new religion. Both Shakers and Mormons believed that there was but one true faith; that there is continuing, modern-day revelation; that time was divided into long dispensations; that their dispensation was the last and greatest; and that their faith was a divine restoration of the primitive Christian church.[11] In addition, his religious journey from Shaker to Quaker to Methodist had opened his mind to other beliefs.

It is clear that Stout's conversion at first was more in his mind than in his heart and was not accompanied by peace and comfort. "All my plans and calculations both spiritually and temporally were now futile. The agitation of my mind was intense and I did not know what to do," he wrote. With the realization that he would suffer disgrace from others and fearful that he would not be able to live up to Mormon precepts (as he confessed had been the case with the Methodists) he chose not to join the church while remaining among the cluster of converts at Farm Creek, where he continued to investigate and indoctrinate himself in Mormonism.

Returning to Stout's Grove he found himself in the peculiar position of preaching the doctrine of the unpopular religion while at the same time not professing to believe what he advocated. Nevertheless, he confessed:

> I was astonished at myself when I saw with what ease and fluency I could confute any one who would oppose me.
> This raised a considerable excitement in the grove.
> Emboldened by my success I soon made it in my way to attack even the ministers who I believed did not understand the Scriptures and I also thought I had always the best of their arguments.[12]

Stout in the meantime had to make a living and in winter 1832–1833 successfully started a school, this time in Stout's Grove. After school was out he returned north to Crow Creek where he raised a crop of corn with Joseph Phillips, with whom he had served in the Black Hawk War.[13] In his spare time he seized the opportunity to study principles of Mormonism with a small group of church members who lived near the mouth of the stream. Attending weekly meetings with the local Mormons, Stout "became intimate with the doctrines they professed and did most devoutly believe it." Still concerned about how faithful he could remain, however, he declined to join the church.

Stout was quite content living at Farm Creek, noting that there also was a "good society" of those who were not Mormons and that he was "well suited" with the people who resided there. The resident with whom he grew especially close was his brother-in-law Benjamin Jones. After storing the good crop of corn that he had raised with Phillips, he moved in with Jones at Farm Creek; and when Nathan Wixom (another Mormon convert) put his Farm Creek saw mill for sale, Jones and Stout bought the mill for six hundred dollars in future lumber as well as the proceeds from Stout's corn crop.

After many years of living without sufficient means, Stout happily admitted that as the year 1833 drew to a close he "assumed a more business-like life and soon became well known in the country." The success with the mill continued through the next season and by fall 1834 he found himself "in comfortable circumstances." Not so comfortable, however, that he felt himself able to rescue his sister Sarah, who after her father left Illinois in 1831 had fallen into poverty and suffered the ignominy of being "the first pauper" of Tazewell County. Hosea and Benjamin were summoned to court to take charge of Sarah, "their poor relation," but they declined, stating an "inability to do so." Thereupon Sarah and another pauper, an old man named Nicholas Miller, were put up for "public sale or private contract," but not one bid was made for them and her immediate fate is unknown (though at some point she moved back to Ohio).[14]

Stout's fate, on the other hand, began to be solidified in mid-year when a group of Mormons, led by Hyrum Smith and Lyman Wight, who were marching through Illinois on their way to Jackson County, Missouri, stayed several days in Tazewell County. The march was in response to the expulsion of Mormons from Jackson County, which had been designated as their "Zion" the previous year.

A gathering to a place of refuge called Zion was a dominant concept of the early days of Mormonism, and at a conference in Kirtland, Ohio, in June 1831 Joseph Smith announced the revelation that directed him and other church leaders to go to Missouri, where the land of their inheritance would be revealed. A second revelation, given on July 20, stated that Zion, the promised land and gathering place for the "Saints" (as Mormons frequently called themselves), was to be built in Independence, Jackson County, Missouri.[15]

The gathering to Zion began almost immediately, and during the spring and summer of 1832 three to four hundred Saints arrived in Missouri to settle in Jackson County. The population of Saints in Jackson County grew rapidly, from approximately three hundred in May 1832 to about twelve hundred the next year. As the Mormon population increased, so also the fear grew among non-Mormons that they might lose control of the county.

What began as isolated hostile incidents against the Saints became more frequent as the Mormon population grew. Before the end of July 1833, threats and violence had escalated to the point that the Mormons had no choice but to bow to the demands of their enemies and agree that the leaders and their families would leave Jackson County before the first of January 1834, and that all of the Saints would be out by the following April 1.

When the news of trouble in Independence reached Kirtland, Joseph Smith immediately counseled the Saints through revelation to remain quiet and peaceable, forgiving the trespasses of others.[16] The

Mormon leaders in Independence decided to heed the advice of their prophet and sought to resolve the conflict through legal means. When opponents of the Mormons saw that the Saints were not leaving but were preparing instead to bring legal action they became enraged and several armed skirmishes occurred in which two non-Mormons were killed. The local militia was called out and demanded that the Mormons surrender their arms. News spread that the Saints had no weapons, and citizens attacked almost every Mormon settlement in Jackson County, driving the inhabitants from their homes and destroying their property.

Parley P. Pratt and Lyman Wight traveled to Kirtland in February 1834 where they made an appeal to the Ohio Saints to go to the aid of their distressed brothers in Missouri. Smith was impressed and announced to members of the "high council" in Kirtland that he was going to Zion to help redeem it. A revelation received by Smith directed that messengers should be sent out in all direction to gather food, clothing, and money as well as to recruit members to assist their fellow church members in Missouri.[17] The endeavor became known as "Zion's Camp."

Despite pleas from Smith, few in the East volunteered for the camp, though recruitment efforts in Kirtland met with more success. Hyrum Smith and Lyman Wight were sent northwest from Kirtland to seek out more recruits while Joseph's company traveled in a more westerly direction. The Smith-Wight party recruited a small group of volunteers, most of whom were from Pontiac, Michigan, and traveled southwest through Indiana, passing the south shore of Lake Michigan. In Illinois they followed the Illinois River to Tazewell County, where they "camped at the home of a Brother Rich, the father of C.C. [Charles] Rich."[18] During the time they remained in the area, Smith and Wight preached a number of times to the local Saints.

Whereas earlier reports of conflict in Jackson County had given Stout a very negative opinion of Mormons, following the visit by the Zion's Camp party he wrote, "The effect of their preaching was powerful on me and when I considered that they were going up to Zion to fight for their lost inheritances under the special directions of God it was all that I could do to refrain from going." Charles Rich did go, and though Stout remained behind, he and Benjamin Jones were impressed that they should let the group have "one yoke of oxen." [19]

The Smith-Wight group of about twenty left Tazewell County on May 29 and marched to the Salt River settlement in eastern Missouri to join other members of the camp and then on to Jackson County. The camp, however, was disbanded before achieving its objective due to an outbreak of cholera that resulted in the deaths of fourteen camp members.[20] Released from duty, Rich returned to his home on July 16, a scant seven weeks after he had joined Zion's Camp.

Stout most likely chose to stay behind to further his joint business with Benjamin Jones. The remainder of the year was spent in bringing a large number of logs to the mill and "in getting out and selling a large quantity of hewed timber for the Peoria market," in which they did "a good and profitable business" while employing six to eight workers. In the spring they sold the mill and used $150 to purchase a half interest in a mill being built at the mouth of Crow Creek in Putnam County in partnership with Samuel Hadlock, a friend of Charles Rich.[21]

In order to raise the water to run the mill, a dam was constructed that backed water on the only other mill on Crow Creek, owned by Joseph Martin about a quarter of a mile upstream. Martin took legal action, which led Stout to quip, "In this case we bought with our mill seat also a law-suit." The action evidently did not hamper Stout, Jones, and Hadlock, as the trio remained in business together until autumn 1836 while Martin finally abandoned his mill project and went downstream to build a saw mill, which he sold in short order to Hadlock.[22]

Long before selling their interest in the mill, Stout and Jones began preparation for an eventual move back to Tazewell county by purchasing land on the bank of the Illinois River in the town of Wesley City, about three miles below their first saw mill. On October 7, 1835, they purchased together eighty acres for $100; Stout alone purchased an adjacent tract of fifty acres for $62.93 while Jones purchased another seventy-nine acres for $99.55.[23] They moved to Wesley following the sale of the Crow Creek mill and together they established an evidently successful carpentry business.

In May 1837 Joseph Stout, with son Allen in tow, began a return trip to Illinois, from which they had been absent for nearly six years. On a steamboat bound for Peoria, Allen was asked by a man named Smith if his name was Stout:

> I said yes. He said he knew me by Lydia. I asked him if he was acquainted with my folks. He said he was and that Anna had married a Mormon. I asked him what that was, for I never before remembered having heard the name of Mormon spoken. He said it was a religious denomination of folks. I asked if they believed the Bible. He said they pretended to but any man who understood the scriptures could confound them in a moment.[24]

Upon arrival in Wesley City, Allen (and most likely his father) received a steady dose of Mormon doctrine. Unable to procure a copy of the *Book of Mormon*, Allen spent his evenings reading *Doctrine and Covenants*, a book published in 1835 that was a sequence of lectures setting forth basic church doctrine followed by a compilation of important revelations received by Joseph Smith. Allen also went to a number of Sunday prayer meetings but later admitted, "the most satisfaction I could get was what Stout would tell me, for he was as well acquainted with the gospel as he is now, but had not obeyed it yet." Well pleased with the words he heard at a meeting from Lyman Wight, Charles Rich, and Morris Phelps, Allen was converted but, like Hosea, had not yet joined the church, though he and his father quickly made preparations to join the main body of the Saints in Caldwell County in northern Missouri, the latest site of their attempt to establish a gathering place.[25]

Hosea, his sister Lydia and Benjamin Jones had remained behind for a few weeks in Illinois to wrap up some affairs and sell their property and left in August. Hosea arrived in Caldwell County with "a good bag of cash" and purchased two hundred acres of good tillable land upon which he built a house and commenced to farm; Allen lived with Hosea, Lydia kept house, and their father alternately lived with Hosea and Benjamin Jones.[26]

Neither Hosea nor Allen was yet a member of the church, though both were thoroughly committed to the cause. Allen, however, was tormented in both body and mind:

> This fall and winter I was afflicted with a breast complaint—fever sores and a breaking out on my body so I was unable to work at all. My mind was also greatly troubled, for I had become satisfied of the truth of the gospel and wished to embrace it, but still lingered back and had not courage to go forward and be baptized until on the 22nd day of April, 1838, I and Thomas Rich were baptized by the hand of Charles C. Rich.
>
> It seemed to me that I could almost walk and not touch the ground. I was baptized in Lost Creek, five miles south of Far West. Soon after that I had the elders to anoint me and I was healed of both my breast complaint and fever sores, after the bone had been naked all winter on my leg, etc. I had breaking out on my body in consequence of change of climate and water, which was also healed.[27]

Hosea finally was baptized on August 26 by Charles Rich, though he made no special mention of the occasion other than the date, perhaps due to ongoing events: in neighboring Carroll County a committee of non-Mormons had ordered the Saints to leave by August 7, and on August 20, according to John Murdock, "a mob of more than a hundred men came, and ordered us off, but finally gave us ten days and threatened if we were not away in that time they would exterminate us without regard to age or sex and throw our property into the river."[28] For the next ten days citizen groups and vigilantes met with the resolve of "bringing alleged Mormon criminals to justice."[29]

Referring in his autobiography to his baptismal date Hosea wrote, "this was in the time that the mob was harrasing the church and the brethren were then under arms to defend themselves against the violence of the mob." Under the circumstances, it is altogether possible that he, long since converted, finally consented to baptism in order to fight with the Saints in their time of great tribulation. Regardless, from that day forth, using his physical, verbal, and written skills, he was a defender of their faith.

Notes

1. Phelps, "Autobiography," MS 21298, Church History Library.
2. To avoid confusion with several other congregations similarly named, the official name was changed in 1838 to *The Church of Jesus Christ of Latter-day Saints*, and its members have since frequently been referred to simply as the "Saints."
3. Phelps, "Autobiography."
4. Ibid.
5. *Doctrine and Covenants of the Church of Jesus Christ of Latter-day Saints* (hereafter known by the abbreviation *D&C*), Section 52.
6. Murdock, "Journal," MS 1194, Church History Library. Murdock reported that he and Smith took the Chicago Road, and it is assumed that Wight and Corrill did the same since it was the only road around Lake Michigan.
7. Howard, *Illinois: A History of the Prairie State*, 161.
8. Jenson, *Latter-day Saint Biographical Encyclopedia*, 1:373.
9. http://earlylds.com/getperson.php?personID=I16671andtree=Early lds; Spangler, "Early Marriages in Tazewell County," *Journal of the Illinois State Historical Society* 14:145. Rich had been empowered to lead the small branch of the Church in Tazewell County and evidently used that authority to perform the marriage.
10. Stout, *Autobiography*, 50.
11. Andrews, *The People Called Shakers: A Search for the Perfect Society*, 73, 222.
12. Stout, *Autobiography*, 50.
13. Ellsworth, *Records of the Olden Time; or Fifty Years on the Prairies*, 123.
14. *History of Tazewell County*, 246. Allen Stout in his journal stated that Sarah had come from Ohio to Missouri in 1839.
15. *D&C*, 57:1, 3; 62.
16. *D&C*, 98.
17. *D&C*, 103.
18. Smith, *History of the Church of Jesus Christ of Latter-day Saints*, 2:88; Lyman O. Littlefield, "The Prophet Joseph Smith in Zion's Camp," *Juvenile Instructor* 27 (1892):56.

19. Stout, *Autobiography*, 52.
20. Manscill, "Journal of the Branch of the Church of Christ in Pontiac, . . . 1834: Hyrum Smith's Division of Zion's Camp," *BYU Studies* 39, no. 1:181–82.
21. In Rich's journal he mentioned visiting Hadlock on numerous occasions. See Charles C. Rich Collection, MS 889, Church History Library, Charles C. Rich DVD Library.
22. Stout, *Autobiography*, 53; Ellsworth, *Records of the Olden Time*, 360.
23. Illinois Public Domain Land Tract Database, http://www.ilsos.gov/GenealogyMWeb/landsrch.html.
24. Stout, "Journal of Allen Joseph Stout," M270.1 S889s 1889, Church History Library.
25. Ibid.
26. Ibid.
27. Ibid.
28. Murdock, "Journal."
29. LeSueur, *The 1838 Mormon War in Missouri*, 263.

5
Fight and Flight

Southern Missouri settlers in the 1830s derided the prairie lands of northern Missouri as being "fit only for Indians and Mormons."[1] Rather than take offense, the Mormons perceived an opportunity to live in peace away from the molestations such as they had suffered in Jackson County. Residents of Jackson County's neighboring Clay County initially received Mormon refugees with compassion, but following a relatively tranquil sojourn of more than two years it became obvious that the Saints had to move on, and they set their sights on the supposedly undesirable northern prairie.

Alexander W. Doniphan, who had been friendly to the Mormons and at the time was a member of the state legislature, sponsored a Mormon petition in mid-1836 for the creation of a new county out of the northern area of Ray County. The area was sparsely settled, and to the politicians the formation of an exclusively Mormon county was considered an excellent solution to the "Mormon problem." Two new counties, named Caldwell and Daviess after two famous Indian fighters from Kentucky, quickly were formed with a general understanding that Caldwell County would be primarily for the Mormons.[2]

Even before the passage of the bill, Mormon families heeded their leaders' counsel and in August streamed northward into unsettled parts of northern Ray County. An estimated three thousand Saints moved to the region and along Shoal Creek leaders platted and started building the town of Far West, which was intended to be the main Mormon settlement in Caldwell County. On November 1 Charles Rich arrived from Illinois with Lyman Wight in Caldwell County and purchased eighty acres of land in Rockford Township in the center of what would become known as the Rich Branch on Log Creek;[3] on September 12, 1837, Hosea Stout purchased land in the southern portion of neighboring Mirable Township, also part of the Rich Branch.[4]

Not long after he moved to Missouri, Stout met and began to court sixteen-year-old Samantha Peck, whose mother, Phoebe Crosby Peck

Knight, and stepfather, Joseph Knight, were among the earliest converts to the Mormon faith, having been baptized less than three months after the "Church of Christ" was organized.[5] Twenty-seven-year-old Hosea married her (whom he in his writings called Surmantha) on January 7, 1838. By that time the population of Caldwell County had reached approximately five thousand people, all but about one hundred of whom were Mormons. Most residents were farmers producing bountiful crops on the prairies that pioneers from the South had disparaged. Far West, the county seat, seemed to rise almost magically above the high rolling prairie and already was the home of some three thousand Latter-day Saints.

Even as the Mormon population in Caldwell County continued to grow, the leadership of the church for the greater part remained in Kirtland, but that was about to change. Joseph Smith and some of the elders in Kirtland, caught up along with others in a speculative craze that swept the country, borrowed money from banks in Ohio and New York with which to buy land that seemed destined to continue to appreciate in value. In November 1836 they organized the Kirtland Safety Society Bank Company, with Sidney Rigdon as president and Joseph Smith as cashier. When the Ohio legislature refused to grant the bank a charter, the Mormon promoters changed the name of the institution to the Kirtland Safety Society Anti-Banking Company and officers began to issue notes, many of which were used to pay off debts owed by the Mormons. As a result of a national economic depression known historically as the Panic of 1837, the notes became virtually worthless, and since the Anti-Banking Company was operating illegally without a charter, Smith was arrested and fined one thousand dollars and court costs.

In this period of economic distress many members of the church in Kirtland apostatized. Despite efforts to quell the unrest, conditions failed to improve, and finally, beset by continuing legal problems and mounting anti-Mormonism in Ohio's Western Reserve area, in January 1838 Joseph Smith and Sidney Rigdon fled to Missouri. Upon reaching Far West, Smith and Rigdon were joyfully received by the Saints, many of whom regarded the difficulties in Kirtland as God's way of bringing the prophet among them.[6] He was followed by hundreds of Saints from the East, particularly from Kirtland.

Some of the dissenters from Kirtland preceded the prophet to Missouri, including such early organizers of the church as Oliver Cowdery, David and John Whitmer, and Lyman Johnson, and found refuge twenty-five miles from Far West in the home of William McLellin, who had left the church in 1836. Nevertheless, Sidney Rigdon, the second most powerful leader of the church, was incensed to find the dissenters still living among the faithful as he arrived at Far West in early April. Rigdon gradually escalated the rhetoric until he directed a thinly-veiled threat to the dissenters in a sermon, quoting Matthew 5:13 as a warning: "If the salt have lost [its] savour, wherewith shall it be salted? It is thenceforth good for nothing, but to be cast out, and to be trodden under foot of men."[7] On June 18 a document signed by eighty-three citizens, many of them members of a recently organized Mormon society known as the "Danites," ordered Cowdery, the Whitmers, W. W. Phelps, and Lyman Johnson, the leading dissenters, to leave the county or face "a more fatal calamity." The dissenters took the warning seriously and immediately left Far West.

The exact date of the inception of the Danites is unknown, though it seems to have coincided with the document of June 18. Neither Hosea Stout nor his brother Allen signed the document, though Allen admitted to being a member[8] and it is widely accepted that Hosea also belonged.[9] Allen Stout wrote of the organization:

> They [Missourians] swore to some lies and some truths which were calculated to excite the Gentiles against us insomuch that mobs began to rise and commit depredations until we were forced to resort to arms in order to save ourselves and property.
>
> The Church was organized under captains tens, fifties, one hundreds, and one thousands. This made the inhabitants mad to see us making ready to defend ourselves. They called our organization the Danite band.[10]

The Danites did not just bear arms to defend themselves but also had groups providing innocuous community service, such as building houses, gathering scattered families, providing wood and meals to families and caring for the sick.[11] Nevertheless, it was their military activities that established their reputation and created fear in their opponents, as witnessed by Danite Oliver Huntington:

> This society of Danites was condemned by the public like the rest of Mormonism; and there was a great quandary about the Danites, all over the county and among the army; but who and what they were no one was any wiser for anything they heard; and as many stories were in circulation the most horrid and awfully distorted opinions their minds could imagine, and they all thought that every depredation was committed by the Danites; Danites, awful Danites; every mobber was afraid of the thoughts of one of those awful men. And if they were to see a man of their own acquaintance, and were told in confidence

he was a Danite, they would even shun his company and conversation. Such being their opinion and belief of the Danites, and we knowing it, concluded to make the best of it.[12]

Emboldened by their strong-arm success in squelching dissension, the Danites, led by Sampson Avard, redirected their focus to the defense of the church against mobs. A speech on July 4 by Sidney Rigdon further incited the Danites as well as other Latter-day Saints and issued a warning to the enemies of the church:

> We take God and all the holy angels to witness this day, that we warn all men in the name of Jesus Christ, to come on us no more forever; for from this hour, we will bear it no more, our rights shall no more be trampled upon with impunity. The man or the set of men, who attempts it, does it at the expense of their lives. And that mob that comes on us to disturb us, it shall be between us and them a war of extermination, for we will follow them, till the last drop of their blood is spilled, or else they will have to exterminate us: for we will carry the seat of war to their own houses, and their own families, and one party or the other shall be utterly destroyed.[13]

Though Mormon leaders generally were pleased with the speech and Joseph Smith granted permission to have it printed and distributed, none could question its inflammatory nature. Newspapers throughout Missouri published angry editorials in rebuttal. Missourians also became resentful that Mormons had moved into Daviess County, believing that it was understood that they would confine themselves to Caldwell County. According to Allen Stout, the speech "enraged the mob worse than ever."[14] Tensions grew and finally erupted during an election on August 6 in Gallatin, Daviess County. Reddick Allred gave a concise account of the conflict:

> The few ranchers in Caldwell and Davies [sic] counties raised false reports about the lawlessness of the Mormons and at an election in Galiton [sic], Davis [sic] County they forbade any Mormon to vote and surrounded the polls to prevent it, but a fight ensued and the Mormons cleared the way and voted. This was enough to wake up the whole of Jackson, Clay, Ray and Carlton Counties into a howling mob, and they began to make raids upon outside settlements.[15]

Increasing hostilities, both actual and threatened, made it advisable for the Saints to organize into military bodies for self-defense. Acting upon advice from Alexander Doniphan, state militia brigadier general for northern Missouri and a non-Mormon, the Saints formed two such units with Lyman Wight and George Hinkle as commanding officers. Many who belonged to these legitimate units also were members of the Danite clan, although little, if any, effort was made to distinguish between one's activities in either group, each of which was organized into companies of tens and fifties.[16] It is probably at this time that Hosea Stout joined to "defend himself against the violence of the mob." Referring to himself in the third person, Hosea wrote, "He entered the war with the rest of his brethren and was in all the difficulties, which they passed through in Caldwell and Davisse [sic] Counties, with the mob."[17]

In September, trouble broke out in Carroll County where George Hinkle and John Murdock had purchased a large number of lots at DeWitt, planning to develop a Mormon colony to serve as a port on the Missouri River for persons and supplies going to and from Far West. Older inhabitants became alarmed when they learned of the purchases, feeling that the Mormons had violated their agreement to confine themselves to Caldwell County, and demanded that the Saints leave DeWitt, threatening to kill every Mormon who remained in the town after October 1. Church leaders appealed to the governor for assistance, but their pleas were ignored and the tired, hungry Mormons were forced to abandon DeWitt on October 11.

Having been denied help from the governor, church leaders decided to take the offensive and strike back at the Gentiles (a Mormon term for those not of their faith). They attacked and seized the towns of Gallatin and Millport, looting supplies, rounding up livestock and burning buildings, including the US Post Office and the County Treasurer's Office.[18] It may safely be assumed that Hosea took part in the attacks, as he admitted to being in all conflicts in Caldwell and Daviess counties.

Mormon depredations in Daviess County outraged Missourians and angry mobs immediately began to retaliate. Rumors spread among the non-Mormons that the Mormons intended to lay waste to the entire northwestern part of the state. With the war intensifying, Joseph Smith, realizing that outlying settlements could not protect themselves, dispatched messengers to notify these Saints to move into Far West for their safety.

Two days after many of the Saints from the smaller settlements had moved into Far West, a battle took place that was a turning point in what came to be called the "Mormon War." The events precipitating the Battle of Crooked River began on October 23 when Samuel Bogart, a militia captain who also was a Methodist minister, wrote a letter to Major General David R. Atchison, commander of the state militia in northwestern

Missouri, informing him that he and his Ray County troops would patrol the line between Ray and Caldwell counties to protect against Mormon ravages. Bogart and his men overstepped their authority and made incursions into Caldwell County, going from one log home to another, threatening and intimidating Saints along the way. On the night of October 24 Captain Bogart's company went to the home of Nathan Pinkham and took Pinkham, William Seeley, and Addison Green prisoner, alleging that they were Mormon spies.

In response, Judge Elias Higbee at Far West called upon Colonel George Hinkle to raise a company of militia to rescue the prisoners. David Patten, a member of the Council of the Twelve Apostles of the church and a Danite leader who was called "Captain Fearnaught" by the Saints, was placed in command and immediately raised forty men. Charles Rich, second in command, considered forty men to be insufficient for an anticipated fight and rode through the settlements on Goose and Log Creeks to recruit more men.[19] Rich's company left Far West at midnight and headed south; one of the "brethren" (probably Rich himself) arrived at Hosea Stout's home very early in the morning of October 26;[20] Stout and Benjamin Jones and about twenty to thirty others recruited there by Rich gathered with the main company near the home of Jones's neighbor Benjamin Bragg, where they divided into companies of ten.[21] They then went down the road four miles to non-Mormon Randolph McDonald's property where they split into three companies commanded by David Patten, Charles Rich, and James Durphee.[22]

At first unable to locate Bogart's troops, the Mormon militia moved on to Crooked River. With dawn approaching, John Lockhart, a sentry for Bogart, shouted for the Mormons to lay down their guns only to hear a cap burst without a gun firing. Lockhart fired a shot in return and wounded Patrick O'Banion, a non-Mormon who acted as a guide for the Caldwell militia.[23] Patten then ordered his troops to charge, despite attacking from an extremely inferior position, standing on nearly open ground while Bogart's men were situated almost entirely out of sight behind the riverbank and in the trees while having a clear view of their enemy. Nevertheless, Bogart and his troops were taken by surprise and panicked, making a hasty retreat through a bend in the river.[24]

"A more severe battle perhaps never was fought when we consider the smallness of the number, and the shortness of the time which was about 1½ minutes," wrote Albert Rockwood in a letter dated October 28.[25] On the Mormon side, David Patten and Patrick O'Banion died of their wounds, Gideon Carter was killed instantly and nine were wounded.[26] Hosea Stout estimated that thirty or forty of the enemy were killed, though in the fog of war he wildly overestimated the casualties, that amounted to but one dead—the sole Missourian to die in the so-called

"Mormon War"—and six wounded, including Samuel Tarwater, who "received several terrible sabre cuts on the head, neck and face, one of which severed his jaw and upper teeth" and was left for dead, though he survived the mutilation.[27] Nevertheless, the sight of opponents escaping a hail of bullets by diving under the water led Stout to refer to the Mormon practice of baptism by immersion when he wrote, "many a mobber was there baptised without faith or repentance under the messingers of lead sent by the brethren."[28]

Though Stout was well off the mark in estimating enemy casualties, he probably was accurate in writing that those of the enemy not killed in the battle "fled in every direction through Clay and Ray Counties reporting as they went that they had been attacted [sic] by the mormons and the whole of their Company killed and they alone was left to tell the tale."[29] The Mormon victory, however, precipitated their eventual defeat in northern Missouri after exaggerated reports of the battle brought down the power of state government upon their heads. Rumors circulated that fourteen thousand Mormons were armed and might have allies among the Indians beyond the Platte. Reed Peck, a first cousin of Samantha Stout, recalled, "In Richmond [Missouri] the first information received of this battle was that the whole company of 50 or 60 men was massacred and before the report was corrected Amos Rees and Wily C. Williams were far on their way to the Governor with this intelligence."[30]

Missouri Governor Lilburn Boggs, who had been unresponsive to any of the numerous Mormon pleas for protection from mobs, suddenly took aggressive action when the Mormons appeared to have taken the offensive. On October 27, the same day that David Patten was laid to rest at Far West, Governor Boggs responded to the rumors and reports of the "massacre" at Crooked River by issuing his infamous "extermination order" to General John B. Clark, saying:

> I have received . . . information of the most appalling character, which changes the whole face of things, and places the Mormons in the attitude of open and avowed defiance of the laws, and of having made open war upon the people of this state. Your orders are, therefore, to hasten your operations . . . The Mormons must be treated as enemies and must be exterminated or driven from the state, if necessary for the public peace—their outrages are beyond all description.[31]

Three days later, on October 30, a Missouri militia from Livingston County numbering greater than two hundred descended on the small village of Hawn's Mill,[32] though there is no evidence that the militiamen knew of the extermination order at the time. It was about four o'clock on a beautiful Indian summer afternoon when suddenly the army burst out of the timber to the north of the mill and overwhelmed the vastly outnumbered villagers. Screams intermingled with gunshots as some fled into the woods and others took refuge in a blacksmith shop while the mob fired mercilessly. A few managed to escape, but fifteen men and two boys were killed and fifteen others were wounded. One of the youths, ten-year-old Sardius Smith, was found hiding in the blacksmith shop by William Reynolds, who raised his rifle and shot Sardius in the head. Reynolds boasted afterward how the child "kicked and squealed" in his dying agony and justified the murder by saying, "Nits will make lice, and if he had lived he would have become a Mormon." Seventy-eight-year-old Squire Thomas McBride was wounded and surrendered his gun to a Daviess County man named Rogers, who then killed his prisoner and mutilated his body with a corn knife.[33]

Almost concurrent with the Hawn's Mill massacre, approximately three thousand militiamen under the command of General Samuel Lucas—"the whole army," in the eyes of William Moore Allred—camped on Goose Creek, about a mile from Far West, preparatory to storming the town.[34] The next morning Charles Rich, carrying a white flag, and a small company of Mormons rode out of Far West to meet with militia officers within sight of Rich's home. After a short encounter, Rich turned and was "three or four rods away" when Captain Bogart of the militia shot at him.[35] The bullet, while missing its target, delivered a clear message that flight was advisable, and that evening Hyrum Smith told Brigham Young and Brigham's brother Lorenzo that he believed those involved in the Crooked River battle would be tried by a court-martial and shot.[36] Considering himself to be among the endangered, Stout wrote,

> "There was no alternative for them but to escape or fall into the hands of their enemies who had sworn their destruction consequently on the night . . . [of] the 31st day of October, twenty seven of them made their escape about mid-night and proceeded north and at the dawn of day were crossing Grand river a bout one mile above Adam ondi Ahman."[37]

Before leaving, Stout gave his sword—perhaps his most prized possession—to Brigham Young.[38] Later that evening, Stout and Charles Rich met their wives at the home of Rich's sister; the couples parted at one o'clock in the morning, of which Sarah Rich wrote, "So him [Charles Rich] and Hosey Stout made a covenant to stay together untill we should meet again; and Hoseys wife [Samantha] and I made a coven[an]t that her and I would remain together as true friends until we should meet our husbands again, and upon this promise we shook hands with our dear husbands and parted."[39]

Due to the major role he played in the attack at Crooked River, Charles Rich had a higher profile than the other battle participants, and for that reason Samuel Bogart had a particular vendetta against him. Even six months later, as Bogart wrote a letter to the postmaster at Quincy, Illinois, whom he believed might be of help in "feriting out and exposing all afendors of the civil laws of oure land," he put Charles Rich at the top of the list of offenders and added the comment, "I wish to no whare they are."[40] Fear of Bogart's dogged pursuit may have been reason enough for Sarah Rich to want Stout to stay with her husband to help protect him. Regardless, Stout, Rich, and the others—including Joseph Smith's brother Samuel and Brigham Young's brothers Lorenzo and Phineas—departed immediately without food and adequate clothing and supplies.

Early on the morning of November 1, the refugees reached Adam-ondi-Ahman[41] and were provided breakfast by Gardiner Snow, who also gave them fifty pounds of cornmeal, the only food they had for the journey. The same morning, Sarah Rich and Samantha Stout stepped out to go to Sarah's home four blocks away but were stopped by guards who refused to let the women pass, instead forcing them to return to Sarah's in-laws where they had spent the night. The Captain of the Guards, upon discovering Sarah's surname, asked if it was her husband who had been killed by Captain Bogart the day before. Bogart's assassination bullet had missed, but rumors to the contrary persisted and Sarah was happy to play along. The ruse didn't last long, however, and angry militiamen—notably including Samuel Bogart—repeatedly went to the Rich home and threatened to blow out Sarah's brains if she didn't disclose where her husband was hiding.[42]

Upon discovering that Rich and the others had departed, General Clark sent sixty cavalry into Iowa Territory in pursuit. Fortunately for the Mormons, Ervine Hodges reached them first to warn that the troops, with orders to bring them back dead or alive, were only a few miles behind. Even more fortunate was an unexpected and drastic turn in the weather: on the night that Rich and company camped in the timber on one edge of a four-mile-wide prairie while, unbeknownst to them, the militia camped on the opposite side, "snow commenced falling and appeared to come down in sheets instead of flakes." By morning the snow was a foot and a half deep, and the wind created snowdrifts completely covering all tracks, thus making it impossible for the militia to follow.[43]

The harsh elements had delivered them from their pursuers, but in their haste they had left Far West dressed for mild weather, not heavy snowfall.[44] "The weather turned exceedingly cold," wrote Stout, "and many of them being thinly clad suffered beyond description, from having to face the Northern winds."[45] Lorenzo Young recalled, "I had on a thin pair of pants. My wife took a flannel sheet from the bed and with the assistance of the neighbors hastily made me a pair of drawers. These I afterwards gave to my brother Phineas as he seemed to suffer more with the cold than I did. Our bedding was as scanty as our clothing."[46]

Eight of the escapees, suffering more from the cold and privation than they could bear, were willing to chance being caught by the militia rather than perishing from cold and starvation and turned back, fortunately reaching the Missouri River and safety. For those who remained, fewer mouths to feed meant that food supplies lasted longer, though after twelve days of travel in the cold and snow, with the corn meal gone, some resorted to eating the bark of slippery elm trees to subsist. During the final three days before reaching a settlement of whites near the rapids of the Des Moines River they were without food altogether and "were near upon perishing of cold and hunger."[47]

The men previously had split into two groups so as not to overwhelm the settlers on the Des Moines River; traveling onward, the first group reached the Mississippi River a day ahead of the other and crossed without incident, but the second group, which included Stout and Rich, encountered ice floes that prevented their crossing and chose to go down the river to the Quincy ferry, a journey of two days. From there Rich navigated the river in a canoe while Stout and the others stayed another two days and worked for board and returned to the ferry where they met fellow Mormons from Caldwell County, from whom they learned the fate of the church.[48] It was not a happy saga for them.

On October 30, with news of the Hawn's Mill massacre on his mind, Joseph Smith secretly had sent emissaries to arrange for a conference with General Lucas.[49] Colonel George Hinkle and John Corrill met with Lucas the following morning to negotiate a solution to the looming crisis. The militia officers, with Governor Boggs's extermination order in hand, demanded that Mormon leaders surrender for trial and punishment, that Mormon property be confiscated to pay for damages, and that the balance of the Latter-day Saints give up their arms and leave the state.

Colonel Hinkle told Joseph Smith, Lyman Wight, Parley P. Pratt, and George W. Robinson that militia officers wanted to talk to them. They consented but were shocked and felt betrayed when Hinkle turned them over to General Lucas as prisoners. Hyrum Smith and Amasa Lyman were apprehended the next day. Hinkle claimed that he considered this the only way to end the war without bloodshed, but to the Mormons it was treachery and they considered him a traitor.

A court-martial quickly was held and the prisoners were sentenced to be shot the following morning. General Lucas ordered General

Doniphan to carry out the order, but Doniphan was incensed with the injustice of the affair and replied:

> It is cold-blooded murder. I will not obey your order. My brigade shall march for Liberty tomorrow morning at eight o'clock and if you execute those men, I will hold you responsible before an earthly tribunal, so help me God.[50]

Doniphan's refusal to submit to the order spared Smith and his fellow leaders from execution, but they along with more than fifty men, including Allen Stout, Benjamin Jones, and Charles Rich's cousin Thomas Rich, were taken to Richmond to stand trial before Judge Austin King. On November 24, after three weeks of testimony, Allen Stout and twenty-two fellow prisoners who were not implicated in any crime were released, though Stout had "fever sores" on his body and his leg was "nearly rotten so as to render [himself] almost helpless."[51] On November 28 Benjamin Jones and most of the other prisoners were released, outright or on bail, while Joseph and Hyrum Smith, Sidney Rigdon, Lyman Wight, Caleb Baldwin, and Alexander McRae were sent to jail in Liberty, Clay County, to stand trial for treason and murder (of the one Missourian who was killed at Crooked River).[52]

As the prophet and other leaders languished in jail, the church entered a period of uncertainty, with many denying the faith.[53] Referring to the golden calf that Israelites worshipped during Moses's absence on Mount Sanai, Allen Stout wrote to his brother Hosea, "about one half of the church has got to themselves a calf for they think that Joseph will be destroyed and there religion is gone"[54] In response to the unsettling news, Rich wrote to his wife on December 21, "It fills my heart with sorrow to hear of the wickedness and abominations that have been carried on in that place since I left there."[55] Two days later Hosea wrote, "I shall not attempt to say what I think about times more than I am a little stronger in the faith than ever and want all of you to continue in the faith although times looks dark at present."[56]

The times were dark indeed. Not only were the days short and gloomy in the midst of an exceptionally cold winter, but they were filled with turmoil and trepidation rather than joy and celebration. In a letter to his wife dated December 17 Hosea wrote:

> I take this opportunity to write a few lines to inform you that I am well and doing as well as can be expected considering all things. I have not heard anything very particular about you yet

though I am very anxious to hear from you I have not heard from any of our people since we left there I want to hear how [Benjamin] Jones and all the rest comes on . . . I want to know how you all are and what they have done with all our property whether they have taken any of it or not and also where you are living and how you fare.[57]

Stout gave instructions to his wife concerning their property and his affairs in Missouri. Of particular importance to him was the sword he had given to Brigham Young, writing, "I want it very badly let no body know you are going to get it."[58] Just six days before Stout asked his wife in a letter, "let me know whether it is safe for me to come there or not," but already it was clear that he deemed it too dangerous and acknowledged such when he continued, "do not let any one see this [letter] you had best burn it when you read it."[59] Perceiving a danger for Benjamin Jones, Stout wrote in his letter of December 23, "I think that Ben is not wise in staying there." Of Charles Rich's cousin Thomas he added, "I want to see Thomas now worse than ever I did and he must come let what will be the case," but sensing the threat inherent in such a journey he added, "when Thomas starts he had better go by some other name than Rich as that is too well known for common use now on the road here" and suggested that he use instead his mother's maiden name, Ricketts.[60]

Likewise, Charles Rich was too well known—and sought after—for him to risk returning to Caldwell County or Missouri. True to their covenants with their wives, Stout and Rich had remained together throughout their hardships (with the brief exception when Rich crossed the Mississippi River two days before Stout) and now could do nothing more than wait and hope their wives would arrive unharmed. Other than having safely reached Illinois, out of reach of the mobs, there was very little during the Christmas season in which they could take comfort. With Governor Boggs's extermination order still in effect, it was certain that Zion, the gathering place for the Saints, would not be located in Missouri; and with Joseph Smith and other important church leaders in jail, Stout and Rich must have wondered, however briefly, if their religion even would survive.

Notes

1. Stevens, *Centennial History of Missouri*, vol. 2:108.
2. *Missouri House Journal*, 155, 188, 204.
3. Friends from Illinois who also were part of the Rich Branch included Morris Phelps, James Emmett, Lyman Wight, Sanford Porter, Solomon Wixom, and Benjamin Jones. See http://www.jwha.info/mmff/rbranch2.htm.

4. Though Hosea stated in his autobiography that he purchased "200 acres of good tillable land," the only recorded US government purchase of land by Hosea Stout was a forty acre tract on September 12, 1837, in Mirable Township. Missouri State Archives.
5. Samantha Peck was born on October 12, 1821, in Bainbridge, New York, the daughter of Benjamin Peck and Phoebe Crosby.
6. Allen and Leonard, *The Story of the Latter-day Saints*, 110–15.
7. Linn, *The Story of the Mormons*, 360.
8. Stout, "Journal."
9. There is neither an official nor a complete membership roster of the Danite organization and no direct proof that Hosea was a member. In his diary on March 21, 1846, he wrote, "we rode some Danite evolutions of horsemanship as practiced in the War in Davis County Missouri in the fall of 1838." See *On the Mormon Frontier: The Diary of Hosea Stout*, vol. 1:141. While not an admission of membership, inasmuch as his brother as well as best friends Benjamin Jones and Charles Rich definitely were Danite members, it is very likely that Hosea also was a Danite.
10. Stout, "Journal." "Gentile" was the word Mormons used to refer to all outside their religion.
11. "The Last Months of Mormonism in Missouri: The Albert Perry Rockwood Journal," *BYU Studies* 28:23.
12. Huntington, "Autobiography," http://www.boap.org/LDS/Early-Saints/OBHuntington.html.
13. Crawley, "Two Rare Missouri Documents," *BYU Studies* 14: 527.
14. Stout, "Journal."
15. Allred, "Journal," MS 18174, Church History Library.
16. LeSueur, *The 1838 Mormon War*, 112–14.
17. Stout, *Autobiography*, 56–57.
18. Hartley, *My Best for the Kingdom*, 69.
19. Rich, "Extract from Charles, C. Rich's History," *Millennial Star* 26:440.
20. Stout, *Autobiography*, 57.
21. Baugh, *A Call to Arms: The 1838 Defense of Northern Missouri*, 102. Allen Stout had "no arms or saddle" and stayed home. See Stout, "Journal."
22. Rich, "Extract." Hosea Stout in his autobiography stated that the group divided into two companies under Patten and Rich, while Lorenzo Dow Young, in his diary written fifty years after the fact said the third company was commanded by John P. Greene, not Durphee.
23. Baugh, *A Call to Arms*, 103.
24. LeSueur, *The 1838 Mormon War in Missouri*, 140.
25. Rockwood, "Journal entries, 1838 October–1839 January," 25.
26. Charles Rich replaced David Patten in command.
27. *Deseret Weekly* 45:277; Winn, *Exiles in a Land of Liberty*, 141.
28. *Deseret Weekly.*
29. Ibid.
30. Reed Peck, "Mormons So Called," (also known as "The Reed Peck Manuscript"), BX8645.P4, Huntington Library, San Marino, California.
31. The Governor to General Clark, October 27, 1838, in *Document Containing the Correspondence in Relation to Mormon Disturbances*, (Fayette, MO, 1841), 61.

32. Though for more than a century the spelling "Haun's Mill" was used, recent research has shown the proper spelling to be "Hawn's Mill."
33. Moore, *Bones in the Well: The Haun's Mill Massacre, 1838, A Documentary History*, 33–34. The information is taken from a newspaper article, reprinted in the book, by Burr Joyce that was published in the *St. Louis Globe-Democrat* for October 6, 1887, and is considered to be the best single account of the massacre.
34. Allred, "Autobiography," MS 1871, Church History Library. One rod is the equivalent of 16.5 feet.
35. Ibid.
36. Little, "Biography of Lorenzo Dow Young," *Utah Historical Quarterly* 14:57.
37. Stout, *Autobiography*, 58. Lorenzo Dow Young stated that there were twenty, not twenty-seven in the group.
38. Letter from Hosea Stout to his wife Samantha, December 23, 1838, MS 16397, Folder 1, Church History Library.
39. Rich, "Autobiography," MS 1543, 20.
40. Samuel Bogart letter to the Postmaster, April 22, 1839, MS 5704, Church History Library.
41. Adam-ondi-Ahman was a location in Daviess County, Missouri, which according to official teachings of the Church of Jesus Christ of Latter-day Saints is the site where Adam and Eve lived after being expelled from the Garden of Eden. They believe it will be a gathering spot for a meeting of the priesthood leadership, including prophets of all ages and other righteous people, prior to the Second Coming of Jesus Christ. See http://josephsmithpapers.org/place/adam-ondi-ahman-missouri.
42. Rich, "Autobiography," 20.
43. Little, "Biography of Lorenzo Dow Young," 59.
44. Rockwood, "Journal entries, 1838 October–1839 January," 28.
45. Stout, *Autobiography*, 59–60.
46. Little, "Biography of Lorenzo Dow Young," 57.
47. Little, "Lorenzo Dow Young," 57; Stout, *Autobiography*, 60. Stout wrote that the journey took eleven days while Lorenzo Young stated it was fifteen. The discrepancy at least in part can be reconciled by the fact that Stout counted the days of travel "North through a howling wilderness," which suggests that he began his count only after the snow began to fall rather than the day they left Far West.
48. Hosea Stout, *Autobiography*, 60.
49. Letter from George M. Hinkle to W. W. Phelps, August 14, 1844, as quoted in Wilcox, *The Latter Day Saints on the Missouri Frontier*, 346–349.
50. Bushman, *Joseph Smith: Rough Stone Rolling*, 336.
51. Stout, "Journal."
52. Bushman, *Rough Stone Rolling*, 633–35. Of the fifty-three who were arrested, all but four—Captain William Allred, Andrew Whitlock, Daniel Carn, and Sidney Turner—were affiliated with the Danites to some degree according to sworn testimony (some of which, such as in the case of Sampson Avard, was less than truthful). According to the testimony of both George Hinkle and Sampson Avard, Martin C. Allred and William Moore Allred were Danites. See Quinn, *The Mormon Hierarchy: Origins of Power*, 480–85.

53. Rockwood, "Journal entries, 1838 October–1839 January," 27.
54. Letter from Allen Stout to Hosea Stout, January 27, 1839, MS 16397, Folder 1, Church History Library.
55. Letter from Charles Rich to Sarah Rich, January 21, 1839, *Selected Collections from the Archives of the Church of Jesus Christ of Latter-day Saints*, DVD collection, 1:36.
56. Letter from Hosea Stout to his wife Samantha, December 23, 1838, MS 16397, Folder 1, Church History Library.
57. Letter from Hosea Stout to his wife Samantha, December 17, 1838, MS 16397, Folder 1, Church History Library.
58. Letter from Hosea Stout to his wife Samantha, December 23, 1838.
59. Letter from Hosea Stout to his wife Samantha, December 17, 1838.
60. Letter from Hosea Stout to his wife Samantha, December 23, 1838.

6
Refuge in Illinois

Justice in America is supposed to be blind, but as the year 1838 drew to a close in northern Missouri it had one eye open and squarely focused on the Mormons. No charges were ever brought against any of the two hundred militiamen who slaughtered seventeen Mormon men and boys and wounded fifteen at Hawn's Mill, though the identities of many of the "principal actors" were known to the public.[1] On the other hand, dozens of Mormons who were associated with the battle at Crooked River were sought for murder in the killing of one Missouri militiaman. In a similar vein, plundering and burning of homes by Mormons in the conflict was considered a crime while similar destruction by anti-Mormon vigilantes went unpunished. Joseph Smith complained, rightfully, that the law was "always administered against us and never in our favor."[2]

Following their surrender in early November, and with Smith and other leaders in custody, the Mormon men in Far West were required to assemble and to hand over their weapons to the militia. "Far West was searched for arms and ammunitions, they said, but when they found anything they wanted, they took it," wrote Lyman Shurtliff in his autobiography. "During this time we were insulted and abused, both old and young, male and female. We had no peace or safety night or day."[3] Albert Rockwood went further, recording, "this army murdered, plundered, and destroyed."[4] In Caldwell County there were numerous reports of destruction and theft of crops and property, in some instances by the state militia. Rockwood noted, "We are captives in a defenceless condition, suffering the insult, of our Enemies daily, but their comeing among us and taking what or who they please and that too without any precept, or authority."[5]

In a letter to Governor Boggs on December 23, 1838, Austin A. King, judge of the Missouri Fifth Circuit Court, wrote:

> I have recently seen Col. Price, who made known to me the object of his mission to this part of the State. In reference to the lawless depredations said to be practiced [*sic*] on the Mormons, I have no doubt that the charges are, to a certain extent, true . . . In most of the cases of outrage against the property of the Mormons, it has been by persons who pretend, and perhaps truly, that the Mormons owe them, or by persons who say that the Mormons, in their late outrages upon them, have destroyed their property, and they take this means to indemnify themselves. This certainly is an unlawful, and highly objectionable course.[6]

King, however, apparently made no effort to bring to justice the non-Mormons accused of unlawful activity; to the contrary, conditions worsened. Albert Rockwood wrote on November 25, "Our houses are rifled and our sheep and hogs and horses are driven of[f] before our eyes by the Missourians, who come in small companies well armed; here is no law for poor Mormons."[7] In a letter to his brother Hosea dated January 8, 1839, Allen Stout noted, "we are threatened on every side and cal[l]ed every thing that is bad . . . we no not how soon we shal be drove out of the State." In the same letter Benjamin Jones added, "the times is truly harde here we dont know how soon we may haf to leve here for we ar thretned on every hand they ar suing and tarring brothern up on all occasions."[8]

In Hosea's absence, his father Joseph—who evidently had not become a Mormon—lived in his son's house with another family.[9] John Larkey, who in late 1838 married Lydia Stout, also apparently was not Mormon and was permitted to stay.[10] While Mormons who renounced their religion and non-Mormons were allowed to remain, most of the Saints in Caldwell County were forced from their homes and gathered in Far West, which became a refugee camp with insufficient food and housing. In December, the Saints appealed to the Missouri General Assembly to rescind the expulsion order of the governor, to restore their lands and to appropriate funds to pay for the damages they had sustained, but the Assembly appropriated $2,000 to aid in their departure from the state while voting the militia $200,000 to cover its expenses in the war.

With armed patrols threatening, the Mormons had no choice but to move from the state, even in the dead of winter, and in a public meeting on January 26 they agreed to leave immediately. Allen Stout, fortunate enough to harvest his crops, sold corn for seventy-five cents per barrel and thus raised twenty dollars to finance Samantha Stout's journey to Illinois to join Hosea.[11] Like their husbands, Samantha and Sarah Rich kept their covenant to remain together until they reunited with their husbands. Sarah, who was eight months pregnant, wrote of Samantha, "She was like a dear sister to me through all my trials and hardships in Missouri. She, too, passing through hardships and sorrows as well as myself; but she being poor in health and very young, her hardships shortened her days."[12] The two women gathered what little they had and departed in a freezing storm on February 3 with Thomas Rich and Sarah's father, John Pea. Having been unwillingly relieved of most of their possessions by the militia and mobs, the four families were able to fit their entire belongings into two wagons.

Reaching the previously frozen Mississippi River, they found the ice broken and the current running so swiftly on the west side of the river that the ferryboat could not cross. "So of course, I and Sister Stout felt quite down-hearted; we knew our husbands were on the opposite side in Quincy waiting for us," Sarah wrote. The only chance to cross was to make it in a skiff or canoe to an island and from there to cross over the ice that covered the east side of the river. Seeing Sarah pregnant and in poor health, George Grant volunteered to go across to notify her husband Charles of her presence, but as Grant reached the island the ice broke and he fell into the river. As the sun began to set behind them, Sarah and Samantha watched from a distance as two men ran across the ice from the other side to save him. Only later did the women learn that the rescuers were their husbands.[13]

After caring for Grant, Stout and Rich, with a compatriot named Webb, carried a skiff on their shoulders across the ice to an island. Despite the approaching darkness and hazardous ice floes, the men managed to cross the river to meet their wives. "Great was our joy!" exclaimed Sarah Rich. "To meet with our loved companions who were compelled to part with us three months before and flee for their lives from a howling mob."[14]

The men remained with their spouses overnight; with the new dawn they concluded that it was best to cross the river at once, since it was unlikely that the ferry would be able to operate for at least several days while Sarah was nearing childbirth, and so the three couples loaded into a single canoe for the crossing. "Just think of it my dear reader," Sarah rhapsodized, "to see us undertake such a perilous trip across the water running with ice, the cakes of which were so large that some times the men would have to jump back out on the ice in order to push it away and jump back into the canoe again, and by hard work reached the ice on the other side."[15] Stout reported that he and his wife had "met each other in good health and spirits," though in this he told a half-truth, since Samantha was greatly weakened by the ordeal.[16]

The citizens of Quincy treated the Mormons, most of whom were too exhausted and impoverished to travel any further, with kindness, sympathy, and respect. With a quickly burgeoning Mormon population, which before long was triple that of the citizens of Quincy, housing was limited and thus a majority of the refugees lived in makeshift quarters. "A multitude of people, men, women, and children, ragged, dirty, and miserable generally, seemed to be living in tents and covered wagons, for lack of better habitations," wrote the Reverend George Peck as he traveled up the Mississippi River in late spring 1839. "We were informed that they were Mormons, who had recently fled from Missouri"[17]

Hosea and Samantha, however, found shelter at David Nelson's Mission Institute about five miles east of Quincy, which had a modestly sized main brick building surrounded by a number of small one-story structures called student lodges.[18] In 1836 Dr. Nelson, a southerner who had freed his slaves, was driven out of Missouri due to his strong and vocal anti-slavery message. A trained physician who left medicine to become a minister, he settled in Quincy and established the Mission Institute, which was to be a school for the education of missionaries. All teachers were abolitionists (as were the students) and in 1839–1840 the Institute became part of the Underground Railroad, helping Negroes escape from slavery in Missouri.

As was the case with the Mormons, Dr. Nelson had been driven out of Missouri—albeit for a different reason—and shared with the Saints an antipathy toward the citizens of that state. While not necessarily abolitionists, Mormons were anti-slavery, another point in common with Dr. Nelson. The first known case of helping a slave escape from Missouri and sheltering him at the Mission Institute was in 1839, roughly at the time Stout and his wife took up temporary residence there. It is not difficult to imagine the family being taken into the Institute to help protect Stout from Missouri authorities, much the same as transpired with escaped slaves later that year and the next.[19]

Hosea and Samantha remained at the Mission Institute for two months, which happened to coincide with Joseph Smith's arrival in Quincy in April. While the Saints were struggling to survive during the first few months at Quincy, Smith and the other imprisoned leaders (with the exception of Sidney Rigdon, who had been released on bail and fled to Quincy) were still in jail at Liberty, Missouri. On April 6 the prisoners were taken from Liberty to Gallatin for a hearing before Judge Austin King, and five days later a grand jury indicted Joseph and Hyrum Smith, Lyman Wight, Alexander McRae, and Caleb Baldwin for murder, treason, burglary, arson, larceny, and theft. On the way to Boone County, where they had been granted an unexpected change of venue, the five prisoners escaped. According to Hyrum Smith, the guards imbibed whiskey and in their drunken state, very likely by design, allowed them to flee.[20]

Mormon spirits were raised considerably when Smith and his compatriots arrived at Quincy on April 22, 1839, exactly one week after their escape. The presence of the prophet in their midst brought a sense of security, allowing Hosea and Samantha to feel they could move from the Mission Institute to the small town of Payson, about fourteen miles southeast of Quincy. Hosea pointedly wrote that he "worked at the carpenters trade for a support" while at Payson, with a clear inference that he had not worked while at the Mission Institute.

While imprisoned at Liberty, Joseph Smith instructed the Saints to assemble their grievances against Missouri, to organize a committee and to present the information to the US government.[21] Following his counsel, Stout made a record and on May 21—about a month after moving to Payson—appeared before Carlo M. Woods, clerk of the Circuit Court for Adams County, and filed the following claim:

> A Bill of damages against the State of Missouri
>
> | | |
> |---|---:|
> | For moving in the state | $50.00 |
> | For the Loss of 200 acres of land | 2000.00 |
> | For the Loss of Property | 50.00 |
> | For the Loss of Time 6 months, 20 | 120.00 |
> | For leaving the State by orders of the Governor | 500.00 |
> | | $2,720.00 |
>
> This may certify the above is a correct account according to the best of my knowledge
>
> Hosea Stout[22]

Many of the affidavits were similar in form and content to Stout's. He, like other Mormons who were expelled from Missouri by proclamation of the governor, felt justified in asking compensation for having been forced out of the state, and his petition was among the 491 that Joseph Smith later took to Washington, DC, in an effort to gain redress for their losses in Missouri. Smith eventually gained an audience with President Martin Van Buren of New York, who professed sympathy but declined to help, reportedly saying, "Your cause is just, but I can do nothing for you."[23] Giving a more detailed explanation, Van Buren said, "What can I do? I can do nothing for you! If I do anything, I shall come in contact with the whole state of Missouri."[24] His reasoning seemed to be that it was a matter of state's rights, and thus the Saints had to look to Missouri for compensation.

Though later attempts (also unsuccessful) would be made for redress, the message was clear that it was time to put Missouri in the past and to move on. Even while he was imprisoned at Liberty, Smith was making plans to do just that by creating another gathering place. Whereas some church leaders questioned the wisdom of once again congregating en masse, Smith was adamant that the Saints must remain together as a group. The location for such a gathering presented itself, somewhat ironically, because of the path that a few of the comrades of Hosea Stout and Charles Rich followed after fleeing Far West.

While most of the refugees, including Stout and Rich, headed south for the Quincy ferry upon reaching the Mississippi River, Israel Barlow and a few others were attracted to Montrose, Iowa, because of the abandoned Fort Des Moines, which they judged could house forty to fifty refugee families. While there Barlow learned that Dr. Isaac Galland held the deed to much land on both sides of the river. Barlow and his associates crossed the river to the small Illinois town of Commerce, where they met Galland and told him of the plight of the Mormons at Far West.

Galland was sympathetic with the Mormon cause and, sensing a chance to sell much of his property, sent several letters to Joseph Smith while he was incarcerated at Liberty. In March 1839, Joseph Smith wrote from jail to Bishop Edward Partridge in Quincy:

> It still seems to bear heavily on our minds that the Church would do well to secure to themselves the contract of the land which is proposed to them by Mr. Isaac Galland, and to cultivate the friendly feelings of that gentlemen, inasmuch as he shall prove himself to be a man of honor and a friend to humanity.[25]

Galland proposed to sell land both at Commerce on the east side of the Mississippi and directly across the river in Lee County, Iowa. The latter, originally known as the Half-Breed Tract, was set aside by Congress as a refuge for the offspring of frontiersmen and Indians, but the land had been sold and resold to the point that true ownership of the land was difficult to ascertain. Nevertheless, the terms offered by Galland—twenty thousand acres at two dollars an acre with nothing down and twenty years to pay, with properties that the Saints abandoned in Missouri as partial payment—were too attractive not to accept.

The first purchase of about 170 acres of land, in the neighborhood of Commerce, about fifty miles north of Quincy, took place on April 30, 1839, and soon the Saints were flocking to their new gathering place. The site of Commerce (later renamed Nauvoo by the Saints), on a large bend of the Mississippi River at the head of the Des Moines rapids, was among the most beautiful in the region. The beauty of the area, however, could not disguise the fact that it was swampland, full of mosquitoes and with water unfit for human consumption. An early settler, Jesse Crosby, referred to the area as "sickly," and later recorded, "Our enemies had been known to say that we would die all of us if we attempted to settle there."[26] Joseph Smith became well aware of these problems:

> The place was literally a wilderness. The land was mostly covered with trees and bushes, and much of it so wet that it was with the utmost difficulty a footman could get through, and totally impossible for teams. Commerce was so unhealthful, very few could live there; but believing that it might become a healthful place by the blessing of heaven to the Saints, and no more eligible place presenting itself, I considered it wisdom to make an attempt to build up a city.[27]

The swamps were a breeding ground for the *Anopheles* mosquito, a carrier of malaria, and scores of Saints became ill and many died from the disease. Other communicable diseases, notably dysentery, typhoid, meningitis, scarlet fever, and diphtheria, were rampant. When Benjamin Johnson arrived in Commerce in the summer of 1839, he reported, "Nearly every one was sick . . . Nearly all were down with typhoid or malarial fever which it almost seemed would sweep the place with death, for among all the families of the saints it was rare to find one who was able to wait upon and care for another."[28]

Across the river in Lee County, Iowa, the bluffs rose abruptly, almost from the water's edge, and were covered by a fine growth of timber, and the lack of swampland meant less disease than in Commerce. Nestling at the foot of one of the highest of the bluffs was the little village of Montrose, in and around which fifty thousand acres were purchased in June and July 1839.[29] The availability of plentiful and cheap land and healthier environs attracted hundreds, and the Mormon population of Lee County began to swell, even though Joseph Smith had encouraged everyone gathering nearby to congregate instead in Commerce.

On August 5, Hosea and Samantha joined the migration to Lee County, stopping first for a week in Quincy. Anticipating the arrival in Iowa six days hence, on August 6 Hosea wrote his cousin Daniel Capps, of Grainger County, Tennessee, that, although he had been driven from place to place, he at last was settled, which could have been a reference to his emotions as well as his geographical location.[30] In response to a letter written by Hosea very shortly after leaving the Mission Institute, Capps wrote, "I re[a]d yours of the 5th of May which was a ha[r]binger of misfortune and distress; instead of prosperity and tranquility."[31]

Hosea had recently received word that both his sister Sarah and his father, Joseph, had died of consumption.[32] More important to him, however, was the poor health of his wife, who during the stay in Payson "was mostly confined to her bed in consequence of the exposures she had endured from the troubles in Missour[i] and in removing to Illinois in the month of February."[33] But despite his wife's frail condition, after a little more than three months in Payson, he prepared to move to Iowa.

In his letter of August 6 Stout gave his cousin a brief sketch of the principles of his religion. Capps wrote back, "if Be of the Lord it will stand in time and in Eternity."[34] Stout was convinced his religion was of the Lord and would stand the test of time. Moreover, his destination was the newly designated place of gathering for the Saints, and Zion seemed as likely to be found in the two settlements at Hancock County, Illinois, and Lee County, Iowa, as anywhere else. In this spirit of gathering, he wrote the words to a hymn, "O Lord, Our Father Let Thy Grace," that would be included in the section "Gathering of Israel" in an 1841 updated version of the official Mormon hymnal:

> O Lord, our Father let thy grace
> Shed its glad beams on Jacob's race,
> Restore that long lost scattered band
> And call them to their native land.
> Their mis'ry let thy mercy heal,
> Their trespass hide, their pardon seal;
> O God of Israel hear our pray'r,
> And grant that they thy love may share.
> How long shall Jacob's offspring prove
> The sad suspension of thy love,
> And shall thy wrath perpetual burn
> And yet thou ne'er to them return?
> Thy quick'ning Spirit now impart,
> Awake to joy each grateful heart,
> While Israel's rescued tribes in thee,
> Their bliss and full salvation see.[35]

The Mormon population in Hancock County, Illinois, was growing at a swift rate as the Saints gathered and by autumn was sufficiently large to merit holding a General Conference to form the Nauvoo Stake (an administrative unit composed of multiple congregations). Stout crossed the river where he received the priesthood and "was ordained an elder in the Church of Christ at the General Conference of said Church held at Nauvoo October the 5th 1839 under the hands of Elder Seymour Brunson."[36]

To Mormons, the priesthood is the power and authority to act in the name of God. Whereas worthy males typically first receive the Aaronic, or "lesser" Priesthood, in earlier days adult males frequently bypassed that step and were ordained directly to the office of elder in the "higher" or Melchizedek Priesthood. While baptism carries a sense of belonging, receiving the priesthood is both an accomplishment and an enabling, for with it one has the authority to give blessings, heal the sick, confer the gift of the Holy Ghost, and be a "standing minister" to watch over the church, among other duties.[37] The importance of the office was underscored by Allen Stout, who was ordained an elder immediately after his brother and Thomas Rich, when he wrote is his journal, "I got my license as an elder . . . which I now have in Hyrum Smith's own handwriting, which I intend to always try and preserve."[38]

Becoming an elder in the priesthood was a very significant event in Hosea's life, but despite his newly ordained authority he was powerless to help his wife, whose health continued to deteriorate. Unable to recover from the privations suffered in the harsh Missouri winter of the previous year, Samantha died on November 29, just a month after her eighteenth birthday.[39] On March 4, 1840, Hosea again wrote to his cousin Daniel Capps; though his letter is long lost, he obviously still was in a state mourning, as can be ascertained from Daniel's consoling response:

> Yours of the 4th March Which Came to hand 15 of May; instead of hearing from you in the manner I expected and hop'd to "C" what a shock of horror flashed over Me to hear of the irreparable Loss you have sustain'd . . . dear Cousin there is nothing certain in this Life but death;
>
> As man was made to mourn and undergo misfortune of this Life Let us Look beyond the Gloomy appendages of death to that great day of the reserretion of the Lord Jesus Christ where if through Life we've kept the Law of God we may pass through the dark Valley of the Shadow of Death; and rise through faith Victorious over death hell and and the grave and enter into the Joy of our Lord.[40]

Six years later as he visited Samantha's grave, Stout revealed his tender thoughts about his departed mate:

> I went in company with Br John D. Lee to the camp on Sugar Creek This was near to the place where I lived at the time my wife (Surmantha) died and was the place of many a mournful hour to me in days gone by when by her death I was deprived of all and the last bosom friend which I then had on

earth in whom I could implicitly confide . . . When I left this place I went disconsolate and alone mourning her untimely death and my own lonesome condition But I went to Nauvoo to keep the commandments of god and my history from that time to this will show the scenes of peril and want which I went through to roll forth the kingdom.[41]

Stout's words echoed his description of losing his mother ("I lost the only unwavering friend that I had"), but Samantha's death hit much harder, as would be expected with the loss of a spouse. Nevertheless, following the letter of March 4 to his cousin his period of mourning ended abruptly, as within days of its writing he moved to Nauvoo where, on March 8, he was called to serve as clerk pro tem of the Nauvoo High Council, a position that he assumed immediately upon his arrival.[42] It was a small yet noteworthy first step on his road to becoming one of the most important—and notorious—figures in the history of Mormon Nauvoo.

Notes

1. Peck, "Manuscript," 132.
2. Ibid.; LeSueur, *The 1838 Mormon War*, 253.
3. Shurtliff, "Autobiography," http://www.boap.org/LDS/Early-Saints/LShurtliff.html. The original manuscript is found in Harold B. Lee Library, Brigham Young University.
4. Rockwood, "Journal entries, 1838 October–1839 January," 27. Letter to his brother dated November 10, 1838.
5. Ibid.
6. Letter from Judge Austin King to Governor Lilburn Boggs, December 23, 1838, http://josephsmithpapers.org/paperSummary/letter-from-austin-a-king-10-september-1838?p=.
7. Rockwood, "Journal entries, 1838 October–1839 January," 29. Letter dated November 25, 1838.
8. Letter from Allen Stout and Benjamin Jones to Hosea Stout, January 8, 1839, MS 16397, Folder 1, Church History Library.
9. Ibid.
10. Ibid.
11. Stout, "Journal."
12. Rich, "Autobiography," 21.
13. Ibid., 22.
14. Ibid.
15. Ibid.
16. Stout, *Autobiography*, 59.
17. Cannon, *Nauvoo Panorama*, 17.
18. Ibid. Stout called it the "Missionary Institute." See also Kuhns, "Home Education and Missions in the Old Northwest," *Journal of the Presbyterian*

Historical Society 32:21. The description of the buildings at the Institute is given in *The Journal of the Illinois State Historical Society* 21:162.
19. *Journal of the Illinois State Historical Society* 21:157–62; 23:76.
20. Affidavit of Hyrum Smith, *Times and Seasons*, July 1, 1843. Non-Mormons had a slightly different version of the event, and Sheriff William Morgan and former Sheriff William Bowman were roughed up by the citizens of Gallatin due to their neglect of duty.
21. *D&C* 123:1–6.
22. Johnson, *Mormon Redress Petitions: Documents of the 1833–1838 Missouri Conflict*, 359–60.
23. *Warsaw Signal*, April 9, 1845, 2.
24. Bushman, *Rough Stone Rolling*, 393.
25. *The Joseph Smith Papers*, http://josephsmithpapers.org/paperSummary/letter-to-the-church-and-edward-partridge-20-march-1839.
26. Crosby, "History and Biography of Jesse W. Crosby," 7.
27. Smith, *History of the Church*, 3:375.
28. Johnson, *My Life's Review*, (Independence, MO, 1947), 60.
29. Kimball, "Nauvoo West: Mormons of the Iowa Shore," *BYU Studies* 18, no. 2:136.
30. Letter from D. B. Capps to Hosea Stout, January 4, 1840, MS 16397, Folder 2, Church History Library.
31. Letter from D. B. Capps to Hosea Stout, June 6, 1840, MS 16397, Folder 2, Church History Library.
32. Stout, "Journal." Allen noted that his father died at the age of seventy-three and of his twelve children only four remained (Hosea, Allen, Anna, and Lydia). Sarah died about twenty-five miles south of Quincy while Joseph died at the home of his brother Jacob in Missouri.
33. Stout, *Autobiography*, 60.
34. Ibid.
35. *A Collection of Sacred Hymns for the Church of Jesus Christ of Latter-day Saints*, 1841 edition (also known as the "Nauvoo Hymnal"). The hymnal had 304 hymns; of the 143 hymns that were added to earlier editions of the publication, only ten were of Mormon authorship: three each by Eliza R. Snow and Mary Judd Page, and one each by Hosea Stout, Robert B. Thompson, W. W. Phelps, and Austin Cowles. Stout's was listed as hymn 157. Though on the surface the text refers to the Jews (Judah was a son of Jacob) and to Israel, it is important to note that Mormons consider themselves to be members of the "House of Israel" and Stout undoubtedly wrote in context of gathering of Mormons rather than of Jews.
36. Stout, *Autobiography*, 60; "Letterbook 2," *The Joseph Smith Papers*, http://josephsmithpapers.org/paperSummary/letterbook-2?p=170#!/paperSummary/letterbook-2andp=170.
37. *D&C* 20:38–50; 124:137.
38. Stout, "Journal."
39. November 29, 1839, also was the day that Joseph Smith and Judge Elias Higbee met with President Martin Van Buren to present the Mormon's redress petitions. Van Buren rejected the redress plea in February 1840, evidently for political reasons.

40. Letter from D. B. Capps to Hosea Stout, May 17, 1840, MS 16397, Folder 2, Church History Library.
41. Brooks, ed., *On the Mormon Frontier: The Diary of Hosea Stout, 1844–1861*, February 13, 1846, 122.
42. Dinger, ed., *Nauvoo City and High Council Minutes*, 361.

7
Rising through the Ranks

"The site of Nauvoo is one of the most beautiful on the Mississippi River," wrote David N. White, editor of the *Pittsburgh Weekly Gazette*, in 1843. "The river at this place makes a large bend, forming a semi-circle, within which lies the lower part of the city, running back to the bluff."[1] From the banks of the Mississippi, wrote B. H. Roberts, "the ground rises gradually for at least a mile where it reaches the common level of the prairie that stretches out to the eastward, farther than the eye can reach, in a beautifully undulating surface, once covered by a luxuriant growth of natural grasses and wild flowers, with here and there patches of meadows."[2]

Despite the flowery descriptions, in late April 1839 when Joseph Smith led a party north from Quincy to Commerce, the area, according to Smith, "was literally a wilderness" and so unhealthy that "very few could live there."[3] Nevertheless, Smith believed "that it might become a healthy place by the blessing of heaven" and on May 1 purchased the farms of Hugh White and Isaac Galland. Other, larger land purchases followed the first acquisition, the largest of which were on the Iowa side of the river, but Smith had chosen the east bank of the river for his own residence and that became the Saints' new gathering place. "When I made the purchase of White and Galland," wrote Smith, "there were one stone house, three frame houses, and two block houses, which constituted the whole city of Commerce."[4]

By May 1840 about three hundred dwellings had been erected, mostly small wooden dwellings but occasionally brick homes of more imposing size and appearance.[5] In the autumn of that year, a few months after the name of the town officially had been changed to Nauvoo, a census listed 2,450 residents, thus surpassing Quincy as the largest urban area in the region (by comparison, Chicago that same year listed 4,470 residents).[6] The streets were laid out exactly north to south and east to west; each block formed a square of four acres that was subdivided into four one-acre lots.

DOI: 10.7330/9781607324775.c007

Figure 7.1. A Portrait of Hosea Stout, 1845, by Robert Campbell.

Upon his arrival in Nauvoo from Quincy in March 1840, Hosea Stout purchased a one-acre plot at a prime location on Main Street at the intersection of Knight Street, directly down the hill and about four blocks from the future temple.[7] He lived in Nauvoo's third "ward" (a word borrowed from the term for political districts of the frontier municipality that came to denote a Mormon congregation), as did his close friends Charles C. Rich, Thomas Rich (who in 1840 married Henrietta Peck, the sister of Hosea's late wife Samantha), Benjamin Jones, and Hosea's future brother-in-law Allen Taylor. He remained in his position as clerk pro tem of the high council until November 28, at which time the words 'pro tem' were eliminated from the title. As if to celebrate his promotion, he married Louisa Taylor on the following day (a Sunday), exactly one year after the death of his wife Samantha.

Stout's aptitude for keeping full and accurate records was put to good use when on October 1 1842 he was asked by the Nauvoo High Council to help write the record of Far West, though in fact he became the sole recorder or copier of minutes contained in the Far West Record, one of only two general church minute books for the Joseph Smith period.[8] The "Record" is particularly important to Latter-day Saints in providing insights into the nature of several of Smith's revelations as well as significant information regarding church organization.

In the early 1840s, Illinois was about equally divided between the two major political parties, the Whigs and the Democrats. Though Nauvoo was not yet an incorporated city, it was growing rapidly, and the power of the Mormon vote became increasingly evident to political leaders. Because of this, the Mormon leaders were able to obtain support of both parties in passage on December 16 1840 of a very liberal charter by the Illinois State Legislature, which made Nauvoo the sixth city in the state with an official charter.[9] The Nauvoo Charter had the unusual feature of empowering the municipal court to grant writs of habeas corpus, which were used later to free arrested persons, in particular Joseph Smith, regardless of the jurisdiction in which they were apprehended. It provided for the creation of a university and allowed the boundaries of Nauvoo, generous to begin with, to be enlarged easily. But the crowning provision of the Charter gave the city its own militia.

The Nauvoo Legion was created by the city council on February 3, 1841. Though most local militias in the state were organized at the county level, the Nauvoo Legion was a city militia controlled directly by the mayor. Loosely modeled after the Roman Legion, the Nauvoo Legion was divided into two cohorts, or brigades, each commanded by a brigadier general and his staff. A court-martial consisting of the legion's commissioned officers was created and was given extensive authority. Unlike a typical military court-martial, it was not a judicial body but was granted the authority to "make, ordain, establish, and execute all such laws and ordinances as may be considered necessary for the benefit, government, and regulation of said Legion; provided [that] said Court Martial shall pass no law or act, repugnant to, or inconsistent with, the Constitution of the United States, or of this State [Illinois]."[10]

Stout was a previously commissioned officer of the state of Illinois—having been elected on May 16, 1840, second lieutenant in the second battalion of the fifty-ninth regiment of the Illinois militia—and with twenty other commissioned officers was selected as a member of the court-martial, which met for the first time on February 4, 1841, at the office of Joseph Smith.[11] After being called to order by Nauvoo mayor John C. Bennett, the court's first business was to elect Titus Billings and Stephen Winchester "Judges" and Hosea Stout "Clerk of the election," after which general officers were elected, most notably Joseph Smith as lieutenant general.[12] Not only was Smith the Legion's top officer, but his rank was the highest held by any military officer in the United States since George Washington, who also was a lieutenant general. Following the approval of his election by Illinois officials, others discovered what Smith already knew, namely that only a court-martial of his equals could remove him, and he had no equals in military rank in the entire country.[13]

Stout also served as "recorder" or clerk of the legion, not just of the election, and in that capacity authored all written records of the legion's early organizational meetings.[14] On February 11, one week after the legion was organized, he was elevated to the rank of captain to fill the vacancy created when A. P. Rockwood was promoted.[15] When the court-martial assembled for the second time, on February 20, dates were set for general parades, the first of which took place on April 6, the eleventh anniversary of the founding of the church.

Great excitement preceded the parade. "It frequently happens," wrote the semi-monthly Latter-day Saint periodical, *Times and Seasons*, "that our anticipations of pleasure and delight are raised to such a height that even exceeds the enjoyment itself, but we are happy to say this was not the case with the immense multitude who witnessed the proceedings of the sixth of April."[16] Shortly after sunrise "loud peals from the artilery were heard," and by nine o'clock the 650 men of the militia were ready for review. "It was indeed a gladsome sight, and extremely affecting," continued the *Times and Seasons*, "to see the old revolutionary patriots, who had been driven from their homes in Missouri, strike hands, and rejoice together, in a land where they knew they would be protected from mobs and where they could again enjoy the liberty for which they had fought many a hard battle."[17]

Stout composed a special eight-stanza poem, "Legion of Nauvoo," for the occasion, and while there is no evidence that it was read in public, the second through fourth stanzas give clear indication of an expectation that a powerful Legion, backed by the state of Illinois, would help protect the Mormons from their foes:

> Our "Legion" is all powerful, t'is war-like, brave, and grand,
> E're long t'will prove a terror to Boggs and all his clan,
> T'is peaceable and harmless to all who come to view,
> Or, have a mind to settle in the "City of Nauvoo."
> Now should our foes be gathered to drive us from our lands,
> Or try to thwart our purposes, to break the Lord's commands,

The day they come against us, as they before did do,
They'll feel the weight and power of the "Legion of
   Nauvoo."
They'll find that Illinois firm in her place will stand,
And, faithfully, sustain us, in peace upon our land.
They'll find that she doth sanction, all that we want to do,
And, especially she'll strengthen then the "Legion of
   Nauvoo."[18]

Much more important to the Saints than the Legion that day was laying the cornerstone for the temple, the "House of the Lord," the construction of which was one of the primary reasons for gathering to Nauvoo. A revelation in 1833 stated: "I gave unto you a commandment, that you should build an house, in the which house I design to endow whom I have chosen with power from on high."[19] A temple had been constructed in Kirtland and dedicated on March 27, 1836, but it was abandoned when the Saints left the city to go to Missouri in 1838. Three more temples were planned in Missouri—at Independence, Far West, and Adam-ondi-Ahman—though none were constructed. Joseph Smith stated publicly in July 1840 regarding the building of a temple in Nauvoo, "Now brethren I obligate myself to build as great a temple as ever Solomon did, if the church will back me up."[20]

The construction that commenced with the laying of the cornerstone continued for nearly five years. Members were expected to tithe their labor as well as their income, working one day in ten for the church, with much of this tithing labor directed toward the completion of the temple. "Such a multitude of people," dictated the prophet for his personal history, "moving in harmony, in friendship, in dignity, told in a voice not easily misunderstood, that they were a people of intelligence, and virtue and order; in short, that they were *Saints* . . . and that they were blessed and happy."[21] For Joseph Smith it was utopia, though trials for him always seemed to be just around the corner.

On Friday, June 4, 1841, Smith visited Governor Carlin at his residence in Quincy and reported being treated "with the greatest kindness and respect." Carlin gave no hint that he had received a writ for Smith from Governor Boggs, but a few hours after the visit ended he sent Sheriff Thomas King of Adams County and Constable Thomas Jasper of Quincy with a posse to arrest Smith and hand him over to Missouri authorities. When news of the arrest reached Nauvoo on June 6, Stout and six others—including Elijah Abel, a former slave who since 1832 had been a faithful Mormon—started immediately from the Nauvoo landing in a skiff to overtake and, if necessary, rescue Smith. Arriving in Quincy at dusk, the men went to Benjamin Jones's house where they learned that the prophet had obtained a writ of *habeas corpus* and had returned to Nauvoo in charge of two officers while awaiting a hearing on his case.[22] Smith was released when Judge Stephen A. Douglas, future presidential opponent of Abraham Lincoln, decided the case on a technicality and declared the Missouri writ of extradition void.

Three months later, on September 4, Stout was promoted to the rank of major in the Nauvoo Legion.[23] Since the parade of April 6, the Legion had more than doubled in size: in his minutes of the Legion from September 11 he wrote, "The official returns of the Legion show the aggregate to be 1,490 men."[24] During the same period the population of Nauvoo had grown rapidly—the prophet himself had estimated the number at about three thousand early in the year, which seemed to be a fair estimate though the number increased by at least a few thousand more by year's end.

In fact, the latter part of 1841 and early months of 1842 have been regarded as the high tide of Mormon prosperity in Nauvoo.[25] The temple alone cost one million dollars, an astounding amount considering that the typical daily wage was one dollar. By late 1842, Mormons were living in about a dozen settlements on both sides of the Mississippi River near the Des Moines Rapids. A visitor to Nauvoo at this time wrote:

> The incorporated limits of Nauvoo contains, it is said, about seven thousand persons; the buildings are generally small and much scattered. The Temple and Nauvoo House, now building, will probably, in beauty of design, extent and durability, excel any public building in the state, and will both be enclosed before winter.
>
> From all I saw and heard, I am led to believe that, before many years, the city of Nauvoo will be the largest and most beautiful city of the west, provided the Mormons are unmolested in the peaceable enjoyment of their rights and privileges, and why they should be troubled while acting as good citizens, I cannot imagine; and I hope and trust that the people of Illinois have no disposition to disturb unoffending people who have no disposition but to live peaceably under the laws of the country, and to worship God under their own vine and fig tree.[26]

So impressive was the industry in Nauvoo that even the Reverend Henry Caswall, otherwise a very harsh critic of Joseph Smith and Mormonism, was duly impressed at first sight while on a visit to Nauvoo in April 1842:

> Curiosity led me to the river's side, where about forty steamboats were busily engaged in receiving or discharging their various cargoes. The spectacle was truly exciting. The landing-place (or levée, as it is denominated) was literally swarming with life.[27]

Though some non-Mormons lived there, there was no denying that Nauvoo was indeed a "City of the Mormons," a reference often used in the press; as such the attitude of outsiders toward the city was greatly influenced by their opinion of Mormonism, and many frowned upon some newly revealed practices. One such was disclosed by Joseph Smith in a sermon in August 1840 at the funeral of Seymour Brunson, who had ordained Stout an elder in 1839 and also in May 1840 had administered the oath to him, making him a second lieutenant in the Illinois militia. Citing a New Testament scripture that referred to the practice and the necessity for man to "be born of water and the spirit" to enter into the Kingdom of God, Smith announced that church members could perform baptisms for deceased family and friends.[28]

Smith's followers readily accepted the new doctrine and many rushed to the banks of the Mississippi to perform the ordinance, in some cases being immersed repeatedly.[29] Significantly, Hosea chose to be baptized that year only for his mother (his brother Allen stood proxy for their sister Rebecca and their grandparents Samuel and Rachel Stout).[30] Though a sacred event for the faithful, baptism for the dead was a subject of derision to many outsiders—Reverend Caswall, for example, included it in a group of doctrines to which he referred as "awful profanations"—but their contempt paled in comparison to what they held for a much more controversial Mormon practice.

Since the early 1830s shocking rumors had circulated both within and without the Mormon community that plural marriage, or polygamy as it was more popularly known, was being practiced by some of the Saints. The rumors were well founded, for Joseph Smith received a clear understanding of the doctrine in 1831 and shared it with a few associates in Missouri in July of that year.[31] Smith took his first plural wife in marrying sixteen-year-old Fanny Alger sometime in 1833, more than six years prior to the founding of Nauvoo.[32] His second plural marriage took place under an elm tree in Nauvoo on the evening of April 5, 1841, when Joseph Bates Noble performed the marriage of his wife's sister, Louisa Beaman, to the prophet.[33] To avoid attracting attention, Louisa wore a man's coat and hat to the ceremony.[34]

Given the volatile and incendiary nature of the subject, official church pronouncements denied the practice. Joseph Smith even issued a church directive on October 5, 1843, that those "preaching, teaching, or practicing the doctrine of plurality of wives" would be subject to church trial and proclaimed emphatically, "*I have constantly said no man shall have but one wife at a time, unless the Lord directs otherwise.*"[35] While not an absolute disclaimer, the statement served to obfuscate the issue, despite the fact that by that date Smith secretly had taken more than two dozen plural wives.[36]

For his part, Stout was far from confused on the subject. Joseph Smith recorded a revelation (later canonized as *Doctrine and Covenants* 132) concerning the plurality of wives on July 12, 1843, and though the doctrine was not proclaimed as an official teaching of the church until 1852, the revelation was shown to a select few, including members of the high council. In an 1883 letter to Joseph F. Smith, the only son of Hyrum Smith and Mary Fielding, at the time second counselor in the First Presidency of the Church, Stout confirmed what many contemporaries either suspected or knew:

> I can very well remember that in the year 1843 and I think in the month of August; but am not certain as to the day, the High Council met at Prest Hyrum Smith, your father, (as we were expecting) came into the Council with a document, said to be the Revelation on plural marriage, for the purpose of reading it to the Council. I was Clerk of the Council at that time, and supposed it would be filed in the Council for their future use. At that very time I had another appoint to meet, and was excused by the Council, supposing it would be filed there and come into my hands as clerk, I could then peruse it at my leasure.
>
> When I returned, the council had adjourned, and your father had gone, taking the revelation with him. But I saw several of the counsellors, who informed me as to the purport of the revelation which corresponded to what is published and now in the book of Doctrine and Covenants . . . Certain is, it was the one particular town topic then of both friends and enemies.[37]

Many, including some who were or who had been close to the prophet, did not take the subject lightly. William Law, second counselor in the First Presidency and one of Joseph Smith's staunchest supporters, ultimately concluded that Joseph was not a false but a fallen prophet over a question of fidelity related to his practice of plural marriage.[38] Austin Cowles, first counselor in the Nauvoo Stake Presidency, openly rejected polygamy when it was announced to the High Council and resigned his position, ultimately leaving the church.[39] John C. Bennett, once the mayor of Nauvoo and former friend of Smith, traveled widely in an effort to expose the "evils of Mormonism," particularly polygamy.

Already alarmed by the rumors of polygamy, non-Mormons also feared the Mormon's potential political power, since they tended to vote as a group and thus could determine the outcome of any election. In addition, the growing size of the Nauvoo Legion, at the time estimated to be three-to-four thousand in number, gave cause for others to fear that the Mormons might challenge the authority of the state. When first established in 1841, the Legion was divided into two major brigades or cohorts, the first comprised of mounted troops and the second of infantry and artillery. At a meeting of the court-martial on March 12, 1842, on the motion of Stout, the city of Nauvoo was divided into four military districts with boundaries corresponding to those of the four wards in the city; the four companies were then to comprise the fourth regiment of the second cohort.[40] On June 13, 1843, Major Hosea Stout was ordered by Brigadier General Charles C. Rich to notify the battalion that he commanded to meet at the grove in front of the temple ten days hence to be organized into and elect officers for a regiment. As scheduled, the battalion met on the June 23 and was organized into the fifth regiment of the second cohort, at which time Stout was elected colonel of the regiment.[41]

As the Legion grew, mounting responsibilities were heaped upon Stout, most but not all clerical in nature. On June 10, 1843, two weeks before his election as colonel, he was appointed the new secretary of the court-martial, and in July he was appointed to prepare revised laws of the Legion in final form for publication.[42] On September 21 he was authorized by Hyrum Smith to raise a company of light infantry to be attached to his regiment.[43] Four days later he was appointed by Smith to regulate the collection of fines of Legion members, taking over for D. B. Huntington, who was released from the assignment, ostensibly for ineffectiveness.[44] The fines, typically one dollar for each day of nonattendance, were used to help finance an arsenal in addition to what was provided by the state.

Two weeks prior to being appointed to collect Legion fines, Stout was selected, along with William W. Phelps and Henry Miller, to visit Governor Thomas Ford in an effort to obtain public arms from the state for the Legion.[45] The men were rebuffed, as the state refused to provide further arms. Nevertheless, according to the governor in his *History of Illinois*, "the Legion had been furnished with three pieces of cannon and about two hundred and fifty stand of small arms; which popular rumor increased to the number of thirty pieces of cannon and five or six thousand stand of muskets."[46]

The Legion existed to defend the Saints and their city and was prepared to use necessary force and armaments to that end. At a meeting in Nauvoo on November 29, 1843, Joseph Smith, in his role as mayor, "rose to make a confession" that he used all his influence in Missouri to prevent Mormons from fighting when attacked by mobs. "If I did wrong," he declared, "I will not do so any more; it was a suggestion of the head; he would never do so again; but when the mobs come upon you, kill them, I never will restrain you again, but will go and help you." Immediately after Smith sat down, Brigham Young "said he would never put his hand on brother Hosea Stout's shoulder again to hold him back when he was abused."[47] It was a remarkable pronouncement, both in its aggressive tone as well as in singling out Stout and clearly suggesting his proclivity for swift and stern retribution.

The Mormons had grown weary of the mistreatment—persecution, in their eyes—they suffered at the hands of non-Mormons. To that end, on December 7 Stout, W. W. Phelps, and Reynolds Cahoon were appointed to draft a preamble and resolution expressing their sentiments regarding the continuing demands by the state of Missouri for the arrest of Joseph Smith, not to mention kidnapping Mormons in Illinois and transporting them across the Mississippi River to Missouri. After a few minutes the trio returned with a lengthy statement that accused Missouri of a "diabolical, unheard of, cruel and unconstitutional warfare" against the Mormons and solicited Governor Ford "by all reasonable means, to grant us peace, *for we will have it.*"[48]

While the Legion was created to defend the city, keeping peace in Nauvoo itself necessitated the creation of an organized police force. In 1841 when Nauvoo was divided by the city council into four wards, a high constable was established in each ward to help city marshal Henry Sherwood keep the peace. Being located on the Mississippi River, Nauvoo, as was common in many American nineteenth century river towns, had a riverfront that often served as a gathering spot for troublemakers and drunks.[49] The marshal and constables were deemed insufficient to defend the city from steadily growing threats, particularly after Governor Ford, in a letter of December 12 1843, forbade the Nauvoo Legion from suppressing, preventing, or punishing individual crimes. In response, on December 29, 1843, forty men were selected to act as city policemen, with Jonathan Dunham the captain or "High Policeman," Charles C. Rich First Lieutenant and Hosea Stout Second Lieutenant. The fact that Dunham, Rich, and Stout also were the top three ranking officers of the second cohort of the Legion, inevitably created a close relationship between the two organizations.[50]

Stout immediately jumped into the role as a policeman, evidently working double shift at first: on January 8, 1844, just ten days after the creation of the Nauvoo Police, Mayor Joseph Smith issued a police receipt that stated, "This may certify that Hosea Stout has done twenty days duty as policeman." For his service Stout was to be paid twenty dollars by the city treasurer.[51] In addition to his daily duty as policemen, Stout was ordered on January 13 to prepare the revised laws of the Legion for press and to sell printed books of the laws at the lowest possible price. A month later, on February 10, it was further determined that Stout would publish up to five hundred copies of the books at his own expense.[52]

While the police and Legion prepared to protect Nauvoo and Joseph Smith from enemies, a major fissure began to appear from within their own ranks. An article entitled "Buckeye's Lamentations for the Want of More Wives" appeared on February 7 in the *Warsaw Message*. In the eyes of Smith, the piece not only exuded "a very foul and malicious spirit," but evidently it was produced by Wilson Law, the Legion's ranking major general whose sole superior was Smith himself.[53] Law and his brother William, who was second counselor to Joseph Smith in the church's First Presidency, were deeply opposed to the doctrine of plural marriage and had embarked on a campaign to expose Joseph as a fallen prophet. Other leaders joined in and their followers grew to number approximately two hundred.

At the April conference, the conspirators sought the downfall of Smith but were unsuccessful. The leaders of the conspiracy were exposed in the *Times and Seasons* and on April 18 Robert D. Foster, Wilson Law, William Law, Jane Law, and Howard Smith were "unanimously cut off" from the church "for unchristianlike conduct."[54] Though the Nauvoo Legion technically was a state militia, in reality it was run by Mormons and therefore it was deemed inappropriate for Wilson Law, who had been excommunicated, to hold the lofty position of major general. Thus, on April 29, he was suspended from his office to await a trial before a court-martial of the Nauvoo Legion; Hosea Stout and six other officers were appointed to sit as a court-martial, while Charles C. Rich was ordered to take command of the Legion.[55] The outcome of the court-martial was predictable, and on May 9 Law was cashiered from the Legion.[56] The ouster of Law had almost immediate implications concerning Stout and his leadership position in the Legion, as did, indirectly, the presidential candidacy of Joseph Smith.

Early in 1844, several candidates for president appeared, including John C. Calhoun, Martin Van Buren, and Henry Clay. Smith sent inquiries to each regarding their policy toward the Saints should they be elected. Only Clay and Calhoun responded and both prompted angry replies from Smith, who declared his own candidacy. At the April conference, attended by as many as twenty thousand people (far exceeding the population of Nauvoo), speakers endorsed and the congregation unanimously affirmed Smith's candidacy. More than three hundred elders volunteered to preach the gospel and campaign for Smith and were appointed by the Council of the Twelve to serve in different states. Among those selected was Charles C. Rich, who in May was sent to Michigan.[57] At about the same time, on May 17, Stout served as a delegate from his birthplace, Mercer County, Kentucky, at a state convention in Nauvoo where it was moved, seconded, and "carried by acclamation that General Joseph Smith, of Illinois," be their choice for President of the United States.[58] A national convention was set to meet at Baltimore on July 13, ostensibly to be attended by Stout and his fellow delegates, but plans to do so were obviated by increasing threats of violence and finally murder.

Previously, on April 28, William Law, Wilson Law, former member of the high council Austin Cowles, and several others appointed a committee to visit families in Nauvoo to gauge interest in a new church with William Law as president and Cowles and Wilson Law as counselors.[59] Disgruntled members joined anti-Mormon forces in advocating repeal of the Nauvoo Charter and vowed to overthrow Mormon rule in the city. Their crowning blow and the most immediate cause of violence came with the publication in Nauvoo of an opposition newspaper.

A printing press arrived on May 7 at a building on Mulholland Street owned by one of the dissenters, Robert Foster. Three days later a "Prospectus," given the name *Nauvoo Expositor*, was printed and circulated in the city with the promise of a first edition to be printed on Friday, June 7. The newspaper arrived on schedule and was filled with accusations supporting William Law's viewpoint that Joseph Smith was a fallen (not a false) prophet, particularly attacking Smith and his associates for immorality connected with the practice of plural marriage.

The city council convened immediately and decided the newspaper was a public nuisance that, if not stopped, would incite mob action. Joseph Smith, as mayor of Nauvoo, ordered city marshal John Greene and police captain Jonathan Dunham (who, while Charles Rich was in Michigan, also was the acting commander of the Nauvoo Legion) to destroy the press and burn any remaining newspapers. The order was executed early in the evening of June 10 by two companies of the Legion.[60]

The demolition of the press was a clear violation of property rights, which aroused the non-Mormon public and enemies of the church and led them to proclaim the destruction of the *Expositor* a violation of freedom of the press. The publishers of the *Expositor* quickly (on June 11) swore out a complaint of riot against Joseph Smith, Greene, Dunham, Stephen Markham, and several others. Citizen's groups in Hancock County, already agitated even before the *Expositor* affair, called for the removal of the Saints from Illinois. Nowhere was the attack more vehement than in the *Warsaw Signal*, where Thomas Sharp, an incessant critic and foe of the Mormons, called for citizens to arise, stating that "war and extermination" were inevitable.[61]

The extreme danger of the situation was apparent to Joseph and Hyrum Smith, both of whom along with several others were arrested on June 17, though discharged on the same day, for misdeeds in the destruction of the *Expositor*. Also on June 17 Stephen Markham gave an affidavit before the city recorder that a mob was gathering "to make an immediate attack" on Nauvoo;[62] later that afternoon Hosea Stout—who in Rich's absence was acting brigadier general and commander of the second cohort—was ordered by Dunham to assemble his regiment at the Masonic Hall "armed and equiped in the best possible manner for defence."[63] Stout's regiment met, as ordered, at six o'clock each evening from June 18 to 20 to protect the city, standing watch the first two nights until 8:00 AM and the third night (and day) until 1:00 PM in the afternoon.[64]

As might be expected, with the Saints openly preparing for an expected conflict, non-Mormons in surrounding communities became concerned about the situation in Nauvoo. As a result of the turmoil, on June 20 Governor Ford went to Carthage, about twenty-three miles southeast of Nauvoo, in an attempt to neutralize the situation. The Governor wrote a letter to Joseph Smith in which he insisted that only a trial of the city council members before a non-Mormon jury in Carthage would satisfy the people, and promised complete protection for the defendants if they would surrender.

In counsel with his closest friends, however, Smith decided that the best course of action was for him and his brother Hyrum to leave Nauvoo:

> The way is open. It is clear to my mind what to do. All they want is Hyrum and myself; then tell everybody to go about their business . . . We will cross the river tonight, and go away to the West.[65]

Expecting an attack, on June 22 Smith instructed Major General Dunham to have Stout's regiment work in shifts of three or four hours the following day. Late that night, Joseph and Hyrum, accompanied by Willard Richards and Orrin Porter Rockwell, crossed the Mississippi River in a skiff.[66] The boat was so leaky and the river so high that it took nearly the entire night to get to the other side. However, several of Smith's friends in Nauvoo, including his wife Emma, sent word across the river begging the men to return, assuming that the Smith brothers were guilty of nothing and thus surely would be acquitted.

Smith, however, realized what others apparently did not, namely that going back to Nauvoo was in essence a death sentence. Seemingly surprised that others could not perceive the danger and would not support his escape, he stated, "If my life is of no value to my friends it is of none to myself."[67] The next day Smith and his brother Hyrum returned to Nauvoo and, on June 24, Joseph was charged with treason for having declared martial law in Nauvoo. That evening, the two brothers rode from Nauvoo to surrender at Carthage. Passing the Mansion House, Joseph turned to a group of men and said, "Boys, if I do not come back, take care of yourselves, for I go as a lamb to the slaughter." As he passed his farm on the eastern outskirts of the city, he declared, "If some of you had got such a farm and knew you would not see it any more you would want to take a good look at it for the last time."[68]

There was great commotion in Carthage as Joseph and Hyrum surrendered and were ushered to the Carthage Jail, accompanied by eight of their friends. At the jail, Joseph gave to James Allred the sword he had unsheathed during his final speech to the Nauvoo Legion, saying, "Take this—you may need it to defend yourself."[69] Soon afterward, Smith's friends, with the exception of apostles John Taylor and Willard Richards, were forced to leave the jail. Realizing the imminent danger and fearing for his life, Smith wrote an official order to Jonathan Dunham "to bring the Legion and reserve him [Joseph] from being killed," but Dunham, probably fearing a massive armed confrontation both in Carthage and Nauvoo, kept the order to himself and the Legion remained in the city, believing all was well.[70]

Governor Ford meanwhile had offered protection for the prisoners and knew of the potential for conflict in Carthage but evidently was unaware of a plot to kill Joseph Smith and believed that no harm would come to him. But as the governor on June 27 was in Nauvoo addressing the Saints, a large group of men, with blackened faces to hide their identity, rushed the jail. The prisoners fought off the attackers in their second-floor cell with a cane and fired shots from a pistol that had been smuggled to them, but they were no match for the mob. One shot fired through the door struck Hyrum Smith in the face, mortally wounding him. John Taylor was wounded five times, but the bullet that might have killed him hit the watch in his vest pocket.[71] Joseph Smith, seeing that there was no safety in the room, tried to jump from the open window but was shot. Exclaiming, "Oh Lord, my God!" and flashing the secret distress signal of the Masonic order to which he belonged, Joseph fell two stories to the ground, whereupon the mob dragged him to against a wall and shot him again, killing him.[72]

Responding to the scream, "the Mormons are coming," the mob made a hasty exit from the murder scene and dispersed into the woods. Perhaps aware that Brigadier General Hosea Stout was in command of the large second cohort of the Legion and knowing his reputation, members of the murderous horde had ample reason to fear a counterattack, though the reality proved to be exactly the opposite. Early in the morning of June 27, Major General Dunham ordered Stout to have officers and soldiers of the second cohort to be ready for action at an hour's notice but not to assemble until ordered. Later in the morning Dunham issued a further order to Stout to assemble the whole of the second cohort by noon on the parade ground north of the partially-built temple, fully armed but with the specific mandate that "no gun or musket must be loaded or discharged without further order."[73]

About two-thirds of the Legion turned out to parade, though they were dismissed when an emissary of the governor arrived with a message that seemed to indicate there was no immediate danger to Smith. When the delayed news of the murders finally arrived in Nauvoo at daylight the following morning, General Dunham immediately issued orders for the whole of the Legion to assemble on the parade ground at 10:00 AM, at which time he addressed members of the Legion, exhorting them "to keep quiet, and not to let their violently outraged feelings get the better of them."[74]

The bodies of Joseph and Hyrum were brought back to Nauvoo in the early afternoon and were taken to the Mansion House[75] in a procession accompanied by Joseph Smith's militia staff, Major General Dunham and his staff, Brigadier General Hosea Stout and his staff, the martial band, and a crowd of several thousand.[76] Among those to address the gathered multitude was Willard Richards, who miraculously had emerged from Carthage Jail virtually unscathed. Though Governor Ford feared a Mormon uprising, and many were "so enraged at the mob that they wanted to go out and slay them," Richards exhorted the crowd to remain calm and keep the peace, saying, "Brethren, think! Think! Think! Think before you act."[77]

The call for peace was timely, for after the slayings many Saints shared the enraged and vengeful emotions of Allen Stout:

> Their [Joseph's and Hyrum's] dead bodies were brought to Nauvoo where I saw their beloved forms reposing in the arms of death, which gave me such feelings as I am not able to describe. But I there and then resolved in my mind that I would never let an opportunity slip unimproved of avenging their blood upon the head of the enemies of the Church of Jesus Christ. I felt as though I could not live. I knew not how to contain myself and when I see one of the men who persuaded them to give up to be tried, I feel like cutting their throats. And I hope to live to avenge their blood, but if I do not, I will

teach my children to never cease to try to avenge their blood and then their children and children's children to the fourth generation as along as there is one descendant of the murderers upon the earth.[78]

Hosea Stout, who in honor of the slain leaders had given his son (born on July 4, a week after the martyrdom) the name Hyrum, laid blame for the murders squarely on Thomas Ford and the state of Illinois:

> I well remembered the never to be forgotten 27 of June, 1844, when [Joseph Smith] fell a sacrifice to the violence of a mob while the constituted authorities of this State winked at their deeds after the honors of the govornor and faith of the State had been pledged for his protection and his blood is now to be seen on the floor of the jail at Carthage where it cries to God for vengeance on this Nation who rejoice at his fall.[79]

Hosea's harsh feelings toward the governor and the state troops who failed to protect Joseph Smith did not diminish over time, as he later wrote, "To all Such men officers and governments I can truly say that it is my hearts desire and prayer to God for Christ's and his kingdom's and people's sake that they may be speedily damned to the lowest degredation of Hell."[80] In his defense, Ford claimed he was powerless to prevent the crime and suspected that the murder plot actually was timed to have him in Nauvoo where the Mormons would suspect that he planned it and subsequently would assassinate him, ultimately placing so much pressure on them that they finally would be expelled from the state.[81] Regardless, many Saints joined in blaming Ford at least for not paying attention to a warning of a plot to kill their prophet, and yet in the confusion of the days following the murders they also felt a necessity to rely on the governor for their protection. In a letter to Ford on July 2, Jonathan Dunham wrote, "I am sorry to inform you that the mob is still prowling between Warsaw and Golden's Point, waiting for an opportunity to come in and burn and destroy . . . I want you to send about one hundred or two hundred men whom you can depend upon as loyal, to quarter in the woods between here and Golden's Point, so that they can be between us and the mob, and protect us."[82]

The greatest immediate threat to the Saints, however, was internal and stemmed from the leadership void created by Joseph Smith's death, for no plan had been made for succession and all apostles with the exception of John Taylor and Willard Richards were on missions in the eastern states. One name that arose was Smith's youngest brother, Samuel.

Joseph's scribe, William Clayton, remembered the prophet having said that if he and Hyrum both were taken, Samuel would be Joseph's successor.[83] The idea of Samuel's succession was terminated, however, by his sudden death on July 30, though his passing was not without eventual controversy involving Hosea Stout.

Sometime after the death of Samuel Smith, the lone surviving brother, William, learned from Samuel's widow that Stout had acted as nurse for his brother and was said to have administered to him a "white powder" daily until his death. William, who later became disaffected from the church and was excommunicated, claimed in a letter written in 1857 that his brother was poisoned by Stout upon the order of Brigham Young and Willard Richards, ostensibly to remove him from the succession picture.[84] It is possible that the white powder was calomel, a mercurous chloride compound that was a purgative commonly used in early nineteenth century medicine that, in the prophet's words, "on an empty stomach will kill the patient," and an overdose of which was deemed responsible for the death in 1823 of Alvin, the eldest of the five Smith brothers.[85] Nevertheless, William Smith, long after the fact, accused Stout of being a co-conspirator in the alleged murder of his brother Samuel.

A few days after Samuel Smith's death, on August 3, Sidney Rigdon arrived at Nauvoo from Pittsburgh, and Brigham Young arrived three days later. On August 8, in a speech to a large assembly, Rigdon asserted that he, as the only remaining counselor in the First Presidency, should assume the leadership of the church. After Rigdon finished, Brigham Young arose to address the crowd; though no contemporary accounts made note of it, many of those present, including Stout's brother-in-law Pleasant Green Taylor, later recorded that they saw Brigham Young transfigured as Joseph Smith standing in front of them:

> He, as well as hundreds of others, arose to his feet and felt sure that Joseph had been resurrected; and even after Brigham began to speak, he still thought it was the Prophet Joseph who was speaking to them.[86]

William M. Allred, who also was present, recorded the event with a slightly different slant:

> After Rigdon got through Brigham got up and spoke with such power that it convinced nearly all that were present that the mantle of Joseph had fallen on him. I was perfectly satisfied.[87]

Most of the Saints, like Allred, were "perfectly satisfied" that the leadership of the church should be given to the Quorum of the Twelve Apostles, with Brigham Young at its head. Members of the Twelve met in council the day after they were sustained and began to set in order the organization and affairs of the church. With the Quorum of the Twelve in control, chaos in Nauvoo began to subside. On August 10, Stout—who recently had been appointed captain of the police—met with the city council to report that "the police were willing to watch the city while it was necessary and all they wanted was to live [i.e., have their living provided for] while they did it." The council "subscribed about $80" to pay Stout and the police.[88]

After Stout was promoted to police captain, the institution began to take a more prominent role in law and order in Nauvoo as Brigham Young and other apostles apparently perceived the police as a legal and legitimate way to maintain a body of armed men in the city while being able to deny any renewed Mormon militarism.[89] At the same time, Stout maintained an active involvement in the Legion, particularly after Charles C. Rich was advanced on August 20 to the rank of major general, thereby effectively becoming the chief military officer in Nauvoo after Brigham Young, who replaced Joseph Smith as lieutenant general, delegated much of the responsibility for running the Legion to his second in command. Rich, fearing new violence from enemies of the Mormons, immediately commenced strengthening his militia. At a meeting on August 31, at which Rich presided and Stout was chosen as secretary, Legion officers resolved to "let our religion be our protection," as Governor Ford previously had suggested, but with the proviso, "with such arms as we procure for ourselves until we can receive our proportion of the public arms according to the Charter of said Legion."[90]

To that end, on October 16 at the request of General Rich, Stout inspected a lot of one hundred muskets that had been purchased at New Orleans for the Legion. Arms in hand, three days later Rich ordered Stout to raise one hundred minutemen to protect the "brethren" who were bound over to the Carthage Court for the destruction of the *Expositor*.[91] With the approval of Governor Ford, Rich sent a party of thirty armed men to Carthage to "protect the court" and "suppress all mobs which might rise in Hancock County."[92] When a grand jury handed down an indictment against those who actually had participated in the destruction, but not against city council members as had been feared, Rich ordered the troops to return to Nauvoo.

It was the last hurrah of the Nauvoo Legion as a state-sanctioned militia. From the inception of the Nauvoo Charter there had been serious criticism in many quarters that too much power had been conferred on the Mormon-controlled city government, and many remained fearful of the Legion, whose power and independence originally were granted by the Charter. With anti-Mormonism pervading the state, the Illinois Legislature on January 24, 1845, repealed the Charter by a nearly two-to-one margin, an action that was viewed by Stout as "not only cruel and tyrannical but unprecedented in all civilized nations."[93]

Nauvoo had been deprived of its legal government and police force as well as the Nauvoo Legion, with no provision for an alternative to prevent lawlessness within the city. It marked the beginning of the final and decisive campaign by anti-Mormon extremists to drive the Saints from the state. The peaceful interlude that had reigned in the months following the murder of Joseph and Hyrum Smith was waning, and it was increasingly clear that it was just a matter of time before the Saints would be forced to abandon their beloved Nauvoo.

Notes

1. Hallwas and Launius, *Cultures in Conflict*, 42
2. Roberts, *The Rise and Fall of Nauvoo*, 3.
3. Bushman, *Rough Stone Rolling*, 384.
4. Flanders, *Nauvoo: Kingdom on the Mississippi*, 39.
5. Pooley, "The Settlement of Illinois from 1830–1850," 224.
6. Leonard, *Nauvoo*, 179.
7. Nauvoo Land and Records Research Center (http://www.historicnauvoo.net/#!land-and-records/c1u53). Hosea's home was on Block 85, lot 1, on the southwest corner of the intersection of Main and Knight streets, four blocks directly downhill from the site of the future temple.
8. Cannon and Cook, eds., *Far West Record*, 134. The other minute book is the Kirtland Council Minute Book.
9. The others were: Chicago, Alton, Galena, Springfield, and Quincy.
10. Launius and Hallwas, *Kingdom on the Mississippi Revisited: Nauvoo in Mormon History*, 50.
11. Nauvoo Legion Files, 1841–1845; MS 3430, Church History Library. Other notable members of the court-martial were Hosea's close friends Charles C. and Thomas Rich.
12. Nauvoo Legion Files, folder 1.
13. Quincy, *Figures of the Past*, 383–84.
14. The records of the meetings of February and March 1841 were recorded by Stout on December 8, 1843; he added that proceedings of meetings in 1841 subsequent to March 9 had been "lost or mislaid." See Nauvoo Legion Files.
15. Stout, *Autobiography*, 60.
16. *Times and Seasons* 1–2 (April 15, 1841), 360.
17. Ibid., 382.
18. *Journal History of the Church of Jesus Christ of Latter-day Saints*, April 6, 1841, Church History Library.
19. *D&C* 95:8.
20. Joseph Smith sermon, July 19, 1840, recorded by Martha Jane Knowlton, *Brigham Young University Studies* 19 (Spring 1979):394.

21. Bushman, *Rough Stone Rolling*, 424.
22. *The Joseph Smith Papers*, History, 1838–1856, volume C–1 (November 2, 1838–July 31, 1842), http://josephsmithpapers.org/paperSummary/history-1838-1856-volume-c-1-2-november-1838-31-july-1842?p=377#!/paperSummary/history-1838-1856-volume-c-1-2-november-1838-31-july-1842andp=377. The other men on the rescue expedition were Tarleton Lewis, William A. Hickman, John S. Higbee, Uriel C. Nickerson, and George W. Clyde.
23. Nauvoo Legion Files, folder 10.
24. *The Latter-day Saints Millennial Star*, 18:663.
25. Pooley, "Settlement of Illinois," 512–13.
26. *Millennial Star* 19:230.
27. Caswall, *The City of the Mormons; Or, Three Days at Nauvoo in 1842*, 3–4.
28. 1 Corinthians 15:29, John 3:5.
29. Caswall, *City of the Mormons*, 55.
30. Black and Black, *Annotated Record of Baptisms for the Dead, 1840–1845, Nauvoo*, 6:3527–3529. Hosea's brother Allen was baptized in 1840 for his sister Rebecca for his grandparents Samuel and Rachel Stout, in 1841 for his sister Mary (whom they called Polly), and in 1843 for his father, Joseph; Hosea was baptized in 1841 for his grandparents Daniel and Pleasant Smith and in 1843 for his great-grandfather Daniel Chancy, his great-uncle Samuel Chancy, his cousin Jesse Stout, his aunt Margaret Stout, and his great-grandfather Peter "the Quaker" Stout.
31. Leonard, *Nauvoo*, 344.
32. Compton, *In Sacred Loneliness: The Plural Wives of Joseph Smith*, 33, states that the marriage took place in February or March 1833.
33. Leonard, *Nauvoo*, 345.
34. Turner, *Brigham Young: Pioneer Prophet*, 88.
35. Van Wagoner, *Mormon Polygamy: A History*, 70.
36. A well-documented record of Joseph Smith's plural wives is in Compton, *In Sacred Loneliness*. Compton identified thirty-three wives, while in 1887 Andrew Jenson, Assistant Historian of the Church of Jesus Christ of Latter-day Saints, calculated the number to be twenty-seven. The most recent authoritative study, by Brian C. Hales, lists the number at thirty-five. See Hales, *Joseph Smith's Polygamy*, 2:263–13.
37. Letter from Hosea Stout to Joseph F. Smith, July 24, 1883, Church History Library.
38. Brodie, *No Man Knows My History: The Life of Joseph Smith, the Mormon Prophet*, 369–70.
39. Compton, *In Sacred Loneliness*, 549.
40. Nauvoo Legion Files, folder 1.
41. Nauvoo Legion Files, folder 1. According to John Sweeney Jr. in his thesis for a Master's degree at Brigham Young University, "A History of the Nauvoo Legion in Illinois," a battalion in the Legion was to be no larger than 256 men and a regiment a maximum of 512. A maximum of five regiments could be in a cohort. Charles C. Rich was elected Brigadier General in the Nauvoo Legion on September 4, 1841, to fill the vacancy of Don Carlos Smith, who was recently deceased; at the same time, Hosea

Stout was elected Major. See *The Joseph Smith Papers*, History, 1838–1856, volume C–1 (November 2, 1838–July 31, 1842), http://josephsmithpapers.org/paperSummary/history-1838-1856-volume-c-1-2-november-1838-31-july-1842?p=397#!/paperSummary/history-1838-1856-volume-c-1-2-november-1838-31-july-1842andp=397.
42. Nauvoo Legion Files.
43. Letter from Hyrum Smith to Hosea Stout, September 25, 1843, Hosea Stout papers, MIC A 200, Utah State Historical Society.
44. Ibid.
45. Bennett, Black, and Cannon, *The Nauvoo Legion of Illinois: A History of the Mormon Militia, 1841–1846*, 205; Smith, *History of the Church*, 6:31.
46. Ford, *History of Illinois: From Its Commencement as a State in 1818 to 1847*, 268.
47. *Millennial Star* 22:392; Smith, *History of the Church* 6:94.
48. *Journal History*, December 7, 1843.
49. Allaman, "Policing in Mormon Nauvoo," *Illinois Historical Journal* 89, no. 2: 92.
50. Smith, *History of the Church*, 4:305–8; 6:113, 149–50.
51. Nauvoo City Records, MS 16800, Church History Library. Another receipt given Stout six days later on January 14, indicated six days of service for six dollars.
52. Bennett, Black, and Cannon, *Nauvoo Legion in Illinois*, 159–60; Nauvoo Legion Minutes, folder 1, p. 5, 80.
53. *Millennial Star*, 22:763.
54. Leonard, *Nauvoo*, 357–61.
55. Smith, *History of the Church*, 6:348. On May 4 Stout served on another court-martial, this time for Robert D. Foster. At the time, Jonathan Dunham and Stout both had the rank of colonel. See *Latter-day Saints Millennial Star*, 23:423
56. Ibid., 6:362.
57. Ibid., 6:334–40.
58. Ibid., 6:389–90.
59. Ibid., 6:346–47
60. Leonard, *Nauvoo*, 363–66.f
61. *Warsaw Signal*, June 12, 1844, 2.
62. Smith, *History of the Church*, 6:492.
63. Nauvoo Legion Minutes, folder 20, pp. 22–23.
64. Ibid., 23–24.
65. Smith, *History of the Church* 6: 545–46.
66. Willard Richards was an early Latter-day Saint leader and apostle who later served as a counselor to Brigham Young in the First Presidency from 1847 until his death in 1854; Orrin Porter Rockwell was a close friend of and bodyguard for Joseph Smith.
67. Smith, *History of the Church* 6:549.
68. Ibid., 6:558.
69. Munson, "Early Pioneer History," 2.
70. Stout, "Journal."
71. Some scholars believe that Taylor's watch actually was broken as he hit a windowsill.

72. Smith received a total of four lead balls.
73. Nauvoo Legion Minutes, folder 20, pp. 24–25
74. Smith, *History of the Church* 7:131–34.
75. The Mansion House was built by Joseph Smith and was used as his personal home, a public boarding house, a hotel, and as a site for the performance of temple ordinances.
76. *Millennial Star* 24:503; Bennett, Black, and Cannon, *Nauvoo Legion in Illinois*, 249.
77. Allred, "Autobiography."
78. Stout, "Journal."
79. Brooks, *On the Mormon Frontier: The Diary of Hosea Stout*, November 4, 1844, 8.
80. Ibid., September 30, 1845, 1:79.
81. Ford, *History of Illinois*, 349.
82. *Millennial Star*, 24:679.
83. James B. Allen, *No Toil Nor Labor Fear: The Story of William Clayton*, 157.
84. "A Letter from William Smith, brother of Joseph, the Prophet." *Daily Illinois State Journal* (Springfield, IL), June 3, 1857, http://www.sidneyrigdon.com/dbroadhu/IL/sang1845.htm. D. Michael Quinn, though believing Stout capable of the murder, in a footnote wrote: "Even if someone's diary described Stout's administration of a 'white powder' to Samuel H. Smith, that would not prove the powder was poison instead of medicine. Even if a forensic examination of Samuel's exhumed remains showed a residue of poison, that would not prove Hosea Stout was the murderer." See Quinn, *Mormon Hierarchy*, 384n54.
85. "Remarks of the Prophet to Saints Newly Arrived from England, April 13, 1843," Hallwas and Launius, *Cultures in Conflict*, 38. Calomel was used in medicine in the United States as a diuretic and purgative from the late 1700s through 1860. See http://en.wikipedia.org/wiki/Mercury(I)_chloride.
86. Taylor, "Record of Pleasant Green Taylor."
87. Allred, "Autobiography."
88. Smith, *History of the Church*, 6:247–48. The specific date of Stout's appointment as police captain is not known.
89. Allaman, "Policing in Mormon Nauvoo," 94.
90. Nauvoo Legion Minutes.
91. Brooks, *Mormon Frontier*, entries of October 17 and 20, 1844, 5.
92. Ibid., October 24, 1844, 6–7.
93. Ibid., January 30, 1845, 18.

8
Policing Nauvoo

"Today was the beginning of another year," Stout wrote in his journal on New Year's Day 1845, "and God grant that it may not prove as ominous to the Saints as the year just gone."[1] He received a divided response to his entreaty: on a personal and religious level it was an eventful year for him, but overall the picture for the Saints in Nauvoo was far from rosy. In many ways the city had never seemed so prosperous as the residents made a determined effort to build homes and shops and to cultivate their farms, but in the end they realized that all would have to be abandoned.

Nothing was more important to the Saints in 1845 than the completion of the temple, which was vital in order to provide the opportunity for as many as possible to receive their endowments, which are comprised of a course of instruction, ordinances, and covenants given only in dedicated temples. Church members were expected to tithe their labor, namely to donate one workday in ten for the construction of the temple. "Great numbers of carpenters, masons, and other workmen are daily engaged in this arduous undertaking," wrote John Taylor.[2]

Despite his carpentry skills, however, it is uncertain whether Stout had time to donate. Already chief of police and commanding officer of the second cohort of the Nauvoo Legion as well as secretary of both the Nauvoo High Council and Nauvoo Legion, on December 5, 1844, he was made secretary of the Masonic Lodge.[3] The following month, on January 31, the Nauvoo Mercantile and Mechanical Association was organized in order to provide employment and support of the large numbers of church members who were gathering into the city; among the twelve trustees elected were Stout and Charles C. Rich, who on behalf of the Association rode together on March 13, to a town six miles down the river to organize the women in order to promote home industry and to manufacture products for their own use "without being dependent on the stores."[4] To add to his duties, on March 23, he was appointed to be on a committee to write the history of the Nauvoo Legion, a task that he performed to a major extent by himself.

As involved in civic, police, and militia matters as he was, it would be easy to overlook Stout's complete conversion to Mormonism, his dedication to Joseph Smith's teachings, and his devotion to the goal of performing ordinances in the temple. A major step in his spiritual progression was his advancement in the priesthood. An elder in the Melchizedek or "higher" priesthood since 1839, Stout was "ordained an Elder in the Quorum of Seventies" on October 4, 1844, and within a few days was appointed one of the presidents of the quorum.

The calling of the seventies was missionary service and in preparation they were urged to study the scriptures diligently. In their weekly meetings the seventies also learned about the criteria necessary for entry into the "House of the Lord," as Mormons called their temple. Stout took seriously his spiritual preparation, and it was common for him to juggle talk of security and things sacred, such as on the morning of February 22, 1845, when he went with J. P. Harmon and Bishop George Miller to the unfinished temple to consult on matters of safety and ridding themselves of "traitors" in their midst; immediately afterwards, Stout and Harmon went to the Masonic Lodge where they locked themselves in a room and "talked over some particular matters reletive to our Eternal exaltation in the Kingdom of God."[5]

While deeply involved in affairs related to the safety and success of Nauvoo, Stout never lost his focus on spiritual matters. His obedience extended to the most divisive Mormon practice, the "new and everlasting covenant" of plural marriage. Stout's first step into the realm of plural marriage was on February 14, 1845, when Lucretia Fisher, three months shy of her fifteenth birthday, came to live in his house.[6] The plan, evidently testing whether Lucretia and Hosea's wife Louisa would be compatible, seemingly was successful, and Hosea and Lucretia were married on April 20 at what Hosea described, in a secretive manner, as "a good and friendly meeting."[7]

Stout's second foray into plural marriage came just two months later when on June 30 he married nineteen-year-old Marinda Bennett, to whom he had been introduced by Allen Weeks (who was married to two of Marinda's sisters) eight days earlier; once again Hosea referred to the event in his diary as a sort of social event, complete with "drinking what wine we wanted" but no mention of a marriage.[8] In keeping with the secrecy surrounding plural marriage, to describe the nights spent with Marinda, Stout made ambiguous entries in his journal such as "went to see Allen Weeks and stood patrol guard all night came home in the morning about sun rise."[9]

Though plural marriage was practiced by relatively few men in Nauvoo, it was fairly common among select church leaders: of the seventeen attendees at the meeting of the Nauvoo High Council on August 12, 1843, when the revelation on plural marriage was read, twelve (including Stout) entered into polygamy while still in Nauvoo, while three of the other five left the church. The last of the twelve who embraced the principle—Lewis Dunbar Wilson (who two decades later would become Stout's father-in-law)—first took a plural wife on February 3, 1846, just days before the Saints began an exodus from Nauvoo.[10]

A very important element of the "new and everlasting covenant" was that marriage would be "for time and all eternity," and to that end Stout was sealed on May 4, 1845, to Lucretia Fisher.[11] In keeping with the secrecy surrounding the practice, Stout guardedly described the event in his journal as going "to meeting with my wife." Interestingly, on the same day as the wedding he issued to his wife Louisa an official appointment "to the office of First Assistant to the colonel of the fifth Regiment, Second Cohort, Nauvoo Legion of the state of Illinois," though inasmuch as the Legion no longer was a legal entity recognized by the state, the title was somewhat empty.[12]

The police force also was legally though not in actuality disbanded with the loss of the Charter. Perhaps in anticipation of the state legislature's vote rescinding the Charter, a meeting of top church officials took place on November 11, 1844, at which it was decided to raise an additional four hundred policemen to guard the city;[13] the new force became known as the "new police" while Stout remained captain of the "old police." On January 14, 1845, the Nauvoo city council, under Mayor Daniel Spencer (who had replaced Joseph Smith in the office), formally approved an enlargement of the "new police" up to a total of five hundred; by that date, 118 policemen had been sworn in, including Brigham Young.[14] Nevertheless, on March 16—more than seven weeks after the repeal of the Charter—Young announced a plan for Nauvoo to be reorganized as the "City of Joseph" but stated clearly, "We have no police."[15]

The status of the police at the time was not as clear-cut as Young intimated. On February 8, Stout met with the "old police" and reported he had been assured by the city council that he would govern the police "as heretofore in all matters." Though the "old police" had served during the winter months without any remuneration, Stout also was told that they would be afforded "a small compensation" and was encouraged to "persevere in the discharge of our duty as policemen." He noted in his diary,

> To stand at the head of so worthy and honorable a company of brethren who possess the inteligence which they do and hold so honorable a standing in society as they, who are willing to be dictated by me in all cases without a dissenting voice

in a matter of so vital importance as the safety of the Temple and the lives of the Twelve [Apostles] at this critical and trying time places me in a position and responsibility which is more easy to be imagined than described.[16]

The unpaid "old police," acting in an extralegal capacity, within a matter of weeks had the opportunity to defend the safety of both the Twelve and the temple. On February 19, Stout wrote apostle Willard Richards that the "old police" would guard the apostles "against the violence of midnight assassins, who stalk abroad, as wolves in sheeps clothing."[17] True to his word, on February 25, upon hearing that Brigham Young, Heber C. Kimball, and others might be attacked on the way back to Nauvoo, Stout immediately went with seven of the "old police" to Macedonia, a distance of twenty-five miles, to provide protection, though the anticipated mob failed to materialize.[18]

The important duty on a daily basis for the police was protecting the temple. Demonstrating conclusively that they would not tolerate any breach of security in the temple, the "old police" on the night of April 2 "beat a man almost to death" in the edifice. Stout defended his men, saying, "I was glad of it" and somewhat defused public controversy by stating that he "had given orders to that effect in case anyone should be found in the Temple after night." Brigham Young, upon hearing of the incident and listening to Stout's explanation, "approved of the proceedings of the Police" and said he wanted them to continue guarding the temple.[19]

The military orientation of the "old police" can be seen in an entry in Stout's journal for April 5, when he "met the police to inspect their arms and then took them out and trained them awhile and then marched to the Mansion house."[20] The force, however, was not a legal entity (the reason for Brigham Young's comment of March 16, "We have no police") and therefore was incapable of providing full protection for the city. A plan to rectify this apparently was conceived two days earlier when the "old police" met at the Masonic Hall to reorganize the "new police" under Stephen Markham. Realizing, however, that without a charter the new police organization would not have legal standing, "it was concluded to organize the whole community of Saints in this County into Quorums of 12 deacons and have a Bishop at their head and they could thus administer in the Lesser offices of the church and preserve order without a Charter."[21]

It would appear, based on contemporary reports, that the birth of the quorum of deacons brought into existence a shadowy group known as the "Whistling and Whittling Brigade." Their method of operation to keep the city free of unwanted characters, as recorded by Sheriff Hawkins Taylor of Lee County, Iowa (directly across the Mississippi River from Nauvoo), was both simple and effective:

> They all had great bowie knives and would get a long piece of pine board and get up close to the officer and pretend to be cutting over it and cut near the officer. In the meantime, small boys would get tin pans, old bells and all sorts of things to make a noise with and surround the officer. No one would touch or say a word to him, but the noise drowned all that he would say. The result would be that he would get out of the city as soon as possible and never come back again.[22]

Mosiah Hancock wrote of his youthful activity with the band, "We all had our knives and cut timbers to whittle and make rails from, and knew what tunes to whistle."[23]

An incident from early April gave a graphic illustration of Whistling and Whittling Brigade tactics and results. At the Mormon General Conference of April 6, 1845, Stout was instructed to keep "the 'Old Police' in readiness to suppress any riot or breach of the peace," though the police still were not a legal entity. Dr. John F. Charles attended from Warsaw and took notes of the conference for the *Warsaw Signal*. Stout wrote, "he pretended to be our friend but in reality he was a secret enemy lurking in our midst in the afternoon he was invited to leave which made him so mad that he did not take any more notes that day."[24] Still in Nauvoo the following day, Charles "was set upon by a gang of ruffians, with bowie knives and dirks in their hands whittling sticks, whistling in chorus." Considering himself abused, Charles complained twice to Brigham Young, who according to the newspaper report echoed the words uttered by President Martin Van Buren to Joseph Smith, who had sought redress for property loss in Missouri, "your cause is just, but I can do nothing for you."[25]

The Brigade was short-lived, its demise likely accelerated by the reorganization of the town. On April 16, a square mile around the temple was incorporated as the city of Nauvoo, dropping the briefly held name "City of Joseph." As the new city government was organized, the "old police" officially were appointed to be the regular police of the town, once again with Hosea Stout as captain. One of the final actions of the Brigade came eleven days later on April 27 at a meeting that was attended by Austin Cowles, former member of the Nauvoo High Council who considered Joseph Smith a fallen prophet. Of the occasion Stout wrote:

Old Father Cowles one of [William] Law's apostates was there, a company of boys assembled to whistle him out of Town, but I prevented them. I came home and in the evening went to police, on my way was informed that the old man had been whistled out immediately after meeting.[26]

Within hours of gaining official legal status and taking oath on May 12, the "Old Police" force sprang into action. Two nights previous, at the small settlement of West Point in Lee County, Iowa, John Miller, a Mennonite minister, was murdered in his home and his son-in-law, Henry Liesi, was mortally wounded. Surviving family members identified brothers William and Stephen Hodges as the perpetrators. When news of the murder spread that the murderers were Mormons, angry citizens in Iowa made it clear that the Hodges brothers must be handed over immediately to Iowa officials or the Saints would be driven from Nauvoo.

Earlier in the year such a warning may well have been ignored by defiant Mormons: as recently as April 13, for example, Apostle John Taylor indignantly warned that an attempt by a US Marshal and his deputies to serve a writ on Brigham Young and others would "cost them their lives."[27] The newly sworn-in Nauvoo police, however, took the threat seriously and wasted no time in their pursuit of the Hodges brothers. While visiting Brigham Young on the evening of April 12, Stout was notified by Cyrus Daniels and some other policemen that a hunt was on for the suspects. Within hours, the brothers were found and agreed to surrender the following morning; almost immediately they were transferred to jail in Burlington, Iowa, to await trial.[28]

William and Stephen Hodges were found guilty of murder on June 22 and were sentenced to be hanged, the execution scheduled for July 15. Following the sentencing, a third Hodges brother, Ervine, tried to induce Brigham Young to help the brothers escape from jail; when Young refused, Ervine publicly denounced and threatened him.[29] On the night of June 23 at about 10:00 PM, Ervine was stealthily making his way through a cornfield near Young's house when policemen Allen Stout and John Scott, who were guarding the house, "heard a few blows as if someone was beating an ox with a club, which was followed by shrieks." Scott ran toward the noise and found Ervine, mortally wounded. "I am a butchered man," cried Hodges as he fell.[30] When Scott asked who stabbed him, Ervine replied that they were men from the river whom he took to be friends. As the commotion drew a crowd, a non-Mormon man named Clapp asked again who did it, but Ervine's dying response was that he could not tell.[31]

The next morning, Hosea Stout went to the crime scene and reported that he found a knife a short distance from where Hodges died.

Some, including William Hall, who became vehemently anti-Mormon after living among the Mormons at Nauvoo, later alleged that the murder weapon actually was Hosea's, that he killed Hodges by stabbing him five times with a bowie knife, though Hodges's dying statement that he was killed by "men from the river" likely points to members of a criminal gang with whom the Hodges brothers were known to associate.[32] Historian D. Michael Quinn examined the murder of Ervine Hodges and concluded that Hosea Stout and his brother Allen were involved.[33] In a more recent and thorough examination, historians William Shepard and H. Michael Marquardt agreed that "Hosea Stout was not above committing such an act" but stated, "More realistic evidence indicates that fellow gang member Return Jackson Redden may have murdered Ervine to keep him from revealing gang secrets." In support of their conclusion, Shepard and Marquardt cited contemporary evidence from the *Territorial Gazette and Advertiser* of Burlington, Iowa, that Hodges was murdered by a band of scoundrels to which he belonged; a statement from local sexton William Huntington that Ervine was murdered by some local "ruffians" in the gang to which he belonged; and a letter from Attorney D. F. Miller of Lee County, Iowa, to Judge Charles Mason, who presided at the trial of Ervine's brothers William and Stephen, that Ervine "was killed unquestionably by one of the Band because he threatened exposure."[34]

The day after Ervine Hodges was murdered, Hancock County Sheriff Minor Deming, who had been elected with Mormon support in August 1844, was attacked by Dr. Samuel Marshall, a bitter Mormon-hater, in the lower hall of the courthouse where Hyrum Smith's murder trial had been scheduled. Deming drew his gun and in the struggle shot Marshall in the stomach, killing him. Though it clearly was a case of self-defense, Deming was indicted a day later for manslaughter, the same day, as it turned out, that William Smith, the prophet's brother, attacked Elbridge Tufts, one of Stout's policemen who refused Smith's demand to release an unnamed prisoner.[35] Under the deteriorating circumstances, Stout realized that the "old police" must refrain from any controversy and on July 3 he "met the police and spoke at considerable length to them on the Subject and necessity of their keeping their selves out of all bad company and maintaining an upright and dignified course before the people."[36]

The police seem to have followed Stout's counsel, but the overall situation became increasingly tenuous. Nevertheless, with support from the Saints, ardently pro-Mormon Jacob Backenstos (though not himself a Mormon) was elected on August 11 to succeed Minor Deming as county sheriff. His lopsided victory, 2,334 to 750, further infuriated enemies, and Thomas Sharp unleashed new anti-Mormon attacks in the *Warsaw Signal*. The attacks were effective, as Thomas Ford wrote, "Backintos [*sic*] was hated with a sincere and thorough hatred by the opposite party."[37]

Renewed violence commenced on September 9 when shots were fired at a schoolhouse in Green Plains where a group of anti-Mormons were meeting. Blaming the Mormons, a group of antagonists under the leadership of Levi Williams attacked at Morley's settlement and burned several homes. When word of the burning reached Nauvoo on September 11, General Charles C. Rich immediately gave orders to Stout "to have the Cohort put in readiness to repel an attack in a minutes notice."[38] Though following the repeal of the Nauvoo Charter the Saints had "agreed not to do any more military duty," the legally disbanded Legion had continued to meet on a regular basis in preparation for a possible defense of the city.[39] At a general convention of the officers of the Legion on May 7 to "regulate matters in case we should be attacked by our enemies," Stout "was appointed to act as Brigadier General 2nd Cohort."[40] On June 23 he wrote of going to see the arsenal, which is a clear inference that the Legion was storing weapons and military equipment.

Almost daily Stout fulfilled his twin duties with the Legion and the police. Not wanting to spark the already incendiary conditions, on September 12 General Rich gave orders that the Legion was "to let the mob burn for the time being the houses of the Saints, [and] not to make war on them."[41] Unavoidably, however, with the continued burning of houses in outlying settlements, emotions reached a crisis level in Nauvoo. Of a meeting with the Eleventh Quorum of Seventies on September 14 Stout wrote, "all who were not in good fellowship were not allowed to be present and the police in keeping them away had to flog three who were determined to stay."[42] He had reached a point where his religion and militancy were intertwined. On the same day that his police flogged the three to keep them out of a meeting, he received a note from Rich instructing him that as "President of the Second Corum [Quorum] of Corums" he was to have his quorum "in readiness for all Duties that shall be necessary in all emergencies."[43]

Two days after Stout's meeting with the Eleventh Quorum of Seventies, word came that Sheriff Backenstos had been attacked while moving his family to Nauvoo for their safety. Fighting back, Orrin Porter Rockwell, at Backenstos's command, took aim at Franklin Worrell—who had been sergeant of the guard at Carthage when Joseph and Hyrum were assassinated—killing him with a single shot, therewith producing a new round of anti-Mormon violence.[44] While straddling his duties between the Legion and the police, Stout wrote on September 17, the day after Worrell was killed, "I am composed nor has the late disturbance had any effect upon me. I want this holloings, beating of drums and firing of Guns should cease." Nevertheless, displaying a heavy hand while keeping the peace, he continued, "the Police have their orders from this time to arrest every man or boy in our street found guilty of these acts or any one walking our street after night detain them till daylight and stripping off their clothes show whether they are male or female." He further advised his men, "keep your Guns to yourselves trust no one and when you shoot take good aim."[45]

On the other side of the conflict, also on September 17, in the wake of Worrell's killing, Thomas Sharp issued a call to arms in his newspaper.[46] In response, the Mormons continued to shore up their forces, leading Stout on September 19 to comment, "the Legion appeared officered as before."[47] On the same day, Sheriff Backenstos occupied the courthouse at Carthage with an armed force, then led a search through Carthage for weapons and sealed off the city.[48] Fearful that the action would exacerbate violence, Stout opined, "Backenstos needs our counsel to keep the peace I would advise the officers to preserve the lives of your men do not rashly expose them because the life of a good man is worth 20 of the mob . . . I am for letting the mob go home if they will and then we can have the law upon them and let them come to the Gallows where they ought to be or else in the Peneteniary [sic]."[49]

General Rich immediately ordered Stout to have fifty wagons, each holding eight well-armed men, ready to march to Carthage by six o'clock the next morning. Before the operation took place, however, Andrew Perkins appeared before regimental officers in their Council of War to relay an offer from the enemy that the Mormons could live in peace if they pledged to leave the state by April 1, 1846. The critical situation having been defused, Rich dismissed the troops the troops on the morning of September 20 and they dispersed to their homes—prematurely as it turned out, for the next day Rich gave Stout new orders to call out the fourth and fifth regiments of the Legion, amounting to about four hundred men.[50]

With civil war imminent, on September 22 a delegation of citizens from Macomb, Illinois traveled fifty miles west to Nauvoo to see whether the Saints were willing to leave the state as had been discussed a few days earlier. Applying as much pressure as possible on the Mormons to make a decision, on September 23 Colonel Stephen Markham sent a letter to Brigham Young informing him that fifteen individuals, including Legion leaders Charles C. Rich, Hosea Stout, Stephen Markham, and Jonathan Dunham, Apostles John Taylor and Willard Richards, and Mayor Daniel Spencer were to be tried for treason.[51] Realizing that they had no alternative, on September 24 the Quorum of the Twelve Apostles announced that the Saints would leave the following spring, in Brigham Young's words "when grass grows and water runs."[52]

Accepting the fate of having to leave the state—and the United States, for that matter—Brigham Young addressed an assembly of troops and stated, "I never intend to winter in the United States except on a visit . . . we calculated to go all the while for I do not intend to Stay in such an Hell of a Hole." Further expressing his anger and frustration with the ongoing persecution, Young continued, "We have been peaceful inclined yet nothing appeases the Mob . . . They are as corrupt as Hell from the president down clean through the priest and the people are all as corrupt as the Devil. I will leave them and God grant I may live to get to some place of peace health and safety."[53]

A potential war had been averted, and on September 28 troops sent by Governor Ford arrived at Carthage to keep the peace. As the Legion stood down, Stout turned his focus more to the police, who had received a dressing down from Brigham Young. "There is an evident lack of humility and faith among you," Young told them. Particularly disturbed by their use of liquor, he continued, "I can for see that a reckless spirit is creeping in among you."[54]

Throughout the earlier months of the year, Stout gathered on occasion with his men in the spirit of fellowship at Leonard Schussler's Brewery to get, in Stout's words, "what beer we could drink."[55] Beer was one thing, however, and liquor quite another. Lecturing the police on their use of "ardent spirits" Young said, "I know this from your breath when I have met you and I know that the Spirit of God cannot rest upon a man who is filled with Whiskey for the kingdom of God cannot be built up by Unholy things." He counseled them to be the master of their passions and not to be a slave to them. While admitting to being "in the habits of taking snuff and Tea," in a refrain echoed by many a tobacco addict he added, "yet I am no slave to these passions and can leave these of it they make my brother affronted."[56]

Supporting his leader, on October 8 Stout ordered his captains to drop any man from the police force who had used liquor since Brigham Young's pronouncement or who would use it in the future.[57] While seeking to elevate the performance of his police, however, his ability to lead them was sharply curtailed when he suddenly had to go into hiding. A week before, he was informed that Governor Ford's troops were inquiring after him as the captain of the police. Not willing to wait to discover their intentions, he immediately rode to the home of Allen Weeks to stay the night.[58]

Though he was able to sleep in his own bed for the next week, on October 10 he once again took up residence in Weeks's cellar as smoldering conditions threatened to reignite. Having received orders to have the second cohort ready at a moments warning to defend against troops that were rumored to be coming from Quincy, Stout recorded indignantly, "We were determined not to let them come in and arrest and take away our men to be murdered in cold blood as had been done. If they should try it we were determined to cut them off from the face of the earth though we all should be exterminated by a government who were always so ready to Sanction the doings and acts of the mob."⁵⁹

While sequestered the next day, Stout reflected on his situation and recorded both his affectionate feelings regarding his family and his willingness to be martyred for the cause. "I thought of the tender ties of nature at home of my little ones who prattle round me in childish loveliness," he wrote of his sons William Hosea and Hyrum (his first child, Lydia, died in 1842 at the age of eleven months). Comparing his situation to Joseph Smith's, who often had to hide from his enemies, he continued, "Should they attempt to arrest me I felt determined to Sell my life as dear as I could and try and convince our enemies that the blood of the Saints was not as easily Shed as was our Prophets and Patriarch."⁶⁰

Though he remained in hiding at night for more than a week, Stout was able to venture out during the day and meet with other leaders. The most important business at hand was to organize the exodus from Nauvoo. On October 11 twenty-five companies were organized "for Calaforna or the West"; Stout was apprised that he would be captain of a hundred of the twenty-fourth company, and he and his fellow Saints began preparing for the trek.⁶¹ The organization for his company hit a major snag, however, when differences that had been brewing for some time reached a boiling point. He concluded, "all had originated from a spirit of dissension, which was in the old police." According to Stout, the disaffected policemen (at least five of the forty member force) were to the point where he "could hardly suggest an idea which was not some exceptions taken to it and some had even gone so far as to join some other companies in a clandestine way."⁶²

Not only had Stout lost control of the force, the organization of his company also was in jeopardy due to both the defections and the discord. "There was hardly a move which I could make but some one would either leave or threaten to leave the company," he wrote.⁶³ He tried in vain to resolve the situation as matters seemed to be escalating totally out of control. On the third day of the dispute "the disaffected police were still raging about as usual," and there was no improvement on the fourth. Finally, on the fifth day (December 9), a solution was thrust upon him. "I started in company with A. J. Stout to the police," he wrote, "and on our way we met Brs [Brothers] B[righam] Young and O[rson] Hyde and Br Young told me that it was decided in council for me to go on a mission to England and wanted to know what I thought of it."⁶⁴

At a General Conference on April 7, 1860, Brigham Young admitted, "We have at times sent men out on missions to get rid of them; but they generally come back. Some think it is an imposition upon the world to send such men among them. But which is best—to keep them here to pollute others, or to send them where pollution is more prevalent?"⁶⁵

Though his pronouncement came nearly fifteen years later, it easily could have referred to Hosea Stout in 1845. As Stout went to the temple on December 10—on the evening of which the first endowments were given to the faithful—Young asked him how he felt about going on a mission to England, explaining that "it would be the best thing" that he could do and that it would be the cause of giving him "more power and exaltation than any thing else." Stout responded that he "had no other feelings than to obey council."[66]

As Brigham Young and the Twelve met for prayer in Elder Kimball's room in the temple on the evening of December 19, "the brethren counseled on the propriety of sending certain brethren to England."[67] After a lengthy discussion Young asked specifically, "Is it wisdom to send Hosea Stout and Jesse D. Hunter to England? Elder [Orson] Hyde answered that the people in England expected that any one sent from America would be expected to be something more than ordinary—The subject was dropped at this point."[68] It is obvious how Hyde's response was interpreted, for neither Stout nor Jesse Hunter was sent to England.

After receiving his endowments on December 15, Stout performed sundry duties in the temple almost daily until December 26, on which day he went to the temple at sunrise but was informed that there would be "no work done at the endowment."[69] Brigham Young explained simply, "I feel disposed to rest a few days, and let the Temple rest." William Clayton, however, painted a disturbing picture: "There was a necessity for a reformation of this sort, for some men were doing things which ought not to be done in the Temple of the Lord. Some three or four men and perhaps more had introduced women into the temple, not their wives, and were living in the side rooms, cooking, sleeping tending babies, and toying with their women."[70]

Stout went home for breakfast, after which he returned to the temple, loaded pistols in hand, to help search for and escort out the unwanted guests. From that day forth his time in Nauvoo was occupied with guarding the temple and, occasionally, the city streets. On one particularly notable evening, Stout and John Scott came to the temple and found "a considerable number of the guard were assembled and among them was William Hibbard son of the old man Hibbard . . . He was evidently come as a spy," Stout reported. "When I saw him, I told Scott that we must 'bounce a stone off of his head.' to which he agreed we prepared accordingly and I got an opportunity and hit him on the back of his head which came very near taking his life.[71] Two days later, on January 11, some "scoundrels under the character of Government Troops were driven from the city" and "were told by Capt. Stout that if they came back and were found runing through the streets at Night he would kill them." The offenders "left the city in great rage."[72] The following evening, as an "insolent and insulting" group of men passed the temple, Stout informed them that they would shoot the next set of armed men who came into Nauvoo without first giving notice of their coming.[73]

Through use of force and threats of violence, Stout had created for himself a fierce and unsavory reputation. It therefore was unsurprising that the "mob" had "singled [him] out as an object of their revenge" and was determined to assassinate him.[74] For most of the next week, fearing his enemies, he slept in the temple. With his life seemingly in a downward spiral, with dissension in his police force as strong as ever, on January 31 Stout laid the matter of the "old police" before the Twelve. As typically seemed to be the case, he judged himself to be right and opponents wrong, recording, "I think some thing is wrong in the minds of the Twelve in relation to this matter but how it appears to them I know not. But I feel that I have done my duty in protecting their lives from their enemies both from within and without which thing has brought down the indignation of the mob and also false brethren upon me and my life is threatened by both and diligently sought for . . . I feel that some very unexpected catastrophe is going to happen because of false brethren."[75]

With so much controversy and trouble swirling around Stout, he was relieved from his duty as captain of the twenty-fourth Emigration Company.[76] Fortunately for him, in the midst of his darkness, Brigham Young astutely judged that Stout's assets outweighed his faults and counseled that he was needed. "He said he was satisfied with me in some things that Some said he thought I was wrong in," Stout wrote. "He gave us good instruction in relation to governing men and Said he wanted me to stand in the place I now hold after we get to the West."[77] There was perhaps more practicality than wisdom in Young's counsel: though the exodus was scheduled to take place in the spring, "when grass grows and water runs," conditions in Nauvoo had changed drastically, forcing a departure in the middle of winter. There was not a moment to waste in making preparations for the sudden evacuation of the Saints' beloved city, and much of the responsibility for it would be laid squarely at the feet of the captain of police, Hosea Stout.

Notes
1. Brooks, *Mormon Frontier*, January 1, 1845, 13.
2. "The John Taylor Nauvoo Journal, January 1845–September 1845," *BYU Studies* 23, no. 3:18.
3. Ibid., December 5, 1844, 1:11.
4. Ibid., January 31, 1845, 1:18; March 13, 1845, 1:27.
5. Ibid., February 22, 1845, 1:22.
6. Brooks, *Mormon Frontier*, February 14, 1845, 21. Lucretia was born on May 13, 1830, in Dalton, New Hampshire. It is interesting to note that Charles

Rich, who had entered into plural marriage in January 1845, took as his second plural wife Sarah Jane Peck, the younger sister of Hosea's late wife Samantha, and that Charles's cousin Thomas Rich married the third Peck sister, Henrietta, in 1840.
7. Ibid., April 20, 1845, 35.
8. Ibid., June 22 and 30, 1845, 49–50. Marinda Bennett was born on August 26, 1826, at Bedford, Tennessee, a daughter of Richard and Mary Bell Bennett. The wedding date is given in the Stout family Bible. See Brooks, *On the Mormon Frontier*, op. cit, 50 fn 12. Marinda didn't come to live with Hosea until November 20, nearly five months after the marriage. See Brooks, *Mormon Frontier*, November 20, 1845, 93.
9. Ibid., July 19, 1848, 53.
10. Hales, *Joseph Smith's Polygamy, Volume 2: History*, 140–41.
11. Lucretia Fisher was born March 13, 1831, in Dalton, New Hampshire. The fact that she was only fourteen years old when she was sealed to Hosea might have contributed to the secrecy surrounding the sealing to her. Among members of the Church of Jesus Christ of Latter-day Saints, sealing refers to the marriage of a husband and wife and to the joining together of children and parents in relationships that are to endure forever.
12. "Nauvoo Notebook," Hosea Stout Papers, MSS B 53, box 1, folder 1, Utah State Historical Society.
13. Ibid., November 11, 1844, 9.
14. Historian's Office General Church Minutes, 1839–1877, CR 100 318, January 14, 1845, Church History Library.
15. Moody, "Nauvoo's Whistling and Whittling Brigade," *BYU Studies* 15, no. 4:2.
16. Brooks, *Mormon Frontier*, February 8, 1845, 20.
17. Ibid., February 19, 1845, 31.
18. Smith, *History of the Church*, 7:376.
19. Brooks, *Mormon Frontier*, March 3, 1845, 32.
20. Ibid., April 5, 1845, 32–33.
21. Ibid., March 14, 1845, 27.
22. Hallwas and Launius, *Cultures in Conflict*, 54–55.
23. Hancock, "Autobiography," 26.
24. Brooks, *Mormon Frontier*, April 6, 1845, 33.
25. *Warsaw Signal*, April 9, 1845, 2.
26. Brooks, *Mormon Frontier*, April 27, 1845, 36.
27. Brooks, *Mormon Frontier*, April 13, 1845, 34.
28. Ibid., May 12, 1845, 38.
29. It is quite likely that this is the same Ervine Hodges who in 1838 rode to warn the participants of the Battle of Crooked River, themselves fleeing Far West, Missouri, that a troop of cavalry were in pursuit.
30. Stout, "Journal," June 23, 1845.
31. Dean C. Jessee, "The John Taylor Nauvoo Journal," *BYU Studies* 23, no. 3:51.
32. Hall, *Abominations of Mormonism Exposed*, 32. A good discussion of Ervine Hodges's murder and the Hodges brothers' association in criminal activity is found in Shepard, "The Notorious Hodges Brothers: Solving the Mystery

of Their Destruction at Nauvoo," *John Whitmer Historical Association Journal* 26. See also Shepard, "Stealing at Mormon Nauvoo," *John Whitmer Historical Association Journal* 23:99–104.
33. Quinn, *The Mormon Hierarchy: Origins of Power*, 216n168–71, 227–28.
34. Shepard and Marquardt, *Lost Apostles: Forgotten Members of Mormonism's Original Quorum of Twelve*, 254; "A Brother of the Murders Murdered," *Territorial Gazette and Burlington Advertiser*, June 28, 1845, 2; William Huntington autobiography, typescript, Brigham Young University, *LDS Family History Suite*, CD-ROM (Provo: Infobases, 1996); "Hon. Charles Mason," July 23, 18435, typescript, Iowa State Historical Society, Des Moines.
35. Smith, *History of the Church*, 7:428–29.
36. Brooks, *Mormon Frontier*, July 3, 1845, 50–51.
37. Ford, *History of Illinois*, 408.
38. Brooks, *Mormon Frontier*, September 11, 1845, 62.
39. Ibid., March 14, 1845, 27.
40. Ibid., May 7, 1845, 38.
41. Ibid., September 12, 1845, 62.
42. Ibid., September 13, 1845, 63. A "seventy" was charged with preaching the gospel to the world. A quorum of seventy was a body composed of up to seventy total seventies.
43. Hosea Stout Papers, Utah State Historical Society, September 14, 1845.
44. Brooks, *Mormon Frontier*, September 16, 1845, 64.
45. Ibid., September 17, 1845, 65.
46. *Warsaw Signal*, September 17, 1845.
47. Brooks, *Mormon Frontier*, September 19, 1845, 67.
48. Hamilton, "From Assassination to Expulsion," in *Kingdom on the Mississippi Revisited*, 223.
49. Brooks, *Mormon Frontier*, September 19, 1845, 67.
50. Ibid., September 20 and 21, 1845, 69–71.
51. *Journal History*, September 23, 1845.
52. *Nauvoo Neighbor*, October 1, 1845.
53. Ibid., September 26, 1845, 73.
54. Ibid., September 27, 1845, 75.
55. Ibid., March 5, 25, and 27, 1845, 19.
56. Ibid., September 27, 1845, 74–75.
57. Ibid., October 8, 1845, 83.
58. Ibid., October 1, 1845, 79,
59. Ibid., October 10, 1845, 82–83.
60. Ibid., October 11, 1845, 83.
61. *Journal History*, October 11, 1845; Brooks, *Mormon Frontier*, October 12, 1845, 1:84.
62. Brooks, *Mormon Frontier*, December 5, 1845, 94–95. Jesse P. Harmon, Daniel Carn, Andrew Lytle, John Lytle, and M. D. Hambleton were the disaffected police named by Stout.
63. Ibid.
64. Ibid., December 9, 1845, 97.
65. *Journal of Discourses*, April 7, 1860, 7:228–29.

66. Ibid., December 10, 1845, 97.
67. *Journal History*, December 19, 1845.
68. Smith, ed., *An Intimate Chronicle: The Journals of William Clayton*, December 19, 1845, 219.
69. Brooks, *Mormon Frontier*, December 26, 1845, 100.
70. Smith, *An Intimate Chronicle*, 234–35.
71. Brooks, *Mormon Frontier*, January 9, 1846, 103.
72. Barney, ed. *The Mormon Vanguard Brigade of 1847: Norton Jacob's Record*, 63–64.
73. Brooks, *Mormon Frontier*, January 12, 1846, 105.
74. Ibid., January 23, 1846, 108.
75. Ibid., January 31, 1846, 111.
76. Ibid., January 19, 1846, 107. Hosea wrote, "met the capt of my emegrating company," signifying that he no longer was the captain.
77. Ibid., February 2, 1846, 111.

9
The Trek across Iowa

"I do not profess to be much of a joker," Brigham Young told a congregation, "but I do think this to be one of the best jokes ever perpetrated. By the time [December 1845] we were at work in the Nauvoo Temple, officiating in the ordinances, the mob had learned that 'Mormonism' was not dead, as they had supposed." Young, who with eight other apostles had been accused of harboring a Nauvoo counterfeiting operation, was in his room in the temple one night when he learned that a posse was lurking outside and that a United States Marshal was waiting to arrest him. Thinking quickly, Young asked William Miller to take his hat and cloak and accompany his driver George D. Grant to the carriage.

Supposing him to be Brigham Young, the marshal immediately tried to arrest Miller, who in turn entered the carriage and said, "I am going to the Mansion House, won't you ride with me?" The marshal obliged, and Lawyer Edmonds, who was staying at the Mansion House, recognized the joke and volunteered to accompany Miller to Carthage. When they reached Carthage the Marshal took the supposed Brigham into an upper room of the hotel, placed a guard over him and bragged at having apprehended the Mormon leader. A short time later, however, an apostate Mormon by the name of Thatcher came in and asked the landlord where Brigham Young was. The landlord pointed across the table to Miller, to which Thatcher exclaimed, "Oh, hell! That's not Brigham; that is William Miller, one of my old neighbors."[1]

Young found great humor when retelling the story twenty-five years later, but it was no laughing matter at the time of the event: though there was no clear evidence linking Young to counterfeiting, a clear signal was sent that government officials would not leave Mormon leaders alone.[2] Compounding the situation, a warning was received from Governor Ford that federal troops in St. Louis would intercept and destroy the Mormons. Though unfounded, the report was accepted as genuine and it became obvious that the Mormons had to leave Nauvoo long before the grass was green. To that end, Young informed Stout on February 2, 1846, "we must be ready to leave for the west by next thursday [February 5]."³ Meeting on the same day, the Twelve Apostles and a few others (including Young) agreed, "it was imperatively necessary to start as soon as possible." He then added to the urgency by stating that families should be ready to depart on four hours' notice.⁴

The early exodus proceeded under the direction of Stout and his "old police." Charles Shumway crossed the river on February 4 and was followed two days later by Bishop George Miller and his family, aided by Reddick Allred and a team outfitted by his father Isaac and his brother-in-law Allen Taylor (a brother of Hosea's wife Louisa).⁵ Evacuating the city under desperate circumstances, however, proved to be much more difficult than anticipated, and Stout, perhaps overly optimistic, expressed disappointment that his orders were not strictly followed.⁶

Under normal circumstances, with time not of the essence, none would have attempted to cross the Mississippi on the morning of February 9, when the wind blew hard, rendering the river choppy and dangerous. Nevertheless, the Saints "gathered several flatboats, some old lighters, and a number of skiffs, forming altogether quite a fleet," and were at work throughout the day and night, superintended by Stout and his police.⁷ At noon he took his family to the river and boarded "an old small boat" for the crossing. In mid-stream they witnessed the overturning of a skiff carrying an older man and two boys, followed in short order the shrieks and cries of men and women on a sinking boat. Though all were rescued, the events were cause for great commotion both on the river and in Nauvoo, where a rumor quickly spread that Stout's boat had sunk and that both he and his family had drowned.⁸

Stout was very much alive, though as he glanced back toward Nauvoo he was alarmed to see the temple afire. Brigham Young saw the flames from a distance and said, "If it is the will of the Lord that the Temple be burned, instead of being defiled by the Gentiles, Amen to it."⁹ Fortunately, the fire—which was caused by an overheated stovepipe—was confined to the roof and extinguished before the building sustained major damage, and the city returned to normal. Nevertheless, to Hosea "it seemed that the destroyer brooded over the land and water at this time and was in a fair way to be triumphant."¹⁰

Though Stout alluded to a mystical, biblical "destroyer," his real enemies were far more tangible. On February 12 he was informed "that some of the Carthage troops were in the city [Nauvoo] with writs for some of the brethren" as well as himself, which seemed to validate the fear that led to the early exodus. In response, he immediately called out all the troops belonging to his camp in Iowa and instructed that should any Carthage troops "cross the river after any of us . . . we would put them to death rather than be Harrassed as we had been after we had started to leave their cursed and corrupt government."[11]

Given his reputation, few would have doubted the sincerity of Stout's threat. While awaiting the anticipated attack (which never materialized), he paused to ponder his situation, particularly since the location of the Saints' camp—at Sugar Creek, about nine miles from the ferry crossing—was in close proximity to the home he had shared with his wife Samantha at the time of her passing six years earlier. On the way to camp, on the morning of February 13 in the company of John D. Lee, Hosea visited Samantha's grave; though her death had been the source of "many a mournful hour" to him, he reflected, "Instead of being deprived of my last bosom friend [Samantha] I now had three [wives] equally dear and confiding to me." Considering the direction his life had taken following Samantha's death he mused how "by a succession of dangerous and continual scene and of life devoted to . . . this kingdom from that time to this has brought me to where I am at the Head of the Army of Israel which was raised by my own individual influence and was now marching forth from the gentiles under my command subject to the Head of the Church."[12]

On February 15, Stout returned to Nauvoo where he met the "Head of the Church," Brigham Young, who while preparing to board his boat to cross the river instructed Stout to send members of the Nauvoo guard to Iowa as soon as possible. He returned to the Iowa side of the river just as the temperature began to plummet. Though the Saints at first were "comfortably situated on the bottom land on Sugar Creek," the weather had become increasingly cold and bitter and on February 14 they awoke to deep snow on the ground that was "still falling very fast accompanied by a high North wind."[13] By the time Young arrived, the mud had become so deep that his teams had to be yoked double to pull the wagons up the hill to the Sugar Creek camp.[14] "It is very cold," wrote Patty Sessions on 16 February, "the wind blows we can hardly get to the fire for smoke and we have no tent but our waggon."[15] As the temperature continued to fall, the Mississippi froze over, allowing many to cross quickly by foot over the ice. By the end of the month, however, moderate temperatures began melting the ice, creating large flocs that made the crossing even more time consuming and dangerous than before.

The uncooperative weather and resultant conditions contributed to a lengthy stay of the increasingly large group of Saints at Sugar Creek, as did continuing deliberations regarding which route to take in the journey across Iowa. On the evening of February 24, as the thermometer stood at twelve degrees below zero, Brigham Young met with apostles Heber C. Kimball and Willard Richards "to investigate some dissatisfaction which existed between Bishop George Miller and the guards." Miller accused Stout of instructing guards to kill Miller should he attempt to cross the bridge that led to the tent where councils were held. Stout admitted to the words but claimed they were uttered in jest; Young, Kimball, and Richards evidently believed Stout and concluded that the incident was a misunderstanding.[16] Nevertheless, the day following the incident—perhaps spurred on by Miller's sudden departure that day with his company—Stout tightened his hold on the camp by forbidding anyone from leaving without his knowledge.[17]

It is evident that Stout projected a fearsome image. For example, on March 3, two days after the three thousand Saints comprising the "Camp of Israel" began moving west from Sugar Creek, Stout and Truman Gillett rode into the small town of Farmington, Iowa, to trade for a few articles. Inside the store they noticed a group of men who "manifested every symptom looks could to pick a fuss with us." Stout, however, smugly recorded that he was "armed with 2 Six shooters and a large Bowie knife all in sight which they eyed very close and when I came near any of them they would give me a wide birth [*sic*]."[18]

The camp, for travel purposes, had been divided into units of one hundred wagons and companies of fifty, and from the outset Charles Allen, captain of the third fifty, called his men together and, in an "inflammatory speech" against what Stout had said, declared that he would neither work with nor receive orders from Stout but rather would go directly to Brigham Young.[19] The clash continued for nearly two weeks, with Allen (according to Stout) "instilling a spirit of insubordination" and causing widespread grumbling.[20] Though their dispute finally was settled, rumors of trouble in the camp were carried back to Nauvoo. On March 7 Thomas Bullock recorded in his journal a report that John Taylor was "going to preach his last Mormon Sermon tomorrow being on his way to Nauvoo for that purpose; that Hosea Stout has shot Pres. B. Young and was fastened to a tree, B. Young being dead and great excitement in the camp. Many of the police left the Camp."[21] Acting as clerk for the Twelve Apostles, John D. Lee on March 16 wrote a letter to Orson Hyde dispelling the rumors, saying, "Brigham Young is not murdered; John Taylor has not apostatized; Hosea Stout has not mutinized; the guards have committed no insurrections."[22]

Lee further stated in his letter, "we do not believe that so large a company ever camped together so long upon the face of the earth, as this has, with so much good feeling contentedness, kindness, benevolence, charity and brotherly love as has been, and is still, manifested among this Camp."[23] He should have added patience to his list, inasmuch as the trek progressed at little more than a snail's pace as melting snow created a mess on the wilderness roads. "Traveled the most muddy road I ever saw," wrote Eliza Maria Partridge Lyman on March 5, just five days into the trek.[24] Eliza R. Snow concurred, writing on the same day, "After crossing the [Des Moines] river the road was thro' timber and intolerably muddy, the banks on the side rising almost perpendicularly. The teams had hard work to draw the loads as we ascended hill after hill."[25] And that was before the rain began to fall, which commenced on March 10 and continued off-and-on for about eight weeks, saturating the prairies and turning them into shallow lakes and quagmires while frequently making the roads almost impassable.

Particularly affected by the adverse conditions was Hosea's wife Louisa, who in her eighth month of pregnancy was continually afflicted by pain in her side. In the incessant rain their tent leaked badly and on March 10 he spent the day trying in vain to keep his family dry, noting that their beds were wet, "thus endangering my sick wife."[26] Primarily due to the weather, the companies remained at Richardson's Point for eleven days. "The ground was still wet and muddy. No time for travelling," he noted on March 12; two days later he recorded, "we went or rather waded to President B. Youngs tent."[27] The following day Eliza R. Snow wrote, "So intolerably windy the men failed in their efforts to keep the tent upright . . . I was led to inquire 'How long O Lord?' Is there no reward for patient submission?"[28]

The Saints, who had traveled a meager forty-six miles from Sugar Creek since March 1, began moving again on March 19, covering twenty-six miles in two days. On both days, however, Brigham Young noted, "Very little corn or fodder of any kind to be had at this place."[29] On March 24 Stout reported that more than half of his men were out of provisions and there was no feed for the animals. The next day, though teams returned to camp with thirty bushels of corn, Brigham Young was confounded by reports of prices driven higher by one Mormon bidding against another. "This is one of the many difficulties which are liable to arise in a large camp where there is not a perfect organization and the agents of the different divisions do not understand each others movements," wrote Young.[30]

Young also was frustrated by the movement of advance scouts, particularly George Miller and brothers Orson and Parley Pratt, who were straying much farther than prescribed from the main body of Saints. Consequently Young wrote to the trio, with special emphasis directed at Miller, "We have found to entire satisfaction that the course taken by Brother Miller from the commencement of this campaign, and the course you are now pursuing has already . . . cost us sorrow and trouble . . . You must know that this large body of people cannot be transplanted in a distant country without order in our travels . . . Now this confused state of thing cannot be borne any longer."[31]

Young reproved a council of the captains of tens, fifties, and hundreds on the morning of March 26 for "their want of order" and reorganized the camp into three units of one hundred, with each of those subdivided into six better-structured units of fifty or more wagons each.[32] Not content to stop there, on March 27 Young rebuked Stout, telling him "that his guard was of little use in the camp, and that some of them would sit by the fire and sleep and let the cattle eat pickles out of the tubs and crackers out of the sacks."[33] Stout responded "that he had done the best he knew how, and so had the Guard," and that "the president had never told him what to do, and what he did, he had to guess at." Young retorted, "that was the way for him [Stout] to do, and when he got wrong, then it was for the president to put him right."[34] He further declared that henceforth the guard would be divided and distributed among the companies of fifties; in a seeming vote of confidence, he selected Stout to be the captain of the guard, that consisted of about twelve or fourteen men, in the company of fifty (designated the first fifty) over which he personally presided.[35]

Travel was more orderly following the reorganization but nothing could overcome the wet spring weather. Almost constant rain created interminable mud, leading Brigham Young to comment on March 27 that they had passed through "one mud hole only, which was about six miles in length."[36] The inclement weather, which was bad in March and even worse the first half of April, once again was particularly wearing on Stout's wife Louisa, who not only was in her final month of pregnancy but was suffering from pleurisy. On April 6 he wrote of the terrible conditions:

> This was of all mornings the most dismal dark and rainy . . . This day capped the climax of all days for travelling. The road was the worst that I had yet witnessed up hill and down through sloughs on spouty oak ridges and deep marshes raining hard the creek rising. The horses would sometimes sink to their bellies on the ridges, teams stall going down hill. We worked and toiled more than half the day and had at last to leave some of our wagons and double teams before we could get through.[37]

Times were not good for the Stout family as Louisa's condition steadily worsened ("My wife was almost dead today with pleurasy," he reported on April 8) and Hosea was stricken on April 15 with a case of dysentery that severely weakened him for nearly a month.[38] On that same day, however, he had no choice but to join the Saints as they moved northwest, taking advantage of moderate weather. A week into the journey, on April 22, Louisa gave birth to a daughter, also named Louisa; the primitive conditions of her birth in the wilderness led Stout to remark that she "might be called a 'Prairie chicken.'"[39] At a birth weight of eight pounds, the child was healthy, a description that could not be applied to her two brothers: three-year-old Hosea weighed thirty-three pounds (by contrast his cousin Charles, though thirteen months younger, weighed thirty pounds) and Hyrum, three months shy of his second birthday, scaled in at only fifteen pounds, just seven pounds heavier than his newborn sister.[40] To complicate matters, three days later the children came down with whooping cough.

In the midst of much suffering, hunger, and sickness among many of the Saints, with wagons and equipment in disrepair and with no prospects for better weather, the dream of reaching the Rocky Mountains later that season was fading. A plan therefore was forged to establish farms or way stations along the road. Hundreds of acres were planted at a place that the Saints named Garden Grove. "It was a pleasantly situated place from the first appearance and presented a beautiful thick wood of tall shell bark hickory," wrote Stout, but Garden Grove turned out to be neither as well timbered nor watered as the Saints had hoped. In addition, the place was infested with rattlesnakes—some men killed eight or more of them each day.[41] Hosea's brother Allen recorded, "About these times the rattlesnakes bit a good many of our animals and there was a great deel of sickness in camp on account of the great exposure the saints were forced to undergo."[42]

Immediately after their arrival at Garden Grove, Hosea's family was out of meal and flour and he complained that "the people would not sell flour when they knew we were starving and some sick."[43] When Benjamin Jones, who had gone to local settlements to peddle belongings in order to buy food, didn't return, James Allred and Green Taylor were sent after Jones, leaving Stout destitute for help in herding cattle as the effects of dysentery rendered him scarcely able to walk.[44] More than a week later, Stout, still without food, went with Jones into the woods to talk over their feelings when word was sent that his son Hyrum was failing; the child died that afternoon in his father's arms "with the hooping cough and black canker."[45] Filled with gloom, he wrote:

> I shall not attempt to say anything about my feelings at this time because my family is still afflicted. My wife is yet unable to go about and little Hosea my only son now is wearing down with the same complaint and what will be the end thereof. I have fearful foreboding of coming evil on my family yet. We are truly desolate and afflicted and entirely destitute of any thing even to eat much less to nourish the sick, and just able to go about myself. Arrangements being made to bury him this evening.[46]

On May 13 most of the camp commenced a move to a second, larger settlement called Mount Pisgah, an attractive area of rolling hills "crowned with beautiful groves of timber" about forty miles west of Garden Grove.[47] Brigham Young, aware that Stout's circumstances would not allow him immediately to join in the move, told him that they would send back for him as soon as possible but in the meantime wanted him to continue to keep charge of the public arms, a duty Stout had borne at least since April 11.[48] It proved an onerous burden, for his only wagon was filled with firearms, thus unable to move his personal property.[49] An attempt to build projections on the wagons to carry his possessions failed, and he sought the help of Charles C. Rich, who was preparing to move his family to Mount Pisgah. In Stout's eyes, though Rich agreed verbally to help, in reality he "did not, neither did he seem to take much interest in it any way." Stout assured himself in his diary that he would have helped Rich had the tables been turned but concluded, "it matters not."[50] As events in the near future would prove, however, it mattered very much indeed.

Over the next several days, teams arrived back at Garden Grove to aid in the move to Mount Pisgah, though none were for Stout or Jesse Hunter (who helped Stout guard the guns), making them feel as if they were forgotten. At length Hunter was able to move on to Mount Pisgah but Stout, with but one wagon and that full of guns, had to linger while trying to protect his family from strong winds and nearly constant rain as the health of his remaining son, Hosea, worsened considerably. Meanwhile, still weak and feeble from his illness, father Hosea summoned his strength to look after his cows and horses and to repair the grave of his son Hyrum, which he surmised he would never again see after they moved from Garden Grove.

Finally, on May 28, Stout's brother-in-law William Taylor and Job Hall returned with teams that Jesse Hunter had taken to Mount Pisgah and Stout was able to commence moving his family; they arrived at Mount Pisgah on the evening of June 1 and camped in a "beautiful grove of small hickory" where he and Jesse Hunter intended to plant a crop. The next day he was greeted by Charles C. Rich bearing an order signed by Brigham Young that simultaneously filled him with relief and confusion:

> General order:
> To Major General Charles C. Rich:
> You are hereby authorized and required to take into your immediate charge all the guns, equipments, public teams, wagons and appurtenances thereunto, belonging now in charge of Col. Hosea Stout, or any other person, and if possible forward

them to future headquarters without delay by Col. Stout or some other trusty persons.[51]

"I confess that I did not understand the object of this move," wrote Stout in his diary, "neither did I care for it released me from all public care and responsibility and I felt like a free man with nothing on my mind but to contrive how to take care of my family for the best." But while Rich released Stout from responsibility for the guns, Brigham Young countermanded Rich's instruction and directed Stout and Hunter to accompany the guns to Council Bluffs while leaving their families at Mount Pisgah. "Here again we were entirely disconcerted and now all together gave up the idea of raising a crop," recorded Stout, "and it seemed that it was designed by some over ruling power that we should not 'Sow nor reap' neither enjoy the peace and happiness of a private life any more. We saw nothing but a long train of public cares and responsibility hanging over us for we knew it would not end at the Bluffs."[52]

While Stout fretted about his heavy, church-related burden, he obsessed over the lack of anticipated help from Charles C. Rich, becoming increasingly frustrated with each passing day. On June 5 he tried "to obtain help from Rich who never even used his influence to assist me much less fit me out as Br Brigham had ordered him"; the next day he "Was after Br Rich again to no purpose for he still evaded any help or using any influence"; and on June 7 he concluded, "I plainly saw that Br Rich did not intend to do anything for me."[53] When Rich later in the week seemed to side with John Guthrie in a dispute with Stout over some property in Garden Grove, the long and close friendship unraveled completely: "It appeared to me in every move that Br Rich made while I was here that he was my secret enemy and doing all that he could against me which I consider a very ungrateful thing for I had always been his strong friend and was always ready to step forward to help advance him even when it militated against me as it often did. But let him prosper in it."[54]

Stout had become increasingly paranoid and began to perceive all of Rich's actions as threats against himself. On June 15 he wrote:

> Today I concluded to go in two waggon[s] accordingly I put all the gns [guns] in one and some of my things and the ballance of them in another General Rich had let me have another waggon since he gave up the one to Johnson So when I concluded thus and had arrainged my affairs to go I told General Rich what I had done which brought out the thing I was after last Saturday, for as soon as I told him he seemed surprised and disappointed and told me that he had hoped

that if I could take all the guns in one waggon and go on that he could have the other for Elder W[ilford] Woodruff this explained the whole matter He had been urging me to go on with the guns in one waggon and leave my family without any shelter but a tent which would not shield them from the storm and all this to be done in my absence In fact I have good reasons to believe that he intended to take the tent also but he did not acknowledge that to me Had I not have suspected some rascality I should have left my family and that was what induced me to undertake to move to such a disadvantage

I thought it best to move from hill to hill with my family and effects if it should take me all summer rather than to leave them in Pisgah where such a friend could take some unknown advantage of them . . . I am now perfectly satisfied that he is a most secret and an inveterate enemy of mine and for what reason I know not.[55]

Only Stout's side of the story has been preserved—Rich's single contemporary extant communication regarding Stout during that period was a letter stating, "the ordinance [sic] were in good condition and would soon be on the way for headquarters in charge of Col. Hosea Stout." It is very possible that Stout exaggerated the situation in his own mind, particularly considering the paranoia and persecution complex he displayed in the months preceding his split with Rich, citing in his diary "disaffected police" who had spread "dissensions" against him all winter (February 20); a "spirit of insubordination" among the guard who did not agree with him on certain matters (March 15); suspected though unsubstantiated "certain evil plotting against" him (April 13); and a suspected "disposition" by John D. Lee to "interfear with [Hosea's] private arraingements relative to [his] wagons" (April 19).[56] It is clear nevertheless that, whatever the cause, the deep and abiding friendship between Stout and Charles C. Rich was fractured beyond repair.

Stout was able to trade for a small horse-drawn wagon to go with a larger wagon for his family and another for the guns and on June 20 was able to begin moving his family. For want of a suitable harness, he attached the smaller wagon to the larger one and had "one of the girls" (likely referring to one of his plural wives, Lucretia and Marinda) take charge of the horses.[57] Though still weak from his lingering illness, he evidently drove one wagon while Peter Manning, a Negro boy who was willing to drive a team in order to get to Council Bluffs, handled the other.

While en route, little Hosea's health continually declined; a priesthood blessing, conferred by the "laying on of hands," was ineffective in healing as was an "ordinance performed according to the Holy order and with the signs of the Priesthood."[58] One night, as the rain fell in torrents and ran through the wagon, the child was discovered by his mother to be lying in water and dangerously ill. Three days later, on June 28, the father awoke very early and discovered his child was dying. "He seemed perfectly easy and now had given up to the struggle of death and lay breathing out his life sweetly," noted his father.[59]

As never before, Stout was crushed. "Thus died my only son and one too on whom I had placed my own name and was truly the dearest object of my heart," he wrote and continued to expound on the degree of his loss:

> I have often heard people tell of loosing the darling object of their heart. I have often heard of people mourning as for the loss of an only son But never untill now did I fully feel and realize the keen and heart rending force of their words. I have once lost a companion for life and left without a bosom friend Left alone to lock sorrow and disappointment up in my own breast. Left to smile in the midst of the merry and happy but to smile only to hide and disguise the effects of an overflowing heart of woe. But not then did I feel the loss or mourn as for an only son. This last loss. This loss of my son. This my hopes for comfort in my old age. This the darling object of my heart gone seemed to cap the climax of all my former misfortunes and seemed more than all else to leave me utterly hopeless.[60]

The trek across Iowa had been filled with hardship and disaster for Stout and his family, including severe illness, hunger almost to the point of starvation, the death of his son Hyrum, and the loss of a close friendship with Charles C. Rich, but nothing was as devastating as the death of little Hosea. Suddenly he felt as if he were "Surrounded by every discouraging circumstance that is calculated to make man unhappy and disconsolate." He was "discouraged, desolate . . . left utterly destitute" and had "no reason to expect any thing better in future."[61] In the depths of his despair, the burning question, unspoken but earnestly contemplated, was whether the road he had chosen could ever lead him to peace and happiness.

Notes

1. *Journal of Discourses,* July 23, 1871, vol. 14: 218–19.
2. Regarding counterfeiting, Brigham Young recorded, "A set of Bogus makers who recently commenced operations in this city and who are determined to counterfeit coin here by wagon loads and make it pass upon

the community as land office money, are determined to be avenged upon us, because we would not permit them to pursue their wicked business in Nauvoo, they have scattered through the country circulating their bogus money and spreading lies and every species of falsehood." See Watson, *Manuscript History of Brigham Young, 1846–1847*, January 24, 1846, 20.
3. Brooks, *Mormon Frontier*, February 2, 1846, 111.
4. Watson, *Manuscript History*, February 2, 1846, 25.
5. Allred, "Journal," *Treasures of Pioneer History* 5:301.
6. Brooks, *Mormon Frontier*, February 6 and 7, 1846, 112–13. Hosea instructed the captains of the emigration companies to have their extra teams meet at the Masonic Hall on the morning of February 7, but the turnout was very poor.
7. Watson, *Manuscript History*, February 9, 1846, 30.
8. Ibid., February 9, 1846, 113–14.
9. Watson, *Manuscript History*, 29.
10. Brooks, *Mormon Frontier*, February 9, 1846, 114.
11. Ibid., February 12, 1846, 121.
12. Ibid., February 13, 1846, 122.
13. Ibid., February 14, 1846, 122.
14. Ibid., February 15, 1846, 123.
15. Smart, ed., *Mormon Midwife: The 1846–1848 Diaries of Patty Bartlett Sessions*, February 16, 1846, 34.
16. *Journal History*, February 24, 1846; correspondence of Bishop George Miller with the *Northern Islander*, Saint James, MI, June 22, 1855.
17. Brooks, *Mormon Frontier*, February 25, 1846, 127.
18. Ibid., March 3, 1846, 129.
19. Ibid., March 4, 1846, 130.
20. Ibid., March 15, 1846, 138.
21. Bullock, "Journals, 1843–1849 " *BYU Studies* 31:1, March 7, 1846, 57.
22. *Journal History*, March 16, 1846.
23. Ibid.
24. "Journal of Eliza Maria Partridge Lyman," M270.07 L9865L, Church History Library.
25. "Journal of Eliza R. Snow," MS 1439, Church History Library.
26. Brooks, *Mormon Frontier*, March 10, 1846, 136.
27. Ibid., March 12 and 14, 1846, 137–38.
28. "Journal of Eliza R. Snow," March 15, 1846.
29. *Journal History*, March 19 and 20, 1846.
30. Ibid., March 25, 1846.
31. Letter from Brigham Young to George Miller, Orson Pratt, Parley P. Pratt, "and their brethren," March 26, 1846. In Bennett, *Mormons at the Missouri, 1846–1852*, 36.
32. Brooks, *Mormon Frontier*, March 26, 1846, 143.
33. *Journal History*, March 27, 1846.
34. Ibid., March 28, 1846.
35. Ibid., March 29, 1846; Brooks, *Mormon Frontier*, March 29, 1846, 146.
36. Watson, *Manuscript History*, 106.
37. Brooks, *Mormon Frontier*, April 6, 1846, 149.

38. Ibid., April 8 and 15, 1846, 150, 152.
39. Ibid., April 22, 1846, 155.
40. Ibid., April 23, 1846, 155.
41. Bennett, *Mormons at the Missouri*, 39.
42. Stout, "Reminiscences and Journal," Church History Library.
43. Brooks, *Mormon Frontier*, April 28, 1846, 158.
44. Ibid., May 2 1846, 158–59.
45. Black canker was a Mormon term for scurvy, a disease resulting from a deficiency of vitamin C.
46. Brooks, *Mormon Frontier*, May 8, 1846, 160.
47. Pratt, *The Autobiography of Parley P. Pratt*, 428.
48. Brooks, *Mormon Frontier*, May 13, 1846, 161.
49. Ibid., April 11, 1846, 151. Hosea wrote on that day, "Some of my men went off to make some boards and some to cleaning the publick guns in my charge." It is not known when he was given charge of the guns.
50. Ibid., May 19, 1846, 162.
51. Letter from Willard Richards and Brigham Young to Charles C. Rich, June 1, 1846; Watson, *Manuscript History*, 177.
52. Brooks, *Mormon Frontier*, June 2, 1846, 165.
53. Ibid., June 5–7, 1846, 166.
54. Ibid., June 12, 1846, 166.
55. Brooks, *Mormon Frontier*, June 15, 1846, 167.
56. Ibid., February 20, 1846, 125; March 15, 1846, 138; April 13, 1846, 151; April 19, 1846, 154.
57. Ibid., June 20, 1846, 169. Including a similar reference to "one of the girls" on June 17, Hosea made mention of his plural wives only twice in more than four months after leaving Nauvoo, a clear indication of their relative ages and also of their significance as wives compared to his wife Louisa, who played a major role in his diary.
58. Ibid., June 25, 1846, 170. The ordinance was performed by both men and women who had received their endowment in the temple before leaving Nauvoo and undoubtedly involved a prayer for the healing of the sick.
59. Ibid., June 28, 1846, 171.
60. Ibid.
61. Ibid.

10
Winter Quarters

With good weather and firm ground, the Saints' journey of less than three hundred miles across Iowa in spring 1846 should have taken about four to six weeks; however, hampered by rain-induced poor travel conditions, after nearly four months almost twelve thousand Saints still were scattered across Iowa. Church leaders who had reached the Missouri River hoped in vain that some of the apostles and others could press on to the West before the onset of winter storms, but the more immediate concern was where the main body of refugees would spend the winter. Answers to both concerns began to come into focus with the arrival in Iowa of Captain James Allen of the United States Army.

In 1846, a year after the annexation of Texas by the United States, President James K. Polk set his expansionist eyes on the acquisition of New Mexico and California. Mexican and American troops had a skirmish on April 24, 1846, and three weeks later Congress declared war with Mexico. The Mormons, who had been denied support by the federal government in their struggles in Missouri and Illinois, at first were unsympathetic; Hosea Stout recorded a typical Mormon reaction to the news of the war:

> I confess that I was glad to learn of war against the United States and was in hopes that it might never end untill they were entirely destroyed for they had driven us into the wilderness and was now laughing at our calamities.[1]

Unbeknownst to most of the Mormon exiles, including Stout, several months earlier Brigham Young had authorized Jesse C. Little to meet with national leaders for the purpose of seeking government aid for the migrating Saints. Little arrived in Washington, DC, just eight days after war had been declared and on June 3 met with President Polk; fearing that the Mormons would aid the enemy in the war, Polk authorized Colonel Stephen W. Kearny "to receive into service as volunteers a few hundred of the Mormons who are now on their way to California, with a view to conciliate them, attach them to our country, and prevent them from taking part against us."[2]

Many Saints were deeply opposed to supplying troops to the United States for any reason. "We were all very indignant at this requisition and only looked on it as a plot laid to bring trouble on us as a people," wrote Stout. "I confess that my feelings was uncommonly wrought up against them. This was the universal feelings at Pisgah."[3] On the other hand, Brigham Young recognized several advantages of government service: desperately needed capital for the exodus could be procured as recruits were paid in advance for their term of enlistment; members of the battalion could keep their arms at the end of their enlistment; and, significantly, the Mormons would be permitted to make temporary settlements on Indian lands while preparing for their trek west. A deal was finalized between the government and Mormon leaders for an estimated 543 men to be mustered into the Mormon Battalion at Council Bluffs, Iowa Territory, and on July 21, 1846, the Battalion began what became at the time the longest infantry march in United States military history, a journey of approximately 1850 miles.

With so many able-bodied men gone with the Battalion, it was no longer feasible to reach the Rocky Mountains that year, and thus energies were directed toward finding a suitable winter way station. In early September a site was chosen on the west bank of the Missouri River, approximately four miles north of present day Omaha, for "Winter Quarters," a place not only to spend the winter but a center for planning, regrouping, and preparing for the following year. Almost simultaneously a rumor reached Winter Quarters that a US marshal from Missouri was approaching to arrest the Apostles.[4] Though a false alarm, it hastened the formation of a scaled-down version of the Nauvoo Legion to protect the new settlement, with Colonel Stephen Markham the ranking officer and Lieutenant Colonel Hosea Stout of the first battalion of infantry second in command.[5] The following month a city guard was established by order of Colonel Markham, to be presided over by Stout.[6] Less than two weeks later, Stout also was appointed as clerk of the Municipal High Council, which exercised legislative, executive, and judicial powers in both church and civic capacities.[7]

The appointments should have served as a triumph for a man who in the previous half-year had been a nearly forgotten figure, but tragedy never seemed to be far around the corner for Hosea Stout. During the trek across Iowa, he and his family were destitute, nearly starving. On July 6, when offered assistance that he considered "would amount to begging" on his part, he wrote, "I concluded that I would rather starve than live thus ignominiously in the midst of the Saints."[8] Though Brigham Young told him he "intended to have me provided for," with Young away from the encampment Stout exclaimed, "I had to make my own arraingments [sic] to live or starve before the President returned."[9]

To Stout's surprise and elation, on July 15 by the order of Brigham Young, he procured "1900 pounds of bread stuff" and enough provisions to sustain his family for a year. "My prospects for living seemed to brighten," he wrote, "for he [Young] acted like a friend that was willing to help in time of need."[10] It is impossible to know whether Young was acting more as a friend than as a leader who saw Stout a vital asset, controversial though he might be; nevertheless, on August 1 Stout wrote:

> Br[other] John D. Lee informed me that all those who had been slandering me and propesying [sic] against me were now being put to shame for my course had been entirely satisfactory to Brigham and proven to all people the sincerity and integrity of my motives and that it was Brighams intentions to restore me to responsible and honorable stations again and that he thought it best to let matters go as it has this summer in order to prove to those who were my enemies that I was a good man and true and that he never doubted it himself. This he said he told me for my encouragement.[11]

Further extending a hand of support, on the evening of August 24 Young visited Stout, who had been ill, and "laid hands on me and said that I should get well and that he would let me have any thing which I needed either in food or clothing and that he was my friend and would be to all eternity."[12]

Despite the blessing, Stout frequently was weakened from lingering illness, stating on several occasions, "I was uncommonly sick" or "I was all give out," and even less healthy was his plural wife Marinda, "who had been very sick for some time." On September 23 Stout recorded that Marinda had "the Dropsy and cold on the lungs."[13] Nevertheless, he moved his family on September 24 to the site for Winter Quarters but noted, "At night I was so tired and worn down with fatigue that when I laid down to sleep the fever rose on me and I was out of my senses most of the night."[14]

Two days later, Marinda delivered a stillborn child; though evidently pain-free after the miscarriage, she seemed to have a "death glare of her eyes," and in the early afternoon she died. "She had ever been true and faithful to me from the first of our acquaintance," wrote Stout, "very near and dear to me which made this stroke of adversity more accutely felt by me and the rest of the family. There is now only four of us left and whose turn will be next God only knows."[15]

On November 24 Stout moved his remaining family into a "partly finished" house at Winter Quarters. It was the first day that his seven-month-old daughter Louisa—his "only living child"—ever had been in a house. The dwelling was extremely modest—twelve feet square on the outside and with neither door nor windows yet installed to repel a strong, cold north wind. "The only thing that was any satisfaction to us was that we were out of the tent for if we had been there in addition to our troubles and cold we would have been expecting the tent to blow down every moment," he remarked. And yet, shivering through the first night in his "little shanty," he couldn't help reflecting on the nine months and fifteen days since his family last slept under a roof:

> During which time we have undere went allmost every change of fortune that could be imagined. One half of my family so dear to me has been consigned to the silent grave andwe who yet remain have often been brought to the verge of death often in storms and rains have I stood to hold my tent from uncovering my sick family expecting every moment to see them exposed to the rain and wind which would have been certain death. Often have I lain and contemplated my own sickness and feeble situation, without any thing for myself and family to eat with death staring me in the face and could only contemplate what would become of them in case I was called away . . . How often in sorrow and anguish have I said in my heart. When shall my trials and tribulations end.[16]

Stout was not unique in having trials and tribulations—sickness and poor living conditions were so widespread in Winter Quarters that the area, officially known as the Missouri Bottoms, was widely called "Misery Bottoms" by the Saints. The estimated death rate at Winter Quarters was 113 per thousand, approximately four times higher than at Nauvoo, and yet Winter Quarters, though established as a temporary way station, was remarkable, a small city of more than six hundred cabins and huts with a population by December of 3,483 inhabitants that was built virtually overnight.[17] "Nothing in American history," wrote prominent twentieth century historian Bernard DeVoto, "is like Winter Quarters. An entire people had uprooted itself and, on the way to the mountains, paused here and put down roots. The endless church government went on. Not only the other camps had to be managed from Winter Quarters but all the missions too, in the United States and overseas."[18]

Of course, Winter Quarters itself had to be managed and protected, and neither the Municipal High Council nor the Council of the Twelve Apostles were satisfied with the performance of the city guard, so Brigham Young encouraged the formation of a "Regular Standing Police," which was effected on November 19, with Hosea Stout the unanimous choice to serve as captain of the police.[19] The force, composed of the twenty-six men (including Stout), seemingly was structured in a similar manner as in Nauvoo, about which Stout made a prescient observation:

> It appears by the foregoing organization that the system of the "Old Police" so much feared despised and beloved in Nauvoo is now revived on precisely the same plan and mostly the same men as there was which composed the old Police in Nauvoo and with the same Captain at their head. those who dreaded us because of their wickedness there may well have the same fears now. For the same men and the same organization the same leader, the same circumstances to act on will naturally produce the same results.[20]

Stout's pronouncement was correct, and the execution of one duty in particular made the police even more unpopular in Winter Quarters than in Nauvoo. Police work was basically a full-time job, and so the high council, to which the police directly reported, levied a personal property tax of 0.75 percent on each person and business in the town to pay members of the force. The council voted that the police would be allowed each seventy-five cents for every tour of duty and that Stout, as captain, also be allotted seventy-five cents per day for his services. It was further voted that Stout "be appointed inspector and receiver" and Marshal Horace S. Eldredge "be appointed assessor and collector of the police tax."[21] Brigham Young, weary from widespread grumbling in the settlement, advised that all should "pay their tax whether they belonged to the church or not, or leave the camp."[22] More than a few dissidents heeded Young's advice and fled to Missouri to avoid the police tax, where they openly worked in opposition to the church, while some dissenters who remained in Winter Quarters had "great objections to police."[23]

Perhaps even more unpopular than the tax were the police themselves, who generally were despised, in great part due to their heavy-handed approach to law enforcement. Three months following the formation of the force, the high council, in response to complaints from citizens at Winter Quarters, investigated police actions. "Here the subject of the police was taken up by myself," wrote Stout, who served both as captain of the police and clerk of the high council, "and a long debate ensued which resulted in good for us, for it was understood by the council for us to do our duty," whereupon it was "voted that the police stop the noise of the boys in the street, that they be authorized to whip any who will not obey."[24] Yet despite their unpopularity, the high council found the police were necessary, even when they enforced with violence, and on March 21, 1847, gave an affirming vote to save the force from being disbanded.[25]

The most important daily function of the police was the night watch, with typically five policemen patrolling the city on each of two shifts. Stout's major responsibility during the first months of 1847 was making sure the requisite policemen showed up for duty, frequently a difficult task, particularly on very cold winter nights when the settlement was battered by frigid north winds. Much of his attention during the early months of 1847, however, was focused upon the approaching spring migration of the first pioneer companies to the Salt Lake Valley. On January 14, 1847, as Stout recorded, "The word of the Lord was obtained . . . in relation to our removal." Known among the Saints as "The Word and Will of the Lord," the revelation to Brigham Young outlined the proper organization of the companies and detailed how the pioneers were to prepare for the journey.[26]

Stout expected to be among those crossing the plains that season, though not necessarily with the vanguard company; indeed, on April 18 an epistle from the apostles, under the signature of Brigham Young, directed that an emigration company be formed to follow the first pioneers "as soon as the grass is sufficient to support the teams," and stated, "It is wisdom that the men in the Emegration Company shall be organized into a military body," with Charles C. Rich as Commander-in-Chief, John Scott superintendent of the artillery, Horace S. Eldredge marshal and Hosea Stout captain of the guard.[27] As the departure date approached, Stout endeavored to find out "what was to be done about the guard for the journey and me going for as yet I could learn nothing," but all he got was a royal runaround. "[Isaac] Morley refered me to [Charles C.] Rich and he to [John] Taylor, who requested me not to trouble him about it . . . and refered me to [Alpheus] Cutler and he said he had no time to talk and [Newell K.] Whitney knew nothing about it." Concluding that he was being excluded from the company, he resigned himself to remain at Winter Quarters and immediately bought Abraham Smoot's house, a larger and more comfortable abode than his own.[28] Five days later, however, he received an express letter, signed by apostles John Taylor and Parley P. Pratt, from Rich's company that remained camped on the southwest bank of the Elk Horn River while organizing for the journey:

To

Captain Hosea Stout,

The Council here has made the following vote which is here copied. Moved by Parley P. Pratt and Seconded by John Taylor that Hosea Stout be sent to mount his horse and come on immediately to act in his appointment as Captain of the Guard. Voted unanimously and we will sustain him as a people both temporally and spiritually. This vote was made at a public meeting this morning, and we expect to see Hosea in conformity with this, at this place in 24 hours from the time he gets this notice.

      P. P. Pratt
      John Taylor[29]

Obedience is a cornerstone of the Mormon faith, but the normally faithful Stout, who previously had stated, "If there is any thing in Mormonism that is the voice of the Lord to this people I mean to live up to it," indignantly thumbed his nose at the directive.[30] He wrote,

> I was now cited to mount my horse and leave home as a runaway and leave my family without any means for their subsistence or provisions for myself," he wrote, "only their blank promise to 'sustain me as a people' which was weak indeed and go and take my place as captain of the guard. What guard when not one man had been enlisted or one dime appropriated for it. This looked like oppressive nonsense to me and excited my feeling to the highest pitch. I felt insulted abused and neglected in the first place and now more so and I did not intend to comply but least I had wrong feeling I postponed my decision untill morning.[31]

In the morning there was no change in feeling, and Stout finalized his decision of the night before. Not satisfied to let it go at that, on June 20 he appeared before the high council and "let off my feeling uncommonly plain denouncing the course that had been taken with me by the authorities and held up the way they had departed from Brigham's instructions." Orson Hyde, by that time the sole remaining apostle in Winter Quarters and therefore its de facto leader, suggested that Stout should take ten men as a guard and overtake the company; surprisingly, considering his bitter words to the council just moments before, Stout agreed to do so, but after further consideration Hyde deemed that Stout's presence in Winter Quarters was more valuable and the matter of him going to the West that season finally was laid to rest.[32] Hyde, who relied heavily on

Stout, then wasted no time in putting him to work, sending him on a mission to avenge the murder of an unarmed Mormon who was murdered by members of the Omaha tribe.[33] It was a mission for which Stout seemed particularly well suited given his experience among the Native Americans in the region.

Brigham Young's objective had been to live in peace among the Indians, but relations, particularly with the Omaha, deteriorated seriously in the first several months of the year 1847. Winter Quarters itself was established on Indian land located between the Oto tribe on the south and the Omaha on the north, with the Pawnee directly to the west.[34] Despite permission of the federal government to settle there as well as treaties with the Omaha and Oto, the Mormons soon were troubled by Indian depredations, particularly theft, and were in the middle of intertribal clashes, but they desired to live in harmony with their neighbors while preparing for their trek west and patiently tried to avoid conflict. Moreover, Mormon theology and, more specifically, the *Book of Mormon* prepared the Saints for positive interaction with the Indians.

First published in March 1830, the *Book of Mormon* was central to the new religion. It provided a sweeping historical context for the New World, at once explaining the origin of the Native Americans and relating the New World to a divine plan for humankind. The new book taught that Native Americans were remnants of the house of Israel, to whom great promises have been extended. Referring to these people as "Lamanites," a *Book of Mormon* prophet declared: "At some period of time they will be brought to believe in his [God's] word, and to know of the incorrectness of the traditions of their fathers; and many of them will be saved."[35] The first members of the church fully believed these promises and were moved to bring about their fulfillment, though at Winter Quarters it was neither the time nor the place for proselytizing.

There were, however, a handful of earlier Native American converts to the religion, among whom were Joseph and George Herring, brothers who were baptized at Nauvoo.[36] Stout befriended them, helped them move in August 1846 to western Iowa in order to spend the winter among the Pottawattamie and even became an occasional hunting companion of Joseph.[37] On October 15, 1846, after a long day's journey, Stout spent the night at Council Point, Iowa, with his "two Mohawk friends," noting that never had he been "better received and entertained by my white brethren."[38] For unknown reasons, however, the Herring brothers had a major change of heart toward the religion and Joseph, in a drunken stupor while staying at Stout's home in January 1847, expressed dissatisfaction with the Twelve in general and threatened specifically to kill apostle Wilford Woodruff. The following day, still drunk, Joseph Herring got into a scrape with John Blazzard and tried to "dirk" him.[39] Then on January

17, Herring repeated his drunken threats while again staying with Stout, prompting Brigham Young and the Twelve Apostles to excommunicate him. Having relocated to Fort Leavenworth, Herring sent a friendly letter to Stout in March in which he stated, "you all think you know whole concerning of the red mans tradition; you will find out not exactly what you think of."[40] The following month Stout received another friendly yet somewhat contradictory letter in which he was requested "to attend the great indian council this summer at the Salt Plains and still says I am the only one who can do any thing among the indians."[41]

Stout didn't attend the council and his importance in Indian relations appears to have been overstated by Herring, but he did his best to maintain harmony with them nevertheless. In January 1847, for example, Henry W. Miller and Arza Adams stumbled upon the bodies of more than seventy Omaha who had been slaughtered by the Sioux. Most of the dead had been stripped of their robes, moccasins and leggings by the rival tribe, but Miller and Adams inappropriately took what remained. "If it is true," wrote Stout upon hearing of the incident, it was "a just cause of resentment on the part of the Omahas." Fearing "revenge for this most sacralagious [sic] insult to their dead friends," Stout reported the event to Willard Richards, and he to Brigham Young, who in turn sent letters to the Omaha agent, the Omaha interpreter, and the guilty parties. Restitution swiftly was made and, likely due to Stout's efforts, conflict was averted.[42]

The Omaha, for their part, constantly raided the Mormon settlements in search of easy food. Stout, whose police were responsible for guarding against Indian theft, wrote on April 18 that the Omaha were "committing unheard of depredations, by driving off our cattle . . . The amount of cattle killed by them the past winter and spring is incredible."[43] Brigham Young maintained a strict policy that killing an Omaha in response to theft would be considered murder, but harsh measures short of taking lives were adopted to stem the thievery, as armed men guarded the cattle and Stout was ordered to take a company of ten men to reconnoiter the countryside for Omaha lying in wait, "armed with horse whips &c to give them a severe flogging in case we found."[44]

The theft problem persisted and on May 9 Stout was voted captain of a company of "ten tough Rangers" to guard against Omaha depredations.[45] The next day the men ran into a group of forty friendly Oto, whose chief, Capt Caw, was acquainted with Stout. "He was very glad to see me," wrote Stout. "They all seemed to want to shake hands with me. I suppose he told who I was." Violating a standard Winter Quarters policy not to feed the Indians for any reason, Stout's company, at the request of Capt Caw, donated three head of cattle, with the intent of gaining favor among the Oto, thereby violating yet another policy, namely not to take sides with one tribe against the other. Before departing, Capt Caw gave a lengthy speech stating his good feelings for the Mormons while "deprecating at the same time the rascalty of the Omaha's" and then set out for the Omaha village with a message in hand from Stout that the Mormons were armed and prepared to thwart any attempt to rustle cattle.[46]

The message to the Omaha backfired, as they matched the Mormons' hostile attitude and considered themselves to be at war with them. Nevertheless, Young Elk, whose father Big Elk the Younger became chief of the Omaha following the death of Big Elk the Elder, sought to avoid conflict and came with a group of his tribesmen to Winter Quarters "to make offers of peace and to present the good desires and wishes of old Elk [Big Elk the Elder]," as well as to return a number of stolen horses and thereby receive ransom that the owners had promised. Stout reported the Indians' intentions to apostle Parley P. Pratt, who refused to receive the visitors and instructed Stout to tell them that the Mormon "chiefs" were mad and wanted neither to see nor have anything to do with them. Apostle John Taylor took the same position, so Stout and Cornelius Lott, who happened to pass by at the time, were sent to meet alone with the Indians, who delivered the horses and received their pay.

Immediately after the exchange was made, the two parties formed into a "regular council," with the Omaha on one side and Stout, Lott, and some members of the guard on the other. Young Elk commenced by stating that he was ready to hear anything the Mormons had to say, whereupon Lott acrimoniously replied that the Omaha were not living up to their agreements. Though the talk became increasingly hostile, Stout reported that Young Elk kept "down his feeling admirably well and coolly related how he had been sent in by his father to . . . enter into a better understanding of peace and had been stoped on the prairie like wild beasts . . . He spoke very sharp at this ill treatment and laid it to our chiefs and said that if the 'Big Red headed' chief (Brigham) was here it would not be so but he would have taken them in and fed them and spoke friendly."[47]

Ten days later Young Elk peacefully returned with his father Old Elk and eighty "chiefs and braves" to meet with the Mormons and were received by Stout and his men in a confrontational formation "according to the Danite system of horsemanship" with Stout in the center of the line. The Indians who knew Stout told the others that he was "a war chief or captain" and all came to shake hands with him first. A council was held that evening, at which Young Elk and Old Elk were reminded of promises and agreements that had been made; though "the best of feelings seemed to exist" between the parties, Stout, after dining with the two tribal chiefs, worked late into the night to strengthen the guard, but no attack was forthcoming.[48]

The peace didn't last long, however, as later in June word arrived at Winter Quarters that some Omaha had murdered Jacob Weatherby, the first bloodshed between Mormons and Indians at the Missouri River. Orson Hyde gave Stout, who had just made his final decision not to go west that year, charge in raising and commanding a company of fifty men; they were joined a few miles south of Winter Quarters by another hundred men gathered from Council Point, "with the intention of making war on the Omahas in case they did not give up the murder[ers]."[49] Young Elk promised Hyde that the murderers, along with twelve stolen horses, would be delivered up, but overall command for the mission was given to R. B. Mitchel, subagent for the Pottawattamie tribe, who dwelled on the opposite side of the river and lacked authority to act among the Omaha. Moreover, Stout considered Mitchel to be "a most famous rascal and an inveterate enemy to us" and was leery of a conspiracy by Mitchel to justify federal intervention:

> It would have therefore been very easy for him to played the game to engage us in a war with the Omahas and leave us in the difficulty . . . Moreover in case he led us into an engagement and did not mention his position or attempt to desert or betray us we would have put him to death instanter."[50]

Stout was fully aware of the risks inherent in the mission and told his men, "it's a delicate job we are going on, and we may lead the church into a scrape."[51] John D. Lee, a member of Stout's company, wrote that Mitchel "only wanted a pretext to justify them in calling the militia on us."[52] The skeptical Mormons brought the mission to an abrupt end without incident, at which time Stout concluded, "so this expedition was but the result of folly and ignorance," and his company proceeded back to Winter Quarters.[53] Jacob Weatherby's murderer would not be brought to justice, but at the very least conflict with the federal government as well as with the Omaha had been averted. Though the Omaha "would linger around town begging and stealing all they could get" and "were very troublesome," relations between the Omaha and the Mormons greatly improved during the second (and final) year at Winter Quarters.[54]

Notes
1. Brooks, *Mormon Frontier*, May 27, 1846, 163–64.
2. Polk, *James K. Polk: The Diary of a President, 1845–1849*, ed. Allan Nevins, 109
3. Brooks, *Mormon Frontier*, June 28, 1846, 172.
4. Ibid., September 19, 1846, 194.
5. Ibid., September 22, 1846, 196.

6. Ibid., October 10, 1846, 204.
7. Winter Quarters Municipal High Council Minutes, October 23, 1846, holograph, folder 2, vol. 1: DVD 19.
8. Ibid., July 6, 1846, 175.
9. Ibid.
10. Ibid., July 14, 1846, 170
11. Ibid., August 1, 1846, 184.
12. Ibid., August 24, 1846, 187.
13. Ibid., September 23, 1846, 201. Dropsy, also known as water on the brain, is a collection of serous fluid in the cellular membrane of the brain. Symptoms of dropsy on the brain include pain in the head, dilation of the pupils, nausea, vomiting, slowness of the pulse, convulsions, loss of appetite, and increase in the size of the head.
14. Ibid., September 25, 1846, 202.
15. Ibid., September 26, 1846, 202. The four left in the family were: Hosea, his wife Louisa and her daughter (also named Louisa), and his wife Lucretia Fisher. Hosea never again directly mentioned Lucretia, though a journal entry on August 5, 1847, stated that his family was "now but two"—namely Louisa and himself, which was an indication that sometime in the preceding eleven months Lucretia had left him.
16. Ibid., November 24, 1846, 213.
17. Bennett, *Mormons at the Missouri, 1846–1852*, 141; Lund, "Pleasing to the Eyes of an Exile: The Latter-day Saint Sojourn at Winter Quarters, 1846–1848, *BYU Studies*, 39, no. 2:128–30. The population figure taken from a ward-by-ward census of the city in December 1846.
18. DeVoto, *The Year of Decision 1846*, 449.
19. Brooks, *Mormon Frontier*, November 19, 1846, 210–11.
20. Ibid., November 19, 1846, 212.
21. Winter Quarters Municipal High Council Minutes, November 29, 1846.
22. Brooks, *Mormon Frontier*, December 20, 1846, 219.
23. Ibid., January 2, 1847, 222. Stout noted that most opposition in Missouri was from the dissenters and that "otherwise the Missourians are very friendly."
24. Ibid., February 14, 1847, 236; Winter Quarters High Council Minutes, February 14, 1847.
25. Winter Quarters High Council Minutes, March 21, 1847.
26. *D&C*, Section 136.
27. Brooks, *Mormon Frontier*, April 18, 1847, 249.
28. Ibid., June 10, 1847, 260.
29. Letter from John Taylor and Parley P. Pratt to Hosea Stout, June 15, 1847, Hosea Stout Papers, 1840–1869, MS 4430, Church History Library.
30. Winter Quarters High Council Minutes, LR 6359 21, January 16, 1847.
31. Brooks, *Mormon Frontier*, June 15, 1847, 261.
32. Ibid., June 20, 1847, 262.
33. Ibid., June 22, 1847, 262; Winter Quarters Municipal High Council Correspondence, MS 6359 22, June 22, 1847, Church History Library.
34. A report from T. Hartley Crawford to Secretary of War J. M. Porter on November 25, 1843, estimated the following Indian tribal populations:

Omaha, 1,600; Oto (and Missouri), 931; Pawnee, 12,500; Sioux, 25,000 ("Report of the Commission of Indian Affairs," *28th Congress, 1st Session, vol. 1, serial 431, Senate Documents*, 277–78—quoted in Bennett, *We'll Find the Place*, 113–14).

35. *Book of Mormon*, Alma 9:17.
36. In her autobiography, Helen Mar Kimball Whitney identified Joseph and George Herring as members of the Shawnee tribe. See Helen Mar Kimball Whitney, "Reminiscences and Diary," MS 9670 38–39, Church History Library. According to Whitney, Joseph Herring was ordained an elder at Nauvoo on October 12, 1845.
37. Brooks, *Mormon Frontier*, August 5, 1846, 184; September 20, 1846, 203.
38. Ibid., October 15, 1846, 205.
39. Ibid., January 8–9, 1847, 224. A dirk is a dagger.
40. Letter from J. F. H. Nigesajasha (alias of Joseph Herring) to Hosea Stout, Hosea Stout Journal and Letters, MSS 7418, March 11, 1847, BYU Harold B. Lee Library Special Collections.
41. Brooks, *Mormon Frontier*, April 2, 1847, 245.
42. Ibid., February 1, 1847, 233.
43. Ibid., April 18, 1847, 250.
44. Ibid., April 20, 1847, 251.
45. Ibid., May 9, 1847, 254.
46. Ibid., May 10, 1847, 255.
47. Ibid., May 25, 1847, 256–57.
48. Ibid., June 5, 1847, 259.
49. Ibid., June 22, 1847, 262; *Journal History*, June 22, 1847. Weatherby's death, on June 20, 1847, was the first recorded among the Mormon emigrant companies.
50. Ibid., June 24, 1847, 263.
51. *Journal History*, June 24, 1847.
52. Kelly, ed., *Journals of John D. Lee, 1846–47 and 1859*, June 25, 1847, 180.
53. Brooks, *Mormon Frontier*, June 24, 1847, 264.
54. Ibid., November 8, 1847, 287.

11
The Pinnacle of Violence

Hosea Stout, particularly in the first half of his life, was a man inclined to violent actions. The conditions in his life that produced his pugilistic and violent tendencies as well as his vengeful nature can be traced, through his own writings, back to his early childhood. At the age of four he was sent to live at the Shaker community at Pleasant Hill, Kentucky, where he was subjected to the rigors of Shaker Society discipline. Children were "not allowed to fight and quarrel nor have any disputation among themselves," and transgression of any type resulted in nightly confession for "fear they might die and the 'Bad man' would get them" even though it might cause "a severe reprimand and sometimes a moderate flogging."[1] Whipping was a regular form of punishment, though the most traumatic punishments involved being placed "under the floor in a little dark hole dug out for the purpose of putting roots and in to keep them from the frost," namely a root cellar. "I have been almost scared out of my wits while in this dark and dreary place and would make any kind of a promise they would demand to be liberated and so would almost all the rest," Stout recalled. The mere thought of the "Bad Man" being around his bed at night often caused him to lay, "trembling with fear, not daring to move, and imagined that I could see him ready to take me 'of[f] to his dark hole.'"[2]

The harsh Shaker discipline opened Stout's eyes to the effectiveness of physical force and threats of violence. Reflecting three decades later upon the subject he wrote, "I consider the regulations good and well adapted to keep a large number of boys in subjection."

Particularly while serving as a policeman in Nauvoo and at Winter Quarters, Stout adapted and expanded this Shaker discipline, using physical force and threats of violence to help establish "good order and quietude instead of a continual scene of disobedience" in the community.

Stout also learned from the example of his father, who flogged his son, chained him to a tree and continually administered very harsh discipline; in turn, Hosea practiced on his younger brother Allen the

DOI: 10.7330/9781607324775.c011

lessons from his father. According to his own admission, he never failed to set Allen "at something he could not do and on his failure would most unmercifully beat and whip him and then make him promise not to tell on me, swearing if he did I would kill him the next time I got him out."[3] The lessons, in turn, were passed on to Allen, who two decades later confessed to Joseph Smith that he had a "fiery temper," was "quick to fight," and "had that very day threshed a man."[4]

At times Hosea would wish he could be back among the Shakers, where the work load and the punishments were less harsh, but knowing he could not go back comforted himself "with the idea that I would some day be 'Big enough' to treat my father as he had me and to this end would try and remember all he said to me that I might return the same to him, which was no small comfort to me."[5] A final formative year in his life was his fourteenth, which began with the death of his beloved mother, who had been the only true stabilizing force in his life. Later that year, though at the time disinclined to engage in fisticuffs, he disabled Elihu Millikin in a scuffle with punches and kicks and thereby realized the reward of physical force, stating that he "was ready for any kind of a fight and perfectly regardless of the consequences."[6]

Shortly thereafter, while living with Isaiah Morris, he returned home to visit his family only to find an empty home. His father had taken the rest of the family and had abandoned him. Though he was living with other families, in many respects he was on his own. He began a journey down a dark road but was rescued by the kindness and good example of Eli Harvey and by seventeen became religious, "fairly a Quaker in my heart." When abused, however, by a non-Quaker boy named Samuel Savage and encouraged by classmates who declared that Savage "ought to be whipped," he administered "a most unmerciful beating," only to be severely reprimanded by Eli Harvey and shunned by his fellow students who suddenly sympathized with Savage. It was a great lesson for Hosea:

> I learned that it was not good policy to do fighting for people who had not courage or a disposition to do it for themselves and it proved a useful lessen to me in after life and caused me to begin to observe the inconstancy and ingratitude of mankind and no doubt it has prevented me from falling into worse difficulties by trying to help those who will not help themselves For if you ever do you may depend on being forsaken in times of trouble.[7]

When Stout went to live among the Latter-day Saints in Missouri in August 1837, he found a people with the courage and disposition to fight for themselves. It was not always that way: during the first three years following the founding of the church in 1830, the Mormons were a remarkably pacifist people considering the abuse to which they, and particularly their leaders, were subjected.

On Saturday, March 24, 1832, Joseph Smith and Sidney Rigdon were dragged from their beds in the dead of night in Hiram, Ohio. Smith was strangled until he lost consciousness and lost a front tooth when a member of the mob tried to force a vial of poison into his mouth. Both men then were tarred and feathered and Smith was left for dead. After his friends spent the night "scraping and removing the tar," Smith "preached to a congregation as usual" on Sunday, apparently without a hint of revenge or retribution.[8]

Following a revelation of July 20, 1831, stating that Missouri was "appointed and consecrated for the gathering of the saints," a steady number of Mormons moved to Jackson County with the intent of establishing the "city of Zion."[9] By summer 1833 Mormons comprised nearly one-third of the county's population of 3,300. Citizens feared that Mormons eventually would take over county offices and civic affairs and approved resolutions requiring that no new Mormons move into the county and that those in the county should pledge to leave in a reasonable time. On July 20, six church leaders, denied adequate time to consider the proposal, rejected the plan, which in turn prompted impatient citizens to take immediate action. Bishop Edward Partridge, who Joseph Smith had selected to preside over the Missouri Latter-day Saint settlements, and Charles Allen were dragged to the public square, partially stripped down and then tarred and feathered, and publication of the newly printed *Book of Commandments* was aborted.[10] Nevertheless, Mormons followed their prophet's pacifist example and did not fight back. John Corrill, an early convert who after a few years renounced his membership in the church, wrote, "up to this time the Mormons had not so much as lifted a finger, even in their own defence, so tenacious were they for the precepts of the gospel,—'turn the other cheek.'"[11]

Continuing in the spirit of "turning the other cheek," in August 1833 Joseph Smith pronounced a revelation instructing the Latter-day Saints, "be not afraid of your enemies . . . renounce war and proclaim peace . . . if men will smite you, or your families, once, and ye bear it patiently and revile not against them, neither seek revenge, ye shall be rewarded."[12] The revelation further instructed them to endure and bear patiently a total of three attacks.[13]

Smith's followers sought to live by the revelations to him that counseled them to live their religion in peace with their neighbors. However, after Mormon settlements on the Blue River, about eight miles west of Independence, were attacked on October 31, homes were raided the following night, and a gristmill in Independence was destroyed, the Mormons had been smitten three times and their patience was exhausted. Thus, as Missourians attacked Mormon settlements in the Blue River Valley on November 2, the Mormons fought back; in the process they wounded a Missourian, prompting the local residents to organize for battle while the Mormons began to congregate in larger bodies for protection. Violence peaked on November 4 at the "Battle above the Blue" (referred to also as the "Battle of Blue River"), resulting in the deaths of two Missourians and one Mormon and severe wounding of others. In response, Jackson County leaders called out the militia, and the Mormons were forced to surrender their weapons and begin leaving their homes.[14]

A direct response to the Mormons having been driven from Jackson County came two months later when, after the arrival from Missouri of Parley P. Pratt and Lyman Wight in Kirtland, Ohio, Joseph Smith dictated a revelation that stated, "And inasmuch as mine enemies come against you to drive you from my goodly land, which I have consecrated to be the land of Zion . . . ye shall curse them; And whomsoever ye curse, I will curse, and ye shall avenge me of mine enemies." The revelation commanded Smith to organize at least "a hundred of the strength of my house, to go up with you unto the land of Zion," and that "whoso is not willing to lay down his life for my sake is not my disciple."[15] This was the beginning of "Zion's Camp" which, though it did not succeed in redeeming Zion, signaled that the Latter-day Saints forthwith could fight their enemies rather than remaining pacifist.

During the march to Jackson County, a small group of volunteers for the expedition camped at the home of Stout's friend, Charles C. Rich. In contrast to his previous negative opinion of Mormons, following the visit by the Zion's Camp party Stout wrote, "The effect of their preaching was powerful on me and when I considered that they were going up to Zion to fight for their lost inheritances under the special directions of God it was all that I could do to refrain from going.[16] From his statement it is difficult to ascertain whether Stout was drawn more to Mormon doctrine or to the chance to join them in battle.

The years immediately following the Mormons' removal from Jackson County were relatively peaceful. From 1834 to 1836 they purchased land and established more than a dozen settlements in Clay County. Eventually, threats of hostilities from residents who never anticipated that the Mormons would remain permanently in Clay County resulted in the relocation of the Latter-day Saints to a sparsely populated area in neighboring Ray County and later to newly created Caldwell and Daviess counties. For nearly two years, from August 1836 to August 1838, relations between Mormons and non-Mormons were stable before deteriorating rapidly, fueled by an incendiary speech on July 4, 1838, by Sidney

Rigdon, who proclaimed that the Mormons no longer would suffer abuse at the hands of their enemies. "We take God and all the holy angels to witness this day," Rigdon proclaimed, "that we warn all men in the name of Jesus Christ, to come on us no more forever. For from this hour, we will bear it no more, our rights shall no more be trampled on with impunity. The man or the set of men, who attempts it, does it at the expense of their lives."[17]

The first hostilities broke out on August 6, 1838, at Gallatin, Daviess County, on the occasion of a statewide election, resulting in a bloody fight with whips, clubs, rocks, and knives, causing several serious injuries but no fatalities.[18] On August 7 Dr. Sampson Avard, who in June 1838 formed the Danite, a paramilitary organization of Mormon men that sought to rid the church of dissent and to help combat external threats against the Saints, called for volunteers to follow him to Gallatin. The following morning, Avard, members of the First Presidency, and more than a hundred Mormon men rode out and called on Judge Adam Black, who in a sworn statement later wrote, "On or about the 8th day of August, 1838 . . . there came an armed force of men . . . and surrounded his house and family and threatened him with instant death, if he did not sign a certain instrument of writing."[19] Following the incident, throughout the remainder of August and much of September, vigilante groups began intimidating and harassing Mormon settlers throughout the area.[20]

Significantly, it was in the midst of the burgeoning hostilities that Hosea Stout decided to be become a Mormon. Writing in his autobiography in the third person he recorded, "on the 26th day of August [1838] following he was baptized into the Church of Jesus Christ of Latter Day Saints by Elder Charles C. Rich, this was in the time that the mob was harasing [sic] the church and the brethren were then under arms to defend themselves against the voilence [sic] of the mob. He entered the war with the rest of his brethren and was in all the difficulties, which they passed through in Caldwell and Davisse [sic] Counties, with the mob."[21] Once again the question is whether Stout, married in January of that year to a Mormon woman (Samantha Peck), having lived among the Mormons in Caldwell County for an entire year and seemingly long since converted to their doctrine, decided to be baptized at the time mainly in order to join their fight. The sudden scheduling of his baptism, coupled with his statement four years earlier regarding his urge to join Zion's Camp to help the Mormons "fight for their lost inheritances" would suggest the latter.

It is uncertain exactly when Stout joined the Danites, of which Joseph Smith wrote, "we have a company of Danites in these times, to put to rights physically that which is not right, and to cleanse the Church of verry great evils which hath hitherto existed among us inasmuch as they cannot be put to right by teachings and persuaysions."[22] Stout was perfectly suited to "put to rights *physically*" that which was not right, and he seemed an fit for the Danites, the activities of which, in the words of historian Stephen LeSueur, "reflected a growing spirit of militancy within the Church . . . Joseph Smith's proposal to confiscate the property of all Mormons who refused to take up arms against the Missourians was as radical as the measures advocated by the Danites. The Danite organization was the product of, not an aberration from, Mormon attitudes and teachings."[23]

Though he was very well suited to be a Danite, unlike the organization itself, Stout was not a product of "Mormon attitudes and teachings" but rather a man whose fiery temperament and physical talents were facilitated by the Mormon society. Recognizing those talents, Mormon leaders quickly made him a clerk in the fledgling Nauvoo Legion, formed in 1841 to defend the Saints and their city and prepared to use necessary force and armaments to that end; Stout quickly rose through the ranks all the way to brigadier general following the assassination of Joseph Smith in June 1844. At a meeting in Nauvoo on November 29, 1843, Joseph Smith, in his role as mayor of the city, said "when the mobs come upon you, kill them, I never will restrain you again, but will go and help you"; immediately afterwards Brigham Young said "he would never put his hand on brother Hosea Stout's shoulder again to hold him back when he was abused."[24] Not only were the Mormons more ready than ever to fight back, but their chief firebrand was Hosea Stout.

One month later, when forty men were selected as city policemen, Stout was appointed second lieutenant and quickly ascended to take total control of the force. In this position Stout was enabled to use physical force and threats as he had learned as a child and adolescent, and by placing him in the proper positions in the Nauvoo Legion and in the police forces at Nauvoo and Winter Quarters, Mormon leadership not only took full advantage of his attributes but also approved of his heavy-handed methods. A prime example of this occurred on the night of April 2, 1845, when the police "beat a man almost to death" who had entered the Nauvoo temple without permission. Although Stout was not involved directly in the beating he defended his men, saying, "I was glad of it"; Brigham Young, upon hearing of the incident and listening to Stout's explanation, "approved of the proceedings of the Police" and said he wanted them to continue guarding the temple.[25]

Protecting the temple was a primary duty for the police, and they were prepared to use any and all means necessary in order to do keep it safe. On September 17, 1845, Stout recorded in his journal,

> I want this hollowings, beating of drums and firing of guns should cease. The police have their orders from this time to

arrest every man or boy in our street found guilty of these acts or anyone walking our street after night, detain them till daylight and stripping off their clothes, show whether they are male or female. I am going to propose to . . . make every man a deputy then we may sally forth with our writs in our pockets in any number and arrest these mobbers. When you shoot, be sure and shoot right . . . Keep your guns to yourselves. Trust no one and when you shoot, take a good aim.[26]

As far as is known, none were shot in defense of the temple, but Stout came close to killing a man, bouncing a stone off the head of William Hibbard, "which came very near taking his life."[27]

Church leaders, apparently realizing that Stout was using too much violence in policing the city and the temple, summoned him on January 31, 1846. Stout was puzzled by their concern, writing, "I think some thing is wrong in the minds of the Twelve [Apostles] in relation to this matter . . . I feel that I have done my duty in protecting their lives from their enemies both from within and without."[28] Brigham Young, who needed Stout despite his faults, on February 2 had an earnest discussion with Stout but overall endorsed him and his actions: "He said he was satisfied with me in some things that some said he thought I was wrong in. He gave us good instruction in relation to governing men and said he wanted me to stand in the place I now hold after we get to the west."[29]

It was no surprise, given Stout's violent reputation, that four weeks after the initial exodus from Nauvoo a false rumor circulated in the city that he had killed Brigham Young somewhere along the Iowa trail.[30] That reputation was exactly the reason that Young wanted him to head the police in Winter Quarters as he had done in Nauvoo. When he received that assignment, Stout accurately predicted the result:

> It appears by the foregoing organization that the system of the "Old Police" so much feared despised and beloved in Nauvoo is now revived on precisely the same plan and mostly the same men as there was which composed the old Police in Nauvoo and with the same Captain at their head. those who dreaded us because of their wickedness there may well have the same fears now. For the same men and the same organization the same leader, the same circumstances to act on will naturally produce the same results.[31]

A seven-month period during his reign as chief of police at Winter Quarters, from August 7, 1847, through March 13, 1848, was the most violent phase of Hosea Stout's life. It was preceded immediately by the latest tragedy to strike his family, the death on August 5 of his fifteen-month-old daughter Louisa. Her passing "seemed to complete the dark curtain which has been drawn over me since I left Nauvoo," Stout wrote. "My family then consisted of 8 members and now but two," denoting not only the death of four children and one plural wife (Marinda Bennett) but also the desertion of plural wife Lucretia Fisher. "Now I am left childless but I shall not dwell on this painful subject."[32]

Stout internalized his despair, which seemed only to help foment the rage that soon spewed forth. Stray cattle, sheep, horses, and dogs often ran at large, intruding on private gardens and the public fields that were necessary for community survival, and therefore the strays were impounded by the police and placed in a "stray pen," a move that consistently irritated residents. On August 7, the day after Louisa was laid to rest, Henry Phelps, son of Mormon stalwart W. W. Phelps, attempted to extricate his horse—without permission—from the stray pen and in turn was severely caned by Stout, who in the process broke a "good fancy hickry cain . . . all to pieces." Stout reported the incident to the high council, which, given the serious nature of stray animal damage, nearly always supported the police in such cases and upheld Stout's action.[33]

A few months later, on November 6, Stout once again defended the use of force at the stray pen, tersely recording the incident, "In driving some cattle to the stray pen we were opposed by C. [Charles W.] Patten and others the result was quite a knock down."[34] Patten issued a charge against Hosea and Allen Stout for abusive conduct against him and his family, though the case was settled amicably before the high council. A more serious charge growing out of the skirmish, however, was that Hosea had been unnecessarily violent and in the process had injured Hiram Murdock's arm. Hosea admitted to administering "several blows" with a club but defended his action as self-defense. Some members of the council were split in their opinions, and the matter was referred to Bishop Isaac Clark, who wrote in his record book:

> November 20 1847 Winter Quarters
> A charge preferred by Hiram Murdock against Hosea Stout Capt. of the police guard of the Camp of Israel for unofficerlike and unchristinanlike conduct. For beating him without mercy with a club without any provocation on his part. I have proposed arranging the matter like brothers. He [Hosea] refuses to do so, says he has done well and would do the same against was to do it over.[35]

Stout thought Clark was prejudiced against him, but most upsetting to him was the accusation of John L. Butler that he "could hear the licks distinctly which sounded like beating an old dry Buffalo skin," even though Butler, according to Stout, was about forty rods distant (about one-eighth mile).[36] Clark found that Stout had used excessive force and fined him three dollars, though upon appeal the high council, stating the law must be maintained, found that Stout had acted within the scope of his duties and thus nullified the fine.[37]

Four months passed before Stout was involved in another altercation, but it was his most ferocious. The confrontation, several days in the making, had its inception in a trial in which storeowner J. M. Strode was sued for payment of a debt by Jack Redding, who was represented by Stout. Strode, who lived across the river at Council Point, considered the proceedings to be a farce and threatened to have United States troops from Fort Kearney get involved. He nevertheless sent witnesses and an attorney to represent him, but the judgment by Daniel Carn, who in addition to serving as bishop of Winter Quarters 10th Ward was one of Stout's policemen, was in favor of Redding, much to the dismay of those who sensed favoritism by Carn and protested the verdict.[38]

A face-off ensued, not only between the faithful and the half-hearted but also between residents on opposing sides of the river. A letter from Apostle Orson Hyde demanded that Redding and several others be delivered on suspicion of theft and also asked for police help in the matter "as they had helped to pay the police." Brigham Young, who in October had returned from the Salt Lake Valley to prepare the Saints at Winter Quarters for the 1848 emigration, wrote to Hyde that "if he would take a good smell of the old whiskey barrel to still his nerves and a little mountain opium and then be calm . . . all [would] pass over." Though Young himself remained calm, Stout was incensed by the threats involving US troops and other retribution and stated, "there was as much dissension now as ever I saw in Nauvoo or at any other period of the Church history."[39]

Stout had reached his emotional limit and by March 17 was ready to explode. "The faultfinding spirit was now raging to a great extent," he wrote, "and Strodes store was now all the time filled with those dissatisfied persons who were all the time railing at the authorities . . . and in fact deprecating every thing that was right and righteous until I had become sick and tired of it and so was every good man." Stout previously had suppressed his feelings in public, but on this occasion he entered the store as two of his policemen, Wilbur Earl and John Bills, heatedly were arguing the Strode case with a group of dissenters. Stout pointedly expressed his opinions, in response to which, according to his own account, Simon C. Dalton, Isaac Hill, and a man named Bartlett let loose a "volley of abuse and low scurrilious insults."[40] Dalton's version was that "Hosea was swearing, 'God damn' and such like" and claimed that Hill "reproved him for using such language" whereupon "Stout struck at him." Testifying before the high council, Dalton continued that he saw Stout take a poker and try to hit Hill on the head though the blow was deflected by Hill's arm.[41]

Conflicting testimony was given as to the nature and extent of profanity used by both sides, but nobody disputed Stout's own description of his assault on Hill: "I 'Lit upon Him' determined to stop or kill him. We had a short scuffle when I got him across the counter and had him secured choked untill he could not breath intending to hold on peaceably as I was but was parted by John Lyttle which put an end to the matter now."[42] Stout thought he was defending the faith and was most upset not by his own violent actions but rather by the accusation that in the altercation he had used profane language, a charge he at first vehemently denied, though he told the council, "It is a natural gift for me to swear, but I tried to avoid it." Continuing his testimony before the high council, after asking forgiveness for his swearing, Stout proclaimed, "It has been my duty to hunt out the rotten spirits in this Kingdom . . . Even now I have a list of who will deny the faith. I have not been mistaken for the first time yet, but I do not know when I may make a misdeal. I've tried not to handle a man's case until it was right."[43]

After listening to evidence from all sides, Brigham Young roundly chastised both parties but reserved the greatest criticism for the captain of police.

> I am here to save both Br[other] Hosea and Hill but not to destroy them," he said. "I know it is natural for Br Hill to tantalize. But that is no Excuse for Br Hosea Stout to fight him. He should have said I am A peace maker And magnyfied his office with dignity and honor but instead of that He desended to the spirit of a tantilizer and fell to fighting and swearing . . . I know how Brother Hosea Stout feels concerning the spirits that murdered the Prophets and still hang around Us, but don't you know that devils are going to the mountains as well as Saints? . . . We have good men and bad men among us but if I see a bad man or good man that needs reproof I will give it to him but will I go into a store and strike a man? No . . . we should be saviors benevolent and kind and imitate the example of the savior.[44]

Young then chastised Stout's police force. "I know the policemen here are not Just right for they will get together for hours together make fun, tell tales, drink whiskey and get drunk and that is why they are so angry all the while . . . Now to the Police I say stop your baldadash . . . I mean to reprove the Police. If we don't get better men in the valley I will vote against them. They have confessed they are angry. I want to see the Police officiate in their office without getting angry. If they do not they disgrace their office."[45]

In less than three months Stout would be on his way to the Salt Lake Valley with a large group of Mormon pioneers. While there were no more reported incidents of excessive violence by him or his police during that time at Winter Quarters, his previous actions, combined with the excessive tactics he sanctioned for his police force, made him wildly unpopular, even hated by some, in Nauvoo and particularly at Winter Quarters. Mormonism did not create a violent man in Hosea Stout—that can be credited mostly to his childhood experiences and upbringing—but Mormon leaders put him positions and gave him the permission to be violent, and he took full advantage of the opportunities. After Winter Quarters they would not do so again.

Notes

1. Stout, *Autobiography*. In his autobiography, Stout frequently used the term "bad man," (5) obviously alluding to the "devil," as well as the term "bad place," (3) which Stout identified as "hell."
2. Ibid.
3. Ibid.
4. Lafayette C Lee, Notebook [n.d.]3.
5. Ibid.
6. Ibid., 18.
7. Ibid., 38.
8. Quinn, "The Culture of Violence in Joseph Smith's Mormonism," 18; Bushman, *Rough Stone Rolling*, 178; Johnson, "The History of Luke Johnson," Church History Library; *Latter-day Saints Millennial Star*, December 31, 1864, 834; http://josephsmithpapers.org/paperSummary/history-1838-1856-volume-a-1-23-december-1805-30-august-1834?p=214.
9. *D&C*, 57:1–5.
10. Quinn, "Culture of Violence," 18; Hartley quoted in Rawson and Lyman, eds., *The Mormon Wars*, 30–32; Baugh, *A Call to Arms*, 6–7. The *Book of Commandments* was the precursor to the *Doctrine and Covenants*.
11. Corrill, *A Brief History of the Church of Christ of Latter Day Saints*, 18.
12. *D&C*, 98:14, 16, 23.
13. Ibid., 98:25–26.
14. Quinn, "Culture of Violence," 19; Allen and Leonard, *The Story of the Latter-day Saints*, 96–97; Rawson and Lyman, eds., *The Mormon Wars*, 30–37; Bushman, *Rough Stone Rolling*, 227–28.
15. *D&C*, 103:24–25, 28, 34.
16. Stout, *Autobiography*, 52.
17. LeSueur, *Mormon War*, 48–52.
18. Ibid., 62–63.

19. Gentry and Compton, *Fire and Sword*, 178–79.
20. Rawson and Lyman, *Mormon Wars*, 53–55.
21. Stout, *Autobiography*, 56.
22. Joseph Smith diary, Missouri Journal, March–September 1838, entry of July 27, 1838, *The Joseph Smith Papers*, http://josephsmithpapers.org/paper Summary/journal-march-september-1838?p=47.
23. LeSueur, *Mormon War*, 46; Foote, "Autobiography of Warren Foote," 29–30, Church History Library.
24. *Millennial Star*, 22:392; *History of the Church*, 6:94.
25. Brooks, *Mormon Frontier*, March 3, 1845, 32.
26. Brooks, *Mormon Frontier*, September 17, 1845, 65.
27. Ibid., January 9, 1846, 103.
28. Ibid., January 31, 1846, 111.
29. Ibid., February 2, 1846, 111.
30. Bullock, "Journals, 1843–1849," March 7, 1846
31. Ibid., November 19, 1846, 212.
32. Ibid., August 7, 1847, 268. Lucretia was only sixteen-years-old at the time she left Hosea.
33. Ibid., August 7, 1847, 268–69.
34. Ibid., November 6, 1847, 286.
35. Clark, "Isaac Clark Record Book."
36. Brooks, *Mormon Frontier*, November 16 and 21, 1847, 288; Winter Quarters High Council Records, November 16, 1847.
37. Clark, "Isaac Clark Record Book."
38. Brooks, *Mormon Frontier*, March 11, 1848, 304–5.
39. Ibid., March 14, 1848, 305.
40. Ibid., March 17, 1848, 305–6.
41. Historian's Office General Church Minutes, March 17, 1848, *Selected Collections from the Archives of the Church of Jesus Christ of Latter-day Saints*, DVD 18.
42. Brooks, *Mormon Frontier*, March 17, 1848, 306.
43. General Church Minutes, Church Historian's Office, March 17, 1848, Church History Library.
44. Woodruff, "Journal," March 17, 1848.
45. Ibid.

12
Crossing the Plains

William Clayton, a late addition to the roster of Brigham Young's pioneer camp of 1847, was frustrated by inexact estimates of the mileage traveled by the company each day. A stickler for detail, one day he measured the circumference of the hind wheel of Heber C. Kimball's wagon and, using simple mathematics, found that 360 revolutions equaled one mile. He then tied a red flag to a wheel and dutifully counted all revolutions during the day—more than 9,300—and found that they had traveled 11¼ miles. After a few days, the tedium was too much even for the fastidious Clayton and he consulted with Orson Pratt, who helped to design a set of wooden cogwheels to be attached to the hub of a wagon wheel to make a mechanical count of the revolutions. Appleton Harmon, a master carpenter, then used his ingenuity to construct machinery with a cogwheel that was attached to the wagon wheel, making a complete revolution once every ten miles; the contraption was dubbed a "roadometer," a version of the modern odometer. Clayton then combined his meticulous notes and observations of the journey with odometer readings and subsequently published *The Latter-day Saints' Emigrants' Guide*, a valuable resource for future Mormon as well as non-Mormon pioneers.

Credit for the serendipitous inclusion of Clayton as a member of Brigham Young's 1847 camp belonged, ironically, to Hosea Stout. Clayton, who shared a mutually antagonistic relationship with Stout, recorded in his journal on April 11, 1847, "I told Winslow Farr concerning Hosea Stout's threats to take my life after the Twelve are gone &c," and on April 13 he wrote, "Evening went to the store and told Brigham [Young] and Heber [Kimball] about Hosea Stout's calculations &c." Young decided it best to separate the conflicting parties and wisely told Clayton "to rise up and start with the pioneers in half an hour's notice"; the notice came quickly and the next day Clayton became the 148th member of the vanguard company.[1]

The intention of the first pioneers, who arrived in the Salt Lake Valley on July 22–24, was to survey the valley and to lay the foundation

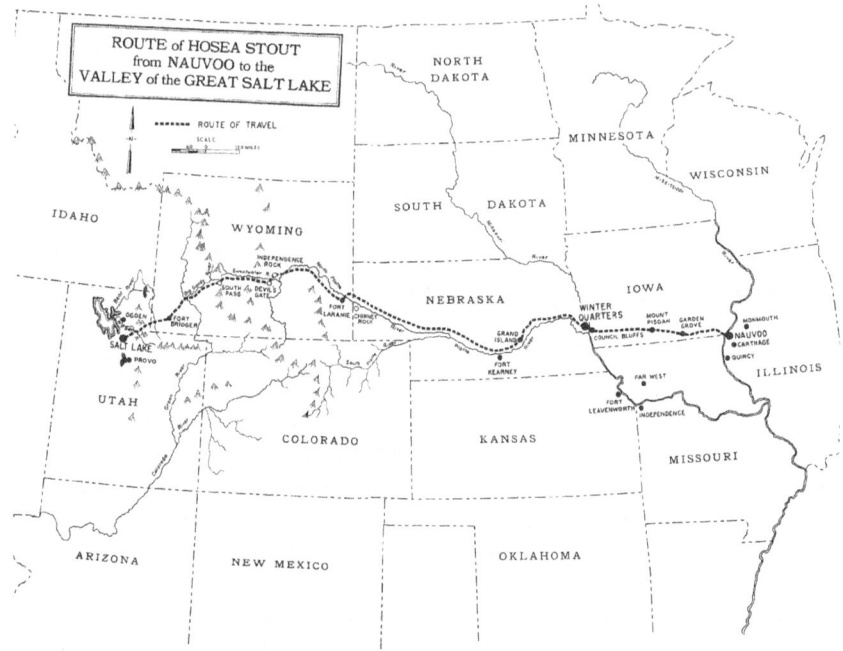

Figure 12.1. Route of Hosea Stout from Nauvoo to the Valley of the Great Salt Lake.

for the arrival of nearly fifteen hundred people in the valley later that summer. Work began almost immediately, and within three weeks a fort had been constructed, complete with a wall and twenty-nine log houses. Wasting no time, on August 3 Young announced initial plans for nearly two-thirds of the advance group to begin the return to Winter Quarters to prepare their families to move the next year.

With lighter loads and familiarity with the trail, the return trip was much quicker and less tedious than the journey west had been: on September 17 Thomas Bullock, the "Clerk of the Camp of Israel," noted that it had taken forty-two days to reach Salt Lake from a certain location but only twenty-three days on the return journey to reach the same spot.[2] The expedition was scarcely trouble-free, however, as on the morning of September 9 the Saints awoke to discover that as many as fifty horses had been stolen by Indians during the night.[3] Following the theft, William Clayton and John Pack were members of a party running ox teams that inexplicably sped up, leaving Brigham Young's main party behind; Hosea Stout, the leader of a relief party of sixteen men from Winter Quarters, experienced intensified contempt for Clayton upon meeting him on the trail on October 14 and hearing his story:

This was but a portion of the pioneers who had been sent ahead with the ox teams to lay up Buffalo meat for the company who were to follow in a short time.

But instead of doing so they proceeded on and were now out of the Buffalo county leaving those who were to follow to shift for themselves. They informed us that the President [Brigham Young] and in fact all those who were behind were attacted by the Souix and robbed of some Eighty horses.

They sent on for this company to stop but they did not

They also said that we would meet them in 40 miles unless they had gone back to the Valley after loosing their animals. Thus deserting them all in this time of trouble. Those who bore the rule in this contemptable act of leaving the Twelve and so many of our Brethren robbed of their Horses in the Black Hills were John Pack and William Clayton with some more to back them up. The main body of this camp were true and faithful Saints and viewed this treacherous act in its true light.

This is their own story and you may immagine our feeling of joy, anger and supprise on meeting them and recieving this intelligence.[4]

Stout's party, not knowing what had become of Brigham Young and his fellow apostles, feared the worst. Young and his companions, on the other hand, were weary and disappointed and merely had halted for a couple of days to recuperate. Very soon after continuing their journey, on October 18, they were met by Stout and his horsemen, who were laden with provisions and fresh horses.[5] "It is useless for me to attempt to describe this meeting," proclaimed Stout. "The whole of us was in a perfect extacy of joy and gladness. They were worn down with fatigue and hunger with many an anxious thought on home and the welfare of their families and the church. Many of their animals had to be lifted up every time they laid down."[6] Reinvigorated, the company was able to proceed to Winter Quarters, arriving on the last day of October, at which time Stout and his men "were formally dismissed by the President with the blessings of God."[7]

One of the first orders of business for Young after reaching Winter Quarters was to complete the organization of the church that, for more than three years following the assassination of Joseph Smith, had been without an official president. In early December the Twelve Apostles, of which Young had been the senior apostle and acting leader, unanimously decided to organize a First Presidency with Brigham Young as the president of the church with Heber C. Kimball and Willard Richards as counselors. A large log tabernacle, sixty feet long and forty feet wide, was built in haste on the east side of the Missouri River at Miller's Hollow to accommodate a general conference, which convened on Christmas Eve. After several days of dancing and numerous addresses and messages from church leaders, the new First Presidency was sustained.[8] This action gave the members a new sense of security. Apostle George A. Smith led the congregation in the shout of praise: "Hosanna, Hosanna, Hosanna to God and the Lamb. Amen! Amen! and Amen!"[9] The rejoicing continued into mid-January, at which time a "Jubilee" of five days duration was celebrated through dance and feasting.

Once the celebration ended, all thought was turned to the upcoming season, which for those in Winter Quarters meant either emigration to the Salt Lake Valley or evacuation of Winter Quarters. Though a majority wanted to emigrate, few families by themselves had the necessary means to cross the plains. Brigham Young's brother Joseph suggested that the journey would be facilitated by teamwork, in which those remaining behind would loan teams and wagons to those making the trip. Brigham took to heart his brother's suggestion and arranged the loan of sixty teams from the Pottawattamie Saints that were to go as far as the Sweetwater River in Wyoming, after which they would be returned under the charge of Stout's brother-in-law, Allen Taylor.[10]

By mid-May great numbers of Saints moved to the banks of the Elkhorn River to get organized for the journey. Stout loaded 3,267 pounds of goods in two wagons, with his wife and infant daughter (two-month-old Elizabeth Ann) in one wagon and a second, driven by Samuel Carn in which Stout slept, and set out for the river on May 17.[11] The plan for the overland expedition called for the formation of three large companies, each to be led by a member of the new First Presidency. On the last day of May, Brigham Young and Heber C. Kimball commenced organizing the people in their companies into hundreds, fifties and tens, and appointing the officers necessary to manage to journey (Willard Richards's company was formed a month later). It was a stirring sight to behold the nearly two thousand people who were camping on the Elkhorn, as Thomas Bullock wrote:

> If any person enquire, 'Is Mormonism down?' he ought to have been in the neighbourhood of the Elk Horn this day, and he would have seen such a host of waggons that would have satisfied him in an instant, that it lives and flourishes like a tree by a fountain of waters; he would have seen merry faces, and heard the song of rejoicing, that the day of deliverance had surely come.[12]

With a total of 397 wagons and 1,229 people, Young's was by far the largest of the three companies and had to be divided into several smaller groups in order to avoid overcrowding at campsites and water holes. On May 31, Lorenzo Snow, William Perkins, Zera Pulsipher, and Allen Taylor were chosen to be captains of hundreds.[13] The term "hundred" loosely referred to the number of wagons and was merely a title, not a description, as Taylor's company actually included 190 wagons and 597 souls, comprising nearly half of Brigham Young's entire company and twice as large as any other "hundred" of the 1848 emigration season. Perkin's company, on the other hand, was comprised of only fifty-seven wagons, primarily because John D. Lee, who had been chosen by Brigham Young to be captain of the second fifty of the unit, was generally disliked and few wanted to go with him.[14]

The 1848 emigration differed little in its route or its encounters on the trail from the 1847 companies. The make-up of the group was very dissimilar, however, consisting of regular families rather than a small, handpicked party of able-bodied men. Fortunately the three main leaders (Young, Kimball, and Richards) traveled to the Salt Lake Valley and back to Winter Quarters in 1847 and therefore had experience in crossing the plains. This was especially important since the Mormons never used professional guides, preferring merely to "trust in the Lord."

The companies of hundred, which were subdivided into groups of fifty and ten, started out at one-day intervals to lessen congestion. Daniel Carn's "Fifty," a division of Allen Taylor's "Hundred" to which Stout's family as well as a number of Winter Quarters policemen belonged, departed on June 5; Stout's "Ten," under Captain Almon Fulmer, led a very long line of wagons that day, a fortunate position in which dust from wagons and livestock was created rather than endured.[15] A wide variety of animals accompanied each of the groups: Taylor's company, for example, had 30 horses, 16 mules, 615 oxen, 316 cows, 63 loose cattle, 134 sheep, 66 pigs, 282 chickens, 19 cats, 31 dogs, 3 goats, 8 geese, 6 doves, and 1 crow, and Snow's company also included two beehives.[16]

Much larger than the 1847 pioneer company, the combined Young and Kimball 1848 companies, with nearly nineteen hundred emigrants, at first were unwieldy and very slow moving. Young summoned his captains on the evening of June 6 and suggested that they "perfect their organizing," forming smaller companies that would travel double file. It was decided that the wagons would be numbered and would move in order, though slower teams would start an hour earlier than the others.[17] At the same meeting Stout was appointed captain of the Night Guard for the overall camp.[18]

The organizational summit must be considered a success, for the very large company ultimately moved at almost the same speed as the much smaller pioneer company the year before. Brigham Young realized how important it was to train leaders for future seasons of emigration, and he proved to be the consummate leader and teacher, never above helping to repair a broken wagon wheel, helping to set a broken leg, or traveling at the rear of the train, the most unpopular of all positions due to the dust created by the hundreds of wagon teams in front. After reaching the Loup Fork, he braved the river's quick current and shifting quicksand and "crossed and recrossed back and fourth, untill he Saw all over safe."[19]

The crossing of the Loup Fork was close to the 98th meridian, almost immediately at the beginning of the Great Plains, a vast high plateau of semiarid grassland over which cold winters and warm summers prevail, with low precipitation and humidity, much wind, and sudden changes of temperature. This was a far different world than most of the Saints had experienced. On June 14 Richard Ballantyne wrote of the excessive heat, "The Lord grant that we many have but little of such weather, as it is wearing and fatiguing to the people. Could not Kindle our fires for fear the Waggons would get burned up."[20] As Allen Taylor's company moved on from the river, Stout recorded: "The ground soft and unpleasant travelling. The day was very hot. One ox of John Alger melted and died."[21]

The unfavorable conditions slowed the progress of the company to about ten miles a day. As they entered an area of several miles of prairie dog villages, grass was meager for the animals and drinking water was becoming scarce so that each day a new well had to be dug, often to the depth of ten feet. Wood also was in very short supply, so the Saints resorted to using another fuel source, as Oliver Huntington wrote: "From this time had to burn considerable Buffalo dung which being pure vegetable burned much like the Irish turf or sod. The dung was thick in most places, and like chips and score blocks, for this and the sake of softening a hard word they go by the name of Buffalo chips."[22]

Fortunately, buffalo chips were practically odorless, but the same cannot be said of a particular animal pest. Mary Pugh Scott remembered, "An English Emmigrant whose sense of smell had left him due to age, was one day hungryly out looking for food, found a strange animal and killed it. (it was furry and black and white) He skinned it and proudly brought it to camp. 'a skunk' and to his amazement everyone fled as he approached and for some days he was an outcast."[23] Stout recorded a similar odoriferous event:

> Tonight about dark a skunk made us a visit Locating himself under my waggons. We endeavored to drive it away without exciting it but knowing the Power it held over us seemed

perfectly tame while we had only to deal mildly with it. At length it went under Judge Phelps waggon and laid down in his harness where we were obliged to let it be in peace.[24]

Skunks were an occasional encounter, but for a number of days buffalo were everywhere. On July 1 Stout wrote, "Saw 1000's of Buffalo today which moved as black clouds in the prairie. It is a sight not to be described and only to be realized by sight."[25] John Pulsipher, traveling in the company with Stout, recorded:

> Buffalo abounds along the Platt[e] River in such vast numbers that it is impossible for mortal man to number them—. The first day or two that we came among them they were in small gangs and now and then an old straggling bull—but as we traveled on the whole country seemed black with them. Sometimes our way seemed entirely blockaded with them but as we approached they would open to the right and left so we could pass through. Thousands of them sometimes would run towards the River, plunge down the bank into the water, tumble over each other and pile up, but all would come out right on the other side of the River and continue the race. Sometimes we would see the Plain black with them for ten miles in width and I don't know how far beyond our sight they extended, all in motion, on the gallop and would pass by us for hours at that speed and then we could see neither end of the herd.[26]

Unfortunately, despite Young's instructions to the contrary, occasionally there was wanton killing of the buffalo by company members:

> The hunting fever seized on the brethren and they, regardless of the previous arraingements, to let hunters kill our meet often ran and left their teams pursuing and shooting at the buffalo all day. Many were killed and left out, and but few brought into camp.[27]

On July 15 Allen Taylor's company camped opposite Chimney Rock, the most famous and recognizable landmark of the entire trail. "Here the Scenery is remarkably interesting and romantic," wrote Richard Ballantyne. "It produces an impression as if we were bordering on a large and antiquated city."²⁸ A few days later the company encountered a large company of Sioux, which Stout described as "very friendly and altogether the best looking and neatest Indians I ever saw. Proud spirited and seemed to disdain to beg and the men would seldom condescend to trade in small articles like moccasins but would have their Squaws do it."²⁹ Traveling the same road a year later on her way to the gold fields of California, Catherine Haun wrote, "The Indian is a financier of no mean ability and invariably comes out A1 in the bargain. Though you may, for the time, congratulate yourself upon your own sagacity, you'll be apt to realize a little later on that you were not quite equal to the shrewd redman—had got the 'short end of the deal.'"³⁰ It would seem that the Sioux were willing to trade for just about anything, as was witnessed by Elmeda Harmon:

> At one time in our journey along the Platte River, a band of Indians came to our camp . . . I noticed a fine looking Indian, evidently the chief, talking to my husband, counting on his fingers as though offering something in a swap or trade. My husband kept shaking his head—no, no. Afterward he told me the chief wanted to buy me, offering him twenty ponies for me.³¹

On July 16 at Chimney Rock a meeting was held, at which time each of Young's and Kimball's companies were divided into four smaller companies to facilitate travel, which was becoming ever more difficult in large groups.³² Daniel Carn was appointed the leader of a diminutive company in which Stout was traveling, consisting of but two tens. It was decided on July 17 that Stout should continue of captain of the guard, though on July 20 he wrote, "Tonight we had no guard out for the first time. after this we do not guard any more." It was a welcome turn of events for Stout, who previously had written, "What a monotonous solitary feeling to go around every night in search of a guard" and on at least three occasions had to court-martial a guard for sleeping while on duty.³³

On July 21, Carn's company, having heard that the greater portion of Young's company had crossed the Platte River the previous day, backtracked two miles through deep, loose sand to reach the point Young had found best for the crossing. Once on the south side of the River, the Saints joined the Oregon Trail, which offered a much better road for travel than the route taken by the 1847 pioneers but far less grass, necessitating taking the cattle across to the north side of the river to feed each evening for several days.³⁴ Despite easier travel in smaller groups on the better road, hardships still abounded as choking dust alternating with frequent drenching rains, occasionally strong winds, and hailstorms.

The climb along the Platte was steadily uphill along a relatively gentle grade, but Fort Laramie marked the end of the high plains and the beginning of a much more arduous upgrade haul to the Rock Mountains. Further complicating matters for Stout, on July 31 his wife Louisa was stricken with "a very severe attack of the mountain fever" (most likely Colorado tick fever), which incapacitated her for three days; then, just as she was recovering, one of their oxen "took the blind staggers and died in a short time." Fortunately, Daniel Carn was able to lend an ox for three days until Carn went ahead with the remaining few members of his company, at which time Stout forged a deal to travel and share oxen with Josiah Arnold.[35]

Though Stout's cattle fared badly and at times seemed close to death, somehow they survived and prospects improved considerably as they approached the Sweetwater Valley with its abundant grass. "It is almost marvelous how Br. Arnold ever reached this place with our loads as we did over the worst road on the whole Journey and such poor feed," Stout recorded, "but our cattle seemed to be in tolerable order and our hopes now brightened."[36] The grass at the Sweetwater Valley was greener and more plentiful than had been encountered since the beginning of the journey, but several cattle perished each day from starvation or poisoning from alkaline water and were left by the roadside, and on August 13 Stout found that another of his oxen had died, dimming his outlook for a swift journey. In the midst of hardships, however, spirits were buoyed greatly when on August 17 an advance team from Salt Lake met the companies with "the joyful information that a large number of teams and waggons were on the way."[37] The promise they brought was of fifty wagons and, perhaps more importantly, 150 yoke of oxen.

While awaiting the arrival of the relief party, Stout was stricken with a severe case of mountain fever and was unable to rise up in his bed for three days and was very weak for three more, forcing his wife to perform twin duties of driving the teams while caring for her infant daughter.[38] Cattle now were dying at the rate of ten per day, and by August 29 the stench became so offensive that the carcasses had to be buried.[39] Fortunately, on the following day forty five wagons and teams arrived from the Salt Lake Valley, at which time the sixty teams borrowed from the Pottawattamie Saints were unyoked and prepared for their return to Iowa under the charge of Allen Taylor.[40]

Responsibility for allotting relief wagons and teams to needy parties was given to Isaac Morley, Reynolds Cahoon, and William Major, who at the start of the journey had been chosen as "Presidents of the Camp." On September 1, a wagon with two yoke of oxen belonging to Bishop Abraham Hoagland was designated for the combined use of Stout and Elisha Groves, whose wife Lucy nearly was killed on the first day of the trek from the Elkhorn River (June 5) when run over by a wagon, breaking her leg and crushing her chest, though miraculously she survived.[41] Heading out immediately, they tackled the steep climb to South Pass, where they were greeted by violent wind and a snowstorm. It took twelve days to reach Fort Bridger, at which point the a very steep hill was rendered dangerous by heavy rains; on September 14 Stout recorded it was "snowing rapidly and so we hurried on to decend out of the clouds and make our decent down a very steep hill for near two miles; our teams literally slid down."[42]

The companies had traveled nearly a thousand miles since leaving Winter Quarters, but the final thirty-six miles, over rugged terrain and boulder-filled creeks, were some of the most difficult of the entire journey. To complicate matters, on September 17 Stout discovered that one of Abraham Hoagland's borrowed oxen was dead, which left him and his traveling companion Elisha Groves "very weak for teams."[43] Fortunately, at that point the companies were able to rest as they stopped and waited for Brigham Young to assume the lead "at the head of the joyful multitude" into the Salt Lake Valley.[44] Unfortunately, the stoppage led to long travel delays, as "the road was crouded for miles having to wait for hours at bad crossings."[45] And that was before Groves broke his wagon tongue on a steep descent and had to stay behind while Stout temporarily forged ahead. It was all a bit too much for Stout, who on September 21 wrote, with a tinge of sarcasm, "Raining disagreeable morning and I was growing very tired of my 'Exalted Station.'"[46]

Stout, suffering from a bad headache, experienced conflicting feelings the following morning when, while gathering his oxen to return for Groves, he was "agreeably disappointed to see him [Groves] drive up having fixed his waggon tongue and borrowed some oxen." As they resumed the journey together they were confronted with some of the roughest terrain they had encountered, traversing another mountain and reaching Little Canyon Creek, which they had to cross "about 18 times over bad places." They finally came to a halt to camp for the night at the mouth of the canyon, about five miles from their promised destination, "waiting with impatience for morning which would terminate our journey."[47]

The companies entered the Salt Lake Valley the following morning, greeted by dark, heavy clouds and strong wind and rain that obscured the view and deposited a fresh blanket of snow on the mountain peaks. As the gloomy weather lifted, from a perch above the city Stout saw that nearly all houses were built in three adjoining forts about a half-mile long and an eighth-mile wide, occupying a small fraction of the barren, flat valley.[48] On the next day, a Sunday, a sizeable congregation assembled under a large "Bowery" to hear President Young, who commended the people for their "industry" and expressed "joy in being able to come here in safety."[49]

By his reckoning, it had taken Stout 130 days to cover the 1031 miles from his home at Winter Quarters to the Salt Lake Valley. "Thus ends this long and tedious journey from the land of our enemies," wrote Stout, "and I feel free and happy that I have escaped from their midst. But there is many a desolate and sandy plain to cross. Many a ruged sage bed to break through. Many a hill and hollow to tug over and Many a mountain and Cañon to pass. And many frosty nights to endure in mid-summer."[50] There would be much more to endure than frosty nights in mid-summer, but after a life's journey that began in Kentucky, with stops along the way in Ohio, Illinois (twice), Missouri, and Nebraska, Hosea Stout finally was home.

Notes

1. Smith, ed., *An Intimate Chronicle: The Journals of William Clayton*, April 11, 13, and 14, 1847, 295. The camp included 142 men, three women, and two children.
2. *Journal History*, September 17, 1847.
3. Arrington, *Brigham Young: American Moses*, 149.
4. Brooks, *Mormon Frontier*, October 8 and 14, 1847, 278, 281.
5. *Journal History*, October 18, 1847.
6. Brooks, *Mormon Frontier*, October 18, 1847, 283.
7. Ibid., October 31, 1847, 286.
8. Ibid., December 22–27, 1847, 291–93.
9. Anderson, *Desert Saints*, 73–74.
10. Ibid.
11. Brooks, *Mormon Frontier*, May 17, 1847, 312.
12. Letter from Thomas Bullock, July 10, 1848, printed in *The Latter-Day Saints Millennial Star* (Liverpool) 10, no. 20, October 15, 1848.
13. *Journal History*, May 31, 1848.
14. Brooks, *John Doyle Lee, Zealot—Pioneer Builder—Scapegoat*, 130. Snow had ninety-nine wagons in his "hundred" while Pulsipher had only fifty-one.
15. Brooks, *Mormon Frontier*, June 2–5, 1848, 314.
16. *Journal History*, June 16, 1848, entry of camp clerk Thomas Bullock.
17. Brooks, *Mormon Frontier*, June 6, 1848. John Harvey was the other captain of Fifty in Allen Taylor's company.
18. Ibid., June 2 and 6, 1848, 1:314; *Journal History*, June 6, 1848.
19. Cleland and Brooks, *A Mormon Chronicle*, July 15, 1848, 39.
20. Ballantyne, "Papers, 1848–1867, 1895," June 1 and 14, 1848.
21. Brooks, *Mormon Frontier*, June 19, 1848, 316.
22. Huntington, "Diary and Reminiscences," June 23, 1848.
23. Scott, "Life Story of Mary Pugh Scott," in Madsen, *Journey to Zion: Voices from the Mormon Trail*, 400.
24. Brooks, *Mormon Frontier*, June 30, 1848, 317.
25. Ibid., July 1, 1848, 317.
26. Pulsipher, "Journal and Autobiography," in Joel Edward Ricks, Cache Valley Historical Material, reel 4, item 88, 33–46.

27. Brooks, *Mormon Frontier*, June 30, 1848, 317.
28. Ballantyne, "Papers," July 15, 1848.
29. Brooks, *Mormon Frontier*, July 12, 1848, 318.
30. Haun, "A Woman's Trip Across the Plains in 1849," Huntington Library, 23.
31. Anderson, ed., *Appleton Milo Harmon Goes West*, 173–74.
32. *Journal History*, July 16, 1848; Brooks, *Mormon Frontier*, July 16, 1848, 318.
33. Brooks, *Mormon Frontier*, July 1, 6, 9, 17, and 20, 1848, 317–19. According to Hosea's journal, the three times guards were found sleeping were June 24, June 27, and July 6.
34. Ibid., July 17–24, 1848, 319.
35. Ibid., July 31–August 6, 1848, 320–21. In a conspiracy in Nauvoo in 1844, Josiah Arnold and Daniel Carn were on guard duty at Joseph Smith's house and prevented assassins from gaining access to the Prophet.
36. Ibid., August 10, 1846, 323.
37. Ibid., August 17, 1848, 323.
38. Ibid., August 19–23, 1848, 323–24.
39. Ibid., August 25 and 29, 1848, 324.
40. *Journal History*, August 20 and September 6, 1848.
41. Bullock, "Journals 1843–1849," June 5, 1848; Brooks, *Mormon Frontier*, September 1, 1848, 1:324.
42. Brooks, *Mormon Frontier*, September 14, 1848, 325.
43. Ibid., September 16–17, 1848, 325.
44. Pulsipher, "Journal and Autobiography," September 18, 1848.
45. Brooks, *Mormon Frontier*, September 18, 1848, 326.
46. Ibid., September 21, 1848, 326.
47. Ibid., September 22, 1848, 326.
48. Ibid., September 23, 1848, 327.
49. Ibid., September 24, 1848, 327.
50. Ibid.

13
Attorney and Legislator

Despite humble beginnings in the Salt Lake Valley, Hosea Stout's ascent to prominence as both a lawyer and a legislative representative was meteoric as well as astounding: on the one hand he had absolutely no legal training or experience, and on the other he was so unpopular, in great measure due to his actions as captain of the police in Winter Quarters and Nauvoo, that he most likely would not have gained public office in a truly democratic election.

Stout was well suited for his first job in the valley, one that he supervised in Winter Quarters. On October 8, 1848, two weeks after his arrival, Stout, David Pedigrew, Almon Fulmer, and Elias Gardner were given the task of rounding up loose cattle and placing them in the stray pen, for which the men were paid fifty cents per animal. The ordinance against strays very much resembled that at Winter Quarters and was equally unpopular, though in Salt Lake there was no police force to assume the duty. As in Winter Quarters, it was vitally important to prevent damage to grains and other crops by stray livestock, but the financial reward for the job was meager at best. "My temporal arraingements were now very much altered," wrote Stout, "and I now had to abandon for the time being the idea of building on my lot as I was about to do."[1]

His one-and-a-quarter acre lot, which he had drawn in a lottery on September 30 and purchased for $1.50, was located on present day Second East near South Temple Street, just two blocks from the site of the future Salt Lake Temple.[2] Unable to build immediately on the lot, Stout instead purchased a house on November 1 from his fellow worker Elias Gardner for forty dollars; though a modest fourteen by eighteen feet in size, he stated it "is plenty of room for me."[3] He was occupied daily for nearly five weeks with "stray penning," but that source of income quickly dried up when, on November 11, Brigham Young notified Gardner that the high council "concluded to stop the stray pen laws." Cleverly straddling the fence between necessity for the stray animal law and the public

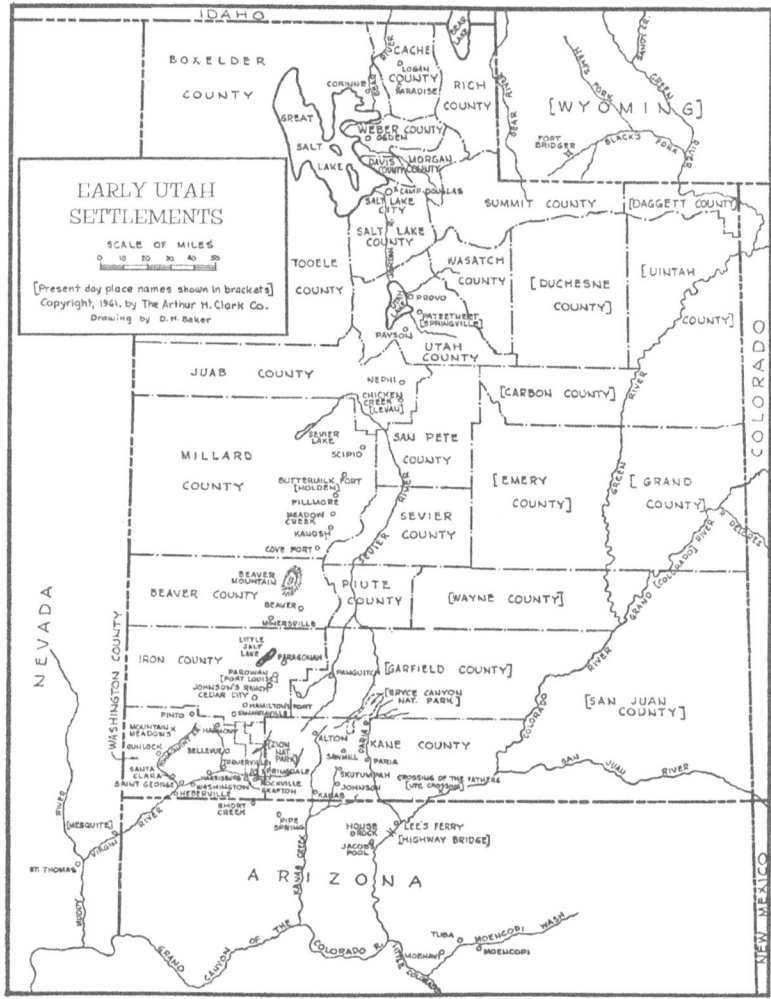

Figure 13.1. Early Utah settlements. Courtesy of University of Utah Press.

distaste for the same, Young secretly rescinded the law and forbade the council members, subject to a twenty-five dollar fine, from divulging the action in hopes that the uninformed citizenry, unaware the law no longer existed, still would comply.[4]

Lacking a job, Stout spent much of his time buying hay and gathering wood in preparation for a severe New England type winter, when "excessive cold commenced on the 1st of December, and continued till the latter part of February."[5] In the midst of the prolonged cold spell, he exhibited a small crack in his militaristic demeanor: after learning

Figure 13.2. Hosea Stout, ca. 1852.

on Christmas Eve that he had been chosen to be on John D. Lee's side in a contest against John Pack's team to see who could rid the valley of the most "wasters and destroyers" (wolves, wildcats, crows, magpies, etc.), Stout declined to participate, saying he was "not feeling very war-like at this time."[6] That did not prevent him, however, from answering the call to go in search of Indians who were suspected of rustling fourteen horses and several head of cattle in the Tooele Valley and taking them to the Utah Valley, about forty-five miles south of Salt Lake City.

Though the Mormons in general and Brigham Young in particular strived to avoid conflict with the Indians, it was deemed that the rogue warriors needed to be taught a lesson. A mounted unit of thirty-five men departed Salt Lake on March 1, 1849; before arriving in the Utah Valley, the group, under the overall command of John Scott, was split into two companies under Hosea Stout and Alexander Williams, with Williams's company reconnoitering the country north along the Jordan River and Stout's company traveling south through the Utah Valley. Though nearly incapacitated by a severe headache, Stout led his men on March 4 to the Provo River, where they encountered friendly Indians; Little Chief, one of their leaders, identified the guilty natives and sent his son to guide the Mormons to their camp.

At dawn on the morning of March 5, at the mouth of a canyon on Battle Creek a few miles north of the Provo River, the posse was divided into four parties and surrounded the Indians. Just before daylight, the natives discovered the Mormon party and screamed for them to go away. Repeatedly refusing bids to surrender, the Indians eventually fired three volleys, which the soldiers returned, initiating the first fight between Mormons and Indians in Utah, a skirmish that lasted for about two hours. Women and children who had been hiding in freezing water gave themselves up, but the battle ended only after four of the native men had been killed. None of the Mormon soldiers were hurt by the "hundreds of arrows" that were shot at rather close range though, according to one report, an arrow had pierced Stout's vest.[7] Reporting on the troop's conduct, Stout wrote, "Our men were perfectly calm and deliberate all the time and did not fire at random as is so common on such occasions."[8] John Brown, a fellow member of the expedition, was much more blunt, writing, "We found them and made an example of four of the principle ones, which had the desired effect."[9]

The company arrived home early in the afternoon of March 6, the day after a convention, orchestrated by the Council of Fifty, had convened to form a provisional state government. The Council of Fifty, named after its fifty members, was a specific outgrowth of the early Mormon belief that the "Kingdom of God" had both a spiritual component, represented by the Church of Christ, as well as a political component. Secretly organized by Joseph Smith in Nauvoo in the spring of 1844, it consisted of Mormons as well as a few friendly non-Mormons and had more or less governed affairs at Winter Quarters. In the Salt Lake Valley it operated significantly behind the scenes from November 1848 to January 1850 and was clandestine enough that John D. Lee, one of its members, referred to it in his journal as the "Council of YTFIF" (fifty spelled backward).[10]

As was the case with many Christian religions, Mormons believed in a millennium that would be ushered in by a second coming of Jesus Christ. Unlike the others, however, Mormons taught that a literal kingdom would need to be established before Christ would come.[11] Brigham Young was committed to the kingdom-building designs of Joseph Smith and on April 6, 1845, with the eleven other apostles, issued a pronouncement that the divine government had been established. The proclamation declared that "the kingdom of God has come . . . even that Kingdom which shall fill the whole earth and stand forever.[12]

The Mormons sought to establish a place of refuge where unity would prevail; to ensure this, political control was deemed necessary.[13] Thus, left to their own desires, the Mormons in the Salt Lake Valley would have preferred independence from the United States while building and strengthening their "Kingdom of God," but on February 2, 1848, just months after Brigham Young's pioneer company had reached the valley, in the Treaty of Guadalupe Hidalgo, Mexico ceded to the United States almost all of the land now included in the states of Utah, Nevada, California, Arizona, Colorado, and New Mexico. Thus the Mormons suddenly found themselves in United States territory, rendering the idea of an independent government unlikely if not impossible. Hopeful that Congress would create a Mormon state, Young met with the Council of Fifty on March 4, 1849, to draft a constitution for a provisional government of the "State of Deseret."[14] The council chose from among their own rank nine to serve as officials in the new government; not surprisingly, the top three offices were filled by the First Presidency, with Brigham Young as governor, Heber C. Kimball chief justice, and Willard Richards secretary of state. An election was held in the Bowery in Salt Lake City on March 12, at which 674 votes were polled in favor of the ordained ticket, for which there was no opposition.[15]

The constitution provided for a militia to be "composed of all able bodied, white male citizens, between the ages of 18 and 45 years."[16] To that end, on April 28 the Nauvoo Legion was organized, divided into two cohorts, one cavalry and one infantry, each with two battalions; the first company of the second cavalry battalion was led by Captain Benjamin Johnson, with Stout his first lieutenant. "This is rising some in the world," he wrote, "Because when the Legion was organized in 1840 I held the office of Second Leut whereas I am now promoted a little." At the same time, Stout marveled that John Pack and John D. Lee, leaders of the great varmint hunt earlier in the year, were nominated as majors in the legion but were "most contemptestously hissed down. When any person in thus duly nominated I never before knew the people to reject it," he recorded, "But on this occasion it appears that they are both a perfect stink in every body's nose."[17]

Organization of the government continued when, pursuant to the provisions of the Constitution of the State of Deseret, the General Assembly met on Monday, July 2, 1849. After being called to order by Daniel Spencer, the Chairman of the Convention, twenty-six of the thirty elected members of the House of Representatives presented their credentials; the last to be seated was Hosea Stout.[18] In reality, it was a selection rather than an election, and even Stout admitted, "By what process I became a Representative I know not."[19]

His two-word journal entry for the July 2, "Around town," suggests that he was not overly impressed with the proceedings.[20] The House also met on July 3, 5, and 6, though Stout "Worked at framing a Barn on the Church farm" each day rather than attending the legislative sessions.[21] Notably, on July 3 the House resolved to "memorialize the Congress of the United States, for a State or Territorial government," which soon developed into a petition for admission "into the Union on an equal footing with other States; or such other form of civil government as your wisdom and magnanimity may award to the people of Deseret."[22] Almon Babbitt, the elected delegate to Congress, left Salt Lake City on July 27 to present the petition for full rather than provisional statehood.

The legislature did not convene for its first true legislative sessions until December 1, 1849. On Tuesday evening, December 4, Stout "received a notification to meet the House of Representatives on Sat next I being a member of that Body," a friendly reminder since he missed the earlier sessions.[23] The most significant accomplishment of the legislature was the creation of the six original counties of Deseret on January 28.[24] More important for Stout personally was the appointment the following day of a number of judges, specifically Daniel H. Wells as Judge of the Supreme Court. Wells, the highest-ranking officer in the Nauvoo Legion, had been serving for the previous nine months as attorney general of the State of Deseret. Inasmuch as Wells was unable to serve simultaneously in the two judicial positions, on Wednesday, February 27, 1850, "by the Joint vote of both houses," he was replaced as attorney general by Hosea Stout.[25]

Like Wells, Stout had no formal legal training. At age twenty-two, after years of sporadic schooling, he opened his own school, not because he felt especially qualified to do so but rather because he decided it was "a last and forlorn hope to a respectable living."[26] He neither attended a law school (of which there were few at the time) nor served a legal apprenticeship; his early experience with legal matters was as a heavy-handed lawman determined to have things done his way rather than as a thoughtful man of the law concerned with proper interpretation and enforcement of statutes. Nevertheless, suddenly he was the top lawyer in the State of Deseret, and that was just the beginning of a momentous, whirlwind nine-day period.

On February 28 the legislature met and passed a bill providing for a chancellor, a treasurer and twelve regents for a state university. The following day, March 1, several absent regents were dropped and Stout was among those selected as a replacement. On March 5 he initiated his first legal proceeding, a suit against Robert Porter and Peter Lish for trespassing, though before he went to court to try that case he was appointed Special Judge Advocate for the Nauvoo Legion and on March 7 presided over the court-martial of John Scott.[27]

Stout needed no introduction to Colonel Scott, having served together as members of a military panel in the court-martial of Robert Foster and Wilson Law, two of the leaders in a conspiracy against Joseph Smith. In addition, exactly one year earlier, Scott had commanded Stout in the expedition to bring justice to Indian rustlers in the Utah Valley. On January 31, 1850, Nauvoo Legion commander Daniel Wells ordered Captain George Grant to go to the Utah Valley to confront members of the Utah tribe who had killed Mormon cattle and stolen horses.[28] Colonel Scott, already censured by authorities displeased with the conduct of his 1849 Utah Valley campaign, was ordered to raise another company to join Grant as soon as possible but he refused to obey.

The expedition proceeded, without Colonel Scott, under the overall command of General Wells, and during five days of battle as many as forty Indians were killed or died from exposure. Scott thereafter was court-martialed for refusing to obey orders and "for using abusive and unbecoming language calculated to discourage the men enrolled" and was cashiered by the court.[29] Later that month, on March 23, Andrew Lytle was promoted to colonel to fill Scott's vacancy in the Nauvoo Legion. Evidently unhappy that Lytle was promoted over himself, Stout immediately resigned his commission as first lieutenant; though General Wells refused to accept the resignation, from that day forth Stout's interest shifted from the military to the legal field.[30]

The three official posts of attorney general, university regent, and judge advocate, as well as his duty as first lieutenant in the Nauvoo Legion, were time-consuming, but the Constitution of the State of Deseret provided compensation only for the governor, while all other officials served at their own expense.[31] To provide for his family Stout first used his carpentering skills in working for Timothy B. Foote on a bridge across Canyon Creek. Though the 1850 United States Census listed his occupation as carpenter, it was the first time he had plied the trade in the six years since the death of Joseph Smith.[32] In July 1849 he worked for three weeks framing and constructing a barn on the church farm and subsequently harvested for Jedediah Grant and John Taylor.[33] In mid-September he commenced working nearly full time on the construction the Council House, a substantial two story edifice that was to be used for both ecclesiastical and legislative purposes, taking time off only for his official duties.

On Friday, March 8, 1850, nine days after assuming the position of attorney general, he worked as a carpenter on the Council House in the morning then switched hats in the afternoon to try his first case in court.

His work on the Council House, however, came to a screeching halt on the following Monday morning as he went "to work as usual but found that the price of labor had so arrainged that I would be allowed only 1.75 per day so I brought away my tools and came home as I did not think I could afford to work at that price considering the relative prices of every other thing."[34] With rising prices in the Valley, Stout could see that he needed a better source of income than carpentering, and the discovery of gold in California and subsequent Gold Rush proved a godsend.

The Mormon Battalion arrived in San Diego on January 29, 1847, after a march of about nineteen hundred miles from Iowa and continued on to Los Angeles, where it was disbanded on July 16, 1847. Some of its members found employment in northern California before resuming the journey to rejoin their families, and a few were working for James Marshall at Sutter's Mill on January 24, 1848, when gold was discovered. Nathan Hawk, returning to his family in Missouri with a small group of Battalion veterans, met Brigham Young on July 27, 1848, near Independence Rock near the Sweetwater River carrying news of the discovery as well as some gold.[35]

Though San Francisco by that time was nearly deserted for the gold fields and the Gold Rush was on, the news didn't reach the east coast and Europe in time for the 1848 emigration season, but 1849 was a different story, as great masses made their way to California to seek riches in gold country, with nearly half of the more than thirty thousand overlanders traveling through Salt Lake City. The Mormons generally did not join the Gold Rush, instead following the First Presidency's admonition "not to scatter around and go off to the mine, or any other place, but to build up the Kingdom of God."[36]

The effect of prospectors pouring into Salt Lake City in 1849 was immediate and profound as Latter-day Saints were able to sell scarce commodities at greatly inflated prices, often at the disapproval of Mormon leaders. Peregrine Sessions, for example, was taken before the Salt Lake High Council on June 23 and found "guilty of taking advantage of the people in the sale of his corn &c" and was ordered to make restitution to those who were overcharged.[37] The following day, Stout visited an emigrant camp and found wagons, harnesses, and surplus clothing and other supplies being sold "cheaper than State prices taking in exchange Horses, mules, saddles, pack saddles &c at very high prices."[38] Quantifying his account, horses worth $25 were being sold for $200 to the emigrants while they in turn sold surplus wagons at a third to a fifth of the original price.[39] The Mormons, who had suffered greatly and had been driven out of Missouri and Illinois by non-Mormons, now were making an economic killing at their expense. Not only were the Mormons able to buy cheaply and sell dearly, but servicing and re-outfitting the overland emigrants provided employment for many, though Stout at first was not one to benefit greatly: for three months after he walked away from the job as a carpenter on the Council House he had no discernible source of income. That changed instantly with the beginning of the 1850 Gold Rush emigration season.

In his service as attorney general (which commenced on February 27, 1850) Stout received no remuneration, but he made himself available for private clients, particularly emigrants to the gold fields of California. Initially the clients were few, and even on the day (April 5) he won an appeal for a client he wrote, following a report of the birth that day of his 9¾ pound son Hosea Jr., "This was better luck than success in legal business."[40] Both his luck and success in the legal business changed rapidly, however, as those headed for the gold fields began arriving in late May.

His first case involving emigrants went to court on June 10, in which he represented a plaintiff suing to recover damages when a ferry carrying his belongings sank while crossing the Weber River; when the ferryman learned that others who suffered the same fate were lining up to sue, he quickly "concluded to pay up and be off."[41] On Friday, June 21, he was attorney for an emigrant plaintiff in a case involving assault and nonpayment of debt in the morning and then represented another emigrant plaintiff in the afternoon, and with that the legal floodgates opened for him. The tribunals, most commonly concerning the division of property, occasionally commenced early in the morning and frequently labored late into the night. After a week of handling cases, Stout wrote, "Disputes are arising among the emergrants . . . while they appeal to the law for a redress of grievances and division of property which is not very interesting to relate."[42] He was almost continuously employed at law by passing emigrants from early June to late August. Nevertheless, to supplement his income, on July 5 he took in several boarders for five dollars a week at the considerable sacrifice of privacy, considering the humble house he constructed on his lot in June 1849 measured only fourteen by sixteen feet with two doors and one window.[43]

Even while representing private emigrant clients, Stout still had to function as attorney general. On one particularly busy Wednesday (July 17) he privately handled the case of one emigrant in the morning, of another at one o'clock p.m. and then represented the state in a trial that commenced at five o'clock in the afternoon, even though he noted that he was "very unwell" both the day before and the day after the trials.[44] From July 1 to 27, according to his diary, he prosecuted ten cases as attorney general and represented emigrant clients in court in nineteen cases, a Herculean task considering the courts were closed on July 2, July 24 (commemorating Brigham Young's 1847 arrival in the Salt Lake Valley) and Sundays; with the extremely heavy load, it is not surprising that on July 26 he was "very sick and at night was out of my senses," and on July 28, after briefly attending a Sunday meeting, he "[c]ame home and went to bed worn out with Lawing the past week and was now quite sick."[45]

Stout remained busy in court until August 22, at which time, with most of the emigrants on their way to California, his private caseload evaporated. On August 27 he stayed with his mother-in-law, Elizabeth Taylor, in Farmington, seventeen miles north of Salt Lake City, while appraising the 2½ acres that he had sowed with wheat as well as another thirty acres that he targeted for future farming. "Went to look at my land this morning," he wrote on August 28, "find it to be fine for farming and contemplate to have more surveyed."[46] On September 12, shortly after his brothers-in-law Joseph and Pleasant Green Taylor arrived from Iowa, he returned to Farmington to hunt for land for himself as well as for his newly arrived relatives. "Came home but found no suitable land," he wrote on September 13. "It is astonishing how the people are taking up the land now in all parts."[47]

At the same time, the US Congress, on September 9 under the Compromise of 1850, established the Territory of Utah to replace the provisional State of Deseret (members of Congress disliked the name Deseret and chose to name the territory after the Utes, the area's largest Native American group). A month later, on October 16, news of the act creating the territory reached Salt Lake City, though without any details. In the meantime, Stout continued to function in his post as attorney general, and in December, as the legislature commenced their second annual session, he once again performed double duty as representative and attorney general. In both positions he was instrumental in the development of judicial practice in Utah, diligently working on legislative committees on the criminal code and civil law while trying the first cases in Utah's county court system.

Though the Constitution of the State of Deseret provided for a supreme court and an ordinance passed on January 9, 1850, created county courts, Brigham Young, in his annual message on December 2, 1850, noted that during the year not a single case had been reported for adjudication before either court.[48] Instead, cases were tried before a justice of the peace (typically but not always a bishop of one of the nineteen Salt Lake City wards) in the Bowery, a large wooden building with adobe walls capable of holding upwards of a thousand people that was used for public meetings.[49] This prompted Young to state in his annual message, "It is highly necessary that a court of probate should be organized," and with the onset of the New Year 1851 the county probate courts began functioning with jurisdiction over probate and, importantly, over criminal and civil matters.[50]

Busily involved in prosecuting cases in county court, Stout was unable to attend concurrent legislative sessions, though he met regularly in the evening with the Committee on Military Affairs to draft a law more effectively organizing the Nauvoo Legion and with another committee drafting a criminal code. "The criminal Law takes more time and calls forth more debate and difference of opinion that anything ever brought up," he wrote on January 15, the night before the code was passed by the legislature.[51] Notably, Section 10 of the criminal law stated, "Be it further ordained, that when any person shall be found guilty of murder . . . and sentenced to die, he, she or they shall suffer death by being shot, hung or beheaded," though beheading never was practiced.[52]

Working within a jury system was a new and not always pleasant experience for Stout, who was accustomed to the previous system in which church and state were totally intertwined. Displeased in one case with the actions of defense counsel James McCabe, Stout "made a very animated plea against the low chicanery of the opposite attorney." Though the defendant, Washington Loomis, was found guilty of stealing a pair of pants, Stout considered the impassioned plea of James McCabe on behalf of his client "a warning never to admit a foul spirit where the Holy spirit should rule and direct either the affairs of State or Church."[53]

The twelve-day special term of the county court ended on January 25; on each of the last two days Stout prosecuted five cases, while two other cases on the docket but not ready for trial were continued until the regular court term in March. Somewhat ruefully he reported, "The sum total of the Rendition of judgements are as follows 33 years and 6 months hard labor, with ball and chain and 240 dollars fine in favor of the State . . . Such is the progress in crime in this onece peaceful valley."[54] His efforts were not without reward, however, as on February 5, the legislature awarded him five dollars for each of the seventeen convictions during the special term of the court.[55] In response, on the following Monday Brigham Young railed in a legislative session "against the practice of any one having any thing for their services either in church or state."[56]

In March, a special term of the Supreme Court convened to hear a case that would have lasting implications. On Sunday, February 5, 1851, in the small town of Manti, Utah, Madison Hambleton, suspecting that Dr. John Vaughn had seduced his wife, shot and killed Vaughn as he exited a church service.[57] News of the murder reached Salt Lake City on February 15, at which time Stout noted that Dr. Vaughn had been accused of immorality the previous summer with the wife of Timothy Foote.[58] The Supreme Court met as a "court of inquiry" before Heber C. Kimball on March 17 to consider the case; Brigham Young spoke convincingly on behalf of Hambleton while Stout, who was the prosecutor, admitted that he "was well satisfied of his justification." Hambleton was acquitted by the court "and also by the Voice of the people present."[59]

It was Stout's final case as attorney general. Official word of a new territorial government reached Salt Lake City on January 27, 1851, with papers stating that Brigham Young had been appointed Governor of Utah, non-Mormons Joseph Buffington and Perry Brocchus and Mormon Zerubbabel Snow justices in the Territorial Supreme Court, Broughton D. Harris secretary of the territory, Joseph L. Heywood marshal, and Seth M. Blair attorney general. Young took the oath of office as governor on February 3, but the transition from the provisional State of Deseret to the Territory of Utah didn't begin until Saturday, March 28, when the legislature met to transact business preparatory to the functioning of the territorial government. The following Saturday, April 5, the legislative government of Deseret was dissolved, completing the transition to territorial government, and Stout noted rhetorically, "I suppose that my office as Attorney General of the State is likewise ended with the State government."[60]

His supposition was correct, and after the conclusion of the short legislative session he spent nearly every day plowing, gardening, and working at home. On May 22, while awaiting mail from the States, he wrote, "I do not know how to make a calculation for the summer untill I learn the news and prospects from the States," anticipating litigation for emigrants as during the previous summer.[61] The mail arrived six days later with news that a great number of emigrants were on their way,[62] but it mattered not, for in the new system he was unable to practice law until admitted to the bar. With no legal practice and "doing nothing as usual now days," Stout traded his horses to his brother-in-law Joseph Taylor for a small farm about eight miles north of the city, briefly intending to give farming another try—"how will it come out?" he mused—but otherwise languished week after week in melancholy.[63]

On July 26 Stout's name was placed in nomination for the House of Representatives from Great Salt Lake County. As was the case with all nominees, he was unopposed on the ballot and on August 4 all candidates were elected.[64] Following the election the monotony of his life continued, as nearly every day his journal entries read simply, "Worked at home." Even on September 17 his entry read, "Worked at home. My wife was delivered of a son about 4 o'c A.M."[65] The son was named Eli Harvey Stout in honor of Stout's friend in Illinois whose mentoring had so positively influenced him.

As the House convened on the first day of autumn, however, Stout's life suddenly became much busier and more interesting. The first job of the legislature was to remedy turmoil caused by the sudden departure of three non-Mormon government appointees. The three officials—two

Figure 13.3. Seth M. Blair (1819–1875). A prominent attorney in territorial Utah, Blair was US District Attorney from 1850 to 1854 and, with Hosea Stout and James Ferguson, co-founded The Mountaineer.

judges and the territorial secretary—trickled in during the summer, with Justice Perry Brocchus not arriving until August 17, 1851. Three weeks after his arrival Brocchus asked for and was granted permission to address the Saints at their General Conference on September 8. After expressing gratitude for the kindness and hospitality of the Saints, he launched into a diatribe against the Mormons, reprimanding them for their lack of patriotism and morality, the latter being an unmistakable reference to the Mormon practice of plural marriage. The audience became infuriated with Brocchus's speech, and after he sat down Young took the stand and rebuked Brocchus for his imprudent remarks, saying he was "either profoundly ignorant or willfully wicked."[66] Young tried to repair the breach through a series of letters, but the damage had been done. Justices Brocchus and Brandenbury and Secretary Harris concluded that they could not fulfill their assignments in Utah and just days after the first meeting of the legislature convened on September 22 they left the territory, later reporting to President Millard Fillmore that Brigham Young had made it impossible for them to function.

In an obvious attempt to incur favor with President Fillmore, the legislature voted that the territorial capital be located 150 miles south of Salt Lake City in the newly formed Millard County whose county seat was named Fillmore. Then, with two of the three federal judges gone, the territorial legislature formed a committee, of which Stout was a member, which filled the judicial vacuum by granting criminal jurisdiction to the territorial probate courts. A bill passed on September 29 that authorized Judge Zerubbabel Snow to hold courts in the districts that were vacated by the departure of Buffington and Brocchus.[67]

The "runaway officials," as the Saints called them, never returned to Utah and their positions remained unfilled until 1853. In the meantime, territorial business proceeded unhindered; on October 1 Stout, who had been out of touch with the legal profession for more than a half-year, was appointed to a committee of three (with Phineas Richards and David Fullmer) to revise and classify the Laws of Deseret, and the laws previously enacted by the provisional State of Deseret were officially incorporated into territorial law.[68] One week later, on October 7, he attended district court, where he was admitted to the bar and "sworn into office, a Councillor and attorney at law and solicitor in chauncery, by Judge Snow upon a motion of [Attorney General] S. M. Blair."[69] Immediately after being admitted to the bar, Stout began attending court daily, getting a crash course in the functioning of a much more formalized legal system than what existed in the State of Deseret. Exactly one week later, on Friday, October 17, a trial—*The United States v. Howard Egan*—took place that became a landmark case in Utah jurisprudence.

Howard Egan was a Mormon stalwart and one of Stout's policemen in Nauvoo as well as one of his fellow officers in the Nauvoo Legion. He was a member of Brigham Young's vanguard company in 1847; after three weeks in the Salt Lake Valley he returned to Winter Quarters to prepare some of his family to cross the plains in 1848. He then returned to Pottawattamie, Iowa, to retrieve one of his plural wives and her daughter; subsequently in spring 1849 he was the captain of a company that bore his name. Upon his arrival in Salt Lake City in 1849, Brigham Young presented him the job of guiding a company of forty-niners across the desert to the gold fields of California. When he returned to the Salt Lake Valley in the spring of 1850, he discovered that one of his wives had been seduced and impregnated by James Monroe.

In September 1851 Egan rode out of Salt Lake in the direction of Fort Bridger and intercepted a wagon train of which Monroe was a member. The affair between Monroe and Egan's wife was generally known throughout the train, and the captain already had advised Monroe to leave, suspecting that Egan would come looking for him. After what appeared to be a friendly chat, Egan drew a pistol and shot Monroe on the right side of his face just below the eye, killing him instantly. Egan rode to the company, divulged his name, confessed his act, and made a short speech, saying "what he did he done in the name of the Lord," that in seducing his wife Monroe had ruined his family and "destroyed his peace on earth for ever."[70]

The case was eerily similar to that of Madison Hambleton, who shot Dr. John Vaughn the previous February, and one in which Stout took keen interest, due in part to his close acquaintance with Egan but also due to the case itself. Attorney General Seth Blair prosecuted for the United States while Apostle George A. Smith, who like Stout had been admitted to the bar though he had no legal training, was counsel for Egan's defense. Smith argued it was "a principle of mountain common law that no man can seduce the wife of another without endangering his own life." Furthermore, he asserted, "The man who seduces his neighbor's wife must die, and her nearest relative must kill him!"[71] The jury agreed and after a fifteen-minute deliberation returned with a verdict of not guilty. Of the verdict Stout wrote, "This is like to be a precident for any one who has his wife, sister, or daughter seduced to take the law into his own hands and slay the seducer and I expect it will go still farther."[72] He was absolutely correct, as on March 6, 1852, the Legislature passed the Justifiable Homicide Act, which stated that killing the person who defiled a "wife, daughter, mother, sister or any other female relative or dependent: would be classified as justifiable homicide."[73]

Subsequent to Egan's trial, the Mormons—and particularly Judge Snow—continued to advocate their own laws, even when they were contrary to the common law. On December 2, Stout "met at the State house with the members of the bar and other gentlemen and Judge Snow to take into consideration the propriety of establishing a law School under the direction of Judge Snow," who gave a short lecture on the nature and origin of government and law.[74] Snow instructed his scholars that they had "a right to make such laws as suited [their] own Convenience Notions and circumstances" and that such laws could be enacted "without any regard to the Common Law of England or the laws which any of the states had adopted."[75] After the meeting it was agreed to establish a "law school," which amounted to a series of five evening classes conducted by Snow during the month of December.

Had Brigham Young been queried about the propriety of a law school in Utah, doubtless he would have been negative, given his inherent dislike of lawyers and litigation. On January 1, 1852, in his "Proclamation: For a Day of Praise and Thanksgiving for the Territory of Utah," he said, "I also request of all good and peaceful citizens, that they abstain from all evil thinking, speaking, and acting on that day; that no one be offended by his neighbor; that all jars and discords cease; that neighborhood broils may be unknown . . . that all may cease their quarrels, and starve the lawyers."[76]

As the legislature convened on January 5, 1852, for a lengthy session that would last two months, a top legislative priority, in response to widespread distrust and disapproval of lawyers, was the creation of a bill to regulate attorneys. A preliminary version of the act was read on February 4 and referred to a committee on laws and ordinances, to which Stout, George A. Smith, and James Brown had been added. On February 17 the House went into a secret session on the subject of attorneys, and on the next day Stout read "An Act for the Regulation of Attorneys" to the House, which promptly passed it.[77] According to the act, the single requisite for an attorney was good moral character; no legal training or experience was necessary, and Section 2 stated that no person would be "compelled by any process of law to pay the counsel so employed for any service rendered as counsel, before, or after, or during the process of trial in the case."[78]

Stout, even while serving as a representative, clearly was focusing increasingly more on the legal profession. Immediately after the legislature adjourned on March 6 he began to attend to legal business on a daily basis. On March 11, after assisting Seth Blair in prosecuting for the state in a case of $900 debt, he switched sides and was retained to defend a man who was being sued for a debt of $338.80; the man, named Lefering, paid Stout fifty dollars in advance for his services, demonstrating that an attorney could be paid as long as he didn't compel the payment.[79]

After nearly three weeks of constantly being in court, on March 23 Stout took a break from his legal affairs as he commenced "preparing the laws for the press," a task he assumed would take about twenty to thirty days.[80] Nearly every day was consumed by reading, indexing, writing marginal notes to, and examining the laws. After a typical morning of reading proof sheets on May 17, he took time out to attend the City Council, having been appointed a member.[81] On June 5, the fifty-seventh day of preparing the laws to be printed, he wrote in his journal, "Indexing still. O tedious!"[82] As his work approached completion at the end of June, he had spent more than seventy days on the task, and only then was he able to engage in "planting suits for golden pilgrims, in the probate Court."[83] It was a rerun of the summer of 1850 for him, when he handled case after case in court.

The month of August was momentous for Stout. In addition to his legislative duties, primarily acting as clerk of the Code Commission, and handling cases in court, on August 2 he was re-elected as a representative when, once again, all candidates ran without opposition and the unenthused Salt Lake public cast only 150 votes.[84] On August 25 he received fifty-six dollars from the US Government for his services in court;[85] though not a large amount, it still was very welcome and greater than the twenty-nine dollars he received earlier in the year for similar service.[86] The colossal surprise of the month, however, came on the first day of a Special Conference on August 28 that was held for the purpose of sending 106 missionaries abroad, when Stout, James Lewis, and Chapman Duncan were chosen to go to China. Stout, who despite his occasionally violent actions was a man of great faith, recorded of the occasion, "The brethren who were chosen all manifest a good spirit and seem to have the spirit of their Calling. I feel well pleased with the mission allotted to me and feel in the name of my master to fill it to the honor and glory of God."[87]

The second day of the conference, August 29, presented another bombshell when Orson Pratt publicly announced the doctrine of plurality of wives. Stout originally learned of the doctrine on July 12, 1843, the day Joseph Smith privately announced it to the Nauvoo High Council, but he had kept it secret; at the conference, he reveled in the fact that it "was publicly read for the first time to the great joy of the Saints who have looked forward so long and so anxiously for the time to come when we could publicly declare the true and greatest principles of our holy religion and the great things which God has for his people to do in this dispensation. I feel that the work of the Lord will roll forth with a renewed impetus. The nations of the earth will be wakened up to an investigation of the truth of the gospel."[88]

Stout was filled with the fire, ready to preach the gospel, and immediately began to prepare to leave for China. The first order of business was to finish a few court cases; notably, on September 8, he granted refuge to eleven-year-old Henry Allen, whom he had represented in a case of abuse against John Hously. After the court ruled the boy should be given up by Hously, to whom he previously had been bound, Stout adopted him.[89]

On September 28, pursuant to a claim he made for his work in preparing the laws and journals of the legislature for printing, Stout was awarded $580 in addition to $42 that he had received earlier, "in all amounting to Six hundred and twenty two dollars in all is 'material aid' just as I am going on a mission for which I feel unusually greatful to my Heavenly father for and feel encouraged to press on to the accomplishing of every duty enjoined on me by the priesthood untill I shall have finished my probation on this earth."[90]

Everything was falling in place for Stout. "Winding up my affairs quite fast to day," he wrote on September 29. "The prospects for my leaving and leaving my family in good circumstances are coming out better than my sanguine expectation." The following day he contracted Daniel H. Wells to build a house, "eighteen feet square with a good cellar," paying in advance $340 and promising another $100 before his departure should the construction proceed on schedule. Soon thereafter his three brothers-in-law, Joseph, William, and Levi Taylor, harvested his wheat, a great accommodation for Stout who had not the time to do it himself. "May they be rewarded an hundred fold for this kind act," he wrote.[91] Scraping together as much money as possible to pay for his new house, he sold his carpenter tools for sixty-five dollars and some of his books for another twenty.[92] "Very unexpectedly did I find myself able to procure the building of a comfortable house for my family before going on a long mission," he wrote. "Otherwise they would have had to remained in the old log ones which will neither screen them from wind snow, or rain This I esteem a special act of providence for when I was first set apart to this mission I did not know how I could procure a scanty outfit without selling my farm or other things which would leave my family very destitute."[93]

Less than a week before his departure, Stout and all three of his children were very ill. "It seems that the destroyer is determined to use up my family on the eve of my leaving," he recorded.[94] The following day, Stout and several others, including adopted son Henry Allen, were baptized.[95] In Stout's case, it was a rebaptism, a practice that began in Nauvoo and became much more common once the Saints reached the Salt Lake Valley, particularly in 1856–1857 during a period known as the "Mormon Reformation."[96] Immediately after his rebaptism, Stout received a special blessing under the hands of Apostle Wilford Woodruff. "This was an interesting day," Woodruff noted. "Spent the whole day in teaching the 44 Elders that were going on foreign Mission to China, Australia, Siam, Hindustan [India], the Isles of the Sea . . . The spirit and power of God rested upon us in a great degree. The Heaven was opened unto us and our minds was filled with visions Revelations and Prophecy and we sealed great Blessings upon their heads."[97] Woodruff's lengthy blessing for Stout read in part:

> Br Hosea in the name of Jesus Christ of Nazareth, and by virtue of the Holy priesthood conferred upon us, we lay our hands upon thy head and set the apart unto the mission whereunto thou art called by the revelations of Jesus Christ through the Servants of God. And we bless thee with the blessings of Abraham Isaac and Jacob, and with the spirit and power of thy mission

Figure 13.4. Hosea Stout residence located on Second East, just south of Brigham Street (South Temple). Hosea rushed to complete the house in 1853 before leaving on his mission to China and returned to find strangers living there, his wife and infant son dead, and his family scattered.

The Lord has opened a way for thy foot steps to go among that people, and thou shalt do a great work there, thy words shall be as the words of the angels of God unto them, and they shall receive them, and thousands shall be brought into the kingdom of God through thy instrumentality.

Thou shalt have power to command the elements and they shall obey thee, Thou shalt have power to perform mighty miracles, and cast out devils heal the sick, and cause the blind to see, the lame to (walk [crossed out]) leap as an hart; for when thou shalt command in the name of the Lord thy commands shall be obeyed, because the eyes of thy heavenly father shall watch over thee for good, and the Holy Ghost shall accompany thee to perform all that they heart desires, therefore be comforted. Though the nation and people may be shrouded in darkness, and the prospects before thee gloomy yet it shall be light, and thy feet shall walk the land whereunto thou art sent, and the angels of God shall prepare the way before thee. Thou shalt find funds, and in a singular manner . . .

> Go thy way trusting in the Lord, and thou shalt return again to thy family and friends with honor and glory upon thy head, and the time thou hast employed in passed days in treasuring up knowledge of Countries and laws, shall be of use unto thee, even a great advantage, and the Lord shall give thee power to obtain a knowledge of their language so as to have access to them, and ordain men who shall assist the in spreading the gospel through that mighty nation.[98]

Stout believed every word of the blessing, though the promises pertaining to success in his missionary work and knowledge of the Chinese language went unfulfilled. The next day—his final Sunday before departing—he was called to preach in the Tabernacle, at which he "bore testimony to the truth of the work of God in the Last Days." Still, with his son Hosea extremely sick, it seemed to him "that the Destroyer is seeking to thwart the purposes of God by afflicting my family but I feel to say in the name of the Lord Jesus Christ that the power of the destroyer shall be rebuked in my family that my children shall be healed and their lives and the life of my wife held precious before the Lord. That they shall be prospered and protected from all evil even untill I return from my mission because I know that it is the will of my heavenly father for it to be so. Which may God seal in the heavens."[99]

Stout's faith was unshakeable and, with his preparation as well as his faith in God, he felt comfortable in his readiness to leave. On October 19, the day before his scheduled departure, he wrote:

> To day I have got my business all wound up to my perfect Satisfaction. I have been prospered beyond my most sanguine expectations in all things since I was appointed to go on a mission to China and I feel that the hand of the Lord is upon me for good notwithstanding the sickness and affliction of my children. I feel the assurance that they will recover and my family be prospered while I am gone. I feel to dedicate my family, my self and my all to the God of Israel invoking his blessings upon them for it will be verily so. I have been enabled to leave my family well provided for in good and clothing besides some Eighty dollars worth of wood on good and responsible men and forty dollars in beef and pork or wood at the option of my wife as well as one hundred and twenty dollars in cash besides a good comfortable house now in progress of building for all of which I feel that the Lord has blessed me with, in a most singular manner.

Besides all this I have deposited with Br Daniel H. Wells, claims on the goverment amounting to seven hundred and seven dollars, which if he succeeds in collecting will amply sustain my family for a long time, yet, independent of all these recourses I have not the least doubt but my family will be well provided for and do well, for I leave them in the hands of the Lord and commend them to his mercy and guardian care which will ever be extended over them and shield them from all harm.[100]

Apostle George A. Smith told the 106 elders (including Stout) who were to serve missions throughout the world, "The missions we will call for during this conference, are generally not to be very long ones; probably from three to seven years will be as long as any man will be absent from his family."[101] Hosea's brother Allen confirmed the anticipated duration of the mission, writing in early 1853, "I did not expect that my brother would return for five years."[102] Hosea felt he had "prospered beyond [his] most sanguine expectations in all things" since being called to go to China, and it seemed a miracle to him that he would be able to provide for his family for such an extended period. And so he prepared to depart, secure in his knowledge that, with "providence" on his side, his family would prosper while he served the Lord on a lengthy and successful mission in China. Fate, unfortunately, had other designs.

Notes

1. Brooks, *Mormon Frontier*, October 8, 1848, 332–33.
2. Ibid., September 30, 1848, 332; Arrington, *Great Basin Kingdom*, 51. Unmarried men were not entitled to a lot, while polygamists were entitled to one for each separate family.
3. Brooks, *Mormon Frontier*, November 1, 1848, 334.
4. Ibid., November 11, 1848, 334–35.
5. "First General Epistle of the First Presidency . . ., " *Millennial Star* 11 (1849): 228.
6. Brooks, *Mormon Frontier*, December 24, 1848, 338; Cleland and Brooks, *A Mormon Chronicle*, 82–84. Hosea was not alone in declining to participate, as a total of only 84 men out of 186 who were chosen took part in the hunt. The two companies killed 2 bears, 2 wolverines, 2 wildcats, 783 wolves, 409 foxes, 31 minks, 9 eagles, 530 magpies, hawks, and owls, and 1,026 ravens; *Journal History*, March 6, 1848.
7. Huff, *Memories That Live; Utah County Centennial History*, 167–68
8. Brooks, *Mormon Frontier*, February 28, March 1–5, 1849, 343–47; Bigler, *The Forgotten Kingdom: The Mormon Theocracy in the American West, 1847–1896*, 67–68.
9. Brown, "Journal Extract, 1849 November–1850 January" March 6, 1849, MS 21607, Church History Library.

10. Arrington, *Great Basin Kingdom*, 31, 50; Cleland and Brooks, *A Mormon Chronicle*, 80.
11. Peterson, *The Mormon Reformation*, 8.
12. *Proclamation of the Twelve Apostles of the Church of Jesus Christ of Latter-day Saints. To all Kings of the World, the President of the United States of America; to the Governors of the Several States, and to the People of All Nations.*
13. Hill, "Mormon Religion in Nauvoo: Some Reflections," 174–75.
14. The name Deseret came from a *Book of Mormon* term for honeybee and signified industry and cooperation.
15. Morgan, *The State of Deseret*, 30–34; Cleland and Brooks, *A Mormon Chronicle*, March 4, 1849, 98–99; Brooks, *Mormon Frontier*, March 12, 1849, 348–49. The officials were: Brigham Young, governor; Willard Richards, secretary; Heber C. Kimball, chief justice; John Taylor, associate justice; Newel K. Whitney, associate justice and treasurer; Horace S. Eldredge, marshal; Daniel H. Wells, attorney general; Albert Carrington, assessor and collector; and Joseph L. Haywood, supervisor of roads.
16. Morgan, *The State of Deseret*, 126.
17. Brooks, *Mormon Frontier*, April 28, 1849, 351.
18. *Constitution of the State of Deseret*, 11.
19. Brooks, *Mormon Frontier*, December 4, 1849, 358. A good possibility is that the representatives were chosen by an inner circle of the Council of Fifty. See Klaus Hansen, "The Theory and Practice of the Political Kingdom of God in Mormon History," 1829–1890, 96–97.
20. Ibid., July 2, 1849, 354.
21. Ibid., July 3–7, 1849, 354.
22. Morgan, *State of Deseret*, 30–39.
23. Brooks, *Mormon Frontier*, December 4, 1849, 358.
24. Morgan, *State of Deseret*, 48. The original counties in 1849 in the provisional State of Deseret were: Davis, Iron, Sanpete, Salt Lake, Utah and Weber. Tooele County was created a short time later, also in 1849.
25. Brooks, *Mormon Frontier*, February 27, 1850, 363.
26. Stout, *Autobiography*, 60.
27. Brooks, *Mormon Frontier*, February 28, March 1, March 5, and March 7, 1850, 363–64.
28. Letter from Daniel Wells to George Grant, January 31, 1850, Utah Militia Records.
29. Brooks, *Mormon Frontier*, March 7, 1850, 364.
30. Ibid., March 23, 1850, 365, footnote 33.
31. Morgan, *State of Deseret*, 34, 124. See Article III, section 12 of the Constitution.
32. Brooks, *Mormon Frontier*, April 4, 1849, 350; 1850 United States Census.
33. Brooks, *Mormon Frontier*, July 3–31, 1849, 354–55.
34. Ibid., March 11, 1850, 364.
35. Owens, *Gold Rush Saints: California Mormons and the Great Rush for Riches*, 202–3.
36. Arrington, *Brigham Young*, 183.
37. Ibid., June 23, 1849, 353.
38. Ibid., June 24, 1849, 353.

39. Arrington, *Great Basin Kingdom*, 68.
40. Brooks, *Mormon Frontier*, April 5, 1850, 366.
41. Ibid., June 10–11, 1859, 371.
42. Ibid., June 28, 1850, 372.
43. Ibid., July 5, 1850, 372–73.
44. Ibid., July 16–18, 1850, 374.
45. Ibid., July 26 and 28, 1850, 375.
46. Ibid., August 27–28, 1850, 379.
47. Ibid., September 12–13, 1850, 380.
48. Morgan, *State of Deseret*, 124, 134; Young, "Governor's Message: Deseret, December 2, 1850: To the Senators and Representatives of the State of Deseret," in Neff, *History of Utah, 1847 to 1869*, 188.
49. Hudson, *A Forty-Niner in Utah with the Stansbury Exploration of Great Salt Lake: Letters and Journal of John Hudson, 1848–50*, 97–98.
50. Neff, *History of Utah*, 188–89.
51. Brooks, *Mormon Frontier*, January 12 and 15–16, 1851, 389.
52. Morgan, *State of Deseret*, 177.
53. Brooks, *Mormon Frontier*, January 23, 1851, 389.
54. Ibid., January 25, 1851, 390.
55. Ibid., February 5, 1851, 392.
56. Ibid., February 10, 1851, 392.
57. Goodell, *A Winter with the Mormons*, 74–75.
58. Brooks, *Mormon Frontier*, February 15, 1851, 393.
59. Ibid. March 17, 1851, 396.
60. Ibid., March 28 and April 5, 1851, 396–97.
61. Brooks, *Mormon Frontier*, May 22, 1851, 399.
62. Ibid., May 28, 1851, 400.
63. Ibid., June 11, 1851, 400.
64. *Journal History*, July 26 and September 18, 1851; Brooks, *Mormon Frontier*, August 4, 1851, 402.
65. Brooks, *Mormon Frontier*, September 17, 1851, 404.
66. Arrington, *Brigham Young: American Moses*, 228; Anderson, *Desert Saints*, 138.
67. Brooks, *Mormon Frontier*, September 26–29, 1851, 405–6.
68. Ibid., October 1, 1851, 406.
69. Ibid., October 8, 1851, 406–7. Snow studied law and was admitted to the bar of the Supreme Court of Ohio in October 1839; Letter from clerk of the court William I. Appleby to Hosea Stout, November 6, 1851, Hosea Stout Papers, Utah State Historical Society.
70. Brooks, *Mormon Frontier*, October 17, 1851, 407.
71. *Journal of Discourses*, 1:97.
72. Brooks, *Mormon Frontier*, October 18, 1851, 408.
73. "Acts, Resolutions, and Memorials," 140.
74. Brooks, *Mormon Frontier*, December 2, 1851, 410.
75. Woodruff, "Journal," 4:85–86.
76. Neff, *History of Utah*, 192.
77. Brooks, *Mormon Frontier*, February 4, 17, and 18, 1852, 423–24.
78. *The Compiled Laws of the Territory of Utah*, 37.
79. Brooks, *Mormon Frontier*, March 11, 1852, 431–32.

80. Ibid., March 23, 1852, 433.
81. Ibid., May 17, 1852, 437.
82. Ibid., June 5, 1852, 439.
83. Ibid., July 13, 1852, 442.
84. Ibid., August 2, 1852, 444.
85. Ibid., August 25, 1852, 445.
86. *Deseret News*, January 2, 1852.
87. Brooks, *Mormon Frontier*, August 28, 1852, 449. Hosea listed Walter Thompson as a fourth missionary called to go to China, but contemporary newspaper and church accounts—including the "Eighth General Epistle of the Presidency of the Church" of October 13, 1852, list only Stout, Duncan, and Lewis as missionaries to China.
88. Ibid., August 29, 1852, 449–50.
89. Ibid., September 8, 1852, 451.
90. Ibid., September 28, 1852, 452.
91. Ibid., October 4, 1852, 452.
92. Ibid., October 11 and 14, 1852, 452.
93. Ibid., September 29–30, 1852, 452.
94. Ibid., October 15, 1852, 454.
95. Ibid., October 16, 1852, 454.
96. Stapley and Wright, "'They Shall Be Made Whole': A History of Baptism for Health," *Journal of Mormon History*, 69–112.
97. Woodruff, "Journal," October 16, 1852, 4:150.
98. Brooks, *Mormon Frontier*, October 16, 1852, 454.
99. Ibid., October 17, 1852, 455.
100. Ibid., October 19, 1852, 455.
101. "Minutes of Conference," *Deseret News*, September 18, 1852, 1.
102. Haven, "Jesse Haven Journals"; Stout, "Journal."

14
Mission to China

In a blistering rebuke of lawyers and "all who love litigation and do not repent," Brigham Young railed from the pulpit of the Salt Lake Tabernacle:

> You men who follow after such a course of things as I refer to, I would not give the ashes of a rye straw for the whole of you, jurymen, witnesses, and every other person who countenances such a place. It is a cage of unclean birds, a den and kitchen of the devil, prepared for hell, and I am going to warn you of it. Some of you wondered why I sent Thomas Bullock to take your names; I wanted to know the men who were coaxing hell into our midst, for I wish to send them to China, to the East Indies, or to where they cannot get back, at least for five years . . . we will send off the poor curses on a mission, and then the devil may have them, and we do not care how soon they apostatize, after they get as far as California."[1]

Had Young delivered the diatribe forty months earlier, before Hosea Stout and his companions (Chapman Duncan and James Lewis) departed on their mission to China, a scepter of suspicion might have been raised that Young was endeavoring to thin the ranks of attorneys in the territory by sending the trio on a lengthy, distant mission since the trio all were involved in the legal system (Duncan was Probate Judge for Iron County and Lewis was District Attorney for the United States Third District). In fact, the remonstration was given on February 24, 1856, thirty months after the missionaries *returned* to San Francisco from China, and evidence for Young's reasoning in sending Stout on the mission clearly points elsewhere.

Prior to Stout's departure, Brigham Young, in his role as governor, gave him a letter of recommendation to take on his journey, stating that he knew Hosea "to be a respectable, high-minded and honorable man."² On October 17 Stout was asked to address the congregation in the Tabernacle, a duty and honor generally reserved for the most prominent church leaders (he shared the pulpit with Jedediah Grant, who in 1854 was made Brigham Young's second counselor in the First Presidency, and Eli Kelsey, who captained a recently arrived wagon train company of about a hundred individuals).³ Three days later Stout departed from Salt Lake City, and on October 24—the fifth day of the journey—Stout was unanimously chosen captain of the company of missionaries headed for Asia and the Pacific, which could not have happened were he not in good standing with church leaders.⁴

The lateness of the season necessitated taking the "Southern Route" to California (rather than crossing the High Sierras), even though it was reputed to be the nation's most difficult wagon road.⁵ The initial leg of the journey through established Utah settlements to Cedar City was relatively easy, though hindered occasionally by rain and mud. The missionaries frequently were sheltered and fed along the way by their Mormon brethren, many of whom were personal friends and aware of their coming. Upon reaching Fillmore, the newly designated territorial capital and site of the partially completed State House, they were treated "with the same warm feelings of hospitality" of home.⁶ Ever the lawyer, while in Fillmore Stout represented Millard County in a lawsuit; in payment he was given a cow, which in turn he sold for twenty dollars worth of corn for his company.⁷

Departing Fillmore, the company fought inclement weather and slippery roads before entering the Parowan Valley. During a four-day sojourn in Parowan, Stout took time to write one letter to Brigham Young and another to his wife.⁸ In his ebullient letter to President Young he reported:

> Our progress thus far has been slow, but we have been preaching in the different settlements and rejoicing among the people, it has seemed that we could not get along faster. The people cling to hear us, to hear our testimony, that they might be strengthened, that we should mingle with them, that they with us might rejoice. We have preached 99 sermons, and we have continually bore our testimony to the truth of this work, yet the elders are full.⁹

To his wife, Stout echoed much the same sentiment. "It is truly heart cheering to see with what alacraty the brethren travel on their way to be gone for years from the tender embraces of their families and all they hold Dear to them on earth to preach," he wrote. "The power and manifestation of the spirit and priesthood of the son of God which has attended us while on our way here is truly astonishing . . . I have preached three times and can say of a surety that the power of the Holy Ghost encircles me round about." In the letter, Stout demonstrated special concern for his adopted son, Henry Allen. "How is Henry doing and is he also happy," he asked. "Tell him to be a good boy and not forget me neither forget his duty and be attentive to his book . . . I feel an interest in his welfare as a father feels for his own son."[10]

James Lewis and Chapman Duncan, Stout's companions to China, joined the company on November 7, bringing it to its full complement of thirty-eight missionaries.[11] The following day the company proceeded on their journey from the settlement at Coal Creek, launching "forth into the Deserts and mountains" beyond the last Utah settlement, for the first time feeling that they had left their homes.[12] The route was well known due to the establishment in 1851 of a Mormon settlement at San Bernardino by Apostles Charles C. Rich and Amasa M. Lyman. "I think we will be near 25 days going through to San Barnidino," Stout wrote to his wife, an estimate that proved to be quite accurate.[13]

Following the "Old Spanish Trail," for three days the missionaries trekked around the north and then west sides of Pine Valley Mountain until they began the descent along the Santa Clara River into the desert. On the fifth day the company executed a difficult six-mile uphill climb over what was known at the time as Conger Hill, passed over a high mountain, descended into the far eastern reaches of the Mojave Desert and kept going until they reached the Rio Virgin, a very challenging one-day trek of twenty-six miles. The difficulty of that journey, however, was surpassed three days later when the terrain forced them to leave the Rio Virgin and conquer Virgin Hill, where twenty men had to assist their animals in pulling up a wagon.[14]

At the Muddy River they were joined by large numbers of Indians, described by Stout as "the most low and contemptible I ever saw and show the most degraded and dishonest disposition."[15] Though a major nuisance, the natives proved harmless and the Mormon party continued on to Las Vegas, where they encountered the Las Vegas River which, unlike the Rio Virgin and the Muddy River, was filled with "clear, beautiful water and [was] a place that nature seems to have designed as a resting place for the weary traveler." Here the company slowed due to the poor health of company chaplain Nathaniel Jones, who was "very weak and sick and feeble."[16] At the same time, Stout was suffering from a toothache so incapacitating that he was forced to ride in the wagon; in desperation, late that night he had the tooth extracted.[17]

After crossing a mountain in heavy snow on November 23, the missionaries overtook a Mormon party led by H. G. Sherwood en route to

San Bernardino, and also met a small party headed by Apostles Lyman and Rich that was bound for Salt Lake City. Continuing their journey, going through the mountains and across the floor of the Mojave Desert began to take its toll on the missionaries as well as the animals, some of which nearly died from drinking brackish, alkaline water. On December 29 both animals and men were refreshed momentarily by a stop at a good watering hole, but as they trudged on Stout declared, "To day I suffered more and was worse worn out and tired than since I have been on my journey."[18]

With more than half of the company out of provisions and the horses failing, they soon reached the summit of the Cajon Pass, a short journey away from the homes of their fellow Saints at San Bernardino. On Friday, December 3, as the company descended the pass, Stout discovered the pleasant southern California climate that defied the calendar. "Since coming out of the Cañnon the weather is very different," he noted, "warm and mellow the wind like the zephyrs of summer, sweet and exhilarating, the face of the country presents the appearance of all in the States, contrasting the green herbage just springing to life, showing that autumn and winter is past. Happy country with no winter."[19] More importantly, upon reaching the settlement, the missionaries felt the comforts of home while resting from the fatigues of their journey.

The settlement at San Bernardino was built on land that was purchased from Mexicans by Charles C. Rich and Amasa Lyman in 1851 for $78,500. "Every one has plenty, while the products of the earth bear a good price in cash," Stout recorded; "nothing appears to hinder the Saints here from soon becoming rich."[20] Upon arrival, he immediately became acquainted with William Stout, who, it was determined, was a distant cousin. For two weeks he and the other missionaries rested, wrote letters and sold wagons, horses, mules, and all else that was not needed for their journey abroad. On December 17 most of the missionaries moved on to San Pedro, where on December 29 they procured passage on the brig *Fremont*, bound for San Francisco for a discounted fare of $17.50 each, less than a third of the normal rate; remaining behind were Elders Stout, Lewis, and Duncan, the three missionaries headed to China, as Hosea searched in vain for his mare.[21]

Stout, like his fellow missionaries, was traveling "without purse or scrip" and had hoped to be able to sell his mare; instead, gratefully he accepted two hundred dollars from his fellow Saints to help finance his journey. On January 3, 1853, the China missionary trio took leave of San Bernardino, traveling through the fledgling town of Los Angeles on their way to San Pedro. On January 9, after a three-day stay in a small brick house with no floor that was "loathsome, lousy and miserable,"[22] they booked cabin passage for fifty-five dollars each and embarked on the

Figure 14.1. Louisa Taylor Stout (1819–1853), second wife of Hosea and mother of eight of his children. Four of her children died in infancy or early childhood.

steamer *Sea Bird*, setting out at about noon in less than favorable weather. "We saw several whales spouting like second hand politicians," Stout wrote, "but we could not get a fair view of them. The rolling sea soon set the passengers to casting up their accounts. I was quite sick before I went on board and before two hours after starting threw my breakfast Jonah like over board having to go to bunk at 4 P.M."[23]

The last communication Stout had received regarding his family was from Horace Clark, who arrived at San Bernardino from Salt Lake City on December 20 with news that Hosea's family was well. Lacking further communication, Stout was unaware that on December 30 his wife Louisa had given birth to a baby son, whom she named Joseph Allen, nor that on January 9, the day the *Sea Bird* embarked from San Pedro, the infant had died. Two days later, as the *Sea Bird* was moored until afternoon in rough seas off the coast near San Luis Obispo, Stout's wife Louisa, seemingly the greatest love of his life, succumbed to erysipelas as a complication of pregnancy and labor, leaving behind three small children. The following afternoon, Brigham Young preached "a comforting sermon" over Louisa's remains, and she was laid to rest with her child.[24] Allen Stout, who didn't expect his brother's return for five years, moved into Hosea's house to take care of his three remaining children and adopted son Henry Allen, though Young soon advised Allen to send them to live with their grandmother, Elizabeth Taylor, which would set the stage for yet another unpleasant episode in Hosea's life.[25]

Totally unaware of the tragedies that had befallen his family, Stout arrived in San Francisco "amid a thousand sail of vessels" on January 13—four days after the previous group of missionaries had arrived aboard the *Fremont*—and set out with the singular objective of raising enough funds to enable the missionaries to make the journey to their various missions.[26] Prior to his arrival, the Elders had raised merely fourteen dollars, but by January 21 donations totaled $6250, mostly due to the generosity of wealthy Mormons John Horner and Quartus S. Sparks, $1000 of which was appropriated for the missionaries bound for China.[27] The following day Stout received his passport from Washington (as did most of the missionaries) and was free to secure passage to China, which turned out to be more difficult that anticipated.[28]

In the midst of making arrangements for the journey, Stout on January 26 took time to write his wife, still unaware of her death. "It is with peculiar feelings that I attempt to address you at this time not having recieved a line from you since I left you," he commenced. Ignorant of the reality he continued, "I must once more commend you and our little ones to the kind providence of our father in heaven whose goodness has not forsaken me nor whose spirit has not been with drawn from me since I left you." Once again demonstrating a specific concern for his adopted son, he wrote, "I want you to remember me to Henry for I have not forgot him. I want him to be a good boy and remember that he has taken upon him to serve the Lord and to shun bad company . . . and when I return I will do him good." After giving assurances that he was filled with faith and the spirit of his mission, he closed, "Kiss all the little ones for me and tell them to remember their pap."[29]

Figure 14.2. Family of Hosea and Louisa Stout.

While in San Francisco, James Lewis received letters from his wife, but by mid-February Stout still had heard nothing from his family or his friends. "Cut off from all communication from home the world seems a blank and I must confess that my anxiety to hear from you is great," he wrote to Louisa on February 20. Noting that the missionaries headed to other countries already had departed, he continued, "This leaves only the China mission here alone, and not only so, but we are lonesome and tired of this scrimpt narrow streeted hotch potch, filthy place. Not wishing to find fault, but it is certainly the most disagreeable place I was ever in, muddy, crowded, planked and broken through the side walks, and the filth eternally sending up a stink offering."[30]

Finally, on February 26 passage was secured for $80 each on the Dutch bark *Jan Van Hoorn*. Prior to departing, on March 1 Hosea at last received two letters from his brother Allen, the latter penned on January 1 and telling of the birth of his son on December 30. Thus as the bark set sail for China on March 9, two months after the deaths of Hosea's son and his wife, the latest intelligence from home was, "Everything is going on as well as could be expected."[31]

The same might be said of the voyage, considering inevitable seasickness of the four cabin passengers (the three missionaries and a Mr. Nash), not to mention the living conditions of sixty Chinese passengers, who were "stowed away in their dens like so many sick pigs."[32] On the open sea, with ample time to meditate, Stout on at least two occasions began to expound in his diary in a prose that was poetic and at times philosophical. On March 12, his first day of the voyage without seasickness, he recorded:

> In the after noon the wind nearley ceased to blow. The ocean became smoothe so that no white caps appeared. Nothing but the smoothe heaving billows came sleepily and lazily along, tilting and rocking the vessel flapping her sails, sporting at our anxiety to go ahead.
>
> How beautiful is the calm Ocean now, like hills and dales ever rising, ever disappearing. Her ever changing heaving bosom, like the never ceasing hopes and fears of the human heart. Sporting at all our attempt to allay them. About sun set the wind ceased and the vessel stopped while we had patiently to contemplate her soft repose.[33]

A similar entry on April 23, the forty-fifth day of the voyage, exposed more clearly his inner feelings:

> This morning the Ocean sleeps. The rolling swells have disappeared and nought but smiling eddies dimple over the wide expanse as though all nature was at rest. The broad blue ocean and the blue vault of heaven face each other in majestic silence while our vessel sleeps. With a warm south breeze playing just perceptibly among her sails, she rests like the smiling infant in her sleeping mother's arms.
>
> Now while nature sleeps let me reflect, let me contemplate the past and think on the future. Now my wife and my little ones, dance playfully before my imagination. Now the scenes of home reveal themselves.
>
> Now the saints in peaceful Utah roll by, busy in their different avocations. Now their fervent prayers ascend on high in my behalf. The kingdom of God rolls to all nations. Millions shout hosanna to hear the glad tidings, and they gather to

geather to that land which is my home, as doves to their windows, while the wicked howl and prepare themselves for the doom which awaits them.[34]

Three days later, more than a dozen Chinese junks were spotted, indicating that the *Jan van Hoorn's* destination was close at hand. Hong Kong, like most non-European foreign destinations for Mormon missionaries in 1853, was a part of the British Empire, though its path to becoming such was unique. In the nineteenth century, China was the main supplier of tea to the British and by 1830 annual imports of Chinese tea into Britain amounted to thirty million pounds, an average of two pounds for every citizen. The massive importation of tea, however, created an immense trade deficit that the Chinese were not anxious to equalize as they shunned importation of European products. Eventually the British found one commodity greatly desired by the Chinese in opium, a nearly inexhaustible supply of which was available from the poppy fields of India.

In the late 1830s, to curb the damage caused by opium on their population, Chinese officials confiscated and destroyed thousands of chests of opium stored in the English merchants' warehouses in Canton. Because of these events on the mainland, Britain required an offshore base of operations under British control and Hong Kong, then a sleepy fishing village whose main export was salt, was an ideal candidate. Under the directives put forth by Queen Victoria, Britain sent a naval expeditionary squadron to China; in 1839, Lord Palmerston, the British Foreign Secretary, initiated what came to be known as the First Opium War in order to obtain full compensation for the destroyed opium. Three years later the British were victorious, and, as a result, on June 26, 1843, the Chinese opened their five ports to foreign merchants and formally ceded Hong Kong to the British.[35]

When the British union flag first was raised over Possession Point on January 26 1841, the population of Hong Kong island was about 7,450, mostly fishermen and charcoal burners; by 1851 the number reached about 33,000 and quickly expanded as large numbers of Chinese emigrated from the mainland due to the Taiping Rebellion, a widespread civil war in southern China that lasted from 1850 to 1864. The overwhelming majority of Chinese and Europeans who came to Hong Kong in those years were single men, including a large British military contingent. In 1845 the census showed only twenty-five families but twenty-six brothels.[36] The vast majority of the women were prostitutes, and by the 1850s Hong Kong was known as a center for prostitution and venereal disease.[37] As the *Jan van Hoorn* arrived in Hong Kong's harbor on April 27, 1853, the deck of the bark immediately was covered with Chinese men seeking employment, women soliciting "washing patronage" and other women seeking "to bargain off their *professional* sex to the crew and all whom it concerned and the lowest possible rates, which seemed on board to range at about one dollar each," though Stout was informed by those who knew from experience that the services actually "could be procured for from ten to twenty cents."[38]

Shortly before leaving San Francisco, Stout and Chapman Duncan had visited a former Presbyterian missionary to China who discouraged the Mormons from going on their mission without means of support, not believing that trusting in the Lord would be sufficient.[39] He turned out to be correct, though the Elders were buoyed by their faith, as Stout related in a letter to Brigham Young:

> To our astonishment we found it as costly living here [Hong Kong] as in San Francisco. We are totally without means of support by labor, a prospect truly gloomy, causing a complete breakdown of our morale had we not evidence within us that we were sent of God to establish the gospel here.[40]

Once on land, the most immediate concern for the missionaries was finding a place to stay in the expensive city on their extremely limited budget. "We found that unless a man has wherewith to pay his way at quite a high price he could have the exquisite pleasure of starving. This we were told in plain and positive language," wrote James Lewis. "Our only chance was to find some liberal-minded person who cared little for popularity."[41]

A ship chandler name Emeny offered temporary quarters, but after four days of searching for lodging, discouragement began to set in as the trio found nothing for less than thirty dollars each per month. Fortunately, a Mr. Duddell was sympathetic to the nature of their mission ("he said he would give all sects a fair chance") and offered "a suit of rooms gratis for at least some three months" at the Canton Bazaar.[42] The rooms, into which the trio moved on May 5, were situated in the third story of "an old decayed mansion, a portion of which had fallen down," but the missionaries gratefully accepted their only offer and acknowledged the hand of the Lord in opening a way to find a home.[43] Having heard that foreigners "will be cheated in both weight and measure and shaved in your change" when purchasing in the markets, the missionaries immediately hired a Chinese servant for $6.50 a month to cook, clean, and shop for them.

Sadly, making favorable living arrangements was the peak of success for Stout and his companions in Hong Kong, though all seemed to start well enough. On the evening of May 6, after spending most of the day indoors due to oppressive heat and humidity, the Elders met with five soldiers—Methodists who worshipped each night in a tower room of the Bazaar—and felt their message was well received, particularly since one of the soldiers closed the meeting with a prayer thanking God that the Mormons "had been sent by his Holly [sic] spirit to visit this dark and benighted land. To comfort those who mourn, and bring many to the knowledge of the truth." Before parting they arranged to have another meeting, on Sunday, May 8, to which they would invite their friends while the missionaries also "would induce as many as we could to come and hear for themselves . . . that this may be an effectual opening to plant the standard of gospel truth in this place."[44]

Had the Elders' vision not been clouded by their missionary zeal they might have perceived the Sunday meeting, at which there were but six soldiers and one citizen, as a indication of the lack of missionary success they would encounter in Hong Kong. Chapman Duncan preached and, according to Stout, "quite boldly declared our principals, and by the way, gave the Sects a tolerabley Severe turn. Whether or not our Methodist friends could see that their religion was declared false, I do not know, but when one of them dismissed meeting, he prayed most fervently for our success, telling the Lord we had been guided by his Spirit here to lead the heathen into gospel light."[45] The following day two of the soldiers dropped by "to reason on the Scriptures," but though the "Methodist brethren" remained friendly, they showed no interest in converting.

Spreading the gospel and gaining converts were the reasons Stout and his companions went to Hong Kong, so the challenge immediately became when, where, and to whom to preach, much of which was governed by the weather. Hong Kong's climate is sub-tropical, tending toward temperate for nearly half the year, but from May to August it is hot and humid with frequent showers and thunderstorms, particularly during the mornings. On May 11 Stout noted, "Trying to day to find some one that I can preach to when it is cool enough to be out."[46] According to James Lewis, the "weather was intensely hot. In the middle of the day, the streets were deserted. The soldiers were not allowed out of barracks, only from 5 to 8 o'clock p.m."[47] Therefore, it was determined that meetings would be held in the evening, and to get the word out, on Friday, May 13, Stout visited the acting editor of the *China Mail*, who was extremely cordial and supportive and suggested that holding meetings on the "green" (the parade ground) would offer the greatest opportunity for large attendance; he further agreed to publish notice of the meetings and to attend them.[48]

The first meeting had to be cancelled due to rain, but, after notices were put in two different papers, a meeting was held as scheduled on Wednesday, May 18. "There were about 100 citizens and as many soldiers present," Stout recorded. "Elder Lewis spoke on the first principals of the gospel, showing also the difference between our religion and the sects of the day. He delivered a powerful discourse, handling the sects quite unceremoniously. The congregation paid good attention and after meeting desired to hear more. We accordingly appointed next Friday at 5 p. m. for another lecture." That meeting was attended by about thirty citizens and two hundred soldiers who "paid good attention and made some inquiries" following the meeting. "There was considerable interest which seemed to be manifested on the occasion," Stout recorded, "and we feel that the ice of superstition is broken and a good work will follow."[49] The following day, he was informed that four or five newspaper editors were present at the meeting, felt encouraged that they paid good attention and expected good publicity to follow. He was wrong.

On Saturday, May 21, the morning after the aforementioned meeting, Stout went to see Andrew Scott Dixson, Secretary of the Victoria Library and Reading room, essentially Hong Kong's first library.[50] Dixson showed him the morning edition of *Friend of China*, which contained three distinctly anti-Mormon articles, two of which railed against the Mormon doctrine of plural marriage, known simply to the outside world as polygamy. Mocking quotes from Orson Pratt's publication *The Seer,* one article—originally printed in newspapers across the United States, including the widely read *New York Weekly Herald* and the religious paper *Advocate and Register*—was particularly damning. Following numerous sarcastic comments the author of the article concluded:

> Such are the abominations of Mormonism, through the confessions of their delegated apostle to Washington. We trust that the government will not much longer tolerate these things. They are in open defiance of the laws and social institutions of the whole country—they are an outrage upon common decency—a monstrous outrage upon woman's rights to a husband of her own—and ought to be abolished before they lead to the disasters of civil war. We trust that General [Franklin D.] Pierce will not overlook the Mormons. They must conform to the laws. It is time they were taken in hand.[51]

After reading the articles, Stout noted, "All these taken together with our exertions on the parade ground, we hope may stir some one at least to become interested to investigate our religion."[52] Once again he was wrong. That evening (May 21) he and Chapman Duncan were guests of Andrew Dixson at a theatrical performance at which they encountered a few Persians who had attended their previous lecture and told their fellow countrymen in attendance that Stout and Duncan were the men who believed in having more than one wife. "We never had mentioned the subject," Stout noted, "but it has been humbugged to day through this city in consequence of what came out in the papers."[53] All interest seemed to dwell on the subject of polygamy, not in investigating the religion as he had hoped.

Stout was not alone in underestimating the negative reaction to polygamy. The privilege of plural marriage was extended to a much broader segment of the Mormon community in Utah than at Nauvoo, but the practice for the first several years was not announced to the outside world, though Brigham Young declared to the Utah Territorial Legislature on February 4, 1851, "I have more wives than one. I have many and I am not ashamed to have it known."[54] Finally, on August 29, 1852, after the practice was openly acknowledged in a General Conference address by Apostle Orson Pratt, Brigham Young spoke on the doctrine and asserted, "It will sail over, and ride triumphantly above all the prejudice and priest-craft of the day; it will be fostered and believed in by the more intelligent portions of the world, as one of the best doctrines ever proclaimed to any people."[55]

Young had judged incorrectly, and fuel was added to the fire when Orson Pratt made his way to Washington, DC, to publish *The Seer*, a periodical defending polygamy. Utah's appointed representative in Congress, John M. Bernhisel, stated two weeks before Pratt's sermon in the Tabernacle, "so far as considering us a religious people, very many here and elsewhere, regard us among the most immoral and licentious beings on the face of the globe" and feared that the issue of polygamy would result in increased negativity toward the church.[56] Unfortunately for the Saints, Bernhisel had correctly judged the situation, and Pratt's publication unleashed a wave of anti-polygamy and anti-Mormon sentiment that tracked across the nation and into foreign countries.

The timing could not have been worse for Stout and his missionary companions, as pejorative newspaper columns were copied from one publication to another and finally made it to Hong Kong in May 1853, just as the Elders were beginning to feel positive about their proselytizing prospects. On May 24, three days following the publication of the three anti-polygamy/anti-Mormon articles in the *Friend of China*, Stout visited William F. Bevan, the editor of the *Hong Kong Register* and found him to be very friendly, but a week later, on Thursday, May 31, he had to be surprised by what appeared in Bevan's newspaper:

> This morning's No of the "Hongkong register" has a long article showing the necessity of having the "Mormonites"

indicted for Blasphemy, and set to "picking oakum and kept on bread and water" but the Editor replies that his prescriptions "savours too much of the dark ages and days of thumbkings" and recommends for the people to let us alone. I confess I admire the Editor's judgement. When the Devil begins to rage and howl, it surely betokens that the Lord has a work to do. Therefore we feel encouraged in opposition.[57]

Once again Stout had misread the state of affairs. At 5:00 PM that day the Elders held a meeting at the parade ground that was attended by about twenty citizens and thirty soldiers, but three meetings held the following week attracted a total of one individual. The damaging publicity, particularly regarding polygamy, had negated any proselytizing opportunities the missionaries might have had and, facing reality, on June 9 they gave up and secured cabin passage on the *Rose of Sharon*, a magnificent English square rigger set to depart for San Francisco in about two weeks. Their mission, despite solid efforts and good intentions, was a complete failure, and they were well aware of some of the major reasons for the lack of success:

> We have decided that our labours in this place be discontinued With all the faith and prayer that we were master of, we have dilligently taught both publickly and privately every one to whom we could in any way obtain access, the truths of the gospel and continued our labors as long as we could obtain audience from even one individual, and we find that no one will give heed to what we say, neither does any one manifest any opposition or interest but treats us with the utmost civility, conversing freely on all subjects except the pure principals of the gospel When we approach that they have universally in the most polite possible manner declined by saying that they did not wish to hear any thing on that subject for they are willing to extend the mantle of charity over all Christian believers and ourselves among the rest, not doubting but we were good men and all would be right with all. And this it is this day we do not know of one person in this place to whome we can bear testimony of the things of god or warn to flee the wrath to come. And as to our staying here to learn the chinese language without one friend or one possible recourse to us appears totally impractable and Paul-like we can truly say that the spirit speaketh expressly, that we preach the gospel no more in Asia for the present. This being the only port which now is safe, for

foreigners, because of the rebelion in china we have no place to fall back on but California, whither we have concluded to sail the first opportunity and there await the orders of the First Presidency, and the dictates of the Holy Spirit to yet learn by what means the Lord will open, to introduce the gospel successfully in this benighted land.[58]

It is clear that the missionaries were ill prepared for what they would encounter in Asia. As was later reported in a letter from the missionaries to Brigham Young, Hong Kong was a British colony and thus they expected to find many English speakers, but by their count the English speaking population was comprised mostly of about a thousand British Empire soldiers (generally from Ireland and Scotland) and only about 250 European citizens—"the would-be *nabobs* of the world, merchants, officers of the civil governments, no common class which are found in English colonies in other parts of the world"—who they found to be almost unapproachable.

The Mormon Elders promptly realized that learning Chinese would not be an option, ecclesiastical assurances to the contrary notwithstanding: before departing on his mission, Stout was given a blessing by Apostle Wilford Woodruff that stated, "Go thy way trusting in the Lord . . . and the Lord shall give thee power to obtain a knowledge of their language so as to have access to them";[59] and on November 7, 1852, Apostle George A. Smith told the assembled missionaries who were on their way to Asia and the Pacific, "Every people to whom they preach, their words shall tingle in their ears, every language they shall engage to learn, they shall learn it, and shall learn it quicker than any one who has learned it hitherto."[60] The promises, however, were no match for the Chinese language, which was far too difficult to learn quickly by individual study, and private teachers were expensive, costing a minimum of twenty dollars a month, and were under the control of missionaries of other religions. Therefore the only Chinese people visited by the missionaries were the few who could speak English. "They are generally in the employ of the missionaries or the government and command high wages," the Elders reported. "They told us they had no time to *talka* religion."[61]

The missionaries' work also was hindered by their arrival in Hong Kong in a season of high humidity, stifling temperatures, and heavy rains. "The heat of the atmosphere was very oppressive," wrote James Lewis, "being reduced in bad health, owing to change of diet, the manner of preparing it and so forth, our spirits were becoming depressed and not perceiving a cheering ray of hope in all our labors." And, above all, they had the misfortune to be missionaries in Hong Kong at the time derisive articles about polygamy and Mormonism made their way across the Pacific and were copied by local newspapers. As Lewis noted following their publication, "Our congregations in the mean time were reduced to a cipher—no one attending."[62]

After deciding to discontinue their labors in China, the three missionaries procured provisions (bread, sugar, potatoes, eggs, rice, etc.) for the voyage and paid parting visits to Andrew Dixson and William Bevan. On Saturday, June 18, they purchased passage for fifty-five dollars each, and on June 22 they set sail on the *Rose of Sharon*, on board with two cabin passengers, two doctors, two cooks, thirty-seven Chinese men, and forty-nine Chinese women who were destined to be prostitutes in California.[63]

Over the first several days of the voyage the breeze changed capriciously, both in direction and intensity, and on July 2, after the ship tacked north and then south without ultimately making progress, Stout displayed a biting sense of humor in describing a "Fowl-tastrophe" perpetuated by the captain:

> While Sailing thus, to break the monotony, kill dull care, and dispel "ennui" the captain with *malice prepense* and without the fear of God before [a fore thought] his eyes, but instigated &c had an innocent goose hung by the hind legs and hoisted to the main top yard, when he took a gun in his hands and willfully, deliberately, pointing in the direction of the said goose, with the said gun, pulled trigger causing the fire to ignite &c causing instant death to the said goose &c against the peace and dignaty of the whole aquatic tribe &c.[64]

To relieve his own monotony, particularly while the ship sat in the doldrums, Stout killed time by "deeply pouring over novels."[65] On July 26, after a number of relatively calm days, he recorded:

> Course and wind same only the ship sometimes bears near south. The obstinate wind keeping us off our course so long we are growing some what impatient in so much that a considerable congregation of the Chinese Courtesan ladies assembled on deck and solemnly invoked or as they say Chin Josh to change the wind, by burning josh sticks and perforating and casting josh paper to the wind, while one of them sat on the Deck, resting her face on her knees, fidgeting and twitching seemed to act as medium while the others were anxiously enquiring in an under tone of her the news from joshs.

which was as near as I could learn, that the wind would change favorably in two days and we would arive at California in two weeks.[66]

Two weeks actually underestimated by half the time it would take to reach San Francisco. Even so, the ship made relatively good progress considering that on August 12 they overtook and promptly left "far astern" the ship *John N. Gosler*, which left Hong Kong on May 27, nearly four weeks prior to their own departure.[67] Finally, on August 23, the sixty-second day of a voyage that lasted longer than their stay in Hong Kong (fifty-six days), they sailed into San Francisco Bay. With great anticipation, Stout visited some local Saints to see if they had reports of his family, but the substantial tragedies he had previously experienced did not measure up to the shocking news that awaited him:

> Earley this morning I went ashore, leaving Brs Lewis and Duncan on Board, and went to visit the Saints in this place finding them all well and rejoiced to see our return but the joy and satisfaction which I expected to be a happy partaker of in their society was only heighten to be overcast in sorrow and deep mourning. Too happy in the anticipation of at last hearing from my wife and children, the last news from whom had left my wife in such critical circumstances had only increased my anxiety to hear how she was now. But my anxiety and better hopes was now doomed to be blasted by the inconsoleable intelligence of her death and the death of her child.
>
> Baffled and disappointed in our hopes and wishes relative to our mission and so soon return I gladly looked forward for consolation in the intelligence from home and a word of comfort from her who was always so ready to console me in the hour of deep distress by proving her self the good angel to administer the balm to the disconsolate
>
> Why attempt to pen grief, disappointment and sorrow totally unutterable; why write the anguish which rends the heart? When the companion of our toils, the partaker of our sorrows, grief, anguish, and despondencies of this mortal life is so rudely torn from our bosom, carrying her last tender offspring with her, while we are absent and in blissful ignorance, of the ravages of the destroyer why should we attempt to depict the feeling which such sad news brings to the heart as this morning beclouds my hopes when I learned that Louisa was no more . . .

> Bereft of her and not knowing how or where my children are with no one who can appreciate my feeling now for who can sympathise with me now only the disconsolate, let me not forget from whence comfort and consolation comes.[68]

Stout, understandably, was fixated on Louisa's death, and two days after his arrival in San Francisco, while engaging in a "social chat" with a large party of Saints, he joined in an "experiment of *Spirit Rappings*," an alleged form of communication with spirits of the dead that began in Hydesville, New York, when in March 1848 mysterious knockings were heard nightly upon the floor of one of the bedrooms in the home of John D. Fox.[69] Two of Fox's daughters made playful efforts to communicate with spirits of the dead using rapping noises and claimed to have succeeded, giving birth to Spiritualism, a movement that spread rapidly across the country.[70] In an unsuccessful attempt to communicate with his late wife Louisa, Stout participated in the spirit rapping, though as a novice he had no idea what was going on and afterwards declared it to be "a negative medium."[71]

Together with Elders Lewis and Duncan it was decided that Stout would return to Salt Lake City to report on their mission to China, and he quickly made arrangements to sail on August 30 to San Pedro on the *Brig Fremont*—the same vessel that carried his fellow missionaries on the reverse voyage the previous winter. "I feel very lonesome now I have parted with the companions whom I have been so closely associated with so long and under such peculiar circumstances," he recorded.[72] Though anxious to go home, after arriving at San Bernardino he discovered that his return trip to Salt Lake City was uncertain due to a major Indian uprising.

Relations between the Ute Indians and the Mormons already were strained when, on July 17, 1853, a Ute man and his wife were trading in Utah Valley near Springville at the home of James Ivie and began to quarrel. Ivie intervened in the dispute and in the ensuing skirmish whacked the warrior on the head with the barrel of a rifle, cracking his skull with a single blow. Though the Indian died a few days later, the incident may have escaped wide notice had not the man been a relative of Walkara (also known as Walker), chief of the Utes, but under the circumstances the death was enough to detonate hostilities that became known as the "Walker War."[73]

The Indians took immediate retribution by killing a settler, Alexander Keel, and the conflict quickly spread and posed enough danger that a "Spanish wall," twelve feet high and six miles in length, was built around Salt Lake City.[74] With that in mind, it was deemed unsafe for a small company to make the journey from San Bernardino, and at a meeting on September 19 only fourteen agreed to join the company. "The prospects for going to the Valley seem dull," he noted. "Such is the unceartinty and dubious situation of the Indians that those who wish to go do not know what to depend upon and there is a probability of the entire party failing to go."[75]

By mid-October Stout still was languishing in San Bernardino and, on the anniversary of his leaving home to go to China, he couldn't help dwelling on his wife:

> To day completes one year since I left home where I was surrounded by all the endearing ties of an affectionate wife, whose ashes now lies mouldering in the dust and my children lonely orphans, my home, with all its kindred ties, no more. I feel a disconsolate blank, my tears dries in their fountain and I groan without a response for only those in like affliction can appreciate the heart felt anguish that burns in his bosom who has had, torn from him the dearest object of his heart the solace of all his cares, the repository of (his [crossed out]) all his joy and sorrow, another self, the wife of his bosom. True I am surrounded by friends who care for me but Home, and family only can make happiness in this world.[76]

After nearly two months at San Bernardino, Stout joined twelve men (including James Lewis, who had arrived from San Francisco the previous week) to make the trip to Salt Lake City, despite the group's small size. After departing on November 3, on the evening of the third day the company was organized by choosing Stout to serve as their captain. The journey presented, in reverse order, all hardships that were encountered on the original trip from Salt Lake to San Bernardino with one exception: on November 21, while camped at Mountain Springs between the Rio Virgin and the Santa Clara River, Hiram Curtis, a camp member, "was shot by an Indian in the breast, with an arrow, from the mountain side, but fortunately was not injured, the arrow being nearly spent."[77]

At long last, on December 8, Stout arrived home "or what more properly might be said where once was my home," since squatters—a family from England—had taken up residence in his house. Once again he became totally preoccupied with his sad state brought about by the premature death of his wife:

> Here, not 14 months since was concentrated all my earthly happiness. Here, the confiding Louisa, the dearest object of

my heart, the solace in all my troubles and my innocent prattling children, was left, in the most perfect enjoyment of earthly bliss. To them I fled as a refuge from trouble and disappointment and how often I have rejoiced that I was thus blessed with that most essential ingredient for man's comfort, a true, faithful and confiding wife, and obedient lovely children There were here then, Here then was my own ocean of affection and love I left them by the command of the Lord to preach the gospel in foreign lands and returned but not to them.

Louisa was no more, the source of my happiness was beneath the cold sod while the very geniuse of desolation and loneliness seemed to brood over the scenes of by gone happiness.

What did I find? Even my brother had removed into the country and not the first vistage of former associations moved on the desolate place.

A family of English saints, total stranger to me resided here and could give no account of neither family or friends.

I gazed upon the sad wreck of all my hopes in silence while my heart sank within me and those around could not refrain from mingling their tears with mine for a few moments when we all hastily with drew from a place so full of sad reccollections as my HOME.[77]

The following day Hosea was taken by his brother Allen to visit his children, who had been well taken care of by his mother-in-law, Elizabeth Taylor. "If grief had dried up the fountain of my tears when I came home how can I attempt to describe my emotions when I embraced those three dear pledges which Louisa had left me of her love and fidelity," he wrote.[79] But though he resolved to "indulge no more in the sad thoughts which burn my brain," he did exactly that when he visited Louisa's grave for the first time:

This morning early I visited Louisa grave, by the side of which rests my son who I never saw and my brother's [son] Charles Heber. Here I must not indulge my feelings in attempting to describe them How calmly, sadly, happily, seemed to rest her ashes. How quiet seemed that heart which once beat for me so warmly Her smiling countenance, but all now rests in death's embrace while I remain as a blank on earth, a monument of disappointed hopes.

> I have followed three wives to their graves and beheld the (silent [crossed out]) earth enclose seven of my own children yet I had hopes of better days but now hope vanished and I must give myself up to inconsolable sorrow[80]

Stout was living alone, having left his children in the care of his mother-in-law ("Mother Taylor"), and for good reason: though clearly a leader of men, left to his own devices in maintaining a household he was totally helpless. On December 30, after the squatters had vacated, he stayed alone in his "new house as the first lesson to my meditated Bachelorship, which leaves any thing but a favorable impression," and he was reminded of the scripture, "it is not good for a man to be alone."[81] His ineptness as a homemaker was amply demonstrated the following day:

> Solatary and alone I arose this morning and commenced the solemn cerimony of getting up my breakfast. This to me was a serious undertaking but however I was relieved for my sister came and finished the job a thing which I was wholy incompetent to do for myself[82]

In desperation, within nine days Stout married Aseneth Harmon Gheen, the widow of William Gheen, a former member of the Nauvoo Legion in Illinois who died the previous year while prospecting for gold on Mormon Island in the Sacramento River.[83] Aseneth entered the marriage with an eleven-year-old daughter, having lost two other children. "This evening about dark a change took place in my fortune which will most likely effect my future life," he presciently wrote of the wedding, though the effect turned out to be quite the opposite of that which he desired and expected.[84]

Stout hoped and anticipated that Aseneth would be a "new mother" to his children, though in essence that amounted to little more than being a nanny. Things seemed to go well at first meeting of Aseneth and Hosea's children on January 15, but the honeymoon was short-lived: on March 18 Aseneth moved back to her previous house with his daughter and the marriage was essentially over. Meanwhile, Hosea's sister Anna came to take care of his children while he prepared to send them to their grandmother Taylor. "Thus almost entirely disbanding my family again," he wrote without the melodrama of previous journal entries. "What next I know not, except that total uncertainty alone lies in the future."[85]

Making arrangements for his children took on a heightened sense of urgency since Stout had just been called to go on a short mission to the Green River in what later would become the state of Wyoming. On March 21 Stout's brother-in-law Joseph Taylor took the children to Mother Taylor's and on March 30 Stout visited and found his children to be well.[86] The following day, however, his world collapsed once again:

> How long affliction, Bad luck, and trouble is to attend I do not know
>
> Just being on the eve of going to green River I came here to see my children for the last time before starting but only found that fickle fortune was yet tampering with me after I vainly supposed I had made permenently arraingements for this summer at least, Mother Taylor has concluded not to take care of my children. My wife not willing too either. The President wants the use of my house this season and here I am left thus unexpectedly disappointed in all my previous arraingements. My children thrown on my hands without a mother's care, while I am totally unprepared to take care of them Without money or provisions for them or even enough to take with me to Green River. What next I know not neither do I know what to do.
>
> I settled with Mother Taylor for the time she had my children which in all is seven months or 210 days She charged me seven dollars per week or one dollar per day 210 dollars. For which I paid her by selling my farm to her for 180 dollars and paid the rest part in cash and the residue in wheat from last year's crop which she already had used.
>
> It is impossible for me to describe my feelings when contemplating the sad dilemma I am placed in at this time when dark clouds of more misfortune and sorrow hang heavily over my head yet. and I can not see one bright ray of future happiness (in the future [crossed out]) not possibly devine when prosperity will smile on me and my little ones or when I can peacibly enjoy their society without fore seeing coming disappointment and trouble.
>
> Hope on Hope ever is a good adage and perhaps it would be well for me to practice on it now.[87]

Mother Taylor's sudden refusal to care for her grandchildren, along with her demand of a ransom for their return, raises a suspicion that Stout in some way was a contributor to his "affliction, Bad luck and trouble," though only his side of the story has been preserved. A week later, Allen Taylor brought the children home, which had to present a hardship as Stout was occupied with legal business while preparing to leave for the Green River mission. Then, on April 28, Aseneth filed a Bill for Divorce in the probate court. Though Stout was present for the hearing, at which "it was ordered and decreed by the court that that the bonds of matrimony existing between the said Asenath Stout and Hosea Stout be dissolved,"[88] he clearly was emotionally uninvolved, and his journal entry of the event stated simply, "Attended probate Court E. Smith Judge."[89]

In three days he would depart for the Green River, for which he "was as yet totally unprepared," though he had more than a month to get his affairs in order. At the last moment, on the day of his departure, everything came together as he was able to obtain sixty pounds of flour to provide his family with the "Staff of life" until his anticipated return on July 1. His sister Anna, who in February 1850 had obtained a divorce from her husband Benjamin Jones,[90] once again came to his rescue by taking care of his small children while adopted son Henry Allen accompanied Stout. For the time being all was well and for once, mercifully, another tragedy was *not* just around the corner.

Notes

1. *Journal of Discourses*, February 24, 1856, 3:239.
2. Letter from recommendation from Brigham Young for Hosea Stout, October 1, 1852, Hosea Stout Papers, Utah State Historical Society.
3. *Journal History*, October 17, 1852.
4. Hyde, "Journal," October 24, 1852, in *Journal History*. The company also included a single man and a couple with one child—all non-Mormons—headed for the gold fields of California, as well as one other man.
5. Lyman, *The Overland Journey from Utah to California*, 1.
6. Brooks, *Mormon Frontier*, October 27, 1852, 458.
7. Ibid., October 28, 1852, 458.
8. Ibid., November 4, 1852, 459.
9. Letter from Hosea Stout to Brigham Young, *Deseret News*, November 7, 1852.
10. Letter from Hosea Stout to his wife, Louisa Stout, November 3, 1852, Church History Library.
11. Brooks, *Mormon Frontier*, November 7, 1852, 460.
12. Ibid., November 8, 1852, 460.
13. Letter from Hosea Stout to his wife, November 3, 1852.
14. Brooks, *Mormon Frontier*, November 16, 1852, 461.
15. Ibid., November 17, 1852, 461.
16. Hyde "Journal," November 18, 1852, in *Journal History*.
17. Brooks, *Mormon Frontier*, November 20, 1852, 462.
18. Ibid., November 29 – December 1, 1852, 463–64.
19. Ibid., December 3, 1852, 464.
20. Ibid.
21. Ibid., December 17–29, 1852, 465–66.

22. Ibid., January 6–9, 1853, 467.
23. Hosea Stout supplemental journal, Hosea Stout papers, 1832–1875, Church History Library. Stout wrote this daily account of January 3–28, 1853, that was more detailed than his regular diary and sent it to his wife.
24. *Journal History*, January 12, 1853.
25. Stout, "Journal."
26. Hosea Stout supplemental journal, January 13, 1853.
27. Brooks, "The Life of Amos Milton Musser," Master's thesis, Brigham Young University, 33.
28. Brooks, *Mormon Frontier*, January 21–22, 1853, 469.
29. Letter from Hosea Stout to his wife Louisa, January 26, 1853, Church History Library. According to his diary the letter was written on January 26, though the letter was misdated January 28, 1852.
30. Letter from Hosea Stout to his wife Louisa, February 20, 1853, Church History Library.
31. Brooks, *Mormon Frontier*, March 1, 1853, 472.
32. Ibid., March 9–10, 1853, 472–73.
33. Ibid., March 12, 1853, 473.
34. Ibid., April 23, 1853, 475.
35. A thorough discussion of this segment of Hong Kong's history is found in Frank Welsh, *A History of Hong Kong*, 42–120.
36. Welsh, *Hong Kong*, 164.
37. Carroll, *A Concise History of Hong Kong*, 56. According to the 1876 census, 5/6 of the almost 25,000 Chinese women in Hong Kong were prostitutes.
38. Brooks, *Mormon Frontier*, April 27, 1853, 476.
39. Ibid., March 3, 1853, 472.
40. Letter from Hosea Stout to Brigham Young, May 16, 1853, in Wayne Stout, *Hosea Stout: Utah's Pioneer Statesman*, 170–73.
41. *Journal History*, December 12, 1854, Letter from James Lewis to *Deseret News*.
42. Brooks, *Mormon Frontier*, 177; Nissim, *Land Administration and Practice in Hong Kong*, 12. The precursor of Hong Kong's central market was the Canton Bazaar, established in 1842 on Queen's Road Central between Cochrane Street and Graham Street. In 1843 the government ordered the Chinese to move to Tai Ping Shan Area and the Canton Bazaar, which was also known as the Middle Bazaar, became a European residential area.

   Mr. Duddell (spelled Dudell in Stout's diary), who gave free rooms to the missionaries, very likely was George Duddell, a land speculator who was notorious in early 1850s Hong Kong for charging excessive rents. A special Land Committee was set up in 1850 in Hong Kong and all who felt they were paying excessive rents were asked to bring their cases before the committee; half the amount of land involved belonged to Duddell.
43. *Journal History*, December 12, 1854, Letter from James Lewis to *Deseret News*; Brooks, *Mormon Frontier*, May 5, 1853, 477
44. Brooks, *Mormon Frontier*, May 6, 1853, 478.
45. Ibid., May 8, 1853, 478.
46. Ibid., May 11, 1853, 478.
47. *Journal History*, December 12, 1854.

48. Brooks, *Mormon Frontier*, May 13, 1853, 479.
49. Ibid., May 18, 1853, 479.
50. "Hong Kong's First," http://hongkongsfirst.blogspot.com/2010_09_10_archive.html. Dixson was Secretary of the Library in 1852–1853 and in 1859 purchased the *China Mail* newspaper.
51. *New York Weekly Herald*, February 5, 1853. General Pierce was President Franklin D. Pierce, who rose to the rank of brigadier general in the Mexican-American War.
52. Brooks, *Mormon Frontier*, May 21, 1853, 480.
53. Ibid.
54. Woodruff, "Journal," February 4, 1851, Church History Library.
55. *Deseret News*, September 14, 1852.
56. Van Wagoner, *Mormon Polygamy*, 82–84.
57. Brooks, *Mormon Frontier*, May 24 and 31, 1853, 480–81.
58. Ibid., June 9, 1853, 482–83.
59. Ibid., October 16, 1852, 454.
60. Ibid., November 7, 1852, 460.
61. *Deseret News*, December 22, 1853; letter from Hosea Stout, James Lewis, and Chapman Duncan to Brigham Young of August 27, 1853. The content and style of the letter are very similar to later letters written by James Lewis, and since Stout was indisposed at the time the letter was written, Lewis seems to be the author.
62. *Journal History*, December 12, 1854, Letter from James Lewis to the *Deseret News*.
63. Brooks, *Mormon Frontier*, June 11–22, 1853, 483–84.
64. Ibid., July 2, 1853, 485. *Malice prepense* is a legal term meaning premeditated or arranged in advance.
65. Ibid., July 6.
66. Ibid., July 11–22, 1853, 487.
67. Ibid., August 12, 1853, 287.
68. Ibid., August 23, 1853, 488–89.
69. Ibid., August 24–25, 1853, 489.
70. It was first mentioned in the church owned *Deseret News* in the edition of February 22, 1851.
71. Ibid., August 25, 1853, 489.
72. Ibid., August 30, 1853, 490.
73. Andrew Jenson, *Encyclopedic History of the Church of Jesus Christ of Latter-day Saints*, 852.
74. Letter from Brigham Young to Hosea Stout, September 30, 1853, *Selected Collections from the Archives of the Church of Jesus Christ of Latter-day Saints*.
75. Brooks, *Mormon Frontier*, September 19 and 30, 1853, 491–92.
76. Ibid., October 20, 1853, 493
77. Ibid., November 21, 1853, 496.
78. Ibid., December 8, 1853, 498.
79. Ibid., December 9, 1853, 499.
80. Ibid., December 14, 1853, 499.
81. Ibid., December 30, 1853, 500.
82. Ibid., December 31, 1853, 500.

83. Youngberg, *Conquerors of the West: Stalwart Mormon Pioneers*, 860. Aseneth Harmon was born November 12, 1823, in Indianapolis, Indiana, a daughter of Henry Harmon and Agnes Green, and died in Pleasant Grove, Utah on June 20, 1899. William Gheen was born on February 27, 1812, in West Goshen, Pennsylvania and died in California on August 19, 1852.
84. Brooks, *Mormon Frontier*, January 9, 1854, 504.
85. Ibid., March 18, 1854, 509.
86. Ibid., March 21 and 30, 1854, 509–10.
87. Ibid., March 31, 1854, 510–11.
88. Salt Lake County Probate Court Record, April 28, 1854, in Hosea Stout Papers, Brigham Young University Special Collections.
89. Brooks, *Mormon Frontier*, April 28, 1854, 513.
90. Ibid., February 7, 1850, 362.

15
Lawyer and Legislator

Legendary mountain man Jim Bridger and his partner Louis Vasquez constructed Fort Bridger on Black's Fork of the Green River in 1843 in present-day Wyoming as a way station and trading post for emigrants traveling westward on the Oregon-California Trail. In 1847 as the first Mormon pioneers stopped there, Brigham Young discussed the merits of settling in the Salt Lake Valley only to find Bridger skeptical that even corn would grow there. Subsequent Mormon pioneers rested at Fort Bridger while on their way to Salt Lake. Gradually, however, Young became convinced that Bridger was his enemy and that he and other mountaineers were responsible for the troubles Mormons were having with Indians in their Utah settlements. "I believe that old Bridger is death on us," said Brigham, "and if he knew that 400,000 Indians were coming against us, and any man were to let us know, he would cut his throat."[1]

In summer 1853, following the onset of the "Walker War," Young, in his dual roles of territorial governor and superintendent of Indian affairs, issued a proclamation that "Every person, whether resident, or non-resident, is strictly forbidden to give trade, or in any way voluntarily put in possession of any Utah Indian, any powder, lead, gun, sword, knife or any weapon, or munitions of war whatever."[2] Fort Bridger, as part of the Utah territory, was subject to this declaration. Having heard that Jim Bridger was selling guns and ammunition to the Indians in violation of his order, Young issued a warrant for his arrest, but before the 150-man posse under Sheriff James Ferguson arrived, Bridger had fled.[3]

The posse proceeded on to the ferries at Green River and in a battle killed a couple of mountaineers.[4] Ferguson then left twenty men in possession of Fort Bridger, where they remained until mid-October. Shortly before they returned home, a mission to Green River was announced at the General Conference in Salt Lake City with stated goals of operating as peacemakers among the Indians, preaching civilization and teaching farming techniques.[5] Unmentioned in the announcement was a financial concern since all emigrants passed through the area and had to cross two rivers on toll ferries that Brigham Young planned to control.

Apostle Orson Hyde, who had been assigned the task of organizing the Green River Mission, read the names on October 8 of thirty-nine young men selected to found a permanent Mormon settlement in the vicinity of Fort Bridger. By the end of 1853 the men, reinforced by a second company, began to secure control of the Green River Basin but opted to establish Fort Supply, located about twelve miles south at an elevation of 7200 feet, rather than occupy Fort Bridger.[6] In March 1854, Hosea Stout, whose mission to China had ended far short of its expected term, was called to go to the Green River Mission with a group, led by Hyde, to strengthen the settlement at Fort Supply.[7]

Ever since summer 1847 at Winter Quarters, Stout had been critical of Hyde, who more than once in his role of attorney in court "became excited and vocalized beyond the bounds of discretion."[8] Three weeks before his call to go to Green River, Stout attended a case in probate court and described Hyde's actions with unusual candor:

> I felt, and so did numbers present express themselves, that Elder Hyde has most shamefully condescended beneath the dignaty of an Apostle to stoop, as he does here before all Israel and play the small intrigueing pettifogger in our lower courts making him self often the butt of ridicule and low abuse. The saints feel justly indignant at his course I left court when the case was submitted to the jury and sincerely hope I may never again see such condescension in our Courts by one of our Apostles.[9]

Nevertheless, Stout put aside his personal feelings and accepted the call. On March 29, Hyde issued instructions to the new recruits to procure as much flour as possible and also "two bushels of mechanic potatoes" per man.[10] This presented a hardship for Stout, who on May 1, as the company readied for departure, admitted to being "totally unprepared, having been disappointed in collecting any means from my creditors." Moreover, his family lacked the necessary provisions that constituted the "Staff of Life." Fortunately, at the last moment he was able to obtain sixty pounds of flour "on credit till the first day of July."[11]

Stout departed Salt Lake City with George Boyd but soon transferred his provisions and luggage to William (Bill) Hickman's wagon.[12] The journey was far from smooth, as careless driving by Hickman resulted in a broken wagon tongue, broken wheel, and broken axle in the space of four days;[13] it was not his driving, however, but actions, including the murder of Jesse Hartley (to which he later confessed) that earned Hickman a measure of infamy.

Jesse P. Hartley was a young lawyer whom Stout had faced ten weeks earlier as opposing counsel in a lawsuit before Judge Elias Smith (Hartley won the case).[14] Shortly after arriving in Utah, Hartley married Mary Ann Bullock, the younger sister of Isaac Bullock, the captain of the second company sent to Green River in 1853.[15] Hartley somehow incurred the wrath of Brigham Young, who at the April 1854 General Conference used strong language against him and cut him off from the church.[16] In his address, Young said Hartley was "a vagrant—a thief, and a robber. He ought to be baptized in Salt Lake with stones tied to him and hold him under 24 hours to wash away one hundredth part of his sins. He ought to be Sent to hell across lots on a mission to preach to the damned."[17] Essentially ostracized, Hartley decided to leave town and join with Stout's company going to Green River.[18] On May 3, the third day of the company's journey, Stout wrote, "This evening Elder Hyde informed the company that Mr J_____ Hartley who did not make his appearance to day with us had most likely had some dishonest intentions by his leaving and wished the guard to renew their diligence least their horses might be stolen."[19]

Unbeknownst to Stout at the time, Hartley was dead, admittedly murdered by Bill Hickman, who later claimed that Orson Hyde instructed him to have Hartley "used up" should he come to Fort Supply. According to Hickman's account, after the murder had been committed "Stout asked me [Hickman] if I had seen that fellow, meaning Hartley. I told him he had come to our camp, and he said from what he had heard he ought to be killed. I then told him all that had happened and he said that was good."[20]

Hickman's book, in which his account appeared, was written seventeen years after the act was committed and presents challenges with credibility since it was edited by John Hanson Beadle, who despised Brigham Young and wanted to produce a sensational book that would sell. Whether Stout actually heard reports that Hartley "ought to be killed" or gave his approval after the fact to the murder is open to debate, but he was not implicated by Hickman or by anyone else in the murder.[21]

After four more days the company arrived at Fort Supply, and Stout was singularly unimpressed:

> Snow squalls and cold west wind Baited at Bridger and proceed on to fort Supply where we arrived at dark. This is the most forbidding and godforsaken place I have ever seen for an attempt to be made for a settlement and judging from the

altitude I have no hesitancy in predicting that it will yet prove a total failure but the brethren here have done a great deal of labor.[22]

The first order of business was to organize the County of Green River, as Probate Judge William Appleby appointed Bill Hickman to the dual roles of sheriff and prosecuting attorney and Robert Alexander as clerk of the probate court.[23] It is uncertain exactly what role Stout was called to perform, for other than occasionally participating in a legal case he was for the most part inactive and bored. "I am doing positively worse than nothing," he wrote on May 18;[24] five days later he recorded, "Lounging around with nothing to do and so lazy that life is almost a drug;[25] and on June 10 he closed a note to W. W. Phelps, "All things jog along slow and easy here, as ever."[26] To compound his boredom, though he received a letter from his friend Isaac Allred in England, he had absolutely no word from home. "My friends seem to forget me it would seem," he wrote.[27]

Not all shared in Stout's boredom at Green River. For example, James S. Brown, who had charge of swimming ten thousand head of cattle across the Green River, reminisced, "From May 13 to July 8, 1854, had been one of the most hazardous, soul-trying, disagreeable experiences of my life, for the short period it occupied. I have written a very brief synopsis of it in the foregoing account; for it might seem impossible to the person of ordinary experience for so many thrilling incidents as I had witnessed to happen in so short a time."[28] Stout, on the other hand, in two months at Green River was involved in only four legal cases, three of which were for the defense and none of which would qualify as thrilling, and was otherwise unoccupied. Showcasing his boredom, one of the highlights of his two-month stay was when Benjamin Hawley returned from Salt Lake on June 11 with the wives of two of the missionaries, thus increasing the female population from two to four. "Since we have been blessed with two more female arrivals the aspect of our society seems to brighten," he wrote.[29] Otherwise, his overall experience at Green River was summed up by his journal entry for June 27: "River rising and every thing else dull."[30]

Stout was not the only unhappy missionary at Green River. John Pulsipher, who traveled in Stout's company across the plains in 1848, wrote of his brother Charles's experience at Green River, "Many of the men were discouraged and dissatisfied and Elder Hyde was not with them and they thought it was a hard, lonesome place, so the next July they were all released to go home unless some wished to stay and save the crops."[31]

Figure 15.1. Alvira Wilson Stout (1834–1910), 1898, sixth wife of Hosea and mother of eleven of his children. She outlived her husband by twenty-one years.

Stout joined the missionary exodus, departing on July 1 in John Mott's wagon, though there is no indication that he had been released from the mission.[32] Upon arrival in Salt Lake City six days later, he found his family thriving and received the expected news that the divorce from Aseneth had been finalized. Unshaken, he recorded simply, "all was well," feeling great relief that the hastily arranged and very unfortunate marriage was at an end.[33] Later that month he visited Louisa's grave and recorded the visit in his journal without the melodrama of his previous journal entries concerning her, perhaps indicating that he finally had made peace with her death.[34]

Figure 15.2. Family of Hosea and Alvira Stout.

Unlike his situation upon returning home from China to his motherless children, this time Hosea's sister Anna proved very capable of caring for his family, so there was no need to rush into another marriage as he had done with Aseneth. Almost exactly one year following the divorce, however, he married twenty-one-year-old Alvira Wilson in a ceremony performed by Brigham Young.[35] Alvira was a daughter of Lewis Dunbar Wilson, who for seven years served on the Nauvoo High Council and with whom Hosea was well acquainted for many years. Despite an age difference of twenty-four years between Hosea and Alvira, the union was successful, as she bore him eleven children, eight of whom grew to maturity.[36]

During the year leading up to his new marriage, Stout was deeply involved in the legal profession, taking time off only for his legislative duties, having been reelected (once again without opposition) on August 7, 1854, to the House of Representatives. Two weeks following the election, he noted the arrival of John Kinney, who had been selected as chief justice of the Supreme Court of the Territory of Utah. In tow was George P. Stiles, whom Stout did not hold in high esteem, referring to him in his journal as "Hon? G. P. Stiles who might be called a *Judicial Cadet* for he came here in expecting *to be* appointed Associate Justice."[37] Unbeknownst to Stout, on August 1 Stiles actually *had* been appointed by President Franklin Pierce as an associate justice of the Utah Supreme Court.[38] At the time a Mormon in good standing, Stiles had been a member of the Nauvoo City Council while Stout served as clerk of the body and in 1844 supported the council's decision to destroy the *Nauvoo Expositor* press, an act that set off a chain of events leading to murders of Joseph and Hyrum Smith.

Stiles replaced Zerubbabel Snow as associate justice while Kinney took over the post of chief justice that was vacated by the resignation due to poor health of Lazarus H. Reed. The third and final member of the Supreme Court appointed by President Pierce was William Wormer Drummond, succeeding Leonidas Shaver, a non-Mormon who had been very friendly to the Saints. Shaver was held in such high esteem that upon his death in June 1855 he was given a funeral fit for a top Mormon leader: "The occasion was a solemn one and called forth more heart felt grief and sympathy than has ever been manifested for any person not a mormon who ever died in our midst," extolled Stout.[39] Judge Drummond, on the other hand, quickly incurred disfavor after his arrival in Salt Lake City on July 9 when it was discovered that he had abandoned his wife in Oquawka, Illinois, and that the woman (Ada Caroll) with whom he arrived in Utah and tried to pass off as his wife actually was a prostitute from Washington, DC.

Though Judge Stiles already had been appointed an associate justice of the Supreme Court, in his first few cases he served as a defense attorney in probate court, three of which were as co-counsel with Stout.[40] On November 7, 1854, Stout went in company with Stiles and Marshal Joseph Heywood to attend the November term of the US Third Judicial District Court.[41] At the time, Stiles and Stout associated affably, and the two men, along with Heywood, even preached together at a Sunday meeting in Parowan the day before court convened.[42]

The year 1855 began pleasantly as the Assembly, along with Governor Young, took time out of their legislative session to throw a party on New Year's Day in the honor of Judge Kinney, his associate justices, and Colonel Edward Steptoe, who had been sent to Utah by Franklin Pierce to replace Brigham Young as governor but ultimately turned down the President's offer. "Great pains and care had been taken to procure and prepare the best the Land could produce or afford to have the best dinner and supper ever got up in the Territory which without doubt was the case," Stout recorded. The feast for the ages included turkey, hares, Beuf ala Mode, chicken, mutton, Fried Steaks, Fried Turkey, fried cutlets, stewed lobsters, potatoes, turnips, parsnips, slaw, fritters, cabbage, pound cake, Washington Cake, Pain-au-Ris, Charlotte Rushe, damson, raspberry, mince and cherry pies, pudding, Blanc Mange, omelets, ice cream, and watermelon.[43] Warm feelings continued through the session, which adjourned on January 19.[44]

Following the conclusion of the legislative session, on January 29 the Supreme Court met, at which time Stout, Joseph Holman and Orson Hyde were admitted to plead at the bar of the court.[45] As the court met the following Sunday, Stout cynically and disapprovingly noted, "Supreme Court was in session every day last week but done but little business except adopt rules and admit persons to the bar who never read, study or even looked into a law book."[46] Stout himself was not among those who never read or studied; quite to the contrary, on March 8 after being assigned to defend Henry Rau for "secreting deserted soldiers" since Rau could not afford counsel, he hit the books and "discovered the law on which he [Rau] was indicted was repealed," leading to a motion to quash and the subsequent release of the prisoner.[47]

In August 1855, three weeks after his marriage to Alvira Wilson, Stout was reelected to the House of Representatives, once again unopposed, as were all candidates. Unsurprisingly, with nothing at stake, only 227 votes were cast in Salt Lake City (the 1856 Census showed 12,730 males in Salt Lake County, most of whom lived in Salt Lake City).[48] Much more important than the election, on October 15, 1855, as the First Judicial District Court of the United States convened for a special term, Stout was appointed special district attorney for the United States, as US District Attorney John L. Payton, who had been appointed to the office on September 13, was nowhere to be found.[49] It was in this office (to which he was reappointed pro tem on November 12, 1855, and again on January 7, 1856) that Stout was involved in legal actions with Judge W. W. Drummond.[50]

On November 5, 1855, Stout started for Fillmore, the new territorial capitol, in company with Deputy US Marshal Anson Call, whose prisoner Levi Abrams was to be tried in Drummond's court for the murder of an Indian named Too-ebe.[51] Six days later, the small company arrived just after dark at Fillmore, where Stout "found His Honor W. W. Drumond and lady all well and in good spirits patiently awaiting our arrival to Court which is to commence to morrow at ten a. m."[52] After Stout was sworn in as US District Attorney pro tem and Joseph A. Kelting as Territorial District Attorney pro tem, Judge Drummond, while charging the grand jury, took the opportunity to rail on the "Laws of Utah in relation to the powers and Jurisdiction of the probate Courts," which in 1852 had been granted jurisdiction for both civil and criminal cases by the territorial legislature:

> He most emphatically declared that under the organic Act of the Territory of Utah the Legislature could not confer, civil and criminal jurisdiction by law on the probate Courts, or any powers whatsoever other matters of Probate proper and

that the judiciary act conferring these powers on the probate Courts, were not only contrary to, and inconsistent with the organic act; but an unwarranted strech of power, not only beyond, but amounting to an abnigation of all law

He also instructed the grand jury that if they found that any of the Probate Judges had exercised civil or criminal jurisdiction that it was their duty to indict not only the judges, but all jurors and officers who had acted under them.[53]

Drummond already had shown indignation not only toward the laws of Utah but also toward the inhabitants of the territory. French naturalist and traveler Jules Remy, who in 1855–1856 spent time in Utah, encountered Drummond and his mistress at Fillmore on November 1, 1855, and wrote of the meeting, "We passed the evening in listening to the anti-Mormon dissertations of Judge Drummond, in which his fair companion took part, who seemed as if she could not say often enough how tired she was of her long stay in Utah."[54] Those "dissertations" were expressed in private, but Drummond's anti-Utah tirade in open court brought forth a sense of outrage. Observer Samuel Richards wrote to his brother Franklin in England, "You have, no doubt, heard of the appointment and arrival of Judge Drummond in this Territory . . . He has the *brass* to declare in open Court, that the Utah laws are founded in ignorance and has attempted to set aside some of the most important ones . . . His course and policy so far seem to be to raise a row if possible, and make himself more notorious."[55]

Drummond's first trial was of Levi Abrams for the murder of the Indian Too-ebe. Remarkably, while in custody of Deputy US Marshal Anson Call on the way to Fillmore, Abrams treated the small company (including Stout), as well as the jurors who were en route to try him in court, to "a luxurious oyster supper."[56] Whether Abrams influenced the jury's outcome with his generosity is unknown, but after prosecuting attorney Stout was unsuccessful in gaining a conviction for murder, Judge Drummond was indignant: "In this case the jury, true to the law of the church, and basely false to the law of the land, found Abrams not guilty," he later wrote to the widow of Captain John Williams Gunnison, who was murdered in the Utah Territory at Sevier River on October 26, 1853, ostensibly by a band of Indians.[57]

While presiding over the trial of an Indian named Enyos for the murders of Captain Gunnison and members of his party, Drummond attempted to get Stout, the prosecuting attorney, to suborn perjury by coming "into court without interpreters and introduce evidence to prove that he [Enyos] had confessed guilty of being at the massacre of Capt Gunnison and party and assisting in the murder and then closing the evidence against him without allowing him the oppertunity of proving his innocence or having the interpreters in court to give him any chance for his life." Stout, believing that "the judge was determined to have him hung guilty or innocent," declined to comply, and the jury returned a verdict of not guilty.[58]

Drummond, by this time incensed with a belief that the juries were stacked against him, became even more active in trying to gain a conviction in the final case of the term. Samuel G. Baker had been indicted on November 19 for the murder of a mute boy named Isaac Whitehouse.[59] On the morning of November 26, Stout commenced a lawsuit against Baker, who was in arrears to the Perpetual Emigrating Fund in the amount of $155.20; Baker "confessed judgement for the amount of the demand" and arrangements were made "to execute his property in favor of the P. E. F. Company." Then, in a very strange twist, Baker's murder case was taken up with Joseph Kelting as prosecutor while Stout, who had just prosecuted Baker, was counsel for his defense.[60]

The trial commenced and occupied the entire day on November 27 and continued on the next, at which time the prosecution rested. Stout was astounded at Drummond's handling of the case: "The Judge took a very active part in the trial against the prisoner and today even took on himself the examination of the witnesses very unbecomingly."[61] For two days the defense presented its case, and on December 1 the jury, after four hours of deliberation, returned a verdict of guilty of murder in the second degree; Baker was sentenced on December 3 to ten years in the penitentiary. Drummond was victorious, but it was not the last he would hear of Samuel Baker.

With a surprising degree of fellowship, the court session of twenty-one days ended on December 1, immediately after Baker was convicted:

> The time having drawn nigh when the court would close, we all like officers of hope, concluded to have a fashionable adjournment, so we ordered a good oyster supper. Brandy and cherry brandy to the tune of some ten or twelve bottles. All pitched in court, officers and bystanders and all got gloriously drunk, and went it till mid night.[62]

With the legislative session commencing in a week in Fillmore, Stout was a captive in the new capitol, bored with nothing to do and not having enough time for a visit home. To relieve the monotony he wrote some letters, including one to Alvira in response to the "few lines" she had written. "In these scant times I must be thankful for small favors for it is the first scratch of a pen I have yet received from you," he wrote with more than a hint of sarcasm. In the letter Stout once again showed great concern for his adopted son Henry Allen, hoping that he would be diligent in his studies "so as to be somebody and not have to drudge through life in ignorance and hard labor as he will if he neglects his books." Concluding the letter to his wife who was not quite half his age he wrote, "I am very anxious to see you all, but I will not call you a baby any more for no doubt you will want to apply that pretty name to some one else," most likely referring to the fact that Alvira was in her sixth month of pregnancy.[63]

The legislature met on December 10 in the new, though not yet completed, State House in Fillmore and was still in session on Saturday, January 5 when Levi Abrams made some disparaging remarks about Drummond's mistress; an altercation ensued, after which Drummond sent his servant Cato to assault Abrams. The affair may have been a set-up by some Mormons to exact a measure of revenge against the judge (Bill Hickman years later admitted such, claiming responsibility in getting Abrams "to swear out a writ"[64]), though, if so, Stout evidently was not privy to the scheme. Samuel Richards described the situation to his brother Franklin:

> Some little excitement prevails in town today. An affair took place between Judge Drummond and a Jew trader here, which was rather amusing at the time, but may be something more than *fun* for the Judge before he gets through with it. A grand jury is meeting this evening, which will bring in a indictment against the Judge and his negro, Cato, for assault and battery with intent to murder; and he will be arrested and brought before the Probate Court on Monday morning next, at 9 o'clock, just at the time he should answer to his name in the Supreme Court, which sits at that hour.
>
> He has virtually ruled our Probate Courts out of power in his decisions, but we will now know whether Probate Courts can act or not, especially in his case.[65]

Drummond was indicted by the probate court as it convened on Monday morning, January 7 at 8:30 AM (half an hour earlier than Richards had predicted), and he immediately retained Hosea Stout, Joseph Kelting, and Aurelius Miner as counsels for his defense. Ninety minutes later Drummond sat on the bench as the Supreme Court reappointed Stout US Attorney pro tem.[66] His opinion of Drummond may have been tainted by the judge's attempt to have him commit perjury in the Enyos case, but his decision to join the judge's defense team might have been a case of the lesser of two evils since Stout despised Levi Abrams, whom in a previous case he had labeled "a mean and contemptible Jew."[67]

By agreeing to defend Drummond, it appeared that Stout would be thrust into the controversy surrounding the probate courts. Though he spent much time arguing cases in those courts, he contended there was a better system, particularly regarding civil suits:

> How much better it would be if saints would always adjust their differences before the proper tribunals of the Church free of costs and in humility and the Spirit of the Lord than to go before the courts of law which so often involves fortunes to the stubborn will of man, engendering an evil spirit and irreconcilable enmity and hatred towards each other which is seldom cured.[68]

On the morning of January 9, 1856, Kinney, Stiles, and Drummond headed to the State House to hold a session of the Supreme Court when a posse intercepted and detained Drummond. "This entirely took the Judiciary aback," Stout recorded. "A parley ensued, the two other Judges remonstrated, The Possee were inexhorable. They would not let Judge Drummond go." The issue was resolved unexpectedly when Judge Drummond withdrew his request for a writ and Levi Abrahms withdrew his suit before the probate court on the condition that Drummond would retract his petition challenging the jurisdiction of the court. "It now seemed that the death Knell of the probate Courts would inevitably be sounded, as Judge Kinney's known and avowed opinion was adversely to the powers of the Probate Courts," wrote Stout, "yet their time had not come for Judge Drummond on the meeting of Kinneys Court with drew the suit and thus the Probates lives."[69]

Two days later, with Drummond back on the bench, the Supreme Court took up the case known as *The People, &c, v. Moroni Green*, in which Green sought to overturn his conviction in October 1855 for assault with intent to murder Nathan Tanner, at which time he had been sentenced to six months imprisonment. Almon Babbittt, an apostate Mormon who in 1853 had been appointed secretary and treasurer of the Utah Territory, was Green's attorney while Stout and Attorney General Albert Carrington represented the people. On January 11 Stout motioned to dismiss the case on the grounds that the plaintiff's papers were so "contradictory and imperfect" that legally there was no case. Seemingly bent on revenge for the way he had been treated, Drummond overruled the motion and told the defense either to allow the case to move forward or have the "priviledge to perfect the plff's [plaintiff's] papers." In protest Stout wrote he was not willing to refine the opposition's papers, which would operate against his own interest, and gave notice that he would neither defend the suit any further nor "disgrace [himself] submitting to such unlawful and unjust rulings of court."[70]

With court adjourned, on Sunday, January 13, Brigham Young took the pulpit at Fillmore, speaking as "Governor of the Territory," not "President of the Church." "The United States judges are not here as kings or Monarchs but as servants of the people," he railed. Demeaning the judges' knowledge, he said, "Some will try to study a hundred sciences of the day and then know no more than a child." Continuing his attack he declared, "Lawyers and Judges should be made to keep the Laws of this Territory as well as other Citizens and if they won't do it put them in the way that they will be made to. And I say to every man who has no business here pack up your goods and go home."[71] Young then said pointedly of Drummond, "The Judge is not here as a king or as a Monarch—he is nothing but a boy."[72]

Young's message evidently got through to Drummond. The Supreme Court reviewed the Moroni Green case the following day and, in an opinion written by Judge Drummond, upheld Green's conviction and ordered "that the Defendant be conveyed to the Penitentiary of Utah Territory by the United States Marshal of the Territory, within ten days . . . to serve for and during six months term of imprisonment in the said Penitentiary of Utah."[73] Immediately afterwards, however, while considering a writ of habeas corpus for William Wall, one of four who had been arrested for contempt, Drummond became "uneasy, and doubting the result of his own doings, became anxious to set in judgement on the case of the prisoners he had caused to be arrested for contempt and . . . called a side session of his own court." Wall was called before Drummond in the presence of Stout and the judge's clerk and was discharged "without costs."[74]

Brigham Young had gotten on Drummond's nerves, and he wasn't done. On February 2 he granted a pardon to Moroni Green,[75] which the judge understandably took as a slap in the face, especially in light of a similar pardon ten days earlier: on January 24 Stout prepared and "had the papers signed for the Pardon of Samuel G. Baker," who immediately was released from prison and came to Stout's house, "rejoicing that his term of ten years had expired so soon."[76] Following the two pardons by the Governor, on February 16, sixteen unopposed candidates from Salt Lake County, who had been placed on the ballot by the church hierarchy, were approved in an "election" for a constitutional convention; in an effort to seem inclusive, US Indian agent Garland Hurt and John Kinney, both non-Mormons, as well as George Stiles were on the slate, while conspicuously missing was the name of William Drummond.[77]

Unlike Drummond, Judge Kinney was on relatively good terms with the Mormons, but that did not prevent him being taken to district court on January 15—the same day the Supreme Court adjourned—in a suit brought by Almerin Grow, an attorney whom Kinney had suspended from the bar. The case was summarily dismissed on a motion jointly filed by Kinney and his defense attorney, Hosea Stout; two weeks later the same complaint was filed in probate court, though it also was dismissed.[78]

The assault on Kinney wasn't confined to the suits brought by Almerin Grow. On January 16, the day after the Supreme Court adjourned, the legislature redefined the judicial districts of the territorial courts and reassigned Kinney to a relatively unpopulated northern area of the territory.[79] Kinney considered the action an "insult to me and my family personally" and felt that he had been "legislated out of office."[80] Rationalizing that he had been forced to leave the Territory, on April 21 Kinney and his family joined a large group of missionaries headed for the States.[81]

After granting the pardon to Moroni Green, Brigham Young broadened his attack against those involved in the legal system. On Sunday, February 24, Stout noted, "Went to meeting President Young spoke against the corrupt practice in Courts and particularly in this last trial on the part of the [plaintiff]."[82] The case to which Young referred was *Thomas S. Williams v. Bradford Leonard*, with Williams and Zerubbabel Snow for the plaintiff and Hosea Stout for the defense. On Thursday, February 21, Stout wrote of "six long winded Lawyers"[83] and noted that "the Presidint and council attended the Court to day to hear the long winded spouters."[84] On Saturday, just after midnight, the jury returned a verdict for Williams, a colorful merchant and lawyer who increasingly was out of favor with the church and later in the year was excommunicated.[85] The following day, Young gave a rebuke of lawyers and the legal system "all who love litigation and do not repent." "Do I say that lying is practised in those places?" he asked rhetorically. "Yes," he answered, "often from beginning to end." In conclusion Young demanded, "Keep away from court houses; no decent man will go there unless he goes there as a witness, or is in some manner compelled to."[86]

With Judge Kinney already gone, Young had to be delighted when Judge Drummond and his mistress took off, on May 17, 1856, ostensibly to hold court in Carson Valley, leaving George Stiles as the only federal judge in the territory.[87] "We are having a very quiet time of it at present," he wrote to George Q. Cannon in San Francisco. "The Indians are peaceable. The judges are absent, and the lawyers and doctors have gone to farming all except Hosea, and I believe he is carpentering."[88]

Young was correct in his supposition regarding Stout, for on the day of Kinney's departure (April 21) he commenced building "another house joining on to the North End" of his house in anticipation of the birth of another child. The son, "fine healthy, and fat, weighing nine and a half pounds," was born on April 27 and given the name Lewis Wilson Stout. "This makes the Eleventh child which has been born unto me, only four of whom are living," he solemnly recorded.[89]

Leaving for the east in the same company with Judge Kinney was US Marshal Joseph Leland Heywood; in preparation for his prolonged absence, on April 17 Heywood appointed both Stout and Alexander McRae as Deputy United States Marshal.[90] "It is not my intention to act as such," Stout wrote, noting that he would have charge of Heywood's business "more to prevent abuse and extravagance than any thing else."[91] There is no evidence that he actually performed any duties as deputy marshal, but rather busied himself in building his house and attending to legal activities.

On August 4 Stout was reelected to the House of Representatives, like the other ten candidates "without a dissenting vote," hardly surprising since all ran unopposed.[92] Later that day, Joseph Troskolawski, an employee of US Surveyor General David Burr, was whipped and severely beaten by two young men. A few days earlier, Brigham Young in a letter to George A. Smith included Troskolawski's name as one who may have signed documents supposed to be used against the Saints in their quest for statehood.[93] "How this affair will come out I do not know," Stout stated. "The law has been violated and the grieveance must be redressed." According to Burr in a letter to Secretary of the Interior Jacob Thompson, however, the grievance was not even addressed:

> The authorities refused or declined to institute criminal proceedings against the offenders; on the contrary, they justified the act on the ground that he had been talking and railing against their religion. We, "the Gentiles," all feel that we cannot rely upon the laws for protection, and are only permitted to live here at the pleasure of the rulers. I think the attack was made upon Mr. Troskolawski, in order to produce a salutary effect upon us "Gentiles," and make us afraid to express our opinions.[94]

A mutual air of distrust had developed between federal officials and the Utah Mormons, and the brewing conflict was about to escalate.

Notes

1. Brigham Young in *Journal History*, May 7, 1849, 1–2.
2. *Deseret News*, August 25, 1853.
3. Alter, *Jim Bridger*, 252–53.
4. Hickman, *Brigham's Destroying Angel: Being the Life, Confession, and Startling Disclosures of the Notorious Bill Hickman, the Danite Chief of Utah*, 93. Hickman ambiguously stated that "two or three" mountaineers were killed.
5. Brown, *Life of a Pioneer, Being the Autobiography of James S. Brown*, 304–5; *Deseret News*, October 15, 1853.
6. Campbell, *Establishing Zion*, 113–16.
7. Brooks, *Mormon Frontier*, March 18, 1854, 509.
8. Hyde, *Orson Hyde: The Olive Branch of Israel*, 317.
9. Brooks, *Mormon Frontier*, February 25, 1854, 507.
10. *Deseret News*, March 30, 1854.
11. Brooks, *Mormon Frontier*, May 1, 1854, 514.
12. Ibid.
13. Ibid., May 2–5, 1854, 514–15.
14. Ibid., February 18, 1854, 506–7.
15. Baskin, *Reminiscences of Early Utah*, 151–52; Green, *Fifteen years among the Mormons: being the narrative of Mrs. Mary Ettie V. Smith*, 309–10. Ettie Smith met Mary Ann, who as a widow was living with her brother at Green River; on November 23, 1856, she married Benjamin Morgan Roberts at Green River.
16. *Millennial Star*, July 22, 1854, 462.
17. Collier, *Teachings of Brigham Young*, 3:287.
18. Baskin, *Reminiscences*, 153.
19. Brooks, *Mormon Frontier*, May 3, 1854, 514.
20. Hickman, *Brigham's Destroying Angel*, 97–98. Hickman's book was written in 1871 while in custody for another murder, after he had been excommunicated, and may have had an agenda in his writing but did not implicate Stout in the murder. Robert Baskin, a Harvard trained lawyer who came to Utah in 1865 and became chief justice of the Supreme Court of Utah, some time later asked Isaac Bullock in Provo "if the matter had ever been investigated by the executive authorities, and he said it had not been, although it was generally known that Hickman had committed the crime. I also asked him why he had not instituted proceedings against Hickman. He shook his head significantly and replied, 'Don't press me for an answer to that question.'" See Baskin, *Reminiscences*, 153.
21. Marquardt, "The Coming Storm: The Murder of Jesse Thompson Hartley," 10.
22. Brooks, *Mormon Frontier*, May 7, 1854, 515.
23. Ibid., May 9, 1854, 516. James S. Brown in *Life of a Pioneer*, 332, wrote that Hosea Stout was prosecuting attorney, but Hosea wrote otherwise and in the few cases in which he was involved typically was counsel for the defense.
24. Brooks, *Mormon Frontier*, May 18, 1854, 517.
25. Ibid., May 23, 1854, 518.

Lawyer and Legislator 239

26. *Deseret News*, June 22, 1854.
27. Brooks, *Mormon Frontier*, June 4, 1854, 519.
28. Ibid., 345.
29. Ibid., June 11, 1854, 519.
30. Ibid., June 27, 1854, 521.
31. Campbell, *Establishing Zion*, 117.
32. Brooks, *Mormon Frontier*, July 1, 1854, 522.
33. Ibid., July 7, 1854, 522.
34. Ibid., July 23, 1854, 523.
35. Alvira Wilson was born on April 21, 1834, in Green Township, Richland County, Ohio. Her parents, Lewis Dunbar Wilson and Nancy Ann Waggoner, were early Mormon converts, baptized on May 23, 1836. Wilson, who went by his middle name Dunbar, served on the Nauvoo High Council from 1839 to 1846 (see *D&C* 124:132).
36. Brooks, *Mormon Frontier*, July 19, 1855, 558. Alvira Wilson was born April 21, 1834, in Green Township, Ohio, a daughter of Lewis Dunbar Wilson and Nancy Ann Wagoner.
37. Ibid., August 22, 1854, 525.
38. Hagan, *Reports of Cases Determined in the Supreme Court of the Territory of Utah*, vol. 1, 1877, iv.
39. Brooks, *Mormon Frontier*, June 30, 1855, 557.
40. Ibid., September 16, 21, and 23, 1854, 527–28.
41. Ibid., November 1, 1854, 530.
42. Ibid., November 19, 1854, 531.
43. Ibid., January 1, 1855, 538.
44. Ibid., January 19, 1855, 549.
45. Ibid., January 29, 1855, 550.
46. Ibid., February 4, 1855, 550.
47. Ibid., March 8, 1855, 552.
48. Anderson, *Desert Saints*, 141; Brooks, *Mormon Frontier*, August 6, 1855, 559.
49. Brooks, *Mormon Frontier*, October 15, 1855, 562. Little is known about John L. Payton. The official Department of Justice history of the office of US attorney for both the Territory and State of Utah states simply, "John Payton served as the U.S. Attorney from September 13, 1855, until the Summer 1856." See https://www.justice.gov/usao-ut/history#payton.
50. Brooks, *Mormon Frontier*, November 12, 1855, 565; January 7, 1856, 583.
51. Ibid., November 5, 1855, 564. Also in the company were Clark Allen Huntington and his father Dimick B. Huntington, who were to serve as interpreters.
52. Ibid., November 11, 1855, 565.
53. Ibid., November 12, 1855, 565.
54. Remy and Brenchley, *A Journey to Great Salt Lake City, Volume 2*, 342. Drummond's "fair companion," Ada Caroll's "long stay" in Utah up to that moment had been a few days less than four months.
55. *Millennial Star*, March 29, 1856, letter of December 7, 1855.
56. Brooks, *Mormon Frontier*, November 10, 1855, 565.
57. Letter from William W. Drummond to Mrs. M. D. Gunnison, April 27, 1857, in Gunnison, *The Mormons, or Latter-day Saints, in the valley of the*

Great Salt Lake, x; Brooks, *Mormon Frontier*, November 15–17, 1855, 566. Some, including Drummond and Mrs. Gunnison, claimed that the murder occurred "under the orders, advice, and directions of the Mormons. See Letter from William W. Drummond to Attorney General Jeremiah S. Black, March 30, 1857, in *New York Times*, April 14, 1857.
58. Brooks, *Mormon Frontier*, November 13–21, 1855, 565–67.
59. Ibid., November 19, 1855, 566.
60. Ibid., November 26, 1855, 567. Hosea was assisted in the defense by John Bair.
61. Ibid., November 28, 1855, 567.
62. Ibid., December 1, 1855, 568.
63. Letter from Hosea Stout to Alvira Stout, December 7, 1855, Hosea Stout Papers, Brigham Young University.
64. Hickman, *Brigham's Destroying Angel*, 110–12.
65. *Millennial Star*, April 19, 1856; letter from Samuel Richards to Franklin Richards, January 5, 1856.
66. Brooks, *Mormon Frontier*, January 7, 1856, 583.
67. Ibid., October 20, 1854, 529.
68. Ibid., February 26, 1855, 551–52.
69. Ibid., January 9, 1856, 584.
70. Ibid., January 11–12, 1856, 585–86.
71. Woodruff, "Journal," January 13, 1856.
72. Arrington, *Brigham Young: An American Moses*, 233.
73. Hagan, *Reports of Cases Determined in the Supreme Court of the Territory of Utah*, vol. 1:17.
74. Brooks, *Mormon Frontier*, January 14, 1856, 587.
75. Pardon of Moroni Green, February 2, 1856, Utah State Archives. From Homer and Michael, "The Federal Bench and Priesthood Authority: The Rise and Fall of John Fitch Kinney's Early Relationship with the Mormons," *Journal of Mormon History* 13:89–108.
76. Brooks, *Mormon Frontier*, January 24, 1856, 590. Record of Baker's pardon is found in the Utah State Archives, Utah Territorial Executive Record Book "B," 44.
77. Brooks, *Mormon Frontier*, February 16, 1856, 592.
78. Ibid., January 15 and 30, 1856, 587–88, 590.
79. Ibid., January 16, 1856, 589; letter from John Fitch Kinney to Attorney General Black, as quoted in Homer, "The Federal Bench and Priesthood Authority," *Journal of Mormon History*, 13:100.
80. Letter from John Fitch Kinney to Attorney General Black.
81. Brooks, *Mormon Frontier*, April 21, 1856, 596.
82. Ibid., February 24, 1856, 593.
83. Ibid., February 21, 1856, 592.
84. Ibid., February 22, 1856, 592.
85. Letter from Brigham Young to George A. Smith, December 7, 1856, Church History Library.
86. Brooks, *Mormon Frontier*.
87. Ibid., May 17, 1856, 596.
88. Letter from Brigham Young to George Q. Cannon, May 30, 1856, *Selected*

Collections from the Archives of the Church of Jesus Christ of Latter-day Saints.
89. Brooks, *Mormon Frontier*, April 27, 1856, 596.
90. Ibid., April 17, 1856, 596.
91. Ibid., April 21, 1856, 596.
92. Ibid., July 17–18, 1856, 598; August 4, 1856, 599.
93. Letter from Brigham Young to George A. Smith, July 1856. The letter was written over several days, with later sections dated July 28 and July 31 and the body of the letter written sometime earlier in the month. Besides Troskolawski, other significant names mentioned as suspects were John F. Kinney, William W. Drummond, David Burr, T. S. Williams, and future United States Marshal Peter K. Dotson.
94. Letter from David Burr to Jacob Thompson, August 30, 1856, *The Utah Expedition: Message from the President of the United States*, 115–16.

16
Reformation and Winds of War

A gathering to the land of Zion was an integral tenet of Mormonism from its earliest days,[1] and yet by 1850—a year after the establishment of the Perpetual Emigrating Fund—there were nearly four thousand more church members in England than in the United States.[2] Though the Fund was created in 1849 to assist Latter-day Saint converts in Europe and the eastern United States in Emigration to the Utah Territory, it was not used to assist Saints in Europe until 1852, and by 1854 the number of "poor" English Saints who were assisted in their emigration quadrupled, from 251 to 1,075.[3] The emigrants were expected to repay the funds once they were settled in the Territory, but many shirked their responsibility, so on April 9, 1855, Hosea Stout was appointed attorney to collect delinquent debts. "There are a number who when they are brought from the old Country here on the avails of this Fund endeavor to leave without paying, forgetting the kind aid received to bring them from bondage to this land of liberty," he wrote.[4]

The emigration to Utah in 1855 was the heaviest to date, as 4,225 Saints (1,161 of whom were aided by the Perpetual Emigrating Fund) crossed the plains,[5] but upon their arrival they found a territory in distress, as a grasshopper plague coupled with drought devastated crops. Stout on May 20, 1855, noted in his journal:

> The drough[t] has been very severe while the grasshoppers cover the land destroying almost all green vegetation both on mountain and valley which presents a dreary prospects for our incoming crops. Whole fields of wheat are swept smooth and appear to be entirely used up yet the people seem to be in good spirits.[6]

The large immigration, in the midst of food shortages, strained the economy and resulted in greatly reduced donations to the Perpetual

Emigrating Fund. During the six years of the Fund's existence, Brigham Young had been considering methods of crossing the plains faster and with less expense; as early as 1851 in the sixth general epistle to the Saints he wrote:

> Families might start from the Missouri river with cows, handcarts, wheelbarrows, with little flour, and no unnecessaries, and come to this place quicker, and with much less fatigue, than by following the heavy trains, with their cumbrous herds, which they are often obliged to drive miles to feed.[7]

In September 1855, after the plan had matured in his mind, Young wrote to Apostle Franklin D. Richards, who was serving as president of the British Mission and also as director of the Perpetual Emigrating Fund's operation in England, suggesting that those traveling by handcart "can come as quick, if not quicker, and much cheaper."[8] A month later, in a general epistle, Young wrote of the European Saints, "let them come on foot, with handcarts or wheelbarrows; let them gird up their loins and walk through, and nothing shall hinder or stay them."[9] The British Saints heeded Young's instructions, as nearly half of the 3,756 Saints who migrated to America in 1856 (of whom all but 213 were from the British Isles) came under the direction of the Perpetual Emigrating Fund Company and were to travel only by handcart.[10]

The five handcart companies—four from England and one from Wales—sailed from Liverpool to either New York or Boston and then traveled on to Iowa City, where they were outfitted prior to crossing the plains. The first two companies, totaling 475 persons under the lead of Edmund Ellsworth and Daniel D. McArthur, arrived in Salt Lake City on September 26, 1856, as Stout recorded:

> To day the Hand Cart Company of saints arrived under the direction of E. Ellsworth and D. D. Mc Arthur The company was escorted in by Prest Young and a large concourse of Saints who met them in Emmigration Kanyon with a treat of melons, fruits vegtables The marched in good order and fine Spirits and seemed to be happy and in excellent health They have drawn their Carts from Iowa City a distance of 1300 miles. Thus men women and children young and old have been their own teams and performed this long journey far out travelling ox trains without incurring the expense for an outfit which would have taken them years of harder labor to procure than

thus coming in Carts. This is a new and improved method of crossing the plains.[11]

The day before the arrival of a third handcart company on October 2 with 314 persons led by Edward Bunker—presumably the last company of the season—the *Deseret News* chimed in, "The journey has been performed with less than the average amount of mortality attending ox trans; and, although somewhat fatigued, stepped out with alacrity to the last, and appeared buoyant and cheerful."[12] Tragically, they and Stout were mistaken in supposing the handcart system to be "a new and improved method," for the day after the *Deseret News* printed their article, Franklin D. Richards and a small group of returning missionaries arrived, bringing word that there were "still 970 Souls back on the plains with handcarts."[13]

Richards had "faith and confidence" that the companies would be "freed from suffering more than they can bear,"[14] but Young did not share his attitude and immediately called a meeting to discuss options in sending relief. The following morning, Sunday, October 5, President Young convened a general church conference and called upon the bishops to raise "60 good mule teams and 12 or 15 wagons" straightaway along with "12 tons of flour and 40 good teamsters."[15] Without hesitation, Mormon scout Ephraim Hanks and some of the missionaries who had arrived the previous day—notably George D. Grant, William Kimball, Cyrus Wheelock, and Joseph A. Young—came to the pulpit to volunteer;[16] two days later, on the morning of October 7, the first of what would be more than two hundred rescue teams moved out from Salt Lake City.

The two companies, under James Willie and Edward Martin, had been delayed at Iowa City and at Florence, Nebraska, while waiting for carts, yokes, tents, and other equipment to be constructed and as a result began their journey very late in the season.[17] Mormon Battalion veteran Levi Savage, a member of Captain Willie's company, advised against starting so late but was outvoted:

> August 12, 1856, Tuesday, Camp of the Saints, Florance, Nebraska Territory. Today we commenced preparing for our journey and ascertaining who wishes to go on this fall and who wishes to remain here. Many are going to stop. Others are faltering and I myself am not in favor of, but much opposed to, taking women and children through when they are destitute of clothing, when we all know that we are bound to be caught in the snow and severe cold weather long before we reach the valley.[18]

Savage was correct. By the second week of October members of the company were exhausted from hunger, fatigue, and bone-chilling temperatures at night. "Our old people are nearly all failing fast," Savage recorded.[19] On October 19, an early-season blizzard forced the Willie Company to halt two miles below Rocky Ridge on the Sweetwater River in Wyoming, nearly three hundred miles from the Salt Lake Valley. On October 21 Grant's party reached the company, one day after they had run out of food. With the aid of the rescuers, the first of the Willie Company entered the Salt Lake Valley on November 9, but at least sixty-eight of their number had succumbed to the ordeal and many others suffered from frostbite.[20]

In the meantime, some members of the rescue party, including George Grant, pushed on in search of the Martin Company, three-fourths of whom were women, children, and the elderly. While an express party of Joseph Young, Abel Garr, and Daniel Jones found the company 150 miles east of South Pass, many rescue teams, held up by the furious storm and believing that the Martin Company must either have decided to winter over or had perished in the storm, turned back toward Salt Lake City.[21] When Ephraim Hanks arrived with news that rescue teams were going the other way, Young and Garr were sent on November 3 as an express team to Salt Lake City to report on the situation and to seek help.[22] On November 11—two days after the Willie Company arrived in the Valley—an express rider reached the city with news that "C. N. Spencer and John Van Cott having been to the Sweet Water and hearing nothing of the last train of Hand Carts had returned and returning had caused all the teams which had gone on the road to help them" and that seventy-seven rescue teams were at Fort Bridger awaiting instruction from Brigham Young. "This news was very unexpected," Stout recorded. "Immediately upon receiving the news the president sent W. H. Kimball, Joseph Simmons, James Furgerson and myself as an express to go and turn the teams East again and for us to find where the Hand cart company was."[23]

The quartet was well chosen for the task: William Kimball, Heber C. Kimball's eldest son and a recently returned missionary from England, had helped outfit the handcart companies at Florence before returning to Salt Lake City and was one of the rescuers of the Willie Company; Joseph Marcellus Simmons, during summer and fall 1855, had been at Fort Supply to control Indians and help with immigration and was very familiar with the region; James Ferguson had led a 150-man expedition to Fort Bridger in 1853 to try to arrest Jim Bridger; and Hosea Stout, who at the age of forty-six was the oldest of all the rescuers, was a stern disciplinarian with abundant leadership experience.[24] The team departed at sunset and met John Van Cott the following morning. Of the encounter, Stout wrote:

Van Cott justified himself for returning and abandoning the Hand Cart Company as he could get no information of them and had concluded they had returned to the states, or Stopt at Larimie, been killed by the Indians or other wise gone to the devil and for him to have gone further was only to loose his team and starve to death himself and do no good after all and as for G. D. Grant and those with him who had gone to meet them they had probably stoped at Ft Larimie. So on these vague conclusions he had not only turned back but had caused all the rest of the teams to return and thus leave the poor suffering Hand carters to their fate.[25]

William Kimball reprimanded Van Cott "severely for his course" and presented a letter from Brigham Young, whereupon Van Cott immediately turned around his wagons and headed east.[26] Whereas in spring 1854 it had taken seven days for Stout to travel to Fort Bridger, this time the team made the journey less than four days, evidently traveling night and day. Following a brief stop of four hours to eat and to kill a cow to provide food for the handcart company, they continued on, in the next two days overtaking several ox teams and suddenly commanding a train of about thirty wagons.[27]

In the week since they left Salt Lake City the weather had been clear and pleasant, but on November 18, exactly a week after leaving Salt Lake City, snow began falling, accompanied by a harsh north wind. Reddick Allred, one of the rescuers of the Willie Company who had refused to turn back toward Salt Lake City but trudged on toward the Martin Company, noted, "As well as I was provided I even lost my toenails from frost."[28] At sundown, after meeting an advance team, several rescue teams were dispatched to usher in the handcart company:

Soon they began to come in, some in wagons, some on horses, some on foot, while some had to be lead or carried on the backs of men.

This presented a sad sight to see men women and children thinly clad poor and worn out with hunger and fatigue trudging along in this dreary country facing a severe snow storm and the wind blowing hard in their face.[29]

The following evening, Stout and Eph Hanks went "to visit and administer to the sick and had an opportunity of seeing the suffering and privations through which they had passed. Some were merry

Figure 16.1. James Ferguson (1828–1863). With Seth M. Blair and Hosea Stout, Ferguson co-founded The Mountaineer.

and cheerfull some dull and stupid some sick some frosted and some lazy and mean but all seemed to be elated more or less with the idea of speedily arriving in the Valley."[30] A day later, on November 20, three four-horse teams arrived to help provide relief, and the entire handcart team was able to move "quite briskly," though after a long day's travel on November 21, as they arrived after dark at Fort Bridger, both humans and animals "were nearly over done with fatigue, hunger and cold" and Stout admitted, "For myself I could scarsely stand alone or keep awake."[31]

Despite the heroic efforts of the rescuers, in "the coldest and most piercing weather" experienced during the journey, many company members died daily from exposure and want of food.[32] By the time the first of the Martin Company reached the Salt Lake Valley on November 28, scores had perished, the final tally of deaths in the company estimated to be between 135 and 150.[33]

Stout arrived in Salt Lake City three days in advance of the handcart company and found "all well with the exception that President Jedediah M. Grant was dangerously sick."[34] For nearly three months, Grant, the very popular second counselor in the First Presidency, had been the driving force behind a call to spiritual rejuvenation that became known as the Mormon Reformation. As new communities were settled, many Saints in Utah had become preoccupied with the struggle to survive on the frontier and often had neglected individual spiritual matters, including attending church. A drought and concurrent grasshopper plague in 1855, along with rapid immigration into Utah, also combined to threaten economic stability. The winter of 1855–56 was uncommonly severe, killing many cattle.

Church leaders, convinced that the problems they faced were divine reminders that not all was well in Zion, preached reform with vigor. An early hint of what was to come was manifested in Provo on July 13, 1855, when Grant, a fiery and fervent orator, told the congregation:

> I wish to see those who profess to be saints act as saints ought to act . . . The church needs trimming up, and if you will search you will find in your wards certain branches which had better be cut off. The kingdom would progress much faster, and so will you individually, than it will with those branches on, for they are only dead weights to the great wheel . . . I would like to see the works of reformation commence, and continue until every man had to walk to the line, then we would have something like union.[35]

Grant's suggested reformation came to fruition the following year. At a prayer circle meeting on September 7, 1856, Brigham Young announced that he wanted his counselors as well as the Twelve to go among the people and preach the gospel. A "Great Reformation" that would have far-reaching implications was launched on September 13 in a four-day conference at Kaysville Ward, about twenty-three miles directly north of Salt Lake City, where Stout's brother-in-law Allen Taylor was serving as bishop. Grant, with Brigham's son Joseph, had been sent to preach repentance and reform, but "when he got there he felt like baptizing and confirming them anew into the church."³⁶ On Sunday morning Grant "delivered a soul-stirring address on the text of Br. Brigham, 'Saints, live your religion,'" and said that those who were not willing to hold to their sacred covenants were encouraged to leave the territory. The next morning, he "enjoined upon the Saints to observe the utmost decorum and reverence while the sacred ordinance of baptism was being attended to." After prayer, he proceeded to rebaptize Bishop Allen Taylor and his two counselors, Reddick Allred and Dorr Curtis, following which nearly five hundred Saints were "immersed under the direction of Prest. Grant, aided by Bishop Taylor."³⁷

Grant and Young next took their thunderous rhetoric five miles southeast to Farmington, where 406 members were rebaptized. They then returned to Salt Lake City and preached reformation in the Bowery. At the same time, John Young began preaching at settlements south of Salt Lake City, starting in Spanish Fork, where four hundred were rebaptized.³⁸ "The spirit of God is like a flame among the Leaders of this people," said Wilford Woodruff of the Reformation, "and they are throwing the arrows of the Almighty among the people. J.M. Grant is pruning with a sharp two-edged sword and calling loudly upon the people to wake up and repent of their sins."³⁹

From mid-September through late November, Grant traveled and preached virtually non-stop, rebaptizing the masses in cold and sometimes icy waters. Through excessive exposure and fatigue he contracted pneumonia; his condition steadily worsened, and on the evening of December 1, 1856, he passed away. Of his funeral three days later Stout wrote, "As a Major General he was buried in the honors of war As a Master Mason he was buried as such and above all as a Saint he lived, died and was buried as such."⁴⁰

Stout neglected to mention that Jedediah Grant also was Speaker of the House of Representatives. Two days after the funeral, Stout and Isaac Bullock started in deep snow for a new legislative session at Fillmore. The first order of business as the legislative session convened was to elect Lorenzo Snow as President pro tem of the Council and Hosea Stout, in a unanimous vote, as Speaker of the House, replacing Grant.⁴¹ After officers were elected, a bill was introduced and passed to change the capitol of the territory from Fillmore to Salt Lake City and the legislators immediately packed their bags.⁴²

The Reformation permeated all walks of life, including the government. On December 19, the second day the territorial legislature met in the Social Hall in Salt Lake City, Stout recorded, "On motion of Mr Rockwood the House adopted the rules of the former sessions of the Council which was to be governed by the dictates of the Holy Spirit."⁴³ According to Isaac Haight, "Both houses met in joint session and

President [Heber C.] Kimball required every member to repent of his sins, and be baptized."[44] Stout confirmed the statement, writing:

> the House went into the Council Chamber where President H. C. Kimball was preaching with great power being filled with the Spirit of God.
> Nearly all the members spoke all being filled with the spirit the meeting lasted till dark The power and testimony of the Elders of Israel exceeded any thing that I have seen in many a day It was truly a pentacost.[45]

Exactly one week later, on December 30, a "joint session met in committee of the whole on the state of the Reformation and passed an unanimous Resolution to repent of and forsake our sins and be rebaptized for their Remission and in conformity therewith." After dinner, the legislators "repaired to the Font filled it with water and some fifty-five were Baptized," including Stout, who was baptized by Franklin D. Richards and confirmed by A. P. Rockwood. "There was an unusual out poring of the spirit of God manifested in joint session on this occasion during the Preaching of Presidents B. Young and H. C. Kimball," Stout recorded.[46] The fire of the Reformation was burning hot and undoubtedly was the driving force behind an incident the previous night that attracted national attention, virtually all of it negative.

On November 16, 1856, Thomas S. Williams was excommunicated from the church.[47] Five weeks later, on December 22, Judge George Stiles suffered the same fate, to Stout's gratification: "Hon? George P. Stiles was tried for adultery found guilty and cut off from the Church root and Branch," he wrote. "Amen to the damnation of that wicked and corrupt Judge."[48] At night on December 29 a mob broke into and ransacked the office shared by Williams and Stiles. "Last night the Law library of Judge Stiles and T. S. Williams was broken open and the books and papers thereof taken away," Stout wrote on December 30. "A privy near by was filled with books a few thousand shingles and laths added and the concern set on fire and consumed."[49] The public was led to believe that official Federal Court records had been destroyed, though that proved not to be the case and the affair was a stunt to anger and deceive the judge.[50] Two days after the break-in, Surveyor General David Burr wrote to Commissioner of the General Land Office Thomas A. Hendricks, "We think the object is to break up the U.S. court if possible and to drive the U.S. Officers out of the Territory."[51] Burr was correct in his assumption. "It is rather warm for the wicked," Brigham Young wrote to George Q. Cannon, editor of the *Western Standard* in San Francisco, "and we expect when spring comes there will be a scattering out of such as cannot abide righteousness."[52]

It is unknown whether Stout was complicit in either the planning or execution of the law office break-in, but six weeks later he along with James Ferguson and Jesse C. Little were deeply involved in a near-brawl that received national attention. On February 10, Stout in one case and Little and Ferguson in another argued for a change of venue in Stiles's court because T. S. Williams, Stiles's law partner, was the opposing attorney in both cases and the three lawyers considered both Stiles and Williams to be hostile. On February 11, the motions for change of venue were withdrawn and instead Stout and Ferguson argued that the US court had no jurisdiction in territorial cases. The following day Stiles overruled their plea but "decided that while sitting as a U.S. Court it could not try Territorial cases" and that US Marshal Peter Dotson could not execute the laws of Utah.[53]

Appearing in Stiles's court on February 13, Surveyor General David Burr challenged Stiles's previous ruling on the matter of jurisdiction. Ferguson responded by calling Burr "a cowardly cur who wished to attack our laws clandestinely but had not courage to do it openly." Williams then introduced a motion asking whether the US courts and the marshal had assumed illegal powers. "To all this cold and deliberate contempt the Judge only overruled it as a matter of course but Mr Furguson and my self took it up and demanded his [Williams's] expulsion from the Bar for that and his incompetence to act as an attorney," Stout wrote. "In fact," he continued, "this was a contest for the supremecy of our laws in our own courts over the unlawful usurpation and rulings of the District Courts . . . At one time the feelings ran so high that several laid off their coats while two gentiles not wishing to take a hand in the contest left the Court."[54] Wilford Woodruff, in a letter to George A. Smith, elaborated:

> It would amuse you to read one of the late scenes while in court . . . It ended in T.S. Williams' resignation and Gen. Burr's dismissal from the bar; and some others, who intended to use the pistols, went out of the house in the form of a sled, using the seat of their honor for runners, dropping their loaded weapons while going out, which they never afterwards found. All has been quiet since, having but little lawing on hand.[55]

It was not Surveyor General David Burr's first clash with Stout: approximately three weeks earlier Burr had been confronted in his office by Stout, clerk of the US District Court James Cummings and territorial marshal Alexander McRae, demanding to know if he had written a letter dated May 12, 1856, reporting "extensive depredations upon the public lands." After Burr affirmed responsibility for the letter, the trio stated "*the country was theirs,* that they would not permit this interference with their rights, and this writing letters about them would be put a stop to." Burr said he could not divine the object of the visit "unless it was to intimidate me and prevent my writing."[56] Understandably shaken by the intrusion and threats as well as news of three murders at Springville, Burr on March 28 wrote to Thomas A. Hendricks expressing his fears and concerns:

> Judge Stiles, the only United States judge remaining here, intends trying to make his escape from the Territory as soon as it is possible to get over the mountains, but he fears attempts will be made to "cut him off." Knowing that our correspondence through the mails was examined, he has been afraid to write an account of affairs here, but intends reporting in person if he can get away. *The fact is, these people repudiate the authority of the United States in this country, and are in open rebellion against the general government* . . .
>
> For the last three months my friends have considered my life in danger. I have been cursed and denounced in their public meetings, and the most diabolical threats made against me . . .
>
> We find our position a critical one. We are by no means sure that we would be permitted to leave, for it is boldly asserted we would not get away alive. The same threats have been made against disaffected Mormons. We were inclined to think them idle menaces, until a few days since, when three men were killed at Springville, sixty miles from this place, for making the attempt. They were shot, *their throats cut, and their bowels ripped open.*[57]

Two weeks later, the Nauvoo Legion was reorganized, a process that began on February 19, 1857, when Stout "met with a committee to draft a new military law" according to "the good old Bible rule of Captains of 10's 100's &c."[58] On April 11 Lieutenant General Daniel Wells issued General Order No. 1, resuming his command of the Nauvoo Legion, thereby activating the military organization that for several years had been dormant. Among the officers chosen were James Ferguson as adjutant general and Hosea Stout as judge advocate.[59]

The reorganization of the Legion was not aimed directly at intimidating David Burr, Judge Stiles, and T. S. Williams, but it may have helped convince the trio of the wisdom of a quick departure from Salt Lake City. Three days after Lieutenant General Wells issued his General Order,

Figure 16.2. Utah Territorial Militia (the Nauvoo Legion). Hosea Stout was an officer in the Nauvoo Legion in Nauvoo and was judge advocate in Utah.

Williams was arrested for breach of peace after his teenage daughter eloped with a son of Heber C. Kimball. "He rages and raves like a mad man," Stout recorded.[60] Worried that Williams might try to carry out a threat to kill the Elder Kimball, Stout vigilantly stood guard nearly all night then the next day triumphantly wrote, "To day T. S. Williams Judge Stiles Genl Burr and P. K. Dotson with nearly all the gentile and apostate Scurf in this community left for the States."[61]

Stout's sentiment toward the departed individuals was hardly surprising given the remarks he had made ten days earlier from the pulpit of the Bowery on Sunday morning, April 5:

> Notwithstanding the blessings we enjoy, some men wish to leave, and they say it is because they are so tied up, there is so much tyranny and abuse that they really cannot stand it . . . I freely confess my feelings, when I see a man who has tasted of the powers of the world to come and then see him give way to the powers of darkness and subject himself to the adversary, it causes a satisfaction in my own breast to see him go away; I consider it a blessing to the cause.
> [Prest. Kimball: You would help such a man, would you not?]
> Yes, I would, and I would sooner see them go than stay.[62]

As a postscript, Stout wrote on April 16, "The fire of the reformation is burning many out who flee from the Territory afraid of their lives This is scriptural. 'The wicked flee when no man pursue' and so with an apostate Mormon he always believes his life in danger and flees accordingly."[63] Brigham Young continued the theme, on June 7 declaring from the pulpit of the Bowery:

> The spirit of the reformation has taken hold on the people; it has kindled the fire of the Almighty in Mount Zion to burn out many of the ungodly that could not stand it and they had fled . . . within the last six months, comparatively a hundred tons of care and anxiety have been removed from my shoulders; and I hope that this fire will continue to burn among this people until curses . . . shall all leave us.[64]

Unbeknownst to Young, sometime in late April or early May President Buchanan, who was convinced that the Mormons were in a state of rebellion, decided to replace Young as governor and determined that a show of military force was the best and quickest way to end the rebellion. On May 28 Lieutenant General Winfield Scott issued orders to put together a force of not less than twenty-five hundred army troops, and by mid-July the troops began their march to a conflict that became known as the Utah War.

"Fellow-citizens of Utah, this is rebellion against the Government to which you owe allegiance," Buchanan later stated in a Proclamation; "it is levying war against the United States, and involves you in the guilt of treason." Though no one incident led to his decision to send troops to Utah, the President gave a few hints at the beginning of the Proclamation: "The officers of the Federal Government have been driven from the Territory for no offense but an effort to do their sworn duty; others have been prevented from going there by threats of assassination; judges have been violently interrupted in the performance of their functions, and the records of the courts have been seized and destroyed or concealed."[65] Though there is no direct evidence that Stout ever made any "threats of assassination" to government officers, without doubt he was deeply involved in the other charges made by the President. As letters and articles regarding the "Mormon rebellion" began flooding the eastern newspapers, Hosea Stout became a household name to readers across the continent.

The Mormons' most damaging antagonist was Judge William Drummond, whose series of letters played a very important role in triggering the national reaction to the situation in Utah. Drummond and his mistress left Utah on May 17, 1856, ostensibly to hold court in Carson City but continuing on to San Francisco. While in California he wrote to San Francisco newspapers mostly under the pseudonym "Amicus Curiae."[66] In a letter to the *Daily Herald* on February 25, 1857, Drummond wrote:

> Again, a man by the name of Baker, (a Mormon,) was tried for murdering a dumb boy, in Judge Drummond's court, at Fillmore city; and although the proof showed one of the most aggravated cases of murder, the Grand Jury, (all Mormons of course,) brought in a verdict of murder in the second degree . . . he started towards the Penitentiary, yet, before the sixth Sabbath he had a full and complete pardon from Gov. Young . . . The reason assigned for the pardon was that he was a Saint, and a d – – d Gentile Judge should not have the pleasure of seeing one of the Saints of God put in prison for the murder of so useless a being as a dumb boy.[67]

Stout, of course, was Baker's defense attorney and likely prompted Brigham Young to issue the pardon. As Drummond returned to the States via Panama he wrote more letters condemning the Mormons, the most damning of which was his letter of resignation on March 30, 1857. The accusations in that letter moved from the general to the specific, citing first the ungovernable nature of the Mormons under the leadership of Brigham Young and that the Mormons looked to him alone as the law by which they were to be governed, supporting his assertions by giving as specific examples the pardons of Baker and Moroni Green that were granted by Young. Drummond specifically singled out Stout in a letter to the editor of the *New York Daily Times* of May 22, 1857, writing of "the unblushing impudence of HOSEA STOUT at the time Judge STILES' Court was adjourned for him by an armed mob." Drummond, irked that Stout had been sworn as US Prosecuting Attorney for the Territory of Utah, made the point that he was "never appointed by the President," though he neglected to mention that Stout was sworn in on May 10 by Judge Stiles himself.[68]

Even before Drummond's resignation, sensational stories were written in Eastern newspapers regarding Mormon abuses in Utah, particularly the disruption of Stiles's court, identifying the two major villains as James Ferguson and Hosea Stout. A lengthy article, written on March 5 but published in the *New York Daily Times* on May 18, 1857, under the title "MORE MORMON OUTRAGE," went into great and embellished detail, selections of which give a hint of what was shaping attitudes in the East:

> The Court was in progress on the 12th [of February] the Mormon members of the Bar and others of the Danite band inveighed Judge STILES into a private room, locked the door, barred the windows, and then with revolvers at his head and knives within an inch of his throat, forced him to promise to uphold them in whatever they did . . .
> The U.S. District Attorney is HOSEA STOUT, an appointee, of course, of the Government at Washington, and a noted member of the Danite Band. Upon the opening of the Court he rose and stated that no Grand Jury would be empaneled . . . Mr. [David] BURR then asked him if he understood him to say that he would be guided by the laws of the Territory in preference to the laws of the United States. Before any reply could be made, an attorney named FERGUSON, jumped up and commenced a most foul and abusive attack upon Mr. BURR, exhausting the stock of even Mormon billingsgate in his malignant trade. He then turned to the Judge, and told him that if he dared to decide against their laws he could sit on that Bench no longer, and the courtroom would be cleared "d – – d quick!" The District Attorney followed in

a violent harangue . . . The room was filled with armed ruffians who constituted the "backers" alluded to. As soon as Mr. BURR and Mr. T.S. WILLIAMS got up to reply, the Territorial marshal ordered them peremptorily to stop; and immediately the whole audience sprang to their feet, and the Danite murderers, who filled the Court, threw off their coats, brandished their knives and revolvers, and created so great confusion that the Judge was obliged to adjourn the Court at once.

The next morning, which was Saturday, the Court opened amid intense excitement. The whole Mormon populace were armed, and had been inflamed to such a degree by the incendiary speeches of FERGUSON, STOUT and others that the least pretence would have been availed of to massacre every Gentile in the place . . .

There can be no doubt that FERGUSON, STOUT, and their Danite bullies, were prompted to the conduct thus related by BRIGHAM YOUNG—for when Judge STILES went to the latter as Governor, and asked him if he would sustain him in the execution of his duties and the enforcement of the laws, he replied that he would not interfere, and would "hold the boys back no longer," but was going to let them have their own way, for the Court had given him too much trouble already.[69]

The report was overstated and incendiary, but such articles were effective in helping to shape public opinion. Even before such sensational stories hit the press, on March 20 Attorney General Black received a confidential letter from Judge John Kinney that in many respects paralleled the letter of resignation that Drummond wrote ten days later. Kinney made six points, the first of which began, "The Mormons are inimical to the Government of the U.S. and to all its officers who are not of their peculiar faith" and quoted Bishop Edwin Woolley, "That they would cut the throats of all the Gentiles, throw their heads into Salt Lake and use their bodies for manure." He accused the Mormons of trying to incite the Indians to murder Surveyor General Burr and charged the Mormons with the murders of unnamed individuals. Kinney concluded the section, "The Governor pardoned one man [Green] who was sentenced to the penitentiary, before he reached there and also another man [Baker] who was sentenced for ten years, after a confinement of thirty days, who was absolutely guilty of murder and ought to have been convicted for that high crime."[70]

On May 29, as mail from the East arrived in Salt Lake City for the first time since the previous November, Stout discovered that "The spirit of the people and rulers of the Nation seem to be hostile and surley towards the mormons."[71] The Sunday meeting at the Tabernacle on June 14 "was taken up in reading to the congregation the different accounts against the mormons as came in last mail," according to Stout. "It appears that there is now through out the U S. the most bitter, revengeful and mobocratic feeling against us that has ever been manifested."[72] When another mail shipment arrived on June 23, Stout reported, "The news paper writers were louder against the mormons than ever whether govt will take notice of the excitement or is not known."[73]

The Mormons tried to fight back in the battle for public opinion, beginning with articles attacking Drummond in George Q. Cannon's *Western Standard* in San Francisco and *The Mormon* in New York City, of which Apostle John Taylor was the editor. A letter to the *Platte Argus* of Weston, Missouri, prepared by Stout for Bill Hickman's signature, questioned why Judge Drummond branded Brigham Young "as a lawless despot only to cover his own iniquity and corruption" and went on to say:

> The Judge when he came here was determined to hang some body and he did not care who, he was disappointed, and so after trading horses in California one year set up his howl to see if he could not scare the U.S. to death about the Mormons and Gov Young. Meanwhile he has been in communication with the few drunken companions he left here and some Government officials settling "a more perfect plan of operations" against the Mormons untill time began to bring to light the frauds and impositions of government of Gen Burr and others causing them to hastily take the line of march Eastward leaving the good people here to wonder what would come next.[74]

Stout also wrote to the *Missouri Republican* "in answer to slanderous reports of Judge Drummond and others."[75] On June 29, in an attempt to smear David Burr's name, Young had William Hooper write to The Commissioner of the General Land Office, stating that Burr had awarded Charles Mogo a very lucrative land contract in deal which was expected to profit about $30,000 and in which Burr was a partner.[76] Two days later, Daniel H. Wells, who had replaced Jedediah Grant in the First Presidency, wrote to instruct Horace Eldredge to have three affidavits besmirching Judge Drummond published in the *Republican* and *New York Herald*. "We trust they will shut up some of their mouths," Wells wrote, "but don't they howl beautifully, wonder how they will feel when they find how completely they have been humbugged by the fellow Drummond. They must have been hungry for mormon news, they snatched at Drummond's lies so voraciously, wonder they did not eat him up as well . . . for he is nothing but a budget of falsehood which any man can see in five minutes in his company."[77]

The Mormon efforts to influence public opinion were of no consequence, however, mostly coming after President Buchanan's decision to send the army to Utah already had been made. On July 24, 1857, as the Saints gathered in large numbers to celebrate the tenth anniversary of Brigham Young's arrival with the first company of pioneers in the Salt Lake Valley, Stout recorded, "Some talk of troops coming."[78] Lorenzo Brown was more explicit in his report:

> But in the midst of this joyful scene there comes a mounted messenger with news . . . News of vital importance to citizens of Utah is quickly but quietly communicated . . . an army is actually advancing on Utah. For what purpose is enquirred by one and all as no one knows.[79]

The Mormons, definitely including Stout, were not spotless in their actions, but they considered themselves to be patriotic Americans and hardly in a state of rebellion, though Stout's account of the Legion's activity on July Fourth—"General training to day by way of celebrating the glorious Independence"—sent a mixed message.[80] On the other hand, reports concerning the state of affairs on Utah, though based on truth, often contained inaccuracies, embellishments, exaggerations, and even falsehoods, and President Buchanan, influenced by public opinion and the correspondence of territorial officials, inexplicably took the reports at face value rather than first investigating the situation before ordering troops to Utah.[81]

Drummond's letter of resignation created the greatest stir, but newspaper editors also "expressed a sense of shock at the treatment given David H. Burr and his surveyors by the people of Utah. They were even more incensed at the destruction of Stiles's court, for they interpreted this act as open defiance of the federal government."[82] Stout, with his involvement in the pardon of Samuel Baker, played a role in Drummond's complaint; he was front and center in the confrontation in David Burr's office that shocked editors across the nation; and he and James Ferguson (and, to a lesser degree, Jesse Little) were openly defiant in Judge Stiles's court, for which they were vilified by the press. While numerous other issues factored into James Buchanan's conclusion that the Mormon people were in revolt, there can be no doubt that Stout had played a prominent role in the president's decision to send troops to quash the "rebellion" in Utah.

Notes

1. *D&C*, Section 29, verses 7 and 8, announced as a revelation by Joseph Smith on September 26, 1830, reads: "And ye are called to bring to pass the gathering of mine elect . . . they shall be gathered in unto one place upon the face of this land . . . "
2. Todd, "More Members Now Outside U.S. Than In U.S." The official membership in England in 1850 was 30,747, while in the United States it was 26,911.
3. Hafen and Hafen, *Handcarts to Zion*, 24–25.
4. Brooks, *Mormon Frontier*, April 9, 1855, 554.
5. Hafen and Hafen, *Handcarts*, 27–28.
6. Brooks, *Mormon Frontier*, May 20, 1855, 555. The type of grasshopper was the Rocky Mountain locust, a species that by the beginning of the twentieth century was extinct.
7. "Sixth General Epistle . . . to the Saints," *Millennial Star* 14:23.
8. Letter from Brigham Young to Franklin D. Richards, September 30, 1855, printed in *Millennial Star*, 17:813–14.
9. "Thirteenth General Epistle . . . to the Saints," *Millennial Star*, 18:54; *Deseret News*, October 31, 1855.
10. Hunter, *Brigham Young The Colonizer*, 109.
11. Brooks, *Mormon Frontier*, September 26, 1856, 601.
12. *Deseret News*, October 1, 1856, 4.
13. Neff, *History of Utah*, 591.
14. *Journal of Discourses*, 4:115.
15. *Deseret News*, October 15, 1856.
16. Bartholomew and Arrington, *Rescue of the 1856 Handcart Companies*, 7–8.
17. *Journal History*, October 2, 1856.
18. Savage, "Journal," August 12, 1856, Church History Library.
19. Ibid., October 8, 1856.
20. Ludlow, *Encyclopedia of Mormonism*, 2:572.
21. Jones, *Forty Years Among the Indians*, 66.
22. *Journal History*, November 3, 1856 (recorded on November 30, 1856).
23. Brooks, *Mormon Frontier*, November 11, 1856, 605; Olsen, *The Price We Paid: The Extraordinary Story of the Willie and Martin Handcart Pioneers*, 389.
24. Bartholomew and Arrington, *Handcart Companies*, 47–9.
25. Brooks, *Mormon Frontier*, November 12, 1856, 605–6.
26. Ibid.
27. Ibid., November 16–17, 1856, 606.
28. Allred, "Journal," November 18, 1856.
29. Brooks, *Mormon Frontier*, November 18, 1856, 606.
30. Ibid., November 19, 1856, 607.
31. Ibid., November 20–21, 1856, 607.
32. Jones, *Forty Years Among the Indians*, 69; Brooks, *Mormon Frontier*, November 22, 1856, 607.
33. Hafen and Hafen, *Handcarts*, 140. According to the Hafens, 13 of 274 perished in the Ellsworth company; 7 of 221 in the McArthur Company; 6 of 320 in the Bunker Company; and 67 of 500 in the Willie Company.

Linda McDowell Carter estimated that between 202 and 267 members of the Willie and Martin companies died, by far the greatest number of all ten handcart companies between 1856–1860. See Bagley, "The Mormon Handcart Disasters," *Journal of Mormon History*, Winter 2009: 108.
34. Brooks, *Mormon Frontier*, November 25, 1856, 607.
35. Grant, July 13, 1855, Provo Conference, in *Deseret News*, October 24, 1855.
36. *Deseret News*, October 1, 1856.
37. Ibid., September 24, 1856.
38. Ibid., October 22, 1856.
39. Woodruff, "Journal," October 9, 1856.
40. Brooks, *Mormon Frontier*, December 4, 1856, 608.
41. Ibid., December 18, 1856, 609. It is notable that three of the top four elected officers of the House were members of Hosea's rescue team (Hosea was elected speaker; James Ferguson, chief clerk; James Martineau, assistant clerk; and William Kimball, sergeant-at-arms).
42. Ibid., December 8, 1856, 606–7; *Baltimore Sun*, March 25, 1857. The Baltimore newspaper identified Hosea as "a member of the Danite Band." Hosea was assumed to be a Danite in Missouri due to his participation in the Battle of Crooked River in 1838 and the fact that John D. Lee claimed all Mormon participants in the battle were Danites. There is neither firm evidence that the same Danite organization was active in Utah nor that Hosea was ever involved in any such organization outside of Missouri, yet newspapers across the nation frequently referred to him as a "member of the Danite Band."
43. Brooks, *Mormon Frontier*, December 19, 1856, 610.
44. Haight, "Journal, 1842–1862," MS 20630, December 30, 1856, Church History Library.
45. Brooks, *Mormon Frontier*, December 23, 1856, 611.
46. Ibid., December 30, 1856, 613.
47. Morgan, *The Great Salt Lake*, 264; Letter from Brigham Young to George A. Smith, December 7, 1856, Church History Library.
48. Brooks, *Mormon Frontier*, December 22, 1856, 611.
49. Ibid., December 30, 1856, 613.
50. Ibid., 613 note 82.
51. Letter from David Burr to Thomas A. Hendricks, December 31, 1856, Utah State Historical Society.
52. *Western Standard*, February 21, 1857, letter of January 7, 1857.
53. Brooks, *Mormon Frontier*, February 10–12, 1857, 621.
54. Ibid., February 13, 1857, 622.
55. Letter from Wilford Woodruff to George A. Smith, *Journal History*, April 1, 1857.
56. Letter from David H. Burr to Thomas A. Hendricks, *Executive Documents, Printed by order of The HOUSE OF REPRESENTATIVES during the First Session of the Thirty-Fifth Congress 1857–58*. In a letter to Hendricks dated June 11, Burr added that James Cummings also was present with Stout and McRae.
57. Letter from David Burr to Thomas A. Hendricks, March 28 1857, *Utah Expedition*, 118–19. The murders were of William Parrish, his son Beetson and Gardner "Duff" Porter. The case, known widely as the Parrish-Potter

Murders, is discussed in a later chapter.
58. Brooks, *Mormon Frontier*, February 19, 1857, 623.
59. *Deseret News*, April 15, 1857. The appointment carried with it the rank of "Colonel of Heavy Artillery of the Nauvoo Legion." See Hosea Stout Papers, Utah State Historical Society, letter from Brigham, June 11, 1857.
60. Brooks, *Mormon Frontier*, April 14, 1857, 625.
61. Ibid., April 15, 1857, 625.
62. April 5, 1857, in *Deseret News*, April 15, 1857.
63. Brooks, *Mormon Frontier*, April 16, 1857, 625
64. *Journal of Discourses*, 4:348.
65. Buchanan, "Proclamation," in *Mormon Resistance*, 332–37.
66. An *amicus curiae* (also spelled *amicus curiæ*; plural *amici curiae*) is someone, not a party to a case, who volunteers to offer information to assist a court in deciding a matter before it.
67. *San Francisco Daily Herald*, February 25, 1857, in Ekins, *Defending Zion*, 285. The article was reprinted verbatim in the *National Era* on April 2, 1857.
68. Letter from Judge William W. Drummond of May 22, 1857, published in *New York Daily Times*, June 26, 1857; Hosea Stout papers, Utah State Historical Society, May 10, 1857.
69. *New York Daily Times*, May 18, 1857.
70. Letter from John Kinney to Jeremiah Black, March 20, 1857, in William P. MacKinnon, *At Sword's Point, Part 1*, 109–11.
71. Brooks, *Mormon Frontier*, May 29, 1857, 627.
72. Ibid., June 14, 1857, 628.
73. Ibid., June 23, 1857, 628.
74. Letter from William Hickman (in the hand of Hosea Stout) to the *Platte Argus*, Weston Missouri, June 30, 1857, Brigham Young File, CR1234/1, Box 47, Folder 46 (Reel 61), Church History Library. Copy of letter courtesy of William MacKinnon.
75. Brooks, *Mormon Frontier*, July 1, 1857, 633.
76. Letter from William H. Hooper to The Commissioner of the General Land Office, June 29, 1857, in Brigham Young Letterpress Copybook, Church History Library.
77. Letter from Daniel H. Wells to Horace S. Eldredge, July 1, 1857, in Brigham Young Letterpress Copybook, Church History Library.
78. Brooks, *Mormon Frontier*, July 24, 1857, 634.
79. Brown, "Journal," MS 270.1 B876b, 283–84, Church History Library.
80. Brooks, *Mormon Frontier*, July 4, 1857, 633.
81. Judge Kinney, for example, in his very influential letter of March 20, 1857, to Jeremiah Black said that Judge Stiles was "a Mormon and a willing tool of Brigham Youngs," apparently unaware that three months earlier Stiles was excommunicated and his law office was vandalized. See MacKinnon, *At Sword's Point, Part 1*, 110. Judge Drummond in his letter of resignation stated "That the records, papers, &c of the supreme court have been destroyed by order of the church." A letter from Curtis E. Bolton, deputy Supreme Court clerk, to Jeremiah S. Black on June 26, 1857, said the records resided "safely in my custody." Drummond charged that Judge Leonidas Shaver was killed by "poisoned liquors given to him under order

of the leading men of the Mormon Church." An inquest into the death, certified by non-Mormon physician Garland Hurt and accepted by a coroner's jury made up of both Mormons and non-Mormons, concluded that Shaver—who, though non-Mormon, was very popular in Utah—had died of natural causes. See Alexander, "Carpetbaggers, Reprobates, and Liars: Federal Judges and the Utah War (1857–58)," *The Historian*, 70, no. 2:209–38. Drummond also stated that "A[lmon] W. Babbitt, was murdered on the plains by a band of Mormon marauders, under the particular and special order of Brigham Young, Heber C. Kimball, and J.M Grant, and not by the Indians, as reported by the Mormons themselves," even though authentic reports had reached Salt Lake City before Drummond's departure that the Cheyenne had massacred Babbitt and his party. See Schindler, *Orrin Porter Rockwell, Son of God, Man of Thunder*, 236–39.

82. Furniss, *The Mormon Conflict, 1850–1859*, 60.

17
Resisting the Feds

Winfield Scott, general-in-chief of the United States Army, when asked in late May 1857 to comment on President Buchanan's decision to put down the rebellion in Utah, replied that it was already too late in the year to send any troops west.[1] General William S. Harney, to whom command of the troops had been given before being recalled to command troops sent to deal with guerrilla warfare in Kansas, had the same concern and preferred to wait until the following year to commence the operation.[2] Both generals had to have been aware of the hazard of a late journey to Utah from reports of the twin disasters of the Willie and Martin handcart companies, yet, in a classic example of how not to initiate a military campaign, the Utah Expedition departed Fort Leavenworth on July 18, 1857, very late in the season and almost exactly a year after the two handcart companies departed Iowa City for their ill-fated trek across the plains.[3]

Conditions in Utah were not investigated before the decision was made to send the troops, so General Harney dispatched assistant quartermaster Captain Stewart Van Vliet with a small escort ahead of the main body of troops to arrange for supplies and to locate a site for a military post near Salt Lake City.[4] An officer with considerable diplomatic skill, Van Vliet seemed a perfect choice for the task. After graduating ninth in his class from West Point in 1840, he served in the Seminole War in Florida and later in the Mexican War, afterwards becoming a quartermaster and assisting in building military posts along the Oregon Trail where he had positive interactions with the Mormons in which he earned their friendship.

Van Vliet, wisely having left his military escort behind, entered the Salt Lake Valley in the company of Mormons Bryant Stringham and Nathaniel Jones on September 8, 1857 (three days after Stout's wife Alvira delivered a healthy, nine-pound son named Brigham Hosea).[5] The captain at first was received cordially, but after he disclosed that an army base would be erected within thirty miles of Salt Lake City to enforce the law while making Utah a military district, church spokesmen reminded him of their previous persecutions and notified him that this time the Mormons would defend themselves.[6] "The Gov[ernor] most distinctly informed what would be the consequences in case of a war with the U. States," Stout wrote of a meeting he attended with church leaders and Van Vliet, "and that he was at liberty to inform the President of the U. S. accordingly."[7]

Earlier in the day "President Young declared the policy he would pursue in case the United States did declare war against the Saints."[8] Stout, perhaps worried that a spy might pilfer the secrets, declined to record Young's policy in his journal that day, but Brigham had no such qualms in spreading the word. On September 14, the same day Van Vliet departed with John Bernhisel for Washington, Young penned a letter that was sent to local military district heads outlining his strategy. The first line of defense would be to take the offensive in a mode of guerilla warfare, laying "waste every thing that will burn, houses, fences, trees, fields, grass, that they cannot find a particle of any thing that will be of use to them, not even sticks to make a fire for to cook their suppers" and to "stampede their animals" and "take the supply trains."[9] Within a week of the date of Young's letter, many miles of grass in front of the troops' advance had been burned,[10] and on September 24 Nauvoo Legion colonels Robert Burton and James Cummings received orders to stampede army horses and cattle, which they began to do posthaste.[11] Particularly effective was Major Lot Smith, who in early October "captured six waggons of our enemies and took the cattle in conformity to the orders to annoy and harrass our enemies and break them down but not to kill any of them."[12] Smith and his militia eventually managed to burn three freight trains (out of forty-one) comprising seventy-four large supply wagons and in seizing about fourteen hundred of the expedition's two thousand head of cattle.[13]

On September 25, Nathaniel Jones, who had accompanied Van Vliet to meet the 2nd regiment of US troops, arrived back in Salt Lake City with a report that Van Vliet tried—unsuccessfully—to dissuade the troops from advancing;[14] armed with that news, on September 26 Lieutenant General Daniel H. Wells, the head of the Nauvoo Legion, called upon his staff to be ready to march on the morrow. "I have been engaged all day in preparing my self to go to meet Uncle's troops," Stout recorded. "If nothing prevents we will start tomorrow and most likely before we return it will be determined whether a legalized government mob can force themselves on us against our will."[15]

Wells decided to erect his defense in Echo Canyon, the eastern portal to the Salt Lake Valley through which the sizeable Utah Expedition troops most certainly would pass. "In front the eye runs down the long bright red line of Echo Kanyon," Victorian explorer and author Sir Richard Francis Burton wrote on his journey to the American West in 1860. "Twin lines of bluffs, a succession of buttresses all fretted and honeycombed, a double row of steeples slipped from perpendicularity, frowned at each other across the gorge."[16] The most formidable section of the canyon, "being surmounted on the West by high perpendicular ledges of rock immediately over looking the road" and with cliffs on the east "very high and difficult of ascent," seemed a perfect location for a defensive stand.[17]

Stout departed Salt Lake City for Echo Canyon on September 27 with Wells and other Nauvoo Legion officers.[18] When word arrived that the US troops were within ten miles of Fort Bridger, Wells took a small group, including Stout, and proceeded in the direction of the fort, but after dining at Cache Cave Station he instructed Stout to return twenty-five miles with Colonel Nathaniel Jones and four other men to put Echo Canyon "in a state for defense."[19] Besides erecting hidden batteries "high in the rocky crags," the militia dug "three impassable ditches 12 feet wide and six or 7 deep filled by means of dams across the Creek which entirely obstructs the road and will keep our enemies exposed to a galling fire." After surveying the surrounding country with Major Joseph Taylor (a brother of Stout's late-wife Louisa) and subsequently reconnoitering some side canyons for the purpose of fortification, Stout concluded that the Echo Canyon defenses were "truly formidable" and proclaimed, "There is no possibility of our being flanked."[20] Whether the Echo Canyon defenses truly were formidable was not important so long as enemy leaders considered them to be so; Colonel E. B. Alexander, commander of the 10th Infantry who in the absence of General Harney had become the de facto commander of the Utah Expedition, was convinced that the canyon would be a death trap, leading him to direct a futile attempt to bypass it by way of Bear River, in the process losing precious time as winter approached.[21]

When Colonels Nathaniel Jones and Robert Burton on October 15 left in pursuit of a better range for livestock, Stout was given charge of the militia in Echo Canyon.[22] On the same day, Richard Yates, assumed by the Mormons to be a federal spy due to his sale of a substantial amount of gunpowder to the approaching Utah Expedition, was captured at Fort Bridger; three days later Stout noted, "At dark W[illiam] A. Hickman came in with Mr Yates a prisoner."[23] That night while Yates was sleeping he was bludgeoned to death by Hickman, a murder to which Hickman later confessed, in the process implicating Stout as a co-participant and giving rise to the arrests in 1871 of Stout, Daniel Wells, William Kimball, and Brigham Young for Yates's murder in a case that captured nationwide attention.[24]

Figure 17.1. Daniel H. Wells, Hosea's co-defendant in the 1872 Richard Yates murder trial.

Exactly one week following Yates's murder, on October 25, General Daniel Wells left orders for Stout to proceed home "at the first chance," even though the previous day he had received orders to march with three hundred troops from Utah County to East Canyon to put it "in a complete State of defence."[25] The reasoning behind the sudden change in orders in the midst of fortifying canyon defenses is unclear, though it may well have been influenced by Alexander's march up Hams Fork to try to enter the Salt Lake Valley by way of Bear River, subsequently making it unlikely that the US troops would attempt to breach the Echo Canyon defenses in the immediate future. That view was challenged, however,

Figure 17.2. Brigham Young.

when on November 8 an express arrived with news that Colonel Albert Sidney Johnston, who had replaced General Harney as commander of the Utah Expedition, was trudging in heavy snow toward Fort Bridger that, along with Fort Supply, had been vacated and burned by its Mormon occupants before they retreated to Salt Lake City.[26] Within two days, thirteen hundred men had been ordered to Echo Canyon to defend against the army's expected invasion,[27] but shortly thereafter Brigham Young received word that the army likely could not advance further toward Salt Lake City until spring, and on the last day of November General Wells issued an order for the vast majority of Legion members to return home from the mountains.[28]

With "Johnston's Army" (as it was known among the Saints) bogged down for the winter, life in the Salt Lake Valley was surprisingly normal. "New Year sets in quiet and peaceable," wrote Stout. "The Spirit of peace and happiness which pervade every breast in the Territory is a perfect miracle."[29] Stout was busily engaged in public service: in addition to being a representative in the territorial legislature, he functioned as a prosecutor in the probate court, as Judge Advocate in the Nauvoo Legion, and "was elected to the same offices as last year to wit Code Commissioner, Regent of the "University of Deseret" and Attorney General."[30] Concurrently, he somehow found time to dig a twenty-two feet deep well in his back yard.[31] Despite his activity and the relative peacefulness in the Valley, Stout was apprehensive about the future: on January 22, 1858, as the joint session of the legislature (that commenced on December 14) came to a conclusion, he noted in his journal, "Thus ends the Seventh Session of Utah's Legislature what will be the Eighth and under what circumstances?"[32]

Of particular concern was a report of January 7 from James Ferguson to Brigham Young expressing apprehension that the barricades in Echo Canyon were not sufficient to defend against the enemy.[33] Ferguson also suggested that the Nauvoo Legion, facing a lack of firearms and gunpowder, should "select some two thousand of the right kind of men" and provide them with excellent rifles.[34] In response, the territorial legislature, demonstrating its close ecclesiastical ties, on January 19 authorized the creation of a standing army of a thousand men to be raised and supported by "levies from the different Wards and Counties."[35]

At virtually the same time, more than three thousand US troops were ordered to march to reinforce the Utah Expedition, bringing its size to more five thousand, nearly a third of the entire US Army.[36] Brigham Young realized that the Saints could not afford to fight the strengthened US Army and decided to pursue a "Sebastopol policy," patterned after the 1855 Crimean War episode in which the Russians, in a hopeless situation, burned the city of Sebastopol and left the ruins for the British and French forces.[37] As early as September 13, 1857, Young preached from the Tabernacle pulpit:

> Before I will suffer what I have in times gone by, there shall not be one building, nor one foot of lumber, nor a stick, nor a tree, nor a particle of grass and hay, that will burn, left in reach of our enemies. I am sworn, if driven to extremity, to utterly lay waste, in the name of Israel's God.[38]

By March 1858, Brigham Young had completed plans to move the Saints in the northern settlements to the White Mountain country—an uncharted desert region to the west of Utah's southern settlements, straddling the present Utah-Nevada border and rumored to be able to support a population of five hundred thousand. "I am going there where we should have gone six or seven years ago," proclaimed Young at a special council on March 21 in the tabernacle.[39] This came even as Colonel Thomas Kane, an old and valued friend of the Mormons, was undertaking a special mission of peace.

In the early winter Kane, hoping to help avoid an armed conflict between the Mormons and the army, had visited President Buchanan in an attempt to persuade him to send an investigation commission to Utah. Buchanan was in no mood to compromise but did give the colonel his unofficial blessing to go to Utah to try to achieve a peaceful solution. In January 1858 Kane, traveling at his own expense and under the pseudonym of Dr. Osborne, went to Salt Lake City by way of Panama, San Francisco, Los Angeles, San Bernardino, and southern Utah—by far the fastest route available in the middle of winter.

Kane arrived in Salt Lake City on February 25, "quite out of health by hard travelling."[40] Though he was warmly greeted, church leaders were skeptical of his ability to bring the conflict to a peaceful conclusion; thus, while Kane met in Wyoming with military leaders and Alfred Cumming, who had been designated by the federal government to succeed Brigham Young as governor of Utah, the Mormons held a meeting at which the decision was made to undertake a great "move south," the most complete account of which was recorded by Stout:

> *Thursday 18 March 1858:* Attended a general Council at the Historians office of the first Presidency, Twelve [Apostles], and officers of the [Nauvoo] Legion The object of which was to take into consideration the best plan of operations to be adopted to counter act the purposes of our enemies, whether to attact them before they come near us or wait untill they come near, or whether it is yet best to fight at all only in unavoidable self defense or in case a large force is sent against us this spring [;] whether to fight or burn our houses and destroy every thing in and around us and flee to the mountains and deserts &c &c &c
>
> It appears that the course pursued hitherto by Gov Young in baffelling the oppressive purposes of Prest Buckhannan has redounded to the honor of Gov Young and the Saints and equally to the disgrace of the President and his cabinet[.] Mormonism is on the ascendancy and now what is the best policy to maintain that ascendancy. If we whip out and use up

the few troops at Bridger will not the excitement and sympathy which is now raising in our favor in the states, be turned against us. Whereas if we only anoy and impede their progress while we "Burn up" and flee, the folly, and meanness of the President will be the more apparrant and he and his measures more unpopular.[41]

Three days later a meeting was held in the Tabernacle at which Brigham Young revealed to the gathered congregation his plan of "fleeing to the desert and mountains." "It was decided to send 500 families from this city immediately to be selected from among those who had never been driven from their homes and from that class to take the poorest and most helpless," Stout recorded. Though his family clearly "did not come in that class who were called upon," Stout gave his name to go with the first company since many were reluctant to volunteer.[42] Unfortunately, on April 5, the day they were to depart, his wife Alvira was stricken with inflammatory rheumatism and rendered unable to walk, forcing the family to remain in Salt Lake City as the "Move South" commenced.[43]

Despite the postponement in their plans, on April 7 M. D. Hambleton took about twelve hundred pounds of Stout's "goods and effects" to Salt Creek in Juab County, the assumed place of the family's relocation. It is clear that Stout thought the move might be permanent. "The garden is growing finely," he wrote on April 17. "Aside from the pending exodus which seems to be our doom I am in a fair way to have the most excellent garden I ever had, but there seems to be no alternative but to leave our houses and fine gardens . . . but such is the fate and always has been with those in every age who would dare to worship the true God."[44]

Though Hosea and his sister Anna were nearly exhausted from sitting up every night with Alvira, who continued to be helpless from her affliction, on April 19 he took the opportunity of accompanying Jesse Little and James Ferguson on a visit to Governor Cumming and Colonel Thomas Kane, who had arrived in Salt Lake City the previous week following Kane's successful peace negotiations with Cumming and Colonel Johnston.[45] It was more than a mere social visit, particularly for Ferguson and Stout, who had been so disruptive in Judge Stiles's court. Cumming "was very much astonished to find that the Utah Library and the Court records were not burned as reported to government," particularly since those reports constituted a major reason for President Buchanan's decision to dispatch the Utah Expedition. Following an "agreeable conversation" on various subjects, the new governor declared his intention to make favorable reports to the government and to do all he could to avoid a collision between the United States and Utah.[46]

Cumming turned out to be amicable and treated Brigham Young with respect, though in his initial appearance before a congregation on April 25 twice he was "roundly hissed" and his notice (which Stout considered a cross "between a Pronunciamento and a Bull) to give safe conduct to all who desired to leave Utah was greeted with skepticism.[47] His subsequent pleas to the Mormons to halt their move south and remain in their homes fell on deaf ears due to their great distrust of the army and of the government. "Is there not some way to stop the moving?" Cumming asked Brigham Young, who replied that "if the troops were withdrawn from the Territory, the people would stop moving, but that 99 out of every hundred of the people would rather live out their lives in the mountains than endure the oppression the Federal Government was now heaping upon them."[48] So deep was the contempt for the troops that as late as May 24, the last day of the Move South, church officials still gave serious consideration to burning structures in Salt Lake City and all settlements to the north.

With Alvira still too ill to travel, on May 5 Stout sent his sister, with his children Elisabeth and Eli, to Salt Creek in the company of John Webster and a load of his goods.[49] On May 23 he sent another eleven hundred pounds of goods with Homer Brown, at the cost of eight dollars. "Times are dull we hardly a neighbour in this vicinity," Stout wrote that day. "The people are moving rapidly and ere many days Great Salt Lake City will be deserted."[50] The following day—the final day for commencing the move south—Stout, in the company of James Ferguson, went to Provo, bringing letters from General Wells stating that various settlements were "very remiss in their duties," before returning the next day to meet his wife and family who had encamped at Mill Creek, just south of Salt Lake City.[51]

While his family trudged slowly toward Salt Creek, Stout returned to the city to attend to some business and to retrieve fifty volumes of legal books.[52] When he finally arrived at Salt Creek, about forty-five miles south of Provo, he found his family well but living "in a little dirty house" that was not nearly large enough to contain more than four thousand pounds of possessions, though it would remain their home for nearly two months.[53] Nevertheless, it was better than the crude accommodations of many, which varied from covered wagons and canvas tents to dugouts and temporary board shanties.

Two days after reaching Salt Creek, Stout received notice that two peace commissioners, Senator-Elect L. W. Powell, former governor of Kentucky, and Major Ben McCulloch, of Texas, arrived in Salt Lake City with a proclamation from President Buchanan offering a free pardon to all Mormons "who will repent of past deeds and do better."[54] While Mormon leaders were relieved by the presence of the commission, they were offended by the contents of Buchanan's proclamation, especially terms such as "treason" and "rebellion" that were contained therein. At a private meeting in Salt Lake City shortly before the arrival of Buchanan's proclamation, "While speaking upon the subject of treason and being tried for treason, he [Brigham Young] said to Hosea Stout, I want to have you get all the history you can on the subject and show it to the Governor of this territory, as he has a right to resist an armed force entering this territory."[55]

While they considered themselves unjustly to have been charged with treason and rebellion, the Mormons also were mystified by President Buchanan's pardon. "By what right he does all this I do not know," Stout exclaimed on June 8, and Charles Lowell Walker wrote that the president's proclamation was "a parcel of Damnd lies from beginning to end."[56] The following week both men were at a meeting in Provo at which Stout concluded that the peace commissioners were sent by Buchanan to "make peace on any terms which would save him from disgrace and his party from ruin"; he also deemed a speech of Powell to the people in Provo to be a "miserable effort to eulogise Utah and Uncle Sam both and altogether was very shallow, and not much liked."[57] Walker was even franker: "Ex Gov Powell said all things were peaceably settled &c and we might return to our homes and a lot more of such like gas, but he lied in his heart and he knew it."[58]

Despite the negative feelings, Brigham Young, in meetings with the commissioners on June 11 and 12, accepted the president's pardon while denying all charges other than burning army supply trains and taking their cattle. At roughly the same time, Albert Sidney Johnston, who had been promoted to brigadier general, made his own proclamation of peace and advised the Saints that "they will find the army (always faithful to the obligation of duty) as ready now to assist and protect as it was to oppose them while it was believed they were resisting the laws of their government."[59] Then on June 14, Governor Cumming made a formal proclamation of the war's end. An editorial in the *Deseret News* responded sarcastically, "We tender our thanks to President Buchanan for pardoning acts committed in holding the wrist to a hand grasping a weapon to destroy our lives, and that too for no breach of law on our part, for we emphatically affirm that all allegations of our disobedience to the Constitution and laws of the United States are untrue."[60]

Before any real peace could be established, it was necessary for the army to enter the Territory and without incident establish a military camp. To that end, General Johnston began advancing his troops on June 13 and triumphantly marched through the deserted streets of Salt Lake City on June 26. Describing the scene, Captain Albert Tracy wrote, "With the exception of a picked few of his "destroyers" of decidedly rough and sinister aspect, left as a police, and with orders to fire the city in case we offered to occupy it, every man, woman, and child, had, under the direction of the prophet, departed—fled! . . . It was substantially a city of the dead, and might have been depopulated by a pest or famine."[61]

The troops halted temporarily eighteen miles west of the city to survey the surrounding countryside for a suitable site for a military post and settled in the Cedar Valley, a few miles west of Utah Lake. Since many displaced Mormons were camping in the vicinity, Johnston decided to pause near the Jordan River until the Saints had returned to their homes. After Brigham Young and church leaders in early July returned to Salt Lake City, "the roads were crowded with people who were following their example"; on July 6, as Stout traveled from Salt Creek to Salt Lake City to check the condition of his house and garden, he met the advance of Johnston's command, who were marching to Cedar Valley where they established a military post called Camp Floyd, in honor of Secretary of War John B. Floyd.[62] Three days later in Salt Lake City, Stout was introduced to the new Chief Justice of the Utah Territory, Delano R. Eckels. "He is a very talkative man who has a great opinion of himself," Stout noted, "but with all I think very superficial and no friend to Utah and her people."[63]

After two days of weeding his garden, Stout returned to Salt Creek with two four-mule teams, courtesy of Brigham Young, to retrieve his family and his possessions.[64] Following his arrival back in Salt Lake City he spent Pioneer Day (July 24) and the following three days "fixing up" his books and putting his house in order, a "great deal of trouble," he reported, though far greater troubles, particularly in the legal arena, lay ahead. Stout's first impression of Judge Eckels as an adversary to the Saints proved correct, but it was Eckels's two associate justices—Charles E. Sinclair and John Cradlebaugh—who became Stout's greatest judicial foes.

Notes

1. Furniss, *Mormon Conflict*, 95.
2. Hafen and Hafen, *Mormon Resistance*, 7.
3. Among newspapers, reports of the handcarts were published in *New York Daily Tribune* on February 24, 1857, and in the *Baltimore Sun* on February 25, 1857; a related article appeared in New York's *Weekly Herald* on March 28, 1857.
4. Hafen and Hafen, *Mormon Resistance*, 38–39.
5. Ibid., September 5 and 8, 1857, 637.
6. Ibid., September 9, 1857, 637; Furniss, *Mormon Conflict* 106.
7. Brooks, *Mormon Frontier*, September 13, 1857, 637.
8. Ibid.
9. Letter from Brigham Young and Daniel Wells to Col. William H. Dame, September 14, 1857, Brigham Young Letterbook, Church History Library. The identical letter was sent to other military district leaders.
10. *Utah Expedition*, 60.

11. Cummings and Burton, Report to Wells, September 27, 1857, Brigham Young Collection, Church History Library.
12. Brooks, *Mormon Frontier*, October 6, 1857, 641.
13. Arrington, *Great Basin Kingdom*, 178.
14. Brooks, *Mormon Frontier*, September 25, 1857, 638.
15. Ibid., September 26, 1857, 630.
16. Burton, *The City of the Saints*, 184.
17. Brooks, *Mormon Frontier*, September 30, 1857, 639.
18. Ibid., September 27, 1857, 638–39.
19. Ibid., September 29, 1857, 639. The other four men were identified by Hosea as H.S. Beattie, William Simmons, Stephen Taylor, and H. Margretts. The men arrived in the canyon on the morning of September 30; that evening at about sunset, a Dane named Frederic Neilsen, "who had been a soldier and a good marksman," took a jaeger rifle and deliberately shot Simmons through the head, killing him instantly. The motive was a mystery since Neilsen and Simmons were known to be good friends. See Brooks, *Mormon Frontier*, September 30, 1857, 639.
20. Ibid., October 5, 6, and 13, 1857, 641–42.
21. Ibid., October 21 and 23, 1857, 643–44.
22. Ibid., October 15, 1857, 642.
23. Ibid., October 18, 1857, 643.
24. The Yates murder case is treated in detail in a later chapter.
25. Brooks, *Mormon Frontier*, October 24–25, 1857, 644.
26. Ibid., November 8–9, 1857, 645.
27. Neff, *History of Utah*, 479.
28. Furniss, *Mormon Conflict*, 146.
29. Brooks, *Mormon Frontier*, January 1, 1858, 650.
30. Ibid., December 15, 1857–January 15, 1858, 649–51.
31. Ibid., January 16, 1858, 651.
32. Ibid., January 22, 1858, 652.
33. James Ferguson, report to Brigham Young, January 7, 1858, in Bigler and Bagley, *The Mormon Rebellion*, 267.
34. Ibid., 270.
35. Brooks, *Mormon Frontier*, January 19, 1858, 652.
36. Bigler and Bagley, *Mormon Rebellion*, 266.
37. Poll, "The Move South," *BYU Studies* 29, no. 4:65.
38. *Journal of Discourses* 5:231.
39. Clifford L. Stott, *Search for Sanctuary: Brigham Young and the White Mountain Expedition* (Salt Lake City, 1984), 57.
40. Brooks, *Mormon Frontier*, February 25, 1858, 653.
41. Ibid., March 18, 1858, 654.
42. Ibid., March 21, 1858, 655.
43. Ibid., April 5, 1858, 656.
44. Ibid., April 17, 1858, 657.
45. Governor Cumming was the only new civil officer to accept Kane's proposal to go to Salt Lake City unaccompanied by the army to establish peace through friendly discussion with Mormon leaders. See Anderson, *Desert Saints*, 180.

46. Brooks, *Mormon Frontier*, April 19, 1858, 657.
47. Ibid., April 25, 1858, 657. A "pronunciamento" was a proclamation while a "bull" signified nonsense.
48. *Journal History*, June 12, 1858.
49. Brooks, *Mormon Frontier*, May 5, 1858, 658.
50. Ibid., May 23, 1858, 659.
51. *Journal History*, May 24, 1858; Brooks, *Mormon Frontier*, May 25, 1858, 659.
52. Brooks, *Mormon Frontier*, May 31, 1858, 660.
53. Ibid., June 6, 1858, 660.
54. Ibid., June 8, 1858, 660.
55. *Journal History*, May 24, 1858.
56. Larson and Larson, eds., *Diary of Charles Lowell Walker*, June 7, 1858, 1:34.
57. Brooks, *Mormon Frontier*, June 8 and 16, 1858, 660.
58. Larson and Larson, eds., *Diary*, June 16, 1858, 1:35.
59. Furniss, *Mormon Conflict*, 197.
60. *Deseret News*, June 23, 1858.
61. "Journal of Captain Albert Tracy," *Utah Historical Quarterly* 13 no. 1 (January 1945):55.
62. Brooks, *Mormon Frontier*, July 4 and 6, 1858, 661.
63. Ibid., July 9, 1858, 661.
64. Ibid., July 16, 1858, 661.

18
The Attorney of the Mormon Church

Christina Rossetti, a daughter of émigré Italian scholar Gabriele Rossetti and his wife Frances Polidori, was one of the most important English female poets of the nineteenth century, best known to future generations for Christmas carols set to words from her poems, *In the Bleak Midwinter* and *Love Came Down at Christmas*. Having suffered frequent and long periods of poor health, Christina eventually came to regard life as physically and emotionally painful and began to look forward to death both as a release and as the possible moment of joyful union with God and with those she had loved and lost. One of her lesser-known yet poignant poems was written on January 16, 1859, upon hearing that her first cousin, Henrietta Polydore, whom she loved but had considered to be lost, was about to re-embark for England:

For Henrietta Polydore

> On the land and on the sea
> Jesus keep both you and me;
> Going out and coming in,
> Christ keep us both from shame and sin.
> In this world, in the world to come,
> Keep us safe and lead us home:
> To-day in toil, to-night in rest,
> Be best beloved and love us best.

Four years later, Christina's brother, the famed English poet and artist Dante Gabriel Rossetti, drew a portrait of cousin Henrietta that remains in the collection of the Victoria and Albert Museum in London. Both the portrait and the poem by Henrietta's cousins were prompted by her return from a four-year stay among the Mormons in Salt Lake City in a case that involved politicians at the highest levels.

The saga began in Gloucestershire, England, in 1854 when the wife of Henry Polydore (uncle of Christina and Dante Rossetti) converted to Mormonism and, without consulting her husband, joined with a group of Mormons immigrating to Utah, taking with her eight-year-old Henrietta, the couple's only child. For nearly four years Mr. Polydore searched in vain for his daughter but received information regarding her whereabouts only after Mrs. Polydore returned to the East in winter 1857–1858. In New Orleans she met John Hyde, an apostate Mormon, who upon learning of the affair informed Mr. Polydore, who in turn asked Lord Malmesbury, the Minister of Foreign Affairs in England, for the aid of the government in his behalf. An application was made to Lord Napier, the British Minister to the United States, who requested assistance from US Secretary of State Lewis Cass in recovering his daughter. Orders then went down through the chain of command from Cass to Secretary of War John B. Floyd to General Albert Sidney Johnston of the Utah Expedition to return Henrietta to her father.

In Salt Lake City, on the day of the 1858 August General Election (in which Stout was reelected to the House of Representatives), Stout was called upon to "attend for the defendant in case before Judge Eckels" in a "Case of Habeus Corpus to recover a minor girl by her father from her mother." The defendant was Henrietta's aunt, Jane Mayer, with whom Henrietta was living in Salt Lake City after Mrs. Polydore's departure for the States. The trial lasted two days, at the conclusion of which the court ordered that Henrietta should be restored to her father.[1]

Serving briefly as court-appointed custodian for Henrietta before she departed Salt Lake City (with her aunt in the company of Judge Eckels and a small escort of US troops) on September 15, 1858, was Albert G. Browne, a war correspondent for Horace Greely's *New York Tribune* who had accompanied the Utah Expedition. Browne later published a thinly disguised account of the affair, *The Ward of the Three Guardians*, in which he wrote, "the writ was served and return was promptly made to it in the aunt's name by Brigham Young's former attorney-general, Hosea Stout, a hot-headed old polygamist, who indiscreetly admitted in the return almost all the facts which we desired to prove."[2]

Stout was no longer a polygamist—twelve years earlier one plural wife died, the second deserted him, and after 1846 he had lived in monogamy—but his temper was enduring.[3] Exactly two months after the Henrietta Polydore *habeas corpus* case, Stout represented R. Gill before Judge Horace Gibbs in a suit against Bradford Leonard. At some point Stout's temper got out of hand, which earned him a quickly scheduled appearance that afternoon in probate court before Judge Elias Smith in *The People v. Hosea Stout:*

The Attorney of the Mormon Church 281

Figure 18.1. Hosea Stout, ca. 1860.

Oct. 2. The Defendant Hosea Stout came before the court and confessed having committed a breach of the Peace by assaulting one B. Leonard, in G.S.L. City, on this date, and asked to have the case investigated.

Whereupon the court proceeded to investigate the above case, and after hearing the evidence ordered the following judgment entered: to wit:—that the defendant H. Stout be fined in the sum of five dollars, and pay the costs of suit, and be discharged.[4]

No record exists as to whether the assault occurred inside or out of the court room, but it was reminiscent of the fracas in Judge Stiles's court in February 1857 when "the feelings ran so high that several laid off their coats while two gentiles not wishing to take a hand in the contest left the Court."[5] Following that melee, Stout, James Ferguson, J. C. Little (each of whom had opposed General David H. Burr in the courtroom that day), along with Aurelius Miner signed a petition that led to Burr's dismissal from the bar for allegedly being a "dishonorable creature."[6] On November 15, 1858, following his return to Salt Lake City and after being readmitted to the bar, Burr tried to settle the score by submitting a motion in the 3rd District Court in Salt Lake County "that the names of James Ferguson, Hosea Stout and J.C. Little be stricken from the roll of attorneys practicing at this Court" for "preferring false, slanderous and infamous charges against a member of the bar in this Court when they knew them to be false" and for "threatening and intimidating a Judge of this Court, interrupting him in the discharge of his official duties and coercing him to adjourn the Court."[7]

Justice Charles Sinclair happily took the case, and on Wednesday, November 17 Stout was served with a notice to appear at the District Court to face Burr's charge. Stout seemed baffled by the affair, writing, "what attorney I preferred charges against and when or what judge or when I threatened &c I am not informed."[8] Before considering the case against Stout and his fellow attorneys, however, Sinclair had something far grander in mind when, on Monday, November 22, he charged the Saints with treason and a variety of other offenses. "The charge was an extraordinary one," Stout recorded. "The court reviewed the subject of treason and intersperced his charge with lengthy quotations from the constitution of the U S. followed by the presidents pardon of 6th April 1856 The whole drift of which seems to indicate that he wishes the grand jury to totally disregard the general pardon of the president and throw the whole transactions of last winter and fall open to Judicial investigation and reopen the breach so lately healed between Utah and the U. S."[9]

On Friday, November 26, the question regarding US officers acting in territorial cases was argued in court between US District Attorney, Alexander Wilson (aided by Charles Maurice Smith) and Attorney General for the Territory of Utah, Hosea Stout (aided by Seth Blair).[10]

As the court reconvened on Monday, Wilson "delivered an address to the grand jury which in nearly every particular conflicted with the charge of the Judge." Sinclair was incensed that Wilson refused to prosecute the Mormons, though Wilson correctly argued that the court "had to observe and respect" President Buchanan's pardon. "They were pale and trembled while their voices faultered while they spoke showing that there was great conflict of feelings existing between them," Stout observed.[11]

Judge Sinclair wasted no time in making another attack, the next day taking up the motion of General Burr to disbar attorneys James Ferguson, J. C. Little and Hosea Stout, though Burr, knowing well that his major antagonist in Stiles's courtroom affair was James Ferguson, withdrew the charges against Stout and Little.[12] No longer a defendant, Stout immediately assumed the role of counsel for Ferguson, but it quickly became clear that Sinclair was aiming at a higher target when he declined Ferguson's offer to resign from the bar. "The proceedings very plainly indicated a desire to avoid an investigation," the newly launched anti-Mormon newspaper *Valley Tan* reported, a fair charge since it was clear that Sinclair's main focus was procuring the testimony of Brigham Young in the hearing.[13]

To the "surprise and disappointment of his enemies," Young responded to a subpoena and attended court on December 3 in his first public appearance since the entry of the US Army into the Valley.[14] "We were informed that the Court was trying to get him to appear as a witness on the morrow," Wilford Woodruff wrote four days prior. "It was expected that there was a plan laid to kill him . . . Hosea Stout had an interview with Sinclair who said He believed that the object was to get Brigham Young out and not to Carry out law or Justice."[15]

With memories of Joseph Smith's fate at Carthage still fresh in mind, Young was accompanied by a cadre of church dignitaries, "their pistols and knives ready for service."[16] "The court was crowded to its utmost capacity," the *New York Times* reported. "In the bar, by the side of Mr. Ferguson, was seated the live prophet himself, Brigham Young . . . During the greater portion of the time he rested his head upon his hand, and his countenance wore a careworn, melancholy expression."[17] Young, however, was not placed on the witness stand, and on January 11, 1859, after several weeks of irregular court sessions, the jury, which included three non-Mormons, found Ferguson not guilty.[18] "Thus ends this miserable and vindictive farce concocted and got up by Burr under the sanction and promised aid and assistance of the court and his accompanying clique," Stout impugned.[19] Brigham Young was much more blunt, observing that "there had not been a Judge in Utah, that had been so completely taken up and set down on his arse in the mud, and had his ears pissed into as Judge Sinclair had been."[20]

Sinclair was defeated and in retribution admitted to the bar a number of anti-Mormon lawyers, including Kirk Anderson, the editor of the *Valley Tan*. Meanwhile, into the breach jumped John Cradlebaugh, the most recent member of the federal judiciary to enter the territory. On his way to Utah he crossed paths with the departing Chief Justice Eckels, whom he found to be "irrationally anti-Mormon," though in time he too became an outspoken foe of the Saints.[21] Though assigned to the southern Utah district centered in Fillmore, the judge, who lacking an eye was referred to mockingly as "One-Eyed Jeffery," elected to open court in Provo.

On March 6, 1859, Stout, accompanied by George A. Smith, Attorney General Seth Blair, Territorial Marshal John Kay, and reporter John Long, left Salt Lake City to attend Cradlebaugh's court.[22] To the surprise and distress of the Mormons, the judge arrived the next day accompanied by one company of US Infantry.[23] "There are about 800 or 1000 troops here," Stout wrote to his wife Alvira. "What their real design is perhaps is not known but they only profess to be here for the purpose of keeping prisoners."[24]

Despite assurances from Judge Cradlebaugh of the peaceful intent of the troops, their "real design" was difficult to discern as court opened on March 8 in the Seminary, a modest religious edifice in Provo, when 110 intimidating soldiers stood in attendance with bayonets drawn.[25] "What influence the presence of this detachment will have upon the Juries and witnesses in criminal proceedings, is yet to be seen," John Kay wrote to Governor Cumming.[26] In charging the grand jury, Cradlebaugh displayed "his venom and prejudice against the people of Utah and particularly the church authorities and the laws of the Territory," particularly denouncing the probate courts and impugning the motives of the Legislature.[27] "It is the first time we people have had a religious tirade forced down our throats by Bayonets, which are bristling all around the Seminary," George A. Smith added.[28]

Cradlebaugh, in his charge to the grand jury, alleged that both the Mountain Meadows Massacre, in which 120 emigrants from Arkansas were executed by a militia composed solely of Mormons in southern Utah in 1857, and the Parrish-Potter murders, also of 1857, were sanctioned by "some person high in the estimation of the people," obviously pointing his finger of accusation at a church leader, most likely Brigham Young.[29] The judge began with the prosecution of the Parrish-Potter murders. William R. Parrish, a longtime church member living in Springville, a few miles south of Provo, had become disillusioned by some events during the active months of the Mormon Reformation and planned to take his sons Orrin and Beetson ("Beason") to California against the wishes of local church authorities. Shortly after nightfall on March 15, 1857, the three Parrish men tried to slip out of town, guided by Gardner "Duff"

Potter, who secretly had been assigned by the bishop at Springville to spy on the Parrish family and report their plans and actions. In an apparent ambush, William Parrish was stabbed to death and his son Beason was fatally shot. "Duff" Potter, mistaken for one of the Parrish sons, also was killed, while Orrin Parrish, though severely wounded, escaped.

Within four days, Stout in Salt Lake City had heard of the murders and noted them in his journal with the cautious comment, "The circumstances and how I have not learned."[30] Much more judgmental was Winslow Farr, in Big Cottonwood on the outskirts of Salt Lake City, who recorded on the same day, "Went to the evening meeting I heard some good preaching and was glad to hear that the law of God has been put in force in Springville on Some men who deserved it."[31] Four weeks later, Stout wrote, "The fire of the reformation is burning many out who flee from the Territory afraid of their lives . . . The wicked flee when no man pursue and so with an apostate Mormon he always believes his life in danger and flees accordingly"[32] Unsurprisingly, David H. Burr, upon hearing of the crime and knowing of "the fire of the reformation," became convinced that his own life was in danger and concluded that he had to leave the territory.[33]

The murders remained an unsolved mystery, and Cradlebaugh, who determined that they were related to an effort to cleanse the community of apostates and other undesirables, anxiously set out to bring justice to the case but was thwarted in his efforts. "There is no place but what has a provision of law that persons found committing crimes can be arrested, brought before tribunals, committed to prison and detained until the court having jurisdiction can try them," he stated in his charge to the grand jury. "Such provision does not seem to be made here."[34]

Court convened on March 10, 1859—two years after the murders were committed. After the grand jury had been chosen and charged, Seth Blair, who had replaced Stout as Territorial Attorney General, inquired of Judge Cradlebaugh whether he should prosecute for the Territory. The judge decided that the US District Attorney was the proper prosecutorial officer, which allowed Blair to join Stout in defending the rights of the accused. Though very early in the trial, observer George A. Smith was impressed enough to write to his brother John, "Blair and Hosea are doing splendid."[35]

Most of the excitement in the first days of Cradlebaugh's court centered around the presence of the troops. "There has been another knock down with the soldiers and citizens," Stout wrote on March 11. "The excitement was promptly quelled by the city marshall ore [sic] there is no doubt but the affair would have terminated seriously."[36] Nevertheless, Stout remained confident in a positive outcome in the court, as he expressed in a letter of March 12 to Brigham Young:

> I shall not say any thing as to the proceedings of the court only that they have undertaken to show the world that the good people are guilty of all manner of crimes and offenses as to the troops being here and posted in the jury room the citizens have but one feeling which is manifesting itself through the city council. The brethren here whoa re from this city are well and O.K. The course taken by His Honor will work its own results and we are all remarkably calm and easy for we can see as we think the final result.
>
> I have never felt more calm and easy in my life as do those who are with me.[37]

On March 16, as the grand jury commenced the examination of witnesses in the Parrish and Potter murders, Stout skipped court to visit Governor Cumming, undoubtedly urging him to take a stand against the presence of the soldiers in Provo. Stout reported that the governor wished "to take the best course to prevent a collision between the soldiers and citizens untill instructions can be recieved from Washington on the subject."[38] The situation worsened on March 18 when several men, including Provo mayor Benjamin K. Bullock were arrested and warrants were issued for others. "There was much feeling manifested by the citizens of Provo at his [Cradlebaugh's] wanton piece of treachery and double dealing of the court," Stout recorded.[39] In response, the city police force was doubled, to which General Johnston countered by sending additional troops to the city.

The explosive situation almost overshadowed proceedings in court where, on March 19, T. S. Williams joined US District Attorney Alexander Wilson for the prosecution while Seth Blair and Hosea Stout were attorneys for the defense. "The U.S. District Court with all its dignaty, dwindled down to that of a committing magistrate's court," Stout noted indignantly, "and while the Grand Jury was in session and enquiring into the same case now proceeded to examine into the cause of these arrests made so uncalled for by His Honor. The day was spent on the case of these prisoners and by their own evidence proved mayor Bullock to be perfectly innocent of the charge so disgracefully prefered against and was acquitted."[40]

Though the mayor had been released, Springville's Captain of Police Hamilton Kearns and Mayor A. C. McDonald were remanded until the next court session two days hence and placed in the hands of the military. After Blair and Stout unsuccessfully pressed the judge to allow the prisoners to remain in the Seminary for the sake of comfort, US Marshal Peter Dotson firmly stated that the prisoners could have blankets and food only if they furnished it themselves.[41] Though they were the only prisoners in custody of the military, on Sunday, March 20, General Johnston sent an additional eight companies of infantry, one of artillery and one of cavalry to Provo. "Their only business here in the first place as declared by the Judge at the opening of court was to take care of prisoners but now they are sending more without even a pretext for so doing," Stout angrily recorded. "The whole affair shows a complete military espionage and their pretences and reasons for bringing them here a farce."[42]

As the threat of armed confrontation between the troops and the Mormons escalated, particularly when several wards in Salt Lake City "notified the males to have their arms and ammunition in readiness."[43] Cradlebaugh, realizing that he would not secure any indictments in the Parrish and Potter murders, discharged the grand jury. "[Cradlebaugh] called in the Grand Jury before they were all assembled," Stout witnessed, "and delivered to them an abusive and slanderous harangue in which he accused them and the whole community of conspiring to not only commit crime but seeking to evade the law. He again took occasion to revert to the church and Territorial authorities in the most abusive manner."[44] In lambasting the grand jury, which he "summarily and insultingly discharged,"[45] the judge said:

> You are the tools, the dupes, the instruments of a tyrannical Church despotism. The heads of your Church order and direct you. You are taught to obey their orders and commit these horrid murders. Deprived of your liberty, you have lost your manhood, and become the willing instruments of bad men. I say to you it will be my earnest effort, while with you, to knock off your ecclesiastical shackles and set you free.[46]

Commenting on Cradlebaugh's speech to the grand jury, the *New York Herald* on May 7 wrote, "In this vindictive and most undignified speech he [Cradlebaugh] has clearly shown himself unfit for the position he occupies."[47] In agreement, the *Philadelphia Ledger* penned, "From the specimen he gave of his temper and fractious feeling, he evidently is an unfit person to preside over a court of justice . . . Judges who act so indiscreetly and perversely in authority should be recalled."[48] Nevertheless, Cradlebaugh, determined to find guilt without the aid of the grand jury, continued to examine witnesses in court and, in several instances, to arrest those who answered summons to appear, in the process acting as "accuser prosecutor, witness, and juror at the same time."[49]

US Marshal Peter Dotson, when sent by Cradlebaugh to serve bench warrants, quickly found that the accused Mormon men had fled to the mountains. On March 25, Stout wrote in a letter to his wife, "The officers are out all the time hunting witnesses and persons to arrest but they make bad progress ever since some were decoyed into court and then arrested . . . it is believed that it is the object of the court to put as many to death as possible. This is the general feeling but still if we keep cool all will come out."[50]

Stout personally had kept "cool," opposing while not antagonizing Cradlebaugh though acting as an agent of the church in defending their interests. His role in the legal proceedings was made clear in a letter to him, dated March 28, from General Daniel H. Wells, leader of the Nauvoo Legion and, more importantly in this case, second counselor in the First Presidency:

> So far from being deceived in relation to those matters which have hitherto transpired, and which are now the subject of court investigation, we have never even been informed in relation thereto neither before nor since, except by common street report. You will have to act according as circumstances develope. Tis true the history of the past as well as the efforts now making admonish us that no stone will be left unturned to trace up and implicate the innocent and feeling not only conscious of the rectitude of our intentions, but also of our acts. We are not at the mercy of those bitter foes who would doubtless luxuriate in our downfall whether guilty or innocent. We are as clear as the noon-day sun, not a line or a word can be traced here in truth.[51]

Wells concluded the letter, "We do not think that many of those who have left their homes have taken refuge in this direction, at least if they have, we do not know it. It cannot last much longer." In this he was absolutely correct, for absent cooperation from the Mormon community, with the men in Springville and environs having fled into the mountains, Cradlebaugh's efforts were doomed to fail. As the trial approached its conclusion, on March 31 Joseph Bartholomew's affidavit was read in court and on the following day Abraham Durfee gave a confession under oath in which he attempted to implicate others while "keeping himself in the mean while perfectly innocent." Stout scornfully recorded that Durfee, like Bartholomew, "has turned states evidence and seeks to save his own neck by implicating others."[52]

The following day, after the prosecution rested, Stout gave his closing statement, as reported in the *Deseret News*:

Mr. Stout commenced his argument by saying that it was the object of the court to find out the guilty party; that it was no uncommon thing for murder to be committed and the guilty party to be among the first sympathisers with the bereft. Mr. Stout then proceeded in a very cool manner to review the evidence before the court, which he did briefly, and concluded by saying: "It is a hard thing for innocent men to be obliged to answer for the guilty. Having answered my feelings upon the subject, I will conclude, trusting the case to the sound judgment of your honor."[53]

Cradlebaugh's judgment was to place five individuals in custody of the US troops. Later that day, Stout wrote to his wife:

The cases which I have been engaged in nearly ever since I have been here was brought to a close this after noon at dark. 5 persons were committed to wit A.F. McDonald, H.H. Karnes [Kearnes], John Daily [Daley], A. Durfee, and J. Bartholemew. The two last turned states evidence and tryed to criminate nearly every body in Springville and make themselves perfectly innocent but how Durfee can escape hanging is more than I can see.[54]

Cradlebaugh justified committing the quintet into custody by saying, "I examined into the truth of said complaint and was satisfied that there is probable cause for believing that said parties participated in the commission of said crimes."[55] While Stout considered Durfee to be guilty and didn't care for Bartholomew's effort to implicate others, he was convinced that Kearnes, McDonald, and, particularly, Daley were "committed without the first shadow of testimony that could possibly be received as legal evidence."[56] Thus a small victory was achieved when, on April 4, at Stout's request Cradlebaugh allowed Daley to be released on bail, which Stout personally posted in the sum of $1,000.[57] Following Daley's release, on April 4 court was closed and the four remaining prisoners (McDonald, Kearnes, Durfee, and Bartholomew) were taken to Camp Floyd. The troops had left the city, the Provo crisis was over, and Stout left for home by way of Camp Floyd, where he stopped to check on the welfare of the prisoners, none of whom ever were prosecuted for the crime.

Cradlebaugh had been unsuccessful in prosecuting anyone for the Potter and Parrish murders and did not take the defeat gracefully: in an act of defiance he dismissed two Indians indicted by the grand jury for rape and two non-Mormons who had been arrested for theft, saying, "When the people come to their reason, and manifest a disposition to punish their own high offenders it will then be time to enforce the laws for their protection."[58] In a final court entry on April 4 the judge left no doubt who he thought was to blame for his failure, writing, "Men high in authority in the Mormon Church, as well as men holding civil authority under the territorial government seem to have conspired to obstruct the course of public justice, and to cripple the earnest efforts of the court.[59] Cradlebaugh's statement came as no surprise to Stout, who wrote, "Thus ended this singular Court its object and aim needs no comment because that has been sufficiently declared by the judge."[60]

After Cradlebaugh's court closed, he and Judge Sinclair received a stern repudiation from US Attorney General Jeremiah Black in a letter dated May 17, 1859, for exceeding their authority in Utah, particularly for Cradlebaugh's use of the military in Provo, specifically stating that only the governor of the territory had the power to requisition troops. "It did not seem either right or necessary," Black lectured the duo, "to instruct you that these were to be the limits of your interference with the public affairs of the Territory."[61] Frustrated by the rebuke and the lack of success in his investigations, Cradlebaugh moved to the Carson Valley to a judicial district comprising a section that a few years later was cut off from Utah and converted into the Territory of Nevada.

Essentially replacing Cradlebaugh was Chief Justice Eckels, who after accompanying Henrietta Polydore east the previous September returned to the Utah Territory on June 16, 1859, promptly setting up court in Nephi, a small town about forty miles south of Provo. In one of his first acts, Eckels informed Stout and Seth Blair that he would issue a writ of *habeas corpus* for A. C. McDonald and Hamilton Kearnes, who had been imprisoned at Camp Floyd since Judge Cradlebaugh closed his court ten weeks earlier.[62] After an exchange of letters in which the attorneys requested that the judge place McDonald and Kearnes in the care of the civil authorities, the two prisoners were released on July 9 in the charge of the sheriff of Utah County, as was Joseph Bartholomew, who the previous day was advised by George A. Smith to "fee up a lawyer," recommending Hosea Stout, to help gain his release from Camp Floyd.[63] At the same time Abraham Durfee, the only suspect to confess his guilt, was set free. "So goes the U. States' system of Justice," Stout mockingly wrote.[64] With the release of the prisoners by Chief Justice Eckels, John Cradlebaugh's legal action regarding the Parrish and Potter murders finally was laid to rest.

Eckels, convinced as was Cradlebaugh that some Mormons had not been punished for their crimes, tried to achieve speedy justice but was thwarted by a lack of funds that forced the closure of his court in less than two weeks. His one conviction was of David McKenzie, a twenty-six-year-old engraver who had been charged with "forgery or engraving a plate for U S drafts."[65] McKenzie was arrested on July 9, the same day the prisoners in the Parrish-Potter case were released. Stout made "four or five different applications to have an interview" with McKenzie but was denied due to "orders from the Judge to let no one not even counsel speak to him."[66]

Stymied in his attempt to visit, Stout left a note for the prisoner, to which McKenzie responded with a lengthy letter pleading for Stout to represent him. Uncertain what to do, Stout asked Brigham Young for counsel and was advised to decline the request. "If he is guilty he ought to be cuffed," Young spoke, "but if my enemies can get him to lie against me or anybody else so they can make a war on me then there will be a fight on hand." Young was correct in his assessment of the situation, for when the counterfeit plate first was discovered it was proposed that a writ be issued for Young as well as the "artist" who created the plates, with the military to be ordered into the city to help with the arrest, though Governor Cumming refused to cooperate and ultimately Young was exonerated.[67]

To protect Young and as well as to keep the peace, Stout declined representing McKenzie, giving the excuse that "the holding of a Court at Camp Floyd in a military Camp was illegal and Contrary to the instructions of Judge Black and President Buchanan."[68] While having turned down the plea for representation, however, Stout appeared in Judge Sinclair's court on August 3 in Salt Lake City with a writ of *habeas corpus* for McKenzie, arguing "if the offence had been committed at all, it was committed in this district." Since McKenzie was to be tried in Judge Eckels's court, Sinclair ruled "that it would make the most utter and entire confusion for a judge at one district to take prisoners by writs of habeas corpus from another" and denied Stout's request.[69]

McKenzie's trial began on August 23 in Judge Eckels's court in Nephi with Stephen De Wolfe, who had been appointed Deputy US District Attorney in consequence of Alexander Wilson's ill health, handling the prosecution. McKenzie believed that Stout would represent him in court, but the next day when Eckels asked if McKenzie's attorneys were ready to proceed, the prisoner replied, "My counsel has not arrived, I do not know why Mr. Stout has not fulfilled his engagement with me, but I will not wait long for him, ere I proceed with my own case." McKenzie secured another attorney, but on August 27 he was found guilty and sentenced to two years in prison, though six months later Judge Eckels changed course and appealed to President Buchanan for executive clemency, stating that McKenzie was "of good moral character" and had "fallen a victim to the duplicity of others."[70]

It is uncertain whether Stout actually had agreed to represent McKenzie at his trial, but it is clear that he had something much more important on his mind at the time:

The history of the last week has been the history of a new system of business to me. On Sunday evening last myself Seth M. Blair and James Ferguson concieved the idea of publishing a news paper in this city to be an independent paper so far as religion and politicks are concerned. On Monday we made arraingements with the Editor of the "Deseret News" for the use of his press and type for the time being and also paper. On Tuesday we Employed J. S. Davis for foreman and set the hands to work and on Saturday we issued 2400 copies of the paper and called it "the Mountaineer" and distributed some 1000 which seemed to take well with all classes of the people. On sunday I was all day doing up and mailing the papers.[71]

After conceiving the idea for publishing a newspaper, Stout and Seth Blair first had a conversation with Brigham Young in his office, suggesting that the paper be called the *Demur*, though the final name chosen was *The Mountaineer*.[72] The purpose of the paper was to counter Kirk Anderson's *Valley Tan*, which from its first issue on November 6, 1858, featuring a vitriolic attack on the legality of polygamy, had criticized Mormons and their beliefs. Rather than answer the criticism, the church-owned *Deseret News* chose to pursue a course of silence instead of arguing with and in the process bringing attention to opposing viewpoints. The editors of the *The Mountaineer*—Stout, Blair, and Ferguson—had a long history of acting in defense of the faith, and with their motto, "Do What is Right, Let the Consequence Follow," they anxiously took on the *Valley Tan*. In the first issue on the *The Mountaineer*—published on the same day that David McKenzie was found guilty and sentenced—the editors explained the purpose of their paper:

> If we shall see slander, we shall tell of it; and if we know ourselves shall not hesitate to tell liars of their falsity . . . We are ready for the contest and we know our side . . . We do not now appear in our religious character, nor as advocates of our faith. We come before our friends as the advocates of the common rights of man. We propose to tell the truth and nothing else.[73]

The second issue of the paper (September 7) took on the federal judges in Utah, stating they "trample the laws under their feet," and in the third issue the judges were labeled "prejudiced" and "baneful."[74] That edition proved to be Stout's last, as he wrote on September 13, "This morning I withdrew from my connexion with the Mountaineer. Leaving that paper in the hands of Ferguson and Blair."[75] In response, the editor of the *Deseret News* punned, "By the last *Mountaineer*, we are informed that Mr. Stout has withdrawn from the concern and left Messrs. Blair and Ferguson to conduct it hereafter. The 'cord' is unquestionably strong enough yet to hold up the youngster and keep it in motion, but evidently not as *Stout* as it was before."[76]

Stout's reason for quitting the newspaper undoubtedly was a conflict of interest due to a federal appointment. On September 17, in letters to Chief Justice Eckels and Justice Sinclair, Alexander Wilson stated that he was leaving for the East because his wife's health would not stand another winter's sojourn in the mountains and his "pecuniary compensation" was inadequate. Wilson's decision to leave might also have been influenced by complaints of the federal judges in Utah that he, a non-Mormon, worked too closely with the Saints, though it must be noted that his first choice as his replacement was his deputy, Stephen De Wolfe, who declined the position to become the editor of the *Valley Tan* and was very critical of the Saints.[77] Of his second choice, Wilson wrote, "I have therefore appointed Hosea Stout, Esq., to perform the duties which appertain to my office in the Territory of Utah, during my absence, or until my successor shall be appointed."[78]

Acting as a deputy US district attorney in Wilson's absence, Stout had to mute the criticism of federal appointees that he had been able to express openly in the *The Mountaineer*. In addition, in the new position he could not afford to be too controversial or to project an image of being too closely allied with the church, particularly given his reputation among non-Mormons as described in the *New York Times*: "In his absence he [Wilson] has deputized HOSEA STOUT, a most bitter Mormon, and the attorney of the Mormon Church and of the Danite organization, to act in his place."[79]

Stout's appointment came at a time of increasing crime and violence in Salt Lake City. Three weeks earlier, Charles Drown and Josiah Arnold were shot while attending spiritualist services at the home of Ivy Eddy: Drown suffered a fatal stomach wound while Arnold was shot in the thigh and died six days later. "ANOTHER HORRID MURDER," screamed the *Deseret News*. "It seems that crime in this city is on the increase, and that there is no end as yet to the shedding of blood."[80] As if to underscore the point, on the day of Stout's appointment, Thomas Ferguson murdered Alex Carpenter; three days later, with Stout on behalf of the prosecution, Ferguson was tried for first degree murder and found guilty by a mixed jury of Mormons and non-Mormons and subsequently was sentenced to hang.[81]

William Hickman, who with T. S. Williams defended Ferguson in court, played both sides of the law, acting as an attorney in court while simultaneously having formed a gang that pillaged the army's livestock. On Christmas Day, 1859 in downtown Salt Lake City, Hickman became engaged in an argument over stolen horses with his long-time friend and protégé, Lott Huntington. Stout's account of the day is remarkable for the blasé description of violence on the day of Peace on Earth: "This was as usual here a very happy Christmas with one exception a renconter ensued between W. A. Hickman [and] Lott Huntington which resulted in a shooting match six men being on the side of Hickman and Lott alone some 60 shots fired."[82] Both protagonists were wounded in the thigh, and Hickman nearly died. So wild had the city become that on New Year's Day Stout remarked, "New years day came and went without any body being killed, or any ill feeling being manifested."[83]

With the dawning of the New Year 1860, the federal government, recognizing that the Utah Expedition was a costly blunder, began drawing down the number of troops at Camp Floyd. General Johnston left Utah in March 1860 and his successor, Lieutenant Colonel Charles F. Smith departed a few months later, leaving the command to Colonel Philip St. George Cooke, who in leading the Mormon Battalion from Santa Fe to San Diego had gained a measure of respect for the Mormons and was much more congenial toward them than his predecessors had been.

The Mormons also looked forward to friendlier courts with the departure of the three federal judges who had fought against the Mormons in Utah. "Chief Justice ECKELS has informed Attorney-General BLACK that he will quit Utah as soon as travel commences in the Spring," reported the *New York Times*. Eckels cited as his reason for leaving "that it is better to have no Government at all in Utah than to have one that only challenges contempt . . . Judge ECKELS' associates on the bench have already quit the country, and when he goes the Territory will be without a single Federal Judicial officer."[84]

Though typically negative toward the Saints in their rhetoric, the *New York Times* wrote objectively of the judicial triumvirate after their departure from the Utah Territory:

> ECKELS, SINCLAIR, and CRADLEBAUGH, in the days of their glory here, adopted a rather austere and restricted policy towards the Territorial Courts, Marshal, and Sheriffs. The rulings of these three Judges virtually ignored the existence of the offices of Territorial Marshal and Sheriff. The United States Marshal was decided to be the proper officer to execute Judicial processes, emanating from the United States Judiciary, whether in United States or Territorial cases. The rigid pushing of these rulings caused the transfer of certain

prisoners from CRADLEBAUGH's Provo Court, in the Spring of 1859, to Camp Floyd, for military safe keeping, which prisoners were subsequently dropped, like hot potatoes, in double quick time, by Gen. JOHNSTON and U.S. Marshal DOTSON, on receipt of advices from Washington, to the infinite delight of the Mormons and the no small chagrin of the Gentiles in general.

The Mormon Judges, lawyers, and politicians urged that the United States Marshal was the proper officer in United States cases, and the Territorial Marshal and Sheriffs the proper officers in all Territorial cases. Whatever may be the legal merits of either side of this question, one thing is certain, that the question, and the action of the Judges thereon, developed a great amount of bad talk and bad blood, and it does seem as though the three Judges and the Marshal, somehow or other, could not sustain themselves in their position . . .

The people of the States have been so accustomed, of late years, to hear startling cross-purpose tidings from Utah, that surely, if only for the sake of variety and of rest, a slight change in the character of the news must be welcome . . . For a little while, then, we must be content if the spitting, snarling, growling, cat-and-dog-customs of the good old times of Judges ECKELS, SINCLAIR and CRADLEBAUGH fall into desuetude.[85]

In fighting successfully against Judge Sinclair in his efforts to prosecute the Mormons for treason and to disbar James Ferguson, and in defending the rights of the men whom he considered illegally imprisoned by Judge Cradlebaugh, Stout had played a role in bringing about the "desuetude" of the judges' "spitting, snarling, growling, can-and-dog customs." In doing so, as far as can be ascertained, he remained notably non-confrontational. Particularly in Judge Cradlebaugh's court in Provo, he followed Brigham Young's counsel for the people to restrain themselves and managed to maintain civil relations, even attending a dinner in honor of Cradlebaugh the night before court adjourned in the Parrish-Potter murder trial.[86]

Alexander Wilson, though he was offered a position as associate justice in the Utah Supreme Court, never returned to Utah, instead resigning his office as US Attorney for Utah and settling in Leavenworth in the Kansas Territory.[87] Thus Stout remained in his position as deputy district attorney through the remainder of Wilson's term, figuring prominently as a prosecuting attorney in the Third District Court in Salt Lake

City while concurrently serving as a representative in the territorial legislature and representing clients in probate court.[88]

It was during this period that Stout ceased keeping a regular journal, making only five entries in 1860 and another five the following year. In one of his final entries in 1861, he wrote of a severe attack of erysipelas that spread to his head and, more particularly, to his eyes, rendering him delirious for four weeks from the end of March and blind and hearing impaired for another two weeks after regaining consciousness.[89] Fortunately, he recovered, but following his illness Stout virtually ceased keeping a journal (save for very simple entries in 1869), recording only the baptism of two sons (Hosea Jr. and Eli Harvey), the appearance of the Great Comet of 1861 and the erection (on July 10, 1861) of the first telegraph pole in Salt Lake City, thus connecting by telegraph the East to the Pacific states.[90] Though he made no mention of it, he regained his senses at exactly the same time news reached Salt Lake City via telegraph and pony express that Confederate batteries on April 12 had opened fire on Fort Sumter in South Carolina, thus marking the beginning of the Civil War.[91] A month later, Governor Cumming departed for his native state of Georgia, and by mid-July the last soldiers left the Utah Territory.

In their haste to leave, the army conducted a fire sale, unloading nearly four million dollars worth of goods for about one hundred thousand dollars. Mormons were permitted to buy livestock, wagons, harness, utensils, food stores, and building material.[92] Despite the windfall, however, church leaders knew that the war would cut off the supply of cotton from the South so they would have to produce their own. Brigham Young's visit to southern Utah in May 1861 convinced him of the possibilities for growing cotton there; he decided to devote the October General Conference to the creation of a "Cotton Mission," but when he asked for volunteers, only one man raised his hand, so a call was issued to 309 families to go south.[93]

In promoting the Cotton Mission, Brigham Young instructed Apostle Orson Hyde to "send good and judicious men, having reference in your selection to the necessities of a new colony and including a sufficient number of mechanics, such as coopers, blacksmiths, carpenters, masons, plasterers, joiners, etc."[94] Though Stout was the highest profile attorney in the Territory, he also was a trained carpenter, in which capacity he was one of three such craftsmen called to the Cotton Mission. Since he still was serving as Deputy US Attorney for Utah, accepting the call to go south would mean setting aside his governmental duties, but there was never a doubt where he placed his loyalty. He had been called by Brigham Young to go to an area that became known as Utah's Dixie, and there he would go and would remain until he was released officially from his mission.

Notes

1. *New York Times*, September 7, 1858; Brooks, *Mormon Frontier*, August 2, 1858, 662–63; September 15, 1858, 665.
2. Browne, "The Ward of the Three Guardians," *The Atlantic Monthly* 39, no. 236 (June 1877):708.
3. Hosea married Lucretia Fisher and Marinda Bennett in mid-1845; by September 1846 Marinda had died as a complication of childbirth and Lucretia had left him.
4. Salt Lake County Probate Court records, October 2, 1858.
5. Brooks, *Mormon Frontier*, February 13, 1857, 622.
6. *New York Daily Tribune*, October 13, 1858.
7. Smith, "Journals," M270.1 S64595s vol. 1–3, Church History Library.
8. Brooks, *Mormon Frontier*, November 17, 1858, 668.
9. Ibid., November 22, 1858, 668–69.
10. *Deseret News*, December 1, 1858.
11. Brooks, *Mormon Frontier*, November 29, 1858, 670.
12. Ibid., November 30, 1858, 670; *Deseret News*, December 1, 1858.
13. *Valley Tan*, December 3, 1858; Furniss, *Mormon Conflict*, 213. The *Valley Tan* began publication on November 6, 1858.
14. *New York Times*, January 3, 1859.
15. Woodruff, "Journal," November 30, 1858.
16. Brooks, *Mormon Frontier*, December 3, 1858, 670; Furniss, *Mormon Conflict*, 213.
17. *New York Times*, January 10, 1859.
18. *Executive Documents, printed by the order of the Senate of the United States, 1859–1860*, 38.
19. Brooks, *Mormon Frontier*, January 11, 1859, 678.
20. Turner, *Brigham Young*, 305; Church Historian's Office, Journal, CR100 1, Church History Library, February 26, 1859.
21. Ibid., 306.
22. Brooks, *Mormon Frontier*, March 6, 1859, 688.
23. Ibid., March 7, 1859, 688.
24. Letter from Hosea Stout to Alvira Stout, March 25, 1859, BYU Special Collections.
25. *Journal History*, March 8, 1859.
26. Ibid., March 9, 1859.
27. Brooks, *Mormon Frontier*, March 8, 1859, 689.
28. *Journal History*, March 9, 1859, letter from George A. Smith to George Q. Cannon.
29. *Deseret News*, March 16, 1859, 9.
30. Brooks, *Mormon Frontier*, April 19, 1857, 624.
31. Farr, "Diary," April 19, 1857, MS 1743, Church History Library.
32. Brooks, *Mormon Frontier*, April 16, 1857, 625.
33. Letter from David Burr to Thomas A. Hendricks, March 28, 1857, *Utah Expedition*, 118–19.
34. *Deseret News*, March 16, 1859.
35. Letter from George A. Smith to John L. Smith, *Journal History*, March 10,

1859.
36. Brooks, *Mormon Frontier*, March 11, 1859, 690.
37. Letter from Hosea Stout to Brigham Young, March 12, 1859, Church History Library.
38. Brooks, *Mormon Frontier*, March 16, 1859, 690.
39. Ibid., March 18, 1859, 690.
40. Ibid., March 19, 1859, 691.
41. *Journal History*, March 19, 1859.
42. Brooks, *Mormon Frontier*, March 20, 1859, 691.
43. Larson and Larson, eds., *Diary of Charles Lowell Walker*, March 22, 1859, 63.
44. Brooks, *Mormon Frontier*, March 21, 1859, 691.
45. *Deseret News*, March 30, 1859.
46. Stenhouse, *The Rocky Mountain Saints*, 408.
47. *New York Herald*, May 7, 1859.
48. Quoted in the *Deseret News*, June 1, 1859.
49. *Deseret News*, March 30, 1859.
50. Letter from Hosea Stout to Alvira Stout, March 25, 1859, BYU Special Collections.
51. Letter from Daniel H. Wells to Hosea Stout, March 28, 1859, Brigham Young Letterpress Copybook, vol. 5.
52. Brooks, *Mormon Frontier*, March 31 and April 1, 1859, 693.
53. *Deseret News*, April 6, 1859.
54. Letter from Hosea Stout to Alvira Stout, April 2, 1859, BYU Special Collections. Displaying a sense of humor tinged with sarcasm, Hosea began the letter, "Unless I learn that you have obtained a divorce I have hopes of coming home next week."
55. *Journal History*, April 2, 1859.
56. Brooks, *Mormon Frontier*, April 2, 1859, 694.
57. Ibid., April 4, 1859, 694; *Deseret News*, April 6, 1859,
58. *Deseret News*, March 30, 1859; *Valley Tan*, March 29, 1859.
59. *Deseret News*, April 6, 1859.
60. Brooks, *Mormon Frontier*, April 5, 1859, 694.
61. Letter from Jeremiah Black to John Cradlebaugh and Charles Sinclair, in Furniss, *Mormon Conflict*, 221.
62. *Journal History*, June 18, 1859.
63. Ibid., July 8 and 9, 1859.
64. Brooks, *Mormon Frontier*, July 10, 1859, 698.
65. Brown, "Journal," July 10, 1859.
66. Brooks, *Mormon Frontier*, July 9, 1869, 698.
67. Firmage and Mangrum, *Zion in the Courts*, 245; Stenhouse, *Rocky Mountain Saints*, 411.
68. Woodruff, "Journal," July 11, 1859; *Journal History*, July 11, 1859.
69. *Valley Tan*, August 10, 1859.
70. *Journal History*, August 30, 1859; March 6, 1860.
71. Brooks, *Mormon Frontier*, August 27, 1859, 701–2.
72. "History of Brigham Young," in *Selected Collections from the Archives of the Church of Jesus Christ of Latter-day Saints*, August 21, 1859.
73. *Mountaineer*, August 27, 1859.

74. Ibid., September 3 and 10, 1859.
75. Brooks, *Mormon Frontier*, September 13, 1859, 702.
76. *Deseret News*, September 21, 1859.
77. Fleming, "Turning the Tide: *The Mountaineer* vs. the Valley Tan," *Utah Historical Quarterly*, vol. 54.
78. Letters from Alexander Wilson to Delano Eckels and Charles Sinclair, September 17, 1859, *Condition of Affairs in Utah*, 63–64.
79. *New York Times*, September 28, 1859.
80. *Deseret News*, August 31, 1859; Brooks, *Mormon Frontier*, August 27 and September 2, 1859, 702; Moorman, *Camp Floyd and the Mormons: The Utah War*, 243.
81. Brooks, *Mormon Frontier*, September 17, 20, and 23, 1859, 703. Ferguson was executed by hanging on October 28, 1859.
82. Ibid., December 25, 1859, 706.
83. Ibid., January 1, 1860, 706.
84. *New York Times*, March 2, 1860. Judge Sinclair previously left Salt Lake City for Washington and Judge Cradlebaugh had relocated to the Carson Valley.
85. Ibid., November 19, 1860.
86. Brooks, *Mormon Frontier*, April 3, 1859, 694; *Journal History*, March 15, 1859.
87. *Journal History*, May 18, 1860; Letter from Alexander Wilson to Hosea Stout, March 12, 1860, Hosea Stout Papers, Utah State Historical Society.
88. Jenson, *Latter-day Saint Biographical Encyclopedia*, 533; Smith, "Journal," April 24, 1860.
89. Brooks, *Mormon Frontier*, March 29, 1861, 707.
90. Ibid., June 21, June 30, and July 10, 1861, 707. For months he had made irregular entries—only six for the entire year 1860 and another five random in 1861 before laying down his journalistic pen forever with the exception of a number of rather mundane entries in 1869.
91. *Deseret News*, April 24, 1861.
92. Anderson, *Desert Saints*, 212.
93. Campbell, *Establishing Zion*, 254. Twenty-three Swiss families also were called to go to Santa Clara, but they were to grow fruit and grapes rather than cotton.
94. Ibid., 256.

19
The Cotton Mission

On a fine Sunday in the fall of the year 1861, Bishop Reuben Miller and his counselor Alexander Hill came to visit fellow-counselor Robert Gardner at his farm near Salt Lake City. After being shown around the farm Bishop Miller remarked, "I am glad to see you so well recovered from being broke. You are nearly as well off as you were before you lost your property and went on your mission." Gardner, who dutifully had gone on a mission to Canada in 1857, replied, "I was well off once and it all went. I am almost afraid of another fall." A few hours later, Gardner recalled, "news came of another fall" when neighbors told him they had heard his name and others called to go south on a mission to raise cotton and that he was to start right away. "I looked and spat," he admitted, "took off my hat, scratched my head, thought, and said, 'All right.'"

The next day Gardner went to Salt Lake City and visited apostle George A. Smith in the church historian's office. Smith laughed when Gardner came in and said, "Don't blame anyone but me. The President [Brigham Young] told me to get a list of names suitable for that mission, so I thought of you for one, and thought you would want to go if called so I put your name down. If you don't want to go step to the President's office and ask him to take your name off the list and he will do it." Gardner replied, "I expect he would, but I shan't try him. I have come to find what kind of an outfit is wanted and when to go." Smith responded, "This is the kind of men we want."[1]

Unlike an individual's missionary calling of limited duration, this was an assignment to resettle a family in southern Utah, perhaps permanently, and become a member of a community dedicated to raising cotton and other semitropical plants. Many of the 309 families called in the semiannual conference on October 6, 1861, to serve in the Cotton Mission were men and women who had been faithful in the past, but most had homes established for a decade or more; thus it is not surprising that

Figure 19.1. Allen Joseph Stout (1815–1899), Hosea Stout's younger brother.

a census of the mission in summer 1862 indicated that only 250 of the chosen families actually had responded to the call.[2]

Among those who did answer the call without hesitation were Hosea Stout and his brother Allen. "The first thing I knew I received a letter from my brother," Allen recalled, "stating that him and me were both called to go to the south to raise cotton." Allen rejoiced that he could

Figure 19.2. Hosea Stout, ca. 1870.

"leave that cold country and get where I could raise southern products" but had concerns for his wife, who scaled in at 250 pounds and doubted that she could live in a hot climate. While no record exists regarding the disposal of Hosea's property, he and other missionaries likely suffered the same fate as Allen, who with so many selling at the same time was able only to procure "one yoke of oxen and a one year old heifer" for his place and belongings, the whole of which was worth $1200.[3]

Hosea had an excuse for not leaving immediately, for on October 17—eleven days following the call to the Cotton Mission—Brigham Young "said it was his intention to have Hosea Stout, Horace Eldredge and J. M. Moody return this winter to fill their places in the Legislature" and thus he could have argued that his wife and children should remain in Salt Lake City until the legislative session was complete before moving.[4] Always faithful, however, he prepared immediately to go; on the morning of October 27 he preached in the Bowery along with Joseph Heywood, John Vance, and Brigham Young, giving what amounted to a farewell address, and on the following morning Hosea, Allen, and their families departed for the South.

After a journey of exactly one month, on November 28 Allen Stout arrived at Cottonwood Creek, the site of a small town called Harrisville, where he lived with his wife and seven children in a tent and some wagons.[5] Hosea, on the other hand, made it only as far as Cedar City, where he deposited his wife and family in the care of Bishop Henry Lunt while he returned to Salt Lake City to attend the legislative session.[6] While still in Salt Lake City, on January 6, 1862, Hosea was elected in absentia in Cedar City as a delegate to the constitutional convention.[7] Eight days later, the Legislative Assembly met in joint session in the Representative's Hall and elected Stout district attorney for the Second Judicial District.[8] In doing so, the Assembly evidently overstepped its authority, since the position was a federal, not territorial, appointment. It mattered little, however, for two days later in Washington, DC, Abraham Lincoln sent a message to the United States Senate stating, "I nominate Hosea Stout, of Utah Territory, to be Attorney of the United States for the said Territory."[9] On March 6, his appointment was confirmed by the Senate, at which time President Lincoln wrote a letter stating:

> KNOW YE, THAT, reposing special trust and confidence in the Integrity, Ability and LEARNING of HOSEA STOUT, of Utah Territory, I HAVE NOMINATED, and, by and with the advice and consent of the Senate, DO APPOINT HIM Attorney of the United States, in and for the said Territory; and do authorize and empower him to execute and fulfill the duties of that Office, with all the powers, privileges and emoluments to the same of right appertaining, unto him, the said HOSEA STOUT, for the term of four years from the date hereof, unless the President OF THE UNITED STATES for the time being, should be pleased sooner to revoke and determine this Commission.[10]

Hosea would sign the commission after it arrived in Salt Lake City, but in the meantime his primary intent was to rejoin his family in the southern part of the Territory, though he was unable to do so immediately.

"Such is that state of the weather and my tender health," he wrote Alvira on January 24, "that for me to undertake to travel would only be to be laid up on the road and left with neither health nor home."[11] Four days later he wrote again to his wife:

> Great Salt Lake City—28 Jan 1862
>
> Dear Alvira
>
> How fares my dove and her dear little brood, which I so much want to see and so much ponder and think about. Now that the Legislature and convention are over and I have nothing to do, how I continually cast my anxious eyes to the south and contemplate the long, cold, muddy, dreary road which leads from me to my dear ones so far away. How I do want to know how you are doing. Do you want for any thing to eat drink or wear, to make you comfortable, are you all happy or are you unhappy about any thing but me being gone and do the children learn their books and remember me.
>
> As for me I am well enough, and feel well enough, so far as health, but O: Do I not long to be with you; but O: That cold dreary road, the cold plains the bleak pearcing winds on my tender jaws, how dare I face them. Shall I or shall I wait till I can come in safety and good health. What say you dear Alvira do tell me for I would do as you say.[12]

Despite what he wrote, he clearly was not "well enough" to travel, and that in turn dictated that he remain in Salt Lake City for another three weeks, as George A. Smith noted in an article of February 17 for the *Millennial Star*, "Hosea Stout has been detained in this city by sickness since the close of the Legislature until to-day, when he started for the southern part of the Territory, where his family are."[13] He didn't make it very far, however, for on March 2 he was among four "well known gentlemen" to give a short speech "in favor of sustaining the Constitution of the United States, and the Constitution of the State of Deseret, and considered that this people had proved themselves worthy of a State Government."[14] He then returned to Salt Lake City where, on April 14, he was selected by the House to serve as Representative from Washington County for a term of two years (about half of the other representatives were selected for a term of only one year).[15] Four days later he was sworn in as attorney for the United States for the Territory of Utah. In taking the oath before William I. Appleby, clerk of the US Supreme Court for the Territory of Utah, he solemnly swore to carry out the duties of his office "with a full determination, pledge and purpose without any mental reservation or evasion whatsoever" and to "well and faithfully perform all the duties which may be required of me by law. So help me God."[16] As would be demonstrated during his term, Hosea put little—if any—effort into fulfilling his oath.

While being detained in northern Utah, Hosea missed out on the greatest flood in recorded Utah history, known as the Great Flood of 1862, which resulted from rainfall of biblical proportions that lasted, appropriately, forty days. It started in the Pacific Northwest in November 1861, where heavy rainfall gradually moved south into California as the polar jet stream slid in that direction. "The Pacific slope has been visited by the most disastrous flood that has occurred since its settlement by white men," reported the *New York Times*. "From Sacramento northward to the Columbia River, in California, Nevada Territory, and Oregon, all the streams have risen to a great height, flooded the valleys, inundated towns, swept away mills, dams, flumes, houses, fences, domestic animals, ruined fields and effected damage, estimated at $10,000,000."[17]

On Christmas Day 1861, the storm track shifted to the south and east, bringing heavy rains to most of the Cotton Mission and snow at the higher elevations, including Cedar City (elevation 5,846 feet). "Snow about 8 inches deep," wrote John D. Lee on January 4, 1862, at Harmony (later New Harmony), twenty miles south and six hundred feet lower elevation than Cedar City. "Snowy through the day" he wrote three days later, followed a week later by, "The storm most vehemently raging."[18] In the midst of the severe storm, Allen Stout set out for Cedar City to rescue Hosea's family from the wintry weather by bringing them to the lower elevations and milder climes of Harrisville (later called Harrisburg when the town site was moved after the original hamlet was destroyed in the Great Flood).[19]

Sometime in late May, Hosea finally joined his family in Harrisburg, bringing the population of the hamlet to forty-one, comprised of ten families; on June 12, Apostles Orson Pratt and Erastus Snow organized the residents as a branch of the church, with Hosea's China mission companion James Lewis the presiding elder and Moses Harris (founder of Harrisville) and Hosea his counselors.[20] Hosea's days in the settlement, however, were numbered: on the evening of April 7, 1862, the newly elected mayor and council of St. George met and appointed Hosea city attorney, though he had not yet set foot in the city;[21] then on August 24, he was called to live in St. George (the designated head city of the Cotton Mission which, according to Erastus Snow, "already assumes the appearance of quite a city—all but the houses") where he could properly act as city attorney.[22]

Almost immediately upon his arrival in St. George, on September 7, Hosea joined Apostles Pratt and Snow and three other church leaders in conferring "the Gift of the Holy Ghost" to thirty-nine church members who had been rebaptized by Pratt three days earlier.[23] The ordinance, according to George Isom, was done "In accordance with the request of authorities that new arrivals should commence anew in the Gospel of Christ."[24] Nevertheless, this was the only recorded instance of rebaptism in St. George, and all thirty-nine rebaptized individuals were youth over the age of eight—the minimum age for Mormon baptisms—including Hosea's three oldest children (Elizabeth Ann, Hosea Jr., and Eli Harvey), even though Hosea Jr. and Eli Harvey had been baptized just the previous year.[25]

The goal may have been to build a strong, utopian community by having all "commence anew," but the practicality was that people are not perfect, no matter how faithful, and thus, in addition to functioning as city attorney, Hosea found work as a defense attorney in the probate court.[26] At the same time, he totally neglected his duty as US attorney.

While he was paid $250 per annum for his office, the total amount received being $977.50, there is evidence that Hosea appointed Aurelius Miner on April 18, 1862, to act as deputy US attorney for Utah for at least the years 1862 and 1863.[27] The fact that the appointment of Miner came on the very day of Stout's swearing into the office clearly indicates a knowledge that some, if not all, of his duties as US attorney would go begging while he served in the Cotton Mission. In reality, there is ample evidence that at no time did Hosea defend the interests of the United States in court, and after more than two years of him being missing in action, on June 14, 1864, US Attorney General Edward Bates sent the following letter to President Abraham Lincoln:

> Sir
>
> I have the honor to reply in answer to your note of inquiry of this days date, that there is not, as far as I am aware, any vacancy in the office of United States Attorney for Utah and that no resignation has been received at my office from Hosea Stout Esq. the last appointee, who was confirmed in March 1862—
>
>   I am, Sir, very respectfully
>   Your obedient servant
>   Edw Bates
>   Attorney General[28]

A correspondent for the *New York Times*, after being in the Utah Territory for about a month, confirmed Stout's lack of duty, writing:

> The kindness of the government to this Territory and its people is proverbial. A long time ago it appointed a Mormon by the name of STOUT District-Attorney. He has never presented himself before the court or before any Judge thereof.

If the man had a good excuse for not coming, when he had married a wife, this Mr. STOUT had six good excuses, as he has six wives . . . He showed his shrewdness by staying away and not appointing a substitute, as the court has no power to appoint a prosecutor in his stead, and, therefore, no criminals can be prosecuted in the Supreme or District Courts of the Territory.[29]

The correspondent was mistaken in an important detail—Hosea historically had six wives, but with three of them dead, one having left him and one having divorced him, he had but one current wife. He also overlooked the fact that Stout appointed Aurelius Miner as his deputy at least for the years 1862–1863, but he made a good point regarding the powerlessness of the district courts in the absence of a prosecutor. A clue to that effect came in a letter of March 20, 1863, from George A. Smith to Stout which told of difficulties with government officials—"We have had a little taste of the old time," as he put it—and a military arrest of Brigham Young and the assumption of control by the governor would have been much more difficult to effect in the absence of the US district attorney.[30]

Had Stout decided to carry out any duties connected with his federal assignment while living in St. George, he could have chosen to investigate one of the greatest mass killings of civilians in United States history, the massacre at Mountain Meadows. On September 11, 1857, just thirty miles north of St. George, 120 men, women, and children of the Baker-Fancher emigrant wagon train company were slaughtered by a band of southern Utah Mormons. Though the majority of known militia participants were from Cedar City, more than a quarter of them lived in Washington City or Fort Clara (later Santa Clara), neighboring towns of St. George.[31]

Stout was very familiar with the case. When Judge John Cradlebaugh opened court in Provo in March 1859, at which Stout was present, he sought not only to prosecute the perpetrators of the Parrish-Potter murders but also of the Mountain Meadows Massacre and other crimes that had been committed in southern Utah. "To allow these things to pass over," he stated, "gives a color as if they were done by authority. The very fact of such a case as the Mountain Meadows shows that there was some person high in the estimation of the people, and it was done by that authority."[32] Cradlebaugh, according to Stout, "then proceeded to charge the jury and in doing so he took occasion to display his venom and prejudice against the people of Utah and particularly the church authorities . . . [Cradlebaugh] charged the whole to the authorities of the church and in the plainest terms declared that he was now ready to do anything he could against both the church and people."[33]

Given the judge's threats to their church authorities, it was not surprising that the Mormon grand jury refused to issue any indictments, upon which Cradlebaugh dismissed the jury, condemning them in "an abusive and slanderous harangue in which he accused them and the whole community of conspiring to not only commit crime but seeking to evade the law."[34] The judge subsequently conducted a tour of southern Utah and the Mountain Meadows area with a military escort of two hundred soldiers and as many civilians, but his investigation was halted when President James Buchanan, in response to a protest by Governor Alfred Cumming, decreed that only the territorial governor could request army escorts for judicial investigations.[35]

Shortly thereafter, in early May 1859, Judge Elias Smith issued a warrant for the arrest of Brigham Young as an "accessory before the fact to murder of emigrants at Mountain Meadows."[36] On May 12, 1859, Young appeared voluntarily before Judge Smith and acknowledged the participation of "armed [presumably white] men" in the massacre. Later that evening he met in the President's office with his Counselor Daniel H. Wells, Apostles George A. Smith and Ezra T. Benson, and his leading Mormon attorneys, Hosea Stout and Seth Blair, "discussing a question of accessory."[37] The following day Young was arrested, but there is no record of any further legal action. Nevertheless, the arrest warrant, along with the efforts by Judges Cradlebaugh and Eckels to prosecute the case, made it obvious to Young that he might face prosecution as an accessory—either before or after the fact—to the atrocity at Mountain Meadows and thus he had a personal interest in preventing an investigation of it by an unsympathetic party.

During the next several months, Young appeared to be willing to cooperate with an investigation if he considered it to be fair and impartial. On May 25, 1859, he told George A. Smith that "so soon as the present excitement subsided, and the army could be kept from interfering with the Judiciary, he intended to have all the charges investigated." He further said he "would try to get the Governor and Dist. Atty. to go to Washington County, and manage the investigation of the mountain Meadow Massacre, themselves."[38] Three weeks later, on June 18, he met with Smith and Jacob Hamblin and told Hamblin that the federal judges should preside over the trials of the accused if the would conduct the trials fairly without military interference.[39] On July 5, Young told US District Attorney Alexander Wilson "that if the judges would open a court at Parowan or some other convenient location in the south . . . unprejudiced and uninfluenced by . . . the army, so that man could have a fair and impartial trial He would go there himself, and he presumed that Gov. Cumming would also go." He "would use all his influence to have the parties arrested and have the whole . . . matter investigated thoroughly and impartially and justice meted out to every man."[40] Combined, the statements make it clear that Young would consent to an investigation and subsequent trials but *only* if he trusted that they would be conducted in a fair and impartial manner. In reality he had no such trust.

As more information about the massacre and its participants was gathered it was discovered that most of the Mormon ecclesiastical leaders in Cedar City were suspected of being involved either in the planning or in the execution of the massacre. While on a trip south, on Sunday, July 31, Apostles George A. Smith and Amasa Lyman released from their positions Philip Klingensmith, Samuel McMurdy, and John Morris of the bishopric and Isaac Haight, John Higbee, and Elias Morris of the stake presidency (all but John Morris eventually were legally implicated in the crime).[41] The next day, Klingensmith wrote to George A Smith, asking Smith and Hosea Stout to defend him in the forthcoming "proceedings . . . against me in a case of alleged murder at Mountain Meadows." [42] A few days later, John D. Lee—the only man actually to be prosecuted for the murders—also wrote to Smith and Stout, asking them "to defend my case, providd [*sic*] I should be arrested and brought before the District court upon the charge of aiding in the Massacre at the Meadows."[43] Soon thereafter Isaac Haight made a similar request of the same men.[44]

While Smith and Lyman were in southern Utah, Alfred Cumming, who like US District Attorney Alexander Wilson was sympathetic to the Mormons, advised that John Kay, the territorial marshal, should be deputized, but Judges Cradlebaugh and Sinclair rejected Kay as "a notorious Mormon" and said it would only "end in a Mormon whitewashing."[45] Though Wilson pointed out that Brigham Young had promised to cooperate, Kay was rejected. Further complicating relations between the judges on the one hand and Wilson, Cumming, and Mormon leaders on the other, Chief Justice Eckels decided to hold court in Nephi, two hundred miles from Cedar City, despite the urging of Superintendent for Indian Affairs Jacob Forney to hold it in Cedar City where "nearly all the perpetrators and witnesses reside."[46]

Forney had given "to the Attorney General and several of the United States judges the names of those who [he] believed were not only implicated, but the hell-deserving scoundrels who concocted and brought to a successful termination the whole [Mountain Meadows] affair." Wilson wrote Forney and asked him to send "all the evidence you may have in your possession or under your command, or within your knowledge, in relation to the Mountain Meadow massacre."[47] Wilson's assistant, Stephen DeWolfe (who later became the editor of the anti-Mormon newspaper *Valley Tan*), subsequently reported, "Nothing has yet been done before the grand jury in regard to the Mountain Meadow massacre."[48] Though Eckels had assembled a grand jury mostly of non-Mormons from Camp

Floyd, even with a stacked jury he could not obtain indictments or convictions of massacre participants.[49] Afterwards, the frustrated judge wrote to Secretary of State Lewis Cass that "an Attorney who understood his business and would try, could show that Brigham Young directed the Mountain Meadows massacre."[50]

Wilson agreed with his assistant DeWolfe that the main difficulty in the trial was the distance between Nephi and southern Utah, where most of the witnesses resided. Forney perceived another problem, stating, "It is to be regretted that nothing has yet been accomplished towards bringing these murderers to justice" and declared, "no well-directed effort has been made to catch them," reasoning that the murderers likely already had fled since the "names of the guilty were paraded in the newspaper."[51] Wilson soon left the territory for health reasons and appointed Hosea Stout "to my office of public prosecutor," though Stout did not handle any cases related to Mountain Meadows.[52]

The outbreak of the Civil War in 1861 slowed the investigation of the massacre. On March 8, 1863, a year after Stout's appointment US district attorney for Utah was confirmed by the United States Senate, Young reminded a congregation in the Salt Lake Tabernacle that he told Governor Cumming he would pledge to protect the court and allow the guilty to "suffer the penalty of the law" if the accused were brought to trial before "an impartial, unprejudiced judge and jury." The reminder was a smokescreen for Young's true feelings, as he claimed the government "had not touched the matter, for fear the Mormons would be acquitted from the charge of having any hand in it [Mountain Meadows], an our enemies would thus be deprived of a favorite topic to talk about, when urging hostility against us. 'The Mountain Meadow massacre! Only think of the Mountain meadow massacre!!' is their cry from one end of the land to the other."[53] Whatever spirit of cooperation may have existed in 1859 had totally vanished.

One month later, Young, his First Counselor Heber C. Kimball, Apostles George A. Smith and Orson Hyde and a large party headed to southern Utah. On May 6 they visited John D. Lee in Washington City, a few miles east of Stout's residence in St. George, and Young condemned Lee for his role in Mountain Meadows. The company then proceeded on to St. George, where on May 9 Young preached at a quarterly conference. Young remained in St. George a total of four days, during which time one can be sure he met with Stout.[54]

Though Young had publically condemned John D. Lee and had given lip service to being cooperative in finding and prosecuting those responsible for Mountain Meadows, had he seriously wanted even a pro-Mormon inquiry of the matter he would have instructed Stout, one of his most loyal lieutenants, to open an investigation. Why Young did not do so is open to debate. Some historians charge that Brigham Young ordered the massacre.[55] Juanita Brooks, a pre-eminent Utah historian and faithful Mormon, on the other hand presented "reasonable conclusions" about the sordid event:

> While Brigham Young and George A. Smith, the church authorities chiefly responsible, did not specifically order the massacre, they did preach sermons and set up social conditions which made it possible . . .
> While he did not order the massacre, and would have prevented it if he could, Brigham Young was an accessory after the fact, in that he knew what had happened, and how and why it happened. Evidence of this is abundant and unmistakable, and from the most impeccable Mormon sources.
> Knowing then, why did not President Young take action against these men? At the time, he was involved in a war and was too occupied and too far away to do anything about it. After he was relieved of his position as governor, he felt no responsibility, he claimed. He did have the men chiefly responsible released from their offices in the church following a private church investigation, but since he understood well that their acts had grown out of loyalty to him and his cause, he would not betray them into the hands of their common "enemy."[56]

In taking no initiative to open an investigation, Stout also may have been influenced by his own feelings toward the federal judges. In a letter from George A. Smith that Stout received shortly before Young arrived in St. George, Smith wrote of a speech by "Hon. John Cradlebaugh of Nevada, Ex. Judge of Utah," that was "replete with the blackness of hatred."[57] Stout personally had experienced Cradlebaugh's animosity as well as that of other federal judges and without an explicit directive from Brigham Young likely would not have initiated any investigation of Mountain Meadows that might hurt Mormons while helping the government. Young never issued such a directive, and Stout did nothing.

While shirking his duty as US district attorney, Stout stayed busy in his calling to the Cotton Mission. Though he continually had been faithful, had spoken from the pulpit a number of times in the Bowery and the Tabernacle in Salt Lake City, and was a confidant of Brigham Young, he never had held an ecclesiastical position of any stature. That changed on May 7, 1864, when Stout "was chosen a member of the High Council to be the foreman thereof unless John Nebeker comes to reside in St. George."[58] In the Cotton Mission's ecclesiastical hierarchy, it was a calling that was superseded only by the two resident apostles, Orson Pratt and Erastus Snow, and then only by Snow when in late 1864 Pratt was called on a mission to Austria.[59] He remained as president of the High Council for the duration of his stay in St. George, even after the arrival of John Nebeker, who had been ticketed to replace him.[60]

Shortly after his term as US attorney expired in 1866, Stout received a request for his return to Salt Lake City:

> Great Salt Lake City
> June 1, 1866
>
> Hosea Stout, Esq.,
> St. George
> Dear Brother
>
> It is by the suggestion of President B. Young that I write to you to have you return with your family to this City with a view to practice Law for our people and the City. We need your services in this respect, and hope that it will be agreeable to your interests and meet with your favorable consideration.
>
> Should you conclude to come please advise us by return or first mail how soon we may expect you.
>
> With kind regards,
> I remain
> Your brother
> DANIEL H. WELLS[61]

The letter from Wells, a member of the First Presidency, was tantamount to a release from his mission (which was granted formally on November 1, 1866, in St. George, three months after Stout already had returned to Salt Lake City). The timing of Wells's letter, coming so soon after the expiration of his term as US attorney, is suggestive that church leaders may have preferred to keep him away from his appointed governmental duty. On May 13, 1866, a few weeks before Wells's letter inviting him to return to Salt Lake City, Stout spoke at the Bowery in St. George "on the corruption of the government officials Sent to Utah," a long-held opinion but one that could not have been expressed if he still had been a functioning government official.[62]

Stout departed St. George shortly after receiving Wells's letter, leaving unsold his house and property, and arrived in Salt Lake City on July 25. A notice in the *Semi-Weekly Telegraph* announcing his return intimated that he was returning not from a mission but from a long vacation:

> Hosea Stout, Esq., got into the city on Wednesday from the Southern regions, where he has been enjoying his "own vine

and fig-tree" for a time, luxuriating in hot sand, early fruit and delicious grapes "in the season thereof." Many of his old friends will be pleased to see his well known figure moving about as in days of yore.[63]

Almost immediately upon his arrival in Salt Lake City, Stout was installed as the city attorney and soon became involved in a civil case that escalated to a sensational murder, alarming the entire community and drawing national attention. John King Robinson, a physician from Maine, came to Utah in 1864, serving as an assistant surgeon at Fort Douglas. There he met and married Nellie Kay, a daughter of well-known iron and silversmith John Kay. Robinson served as superintendent of the "Gentile Sunday School" following its creation on February 2, 1865, by Reverend Norman McLeod, chaplain of Fort Douglas who preached against Mormonism.[64]

Robinson desired to build the city's first hospital and, in preparation, began constructing a workshop adjoining Warm Springs, about a mile north of any habitation but within the municipality boundary of the city. Shortly after the workshop was completed it was torn down by the city police, who "warned the doctor that it would not be healthy for him to renew his operations there." Robinson contemplated suing the city, disputing the validity of the city charter and the city's claim to ownership of the Warm Springs property, but was turned down by an attorney who feared "personal violence" if he represented the doctor in the case.[65]

Robinson then consulted Robert N. Baskin, a Harvard educated attorney from Ohio who arrived in Utah in 1865 on his way west and decided to stay in Salt Lake City. Baskin's relentless efforts to bring about unwanted change in the Kingdom of God made Mormons consider him their enemy and prompted the Mormon press to label him "a lean, lank, rather dirty and frowsy, red-headed young man, but a lawyer of shrewdness and coolness, and inflamed against Mormonism."[66] Baskin advised Robinson not to bring suit but he agreed to represent him when the doctor pressed forward, believing to have found a loophole in the 1862 Homestead and Preemption acts that would allow him to claim the property.[67]

The action was instituted by Baskin on July 21, 1866, six days before Stout returned in Salt Lake City. On Tuesday, September 4, in the case of *Robinson v. Great Salt Lake City*, Stout as city attorney made an argument before Territorial Chief Justice John Titus that was so complex as to confound the *Deseret News* reporter, prompting the paper to admit, "Our reporter is a little thick-headed at times, and thought perhaps the lawyers knew all about it, as their business is to unravel knotty questions or make them so that they cannot be unravelled."[68] On October 17, final arguments were made in the Third District Court, Chief Justice John Titus presiding. "As our readers have already been informed," it was reported in the *Daily Alta California,* the issues at hand made "it one of the most important questions that has ever been brought before the Courts of Utah."[69] Justice Titus, in a carefully worded opinion, ruled against Robinson, submitting the judgment in writing because he realized the importance of the decision and the possibility that it might "be reviewed and rectified by a higher tribunal, if erroneous."[70]

Obviously upset, on October 20 Dr. Robinson visited the home of Salt Lake City Mayor Daniel Wells, seeking to lodge a complaint regarding the treatment he had received. According to Robinson's sister-in-law (Mrs. S. Crosby, who lived with the Robinsons), Wells asked if he was the Robinson contesting the Warm Springs property and, upon receiving an affirmative answer, promptly ordered the doctor from his house. Robinson acknowledged to Mrs. Crosby that "he had no right to go to the Mayor's house, but he thought he might at least have heard what his business was before ordering him away."[71]

Two days later, at about 11:30 PM, Robinson was awakened by a knocking at the door and the call, "Doctor, come quick; my brother, John Jones has broke his leg; a mule fell on it and smashed it all to thunder!" Ignoring his wife's pleadings not to go, Robinson accompanied the man to the corner of Main and Third South where a skirmish took place in which he was brutalized with a sharp weapon, shot in the head and left in a pool of his blood; two hours later he died at home in his wife's arms.[72]

News of the murder spread quickly by telegraph to California and across the nation, with a general consensus in the national press that the Mormons were responsible for the crime. "Circumstances indicate that he was murdered by the Mormons because he had instituted a suit against the city for the recovery of the Warm Sulphur Springs, claimed by both parties, the Saints evidently concluding that assassination was more effectual than a legal process to get rid of a rival claimant," wrote the *Sacramento Union* on October 25.[73] A headline in the *Baltimore Sun* on October 27 stated simply, "Another Murder in Utah."[74] The *Springfield (Mass.) Republican* reported, "The alarm spread among the anti-Mormon citizens of Salt Lake City by the shocking assassination of Dr. Robinson was even deeper than was obvious. Gentile fears extended to the federal judges, the district attorney and the U.S. marshal . . . One or all are felt to be marked for the next blow from the secret assassins in the interest of the Mormon hierarchy."[75] In the US House of Representatives, on December 9 a resolution of the Legislature of Maine—King's home state—asserted, "the circumstances attending the violent death of Dr. John King Robinson at Salt Lake City, in the Territory of Utah, show conclusively that he was assassinated by a band of Mormons acting under the direction of the leading authorities of that people . . . the continuance of the Mormon power in Utah renders unsafe all citizens of the United States in that Territory who desire liberty of conscience and freedom to pursue honorable employments, such as can be enjoyed in other States and Territories."[76]

In Utah, the murder caused "great consternation" among Mormons and non-Mormons alike.[77] The city offered a reward of $1,000 for the apprehension of the murderers, with an additional $7,000 added from private funds, including a promised contribution of $500 from Brigham Young.[78] Given the importance of the case on both local and national scales, a coroner's inquest was held immediately in Salt Lake City before Probate Judge Jeter Clinton, who doubled as the city coroner, with the assistance of Chief Justice Titus and Associate Justice Solomon McCurdy. In an attempt to demonstrate impartiality, prominent attorneys on both sides were brought into the case, including Mormons Hosea Stout and Seth Blair and non-Mormons Charles Hempstead and John B. Weller, the ex-governor of California. Weller, speaking for the coroner's court, laid suspicion for the murder on the doorstep of church leaders, though Brigham Young vehemently denied the accusation.[79] After lengthy examination and testimony over eight days, the final decision of the coroner's court was given in a simple sentence: "The deceased died by the hands of some persons unknown to the jury."[80] As described in the *New York Times*, "After all this investigation, however, not a clue to the murderer was discovered—nothing which could be fairly considered reliable evidence of who were the perpetrators."[81]

At the close of the inquest on Tuesday, November 6, ex-Governor Weller, dissatisfied with the proceeding, "delivered a lengthy speech, very broadly insinuating that the murder of DR. ROBINSON could be traced to the Tabernacle preachings of the Mormon chief men and elders."[82] Weller addressed the jury and asked them nineteen questions, the first of which was, "If my associate, Judge Stout, the City Attorney, had been murdered under the circumstances Dr. Robinson was, would the police have exhibited a greater degree of vigilance and energy?" Other questions, which left no doubt that the ex-governor suspected complicity of Mormon Church leaders in the crime, included:

> Is there not an organized influence here which prevents the detection and punishment of men who commit acts of violence upon the persons or property of "Gentiles?"
>
> Was the murder committed for the purpose of striking terror into the "Gentiles" and to prevent them from settling in this territory?

Are all legal questions which may arise in this city between "Mormons and Gentiles" to be settled by brute force?

Do the public teachings of the "tabernacle" lead the people to respect and obey the laws of the country, or do they lead to violence and bloodshed?[83]

Weller's lengthy remarks and questions were carefully prepared; in contrast, after Weller concluded, Stout stood to give an extemporaneous rebuttal, beginning by saying, "I feel called upon to make a few remarks, with the permission of the Court." His remarks, however, were not few, and his rebuttal was anything but brief.

As city attorney, Stout first defended the manner in which the police conducted the investigation. While acknowledging that "secret combinations" existed in Salt Lake City "to commit crime, to violate the law, to trample on the rights of citizens and take life," he denied that there was any connection between them and either the police or church authorities. The crime, he said, "struck gloom to the heart of every man in the Territory . . . without respect to party or faith." Citing the Warm Springs case, in which he was personally involved, Stout stated, "it had been hotly contested" but "there were no grounds left for revenge or hard feelings." In a statement that would prove to be very true he continued, "The case is pending . . . Before his death we were contesting with the Doctor; after his death the contest is with the bereaved widow."

Turning to religion, Stout asked, "Why should we turn from investigation the murder of Dr. Robinson to inquire into religion and who dipped the men in the Jordan?" He then countered Weller's aspersions that the case boiled down to a conflict between Mormons and Gentiles. "Such a party spirit has no business in court," Stout contended. "It is told you that no 'Gentile' can successfully contest a case here with a 'Mormon.' The thousands of cases on the records of the courts prove the incorrectness of the statement." He then defended Brigham Young, saying, "I defy any man to produce one solitary example of chicanery or double-dealing in his character or career."

While clearly defending his church and his prophet, Stout attempted to demonstrated his desire for even-handedness and peace in the community. "I am ashamed of the course that has been taken . . . the results can do nothing but increase the acrimony of party feelings, which is a thing I have ever despised. Ever since I returned to the city I have labored to put down this acrimonious party spirit which I found here in the courts and out of the courts." Finally concluding, he said, "I do not acknowledge the 'Mormons' to be a law-breaking community. It is the first time I have had to speak of it in the forum, and I have been a lawyer since before this was a Territory . . . Let us all abide the law . . . Let us cease this party spirit and find out where the wrong is."[84]

The following day, in an article titled "The End of the Inquest," the *Union Vedette,* which was established at Camp Douglas to provide an opposing voice to the church-controlled *Deseret News,* wrote, "Mr. Stout, also engaged in the prosecution . . . came to the rescue of the Mormon authorities and defended them against what he at least enfected to believe is a charge of their actual complicity in the murder. For a time he evinced considerable indignation and much excitement."[85]

As Stout intimated in his lengthy rebuttal to ex-Governor Weller, the case concerning Warm Springs was pending, even after Dr. Robinson's death, though little transpired until July 12, 1869, when Robinson's widow Nellie attempted to take control of the Warm Springs land, prompting the city to file a counter claim.[86] Once again it was Robert Baskin (aided by Charles Hempstead) vs. Hosea Stout (aided by Aurelius Miner), arguing the case in the Third District Court.[87] Arguments continued through December, leading the *Deseret News* to comment, the "case was instituted, as is generally known, on complaint of Dr. J.K. Robinson, in this Court, in September, 1866, Hon. John Titus, Judge. It may with propriety be termed a case of 'long standing.'"[88] In January 1870 the case was decided in favor of the city by the Commissioner of the Land Office at Washington.[89]

Baskin placed the blame on Mormon officials for his defeats in court and Robinson's unsolved murder, leading him to become bent on revenge. "By my investigations before referred to I became convinced that existing evils could only be corrected by adequate legislation of Congress," he wrote in his *Reminiscences,* "and therefore as I had mentally resolved while looking upon the mutilated body of my murdered client, Doctor Robinson, to do all that I possibly could do to place in the hands of the federal authorities the power to punish the perpetrators of such heinous crimes, I drafted the bill."[90]

The bill drafted by Baskin in 1869 was introduced in the US House of Representatives by General Shelby M. Cullom of Illinois, after whom it was named. It included thirty-four sections, each of which was aimed at ending polygamy and Mormon political control of Utah Territory. Prominent provisions of the bill would have prevented those who believed in plural marriage from serving on juries in polygamy trials; placed in the hands of the US marshal and the US attorney all responsibility for selecting jurors; deprived plural wives of immunity as witnesses in cases involving their husbands; and excluded polygamists from voting, being naturalized, or holding public office.[91] The Cullom Bill passed the House on March 23, 1870, but was kept from coming to the floor of the Senate; nevertheless, the near passage of the bill into law caused a great deal of excitement among the Utah Mormons.

On March 31, a mass meeting was held in Salt Lake City to protest against the bill. "Brigham Young set his best speakers at work, as soon as the Cullom Bill was passed," wrote the *Bangor Daily Whig and Courier*, "to prepare the people for protesting, and, as it would seem likely, for resisting."[92] Following a speech by Orson Pratt, Hosea Stout stood to address the crowd. For the first time in more than two decades, he had a personal stake in the subject of polygamy, having married Sarah Cox Jones on May 23, 1868, and would have been greatly affected had the bill passed.[93] Whereas Pratt in his speech took "the view of the matter which is most popular and likely to prevail with the staunch saints," laying out the religious basis of plural marriage, the Eastern press found that "a more sensible view of the matter was taken by Judge Stout":

> He asked whether, with female suffrage established in the Territory, and with railroads opening up the whole settlement to outside influences, Congress could not have been satisfied to let the religion die out, as it surely would do if false, instead of attempting to regulate it in this harsh manner. The same question has been asked here, and it gains greater force when we see the storm of fanaticism the Cullom bill has raised in Utah.[94]

Stout used his skills as an expert lawyer to reason logically and concluded by saying the meeting was "to show Congress that the people felt it was a question of suffering the penalties of this law or of being damned."[95] Fortunately for the Saints, as the bill died in the Senate, the "storm of fanaticism" in Utah passed without the people having to suffer the "penalties" of the law. Though many points of the bill were incorporated into later laws, Baskin's effort to destroy the Mormons was thwarted for the time being, but he was a nimble adversary, ready to seize any opportunity that might present itself. He didn't have to wait long.

Notes

1. Gardner, "Journal," *Heart Throbs of the West*, 10: 311–12.
2. Miller, *Immortal Pioneers*, 17–19; Bleak, "Annals of the Southern Utah Mission," 59–65.
3. Stout, "Journal," 37.
4. *Journal History*, October 17, 1861.
5. Stout, "Journal," 37.
6. *Journal History*, December 8, 1861; letter from Hosea Stout to Alvira Stout, January 24, 1862, BYU Library Special Collections. His family at the time consisted of his wife Alvira, three children of his late wife Louisa Taylor, four children of his with Alvira, and adopted son Henry Allen.

7. *Journal History*, January 6, 1862.
8. *Deseret News*, January 15, 1862.
9. *Journal of the Executive Proceedings of the Senate of the United States of America, from December 2, 1861, to July 17, 1862, Inclusive, Vol. XII*, January 16, 1862, 78.
10. Hosea Stout Papers, March 6, 1862, Utah State Historical Society, 146.
11. Letter from Hosea Stout to Alvira Stout, January 24, 1862, BYU Library Special Collections.
12. Letter from Hosea Stout to Alvira Stout, January 28, 1862, BYU Library Special Collections.
13. *Millennial Star*, 24:236, article of February 17, 1862.
14. *Deseret News*, March 4, 1862. The other "well known gentlemen" were Timothy B. Foote, Esq., Dr. Matthew McCune, and John Borrowman, Esq. [prosecuting attorney for Utah County].
15. *Deseret News*, April 23, 1862.
16. Hosea Stout, oath of office, April 18, 1862. Typescript copy in Hosea Stout Papers, Utah State Historical Society.
17. *New York Times*, January 21, 1862.
18. New Harmony Ward Record, LDS Family History Library, microfilm #26216, item 1.
19. Stout, "Journal," 38.
20. *Journal History*, June 12, 1862.
21. Miller, *The Immortal Pioneers*, 43.
22. Lyman, *Treasures of Pioneer History*, 6:473; Bleak, "Annals of the Southern Utah Mission," 97.
23. Bleak, "Annals of the Southern Utah Mission," 108. The other leaders to take part in the confirmation were Robert Gardner, William Carter, and James G. Bleak.
24. Isom, "Autobiography," MSS SC 1851, BYU Library.
25. Brooks, *Mormon Frontier*, June 21, 1861, 707. They were baptized on June 21 in Salt Lake City by Bishop Edwin D. Woolley.
26. Washington County Probate Court Records, LDS Family History Library microfilm #484838. In all recorded cases in which Hosea was involved in probate court he was counsel for the defense.
27. Letter from W. Neil Franklin, acting chief, Diplomatic, Legal and Fiscal Branch, National Archives and Records Service to Juanita Brooks, January 11, 1963, in Brooks, *Mormon Frontier*, 713.
28. Letter from Edward Bates to Abraham Lincoln, June 14, 1864, The Abraham Lincoln Papers at the Library of Congress.
29. *New York Times*, article of October 4, 1865, printed on November 27, 1865.
30. Letter from George A. Smith to Hosea Stout, March 20, 1863, in Hosea Stout Papers, Utah State Historical Society.
31. Walker, Turley, and Leonard, *Massacre at Mountain Meadows*, 256–64. St. George was not established as a city until 1861, four years after the Massacre.
32. Turner, *Brigham Young*, 306; Bancroft, *History of Utah*, 559–60.
33. Brooks, *Mormon Frontier*, March 8, 1859, 689.

34. Ibid., March 21, 1859, 691.
35. Letter from Black to Cradlebaugh and Sinclair, March 17, 1859, *Senate Exec. Doc. No. 32*, U.S. Congress 36th, 1st Session, 1860; Letter from Floyd to Johnston, May 6, 1859, *Senate Exec. Doc. No. 2*, U.S. Congress 36th, 1st Session, vol. 2; Cradlebaugh, "Utah and the Mormons."
36. Warrant (issued by Judge Elias Smith), May 1859, MS 17213, Church History Library.
37. Bagley, *Blood of the Prophets*, 233–34; *Journal History*, May 12, 1859.
38. Alexander, "Brigham Young, the Quorum of the Twelve, and the Latter-day Saint Investigation of the Mountain Meadows Massacre," Leonard J. Arrington Mormon History Lecture Series No. 12, Utah State University Press, 2007, 18; Church Historian's Office Journal, May 25, 1859, Church History Library; Moorman and Sessions, *Camp Floyd and the Mormons*, 118.
39. Church Historian's Office Journal, June 18, 1859.
40. Ibid., July 5, 1859.
41. Lyman, *Amasa Mason Lyman*, 291, citing Henry Lunt Journal, July 31, 1859.
42. "History of the District of Utah's U.S. Attorney's Office," http://www.justice.gov/usao/ut/history.html#wilson.
43. Cleland and Brooks, *A Mormon Chronicle: The Diaries of John D. Lee*, August 5, 1859, 1:214. The first of Lee's two trials took place in 1875—nearly eighteen years after the massacre—but Stout was not his attorney.
44. Lyman, *Amasa Mason Lyman*, 291. Klingensmith, Lee and Haight were three of the nine men who eventually were indicted for the massacre, but only Lee was tried. In a second trial he was found guilty and was executed by a firing squad at Mountain Meadows.
45. Bigler and Bagley, *Innocent Blood*, 226.
46. *Senate Exec. Doc. No. 32*, U.S. Congress 36th, 1st Session, 1860, August 10, 1859, 10:74.
47. *Utah Territory. Message, 36th Congress, 1st Session. Senate. C Ex. Doc. No. 42.* Message The President of the United States, Communicating, 86. http://www.olivercowdery.com/smithhome/1860s/1860Buch.htm#papersA05.
48. Buchanan, *Territory of Utah*, 56.
49. "First Judicial Court," *Deseret News*, September 7, 1859.
50. Turner, *Brigham Young*, 308, citing Eckels to Cass, September 27, 1859, copy in Box 48, Folder 41, Brigham Young Papers, Church History Library.
51. *Utah Territory*, 86–87.
52. Buchanan, *Utah Territory*, 56; Brooks, *Mormon Frontier*, September 16, 1859, 703.
53. Discourse of Brigham Young, March 8, 1863, *Journal of Discourses*, 10:110.
54. Alexander, "Brigham Young," citing David John Journals, May 6, 1862 [1863], vol. 3:60, MS 21, L. Tom Perry Special Collections, Harold B. Lee Library, Brigham Young University Provo, Utah.
55. Bagley, *Blood of the Prophets*; Denton, *American Massacre: The Tragedy at Mountain Meadows, September 1857*; Krakauer, *Under the Banner of Heaven: The Story of a Violent Faith*.
56. Brooks, *The Mountain Meadows Massacre*, 219.

57. Letter from George A. Smith to Hosea Stout, March 30, 1863.
58. Bleak, "Annals of the Southern Utah Mission," 157, 160.
59. Though Orson Pratt was senior to Erastus Snow in the Quorum of the Twelve Apostles, Snow was the driving force in the Cotton Mission.
60. *Journal History*, November 6, 1864, July 5, 1865, June 5, 1866.
61. Letter from Daniel H. Wells to Hosea Stout, June 1, 1866, Hosea Stout Papers, Utah State Historical Society.
62. Larson and Larson, eds., *Diary of Charles Lowell Walker*, May 13, 1866, 259.
63. *Semi-Weekly Telegraph* (Salt Lake City), July 30, 1866.
64. Bancroft, *History of Utah*, 647; *The Church Review, Salt Lake City, Utah*, 4–5.
65. Baskin, *Reminiscences of Early Utah*, 13; *Deseret News*, October 24, 1866.
66. *Journal History*, November 7, 1871; John Gary Maxwell, *Robert Newton Baskin and the Making of Modern Utah*, 322.
67. Baskin, *Reminiscences*, 14; Bigler and Bagley, *Mormon Rebellion*, 248–49.
68. *Deseret News*, September 12, 1866.
69. *Daily Alta California*, October 21, 1866.
70. *Deseret News*, October 24, 1866.
71. Testimony of Mrs. S. Crosby, *Union Vedette*, October 26, 1866.
72. *Deseret News*, November 14, 1866.
73. *Sacramento Daily Union*, October 25, 1866; *New York Times*, October 26, 1866.
74. *Baltimore Sun*, October 27, 1866.
75. Maxwell, *Robert Newton Baskin and the Making of Modern Utah*, 94.
76. "Resolution of the Legislature of Maine," relating to *The Assassination of John King Robinson, at Salt Lake City*, House of Representatives Miscellaneous Document No. 4, February 28, 1867, Fortieth Congress, Second Session, 1867–'68.
77. *Deseret News*, October 23, 1866.
78. Ibid., October 23, 1866.
79. Firmage and Mangrum, *Zion in the Courts*, 246; *Journal of Discourses*, 11:280–82.
80. *Americana*, vol. 9, part 1, 449.
81. *New York Times*, November 29, 1866.
82. Ibid.
83. *Deseret News*, November 14, 1866.
84. Ibid.
85. *Union Vedette*, November 8, 1866. Enfect is an obsolete word defined as "contaminated with illegality."
86. Brooks, *Mormon Frontier*, July 12–13, 1869, 728.
87. Ibid., October 13–23 and October 31—November 6, 1869, 734–35.
88. *Deseret News*, December 20, 1866.
89. *Millennial Star*, vol. 34, February 22, 1872, 125.
90. Baskin, *Reminiscences*, 28.
91. Ibid., 28–30.
92. *Bangor* [Maine] *Daily Whig and Courier*, April 18, 1870.
93. Sarah Cox was born on February 28, 1832, in Greencastle, Putnam County, Indiana, a daughter of Jehu Cox and Sarah Riddle Pyle. Her brother Isaiah was married to Hosea Stout's daughter, Elizabeth Ann.

Her first husband, David Hadlock Jones, was the son of Hosea's longtime friend, Benjamin Jones, who in turn previously was married to Hosea's sister Anna.
94. *Bangor Daily Whig and Courier*, April 18, 1870.
95. *New York Herald*, April 7, 1870.

20
Last Hurrah

In January 1872 in Washington, DC, James B. McKean, chief justice of the Utah Territorial Supreme Court, declared to Judge Louis Dent, brother-in-law of President Ulysses S. Grant, "the mission which God has called upon me to perform in Utah is as much above the duties of other courts and judges as the heavens are above the earth, and whenever or wherever I may find the Local or Federal laws obstructing or interfering therewith, by God's blessing I shall trample them under my feet."[1] The son of a Methodist clergyman, McKean was said to have come to Utah "with the prestige and experience of an honorable past to lend luster to his local position and light the pathway of duty lying before him."[2] Unfortunately for the Mormons, the duty McKean saw was to force them to obey the laws of the land, particularly in regard to polygamy, and he was ready to "trample" the Territorial laws in order to achieve his goals. "His gospel was one of patriotism, of high civic and domestic ideals," wrote Frank J. Cannon, who, despite his own strong anti-Mormon sentiments, noted "that McKean stretched his authority to cover every act which he conceived might work an injury to the Mormon kingdom."[3]

McKean was appointed chief justice of Utah's Supreme Court by President Grant in July 1870 and arrived in Salt Lake City on August 30. At the time of his appointment, the Cullom Bill already had passed in the House of Representatives but was languishing in the Senate, where it eventually died. Nevertheless, McKean ignored judicial procedures established by the Territorial legislature and instituted a key provision of the failed Cullom Bill by having US Marshal Matthewson Patrick handpick jurors, generally non-Mormons, rather that selecting them from taxpayer lists as required by territorial law.

US District Attorney Charles Hempstead, who had succeeded Hosea Stout in the position, resigned from office in 1871, complaining that his compensation was insufficient while also evidently unwilling to continue prosecuting under the extraordinary rulings of

Judge McKean's court.[4] Though a former editor of the anti-Mormon *Union Vedette*, Hempstead soon became Brigham Young's chief counsel and fought against McKean's method of impaneling juries.[5] After Hempstead's resignation, Judge McKean appointed Robert Baskin—the author of the Cullom Bill and a judicial ally—as the interim US attorney for Utah.[6] Seizing the opportunity, Baskin quickly sprang into action in his crusade against Mormonism, "determined to procure indictments against the officers of the Mormon Church for their violations of the law against polygamy."[7]

Brigham Young was Baskin's target, but he "knew that the indictment of Brigham and others would cause great excitement," so he started small with the arrest of Thomas Hawkins, whose wife entered a complaint after he took a plural wife without her approval.[8] Hawkins was indicted on August 8, 1871, for violation of a territorial law passed in 1852 to punish adultery and "lewd and lascivious association." Acting as though the Cullom Bill had been passed into law, Judge McKean not only had the US marshal pick the grand jury but also allowed Hawkins's wife to testify against her husband (an action not legal under Territorial law), and on her testimony alone he was found guilty and sentenced to three years imprisonment and a fine of $500.[9]

Even while the Hawkins case was being prosecuted, on September 29 an emboldened Baskin secured an indictment against Young for "lewdly and lasciviously associating and cohabitating with women, not being married to them."[10] Young was arrested on October 20, as were his First Presidency Counselors Daniel H. Wells and George Q. Cannon shortly thereafter, also for unlawful cohabitation. A protest was filed under the signature of Young's nine attorneys, including Hosea Stout and recently resigned US Attorney Charles Hempstead, and a motion to quash the indictment was made on the plea that the grand jury was improperly impaneled and therefore not legal.[11] Judge McKean overruled the motion, saying in part, "A system is on trial in the person of Brigham Young."[12] Due to poor health, Young asked the court's permission to make his usual winter trip to St. George, which was granted with the trial set for the following March.

While McKean's immediate target was the eradication of polygamy, Baskin was more intent on damaging Mormonism by going after its prophet. His opening came with the arrest of Bill Hickman for the September 1870 killing of a "Spaniard" (likely a Mexican) in Tooele County who had married one of Hickman's plural wives and subsequently made "heavy" threats against him. To avoid arrest, Hickman fled into the local mountains and during the winter received word that Deputy Marshal H. Gilson offered to meet without arresting him. Finally consenting to meet in April 1871, Hickman was told by Gilson that if he confessed to his

Figure 20.1. Hosea Stout, ca. 1855.

crimes it "would be greatly in [his] favor," and that R. N. Baskin was the man who could help him.[13]

Baskin's motive was obvious: "He conversed about many cases with which I was connected and finally elected the case of Yates as the one on which we could with the greatest safety rely for prosecuting Brigham Young."[14] The crime to which Hickman referred was the murder of Richard Yates in 1857. As a bonus, also implicated by Hickman in the murder were three high ranking Mormons: Daniel Wells, first counselor in the First Presidency; Brigham's son Joseph A. Young; and Hosea Stout, who in April 1870 had been sustained as an alternate member of the Salt Lake High Council.[15]

Over the course of two meetings, Hickman "revealed most of the numerous crimes contained in his published confession," including many murders he committed and admitted to in his book, *Brigham's Destroying Angel*. Following the second interview, Baskin became convinced of the sincerity and veracity of the multiple murderer, who "then gave him a full statement of the case and the names of the witnesses that would make the circumstances complete."[16] In late September 1871, shortly after Baskin had been appointed interim US district attorney, Hickman was arrested, though reportedly he struck a deal and had little to fear:

> Hickman was arrested some time since on a charge of murder in the first degree. He has been told that if he would criminate the leading authorities of the Church on some capital crime, he would be exonerated from guilt and probably receive some consideration; altho charged with murder committed about a year ago with incontestable evidence, he has been at large on parole on his own verbal recognizance.[17]

Hickman told the grand jury the story of Richard Yates, a mountaineer who made a living by hunting and by trading with the Indians. In 1857, Yates sold a substantial amount of gunpowder to troops of the approaching Utah Expedition, resulting in the Mormons branding him as a spy. According to an interview given about a month after his grand jury testimony and published in *New York World* on November 25, 1871 (very likely the most accurate account since *Brigham's Destroying Angel* was heavily edited without Hickman's input by noted anti-Mormon author John H. Beadle), Hickman was commissioned to bring Yates into town before Brigham Young.[18] On October 18, 1857, however, on his way to Salt Lake City Hickman encountered Joseph A. Young, who said his father Brigham "didn't want that fellow brought to the city, but wished him 'taken care of.'"[19] Hickman turned back to the mouth of Echo Canyon and arrived after dark with his prisoner at the camp of Colonel Nathaniel Jones, where Stout was stationed.[20] Of the events that night, Hickman wrote:

> About this time all was still, and everybody supposed to be in their beds. No person was to be seen, when Col. Jones and two others, Hosea Stout and another man whose name I do not recollect, came to my camp-fire and asked if Yates was asleep. I told them he was, upon which his brains were

knocked out with an ax. He was covered up with his blankets and left laying. Picks and spades were brought, and a grave dug some three feet deep near the camp by the fire-light, all hands assisting.[21]

Unwritten in that account was that Hickman committed the murder, though a drawing in *Brigham's Destroying Angel* depicts him killing Yates with an axe while Hosea Stout held a lantern.[22] Newspaper accounts, published across the nation following Hickman's testimony before the grand jury, offered a slightly different description of the event:

> The Mormons regarded him [Yates] as a spy, and some weeks after they arrested him and placed him in the custody of Hickman, to be taken to Salt Lake. D. Wells was then in command of the Mormon troops, and Hosea Stout was Judge Advocate. On the way to Salt Lake a guard killed Yates, as he says, by an order from Brigham Young and Joseph A. [Young], and at the instigation of Wells and Stout.[23]

Solely on the basis of information supplied by Hickman, the grand jury on September 26, 1871, issued an indictment against Brigham Young, Daniel H. Wells, Hosea Stout, and Joseph A. Young for murder in the first degree of Richard Yates.[24] Arrest warrants were issued for the four men on October 28, coincidentally the same day that Judge McKean sentenced Thomas Hawkins.[25] A warrant also was issued for William Kimball, eldest son of Heber C. Kimball, implicated by Hickman for a separate murder. While Wells, Stout, and Kimball were arrested, Brigham Young was out of reach, having left four days earlier for St. George. "The explanation given by his friends was that he had merely left on his usual annual tour to the Southern settlements," reported the *New York Tribune*. "It, however, soon became necessary to admit that his departure was at least hastened by the fears of his friends and advisers that a fair trial on any charge, by the U.S. Courts as at present constituted, was not possible, and that his punishment was predetermined on the attenuated evidence known by the court to exist."[26]

News of the arrests (and of the Hawkins sentencing) hit every major newspaper in the country, often with criticism of the court and the legal process. The Salt Lake correspondent of the Cincinnati *Commercial*, referring specifically to the indictment of Brigham Young, said the court organized a "grand jury to do the work of inquisition, a petit jury to try him . . . This is persecution, because there is no law for it. The Court enacts the Cullom Bill, which never passed Congress, and prosecutes under it by the very man who wrote it."[27] After observing McKean's court, William Pinkney Fishback, editor of the *Indianapolis Journal*, wrote in his paper, "We are convinced that the pending prosecutions are conceived in folly, conducted in violation of law, and with an utter recklessness as to the grave results that must necessarily ensue."[28]

In Mormon circles the reaction to the arrests was predictable. Apostle Wilford Woodruff opined that the prisoners "were as innocent of the Crime as the Savior before his Crucifixion."[29] Probate Judge Elias Smith, after visiting Stout and William Kimball at Camp Douglass, wrote that they "were two victims of the Inquisition known by the name and style of the 'Third District Court'" and that "the whole concern [was] nothing but a vile and wicked persecution."[30] The pro-Mormon *Salt Lake Herald* editorialized, "No intelligent man in Utah today, at all acquainted with the facts or the men, believes for a moment that either Daniel H. Wells or Hosea Stout had anything to do with the killing of Yates nor do we believe that such a jury can be packed even as will find either of them guilty."[31]

The arrested men, thinking that Brigham Young was the real target, evidently also did not believe a jury would find them guilty, as the *New York Tribune* reported "each and all smilingly accompanied the marshal and his deputies to the court-room." Regarding Stout, the *Tribune* article continued:

> Still another *particeps criminis* in this Yates murder, Hosea Stout, is a lawyer, a clever, indolent fellow, but with a good deal of positive force when aroused. He is one of Brigham's counsel in the cohabition [*sic*] case, and is also employed in others of the pending suits. He will have an abundant time for the preparation of his cases in his quiet retreat at Camp Douglas, bail having been refused in his case as well as in the case of Kimball. Stout takes the whole matter good-naturedly, and says that if he killed Yates he did it in his sleep. A friend of Stout, who has known him from boyhood, remarks that if the killing of Yates involved any actual labor, any physical exertion, "Hosea," as he is generally called, had no hand in it, as he is too lazy to exert himself. The fact is the whole matter is made a subject of ridicule by all classes, except perhaps a very limited circle about the court, who affect to believe that there may be something in the charges. The leading spirit in influencing the Grand Jury is, of course, the Prosecuting Attorney [Baskin], who, in this case, happens to be a bitter partisan, a poor lawyer, and a man of very dubious character.[32]

On the day following the arrests, Daniel Wells, who in addition to being a member of Young's First Presidency was mayor of Salt Lake City, asked for and was granted bail in the amount of $50,000 (Baskin had asked for $500,000 but was turned down by Judge McKean, who considered the sum to be exorbitant).[33] "Judge McKean's course in admitting Mayor Wells to bail is admitted in all quarters to be eminently wise and proper," wrote the *Salt Lake Tribune* on November 2, adding, "No fault is found for refusing bail for Stout and Kimball, although it is not deemed that the probability of their guilt is greater than that of Mayor Wells."[34]

While Stout may have appeared to the *New York Tribune* reporter to take "the whole matter good-naturedly," he was very serious about getting out of jail; having been denied bail, on October 30—two days after his arrest—he swore an affidavit before the clerk of the Utah Supreme Court stating "That he, the said Hosea Stout, can only be indicted for the crime aforesaid by a grand jury, duly selected, drawn, summoned, and empaneled according to the laws of the Territory of Utah."[35] Unsurprisingly, his plea to the Utah Supreme Court "that a writ of habeas corpus may issue as provide by law, and that he be discharged from his unlawful imprisonment" fell on deaf ears since the judge, Chief Justice James McKean, personally had impaneled the grand jury, so Stout retained Curtis J. Hillyer to appeal the case to the United States Supreme Court. The importance of the case, known as *Hosea Stout, Plaintiff in Error, v. The People of the United States in the Territory of Utah*, was recognized far beyond the borders of the Utah Territory, as reported in the *San Francisco Chronicle* on January 6, 1872:

> The question whether the Grand Jury which indicted Hosea Stout, the Mormon, for murder, having been summoned by the United States marshal, instead of the County authorities, was a lawful and properly organized body, will be argued in the Supreme Court next Thursday. The decision will determine the validity of the recent Mormon trials, and is looked forward to with great interest.[36]

The case was argued before the US Supreme Court by Hillyer (aided by Thomas Fitch) on December 15, 1871, and January 17, 1872. Hillyer's question to the Court was, "Is the law of the territorial legislature, prescribing the mode of obtaining panels of grand and petit jurors, obligatory upon the district courts of the Territory?"[37] In the decision, handed down and February 5, 1872, four of eight sitting judges determined "the summons in this case wholly void" while the other four reasoned that habeas corpus could be denied if the indictment was "regular in form and for a crime of which the court has jurisdiction." The conclusion, delivered by Chief Justice Salmon P. Chase, was, "*the court being equally divided on this point, the judgment must, necessarily, be affirmed.*"[38]

Stout had lost his appeal on the split decision and remained incarcerated, as did Brigham Young, who on January 2 confounded his enemies by walking into McKean's court and surrendering to US Marshal Patrick. The new prosecuting attorney, George C. Bates, who had been appointed in November 1871 by President Grant to replace Robert Baskin as US attorney for Utah, offered no objection to granting bail to Young as long as it was in the sum of $500,000, but McKean declined the motion, instead allowing him to be confined to a room in his own house.[39]

Meanwhile, Stout, William Kimball, and others were confined to the city hall, though it was more a case of being in custody than in jail since they had ample freedom. In late January 1872, for example, Mr. D. McDonald, a professor from Scotland, delivered a series of lectures on phrenology, a pseudo-science using measurements of the cranium to determine character and mental capacity, at the Tabernacle in Salt Lake City. At the close of his discourse, McDonald asked for subjects, in the process doing a "rushing business."[40] Among those examined was Hosea Stout, who was allowed to leave city hall to attend the professor's lecture.[41] On February 11, Stout and fellow prisoner Brigham Young Hampton visited Brigham Young at his office. "He felt well and told us to be patient and all will be well," Hampton recorded in his journal.[42] On March 6 the prisoners got the guard drunk and proceeded to go to the theater, after which they went home for the night.[43]

The liberal visitation policy, however, was about to change. On March 20, the wives and a few other friends "paid a condolatory visit to the brethren confined in the City Hall, Salt Lake City, carrying along various creature comforts, as well as smiles, cheerfulness and good wishes."[44] The festivities that night went too far, and the next day the prisoners—specifically Stout, William Kimball, and three men who had been indicted for the murder of Dr. John King Robinson—by order of US Marshal Patrick were removed from their quarters at the City Hall, as was Brigham Young from his home, and sent to Camp Douglas. "The prisoners were greatly excited and highly indignant, and the Mormon community generally is excited," reported the *New Hampshire Sentinel*. "The cause of this change was a ball and supper given in the city prison on Wednesday night by friends of the prisoners, when they had music, wine for supper, and a general festive time enjoyed."[45] Brigham Young Hampton, one of the men indicted in the Robinson murder, lamented, "To send us all to Camp Douglas on account of the surprise party . . . [we] were put in prison with 18 other prisoners, the hardest looking lot of men I ever saw . . . We had hardly room to stand up in the jail was so crouded."[46]

In the eyes of the Mormon community, a great injustice had been performed. The prisoners were sent to Camp Douglas, they believed, "to herd in the narrow confines of a military cell with self-confessed assassins and other criminals of the blackest dye. These innocent men, as all who know them are well satisfied, who are committed on the testimony of a self-acknowledged perjurer, are not only placed in jeopardy of life, liberty and possessions, but have to submit to the outrage of being compelled to suffer the society of the vilest of the vile, until the merciless powers who at present hold sway in Utah, see fit to bring them to trial, and all this because a few friends visited and spent a pleasant evening with them, the Marshal himself being present."[47] Fortunately for the prisoners, their incarceration at Camp Douglas was reasonably short-lived due to a case before the US Supreme Court, known as *Clinton v. Englebrecht*, that was argued on March 7, 1872.

Shortly before McKean arrived in Salt Lake City in 1870, Paul Englebrecht violated city ordinances by operating a liquor store without a license, whereupon Alderman and Justice of the Peace Jeter Clinton ordered the police to destroy the entire stock of booze, valued at about $22,000. A suit for recovery of damages was instituted by Englebrecht's attorney, Robert Baskin, which resulted in a judgment for nearly treble damages ($59,000). Clinton appealed to the United States Supreme Court on a claim that was virtually identical to that in *Hosea Stout v. The People of the US in the Territory of Utah,* namely that the grand jury (which was the same in both cases) was selected by the US marshal in violation of territorial law. Unlike the evenly divided Court in the *Stout* case, however, in *Clinton v. Englebrecht* the Supreme Court ruled unanimously in favor of the plaintiff. In presenting the decision of the Court on April 15, 1872, Chief Justice Chase said:

> Upon the whole, we are of opinion that the jury in this case was not selected and summoned in conformity with law, and that the challenge to the array should have been allowed. This opinion makes it unnecessary to consider the other questions in the case.
> *The judgment of the Supreme Court of the Territory of Utah must be reversed.*[48]

One can only speculate how the court could be evenly divided in one case and then, ten weeks later, unanimous in another on the same issue. Newspapers labeled Stout's a "test case," but it also may have served as a mock trial, for C. J. Hillyer was the plaintiff's attorney in both cases and likely learned from his losing experience in *Stout*. In addition, the opposing attorneys in *Stout* were a heavyweight trio of US. Attorney General George H. Williams, Assistant Attorney General C.H. Hill and Solicitor General B.H. Bristow whereas Robert Baskin stood alone for the defense in *Englebrecht*. Lastly, whereas Jeter Clinton and Paul Englebrecht were unknown to the eastern press, Hosea Stout had gained the reputation of a "most bitter Mormon" and was being tried for murder, which may have influenced some of the justices—consciously or subconsciously—into denying habeas corpus for Stout, even if there were true "irregularities in the summons of grand juries."

Englebrecht was a stunning defeat for McKean and his compatriot Baskin, smashing their crusade against Mormonism. In addition to the case at hand, the Court threw out all indictments brought by the illegally impaneled grand jury—a total of 130, several of which involved multiple defendants, including those charged with the murders of Richard Yates and Dr. John King Robinson. "The effect of this decision," wrote the *New York Tribune*, "is to make void all criminal proceeding in the territorial courts of Utah during the past year, and render necessary the immediate discharge of 138 prisoners who have been illegally held, at an expense of from $40,000 to $50,000, which there is no law to provide the payment of, and to affect in the same way all civil cases in which exceptions were taken to the legality of the juries."[49]

The Utah community was deeply divided in opinion regarding the case. Expressing the Mormon view, the *Deseret News* wrote of the prisoners' release, "We doubt whether there be anybody who really and firmly believed them guilty of the charges which were hatched and preferred against them, while the public generally were imbued with a belief in their complete innocence. There is no doubt that all of these gentlemen are perfectly willing that a searching investigation of their cases be entered upon whenever it can be done in a legal and unprejudiced manner."[50] On the other hand, the *Salt Lake Tribune* mockingly wrote, "Hosea Stout, as free as Judge McKean himself, will hang out his law shingle alongside of Tom Fitch and practice in the same courts again. He is no doubt already retained by many of the prisoners with whom he is confined at camp."[51]

The *Tribune* was correct in speculating that Stout would return to practice law, though his partner was Theodore Burmester, not Tom Fitch and, as far as can be determined, he was not retained by his fellow prisoners at Camp Douglas. His return to court, however, was delayed by legal confusion: the *Englebrecht* decision held that the US marshal could not summon jurors and the US attorney could not try cases under territorial law, while the territorial judges ruled that neither the territorial marshal nor territorial attorney could function before them. The end result was a non-functioning system under which no jury trials could be held.[52]

When the courts began to function again in fall 1873, Stout was back in action, almost exclusively as a defense attorney appearing in probate court. In their first substantial trial, the legal team of *Stout and Burmester* defended Solomon Gee who had been charged as an accomplice in a triple murder on July 24, 1873, at the mouth of Bingham Canyon. The evidence against Gee was circumstantial, namely that he was at the place of one of the murdered men on the day of the crime and that he owned a pistol. Stout, it was reported, was persuasive in his argument while his partner was, above all, loud:

> Judge Z[erubbabel] Snow delivered an argument for the prosecution, and was followed by Mr. Hosea Stout, whose arguments were ingenious and well put. Mr. Burmester then followed, also for the defense, and if logic and eloquence consisted of sound he would most certainly be a most powerful reasoned. When our reporter got within half a block of the Court House he could hear him quite plainly. Perhaps some of the jurymen were afflicted with deafness. Apparently he is a strong believer in *sound* philosophy.

At the conclusion of the case, in which Gee was found not-guilty, the *Salt Lake Tribune*, though typically sparing in their praise of any Mormons, wrote, "Messrs Stout and Burmester, counsel for the defense, are entitled to great credit for their devotion to their client's interest. They had a difficult case to conduct, but they went into it with their full force."[53] In his journal on the day of the verdict, presiding Judge Elias Smith wrote, "H. Stout, T. Burmester . . . For the Defence, with zeal and ability and much fairness."[54]

Stout continued to practice law for a few years, though much of the excitement of his life had vanished. In a letter of November 30, 1875, to his daughter Elizabeth, who resided in St. George, he wrote, "Now when I undertake to write to you I hardly know what to write because times are still well and in fact nothing going on or even transpiring except the every day hum drum routine business of life which makes ever day alike. As to day so was yesterday and so will be tomorrow if it should come . . . I would be only too well pleased to make a visit to Dixie and make you all sick of me and so would [wives] Vira and Sarah but how can I and how can they The truth is they could go much easier than I."[55]

Stout had suffered frequently from ill health throughout his adult life and in the letter seemed to allude to the lack of strength for travel, though he was virile enough in his sixty-sixth year to sire his nineteenth and final child (Charles Stephen Stout, born October 30, 1876). Around that time he retired to a small farm near Big Cottonwood Creek of thirteen acres with large peach and apple orchards and five-room house that he purchased from Milo Andrus on October 9, 1869[56] (an article in the *Salt Lake Tribune* on July 21, 1877, referred to him as "formerly a lawyer and now a farmer near Salt Lake City"[57]). While tending his farm, he still was involved in affairs of the local community, first serving on a committee of six individuals in May 1878 to draft resolutions concerning water rights at Mill Creek.[58] The following year he became Justice of the Peace for Big Cottonwood Precinct,[59] and in July 1880 he was selected by the Salt Lake County Court as one of three judges of elections from Big Cotton Precinct,[60] yet nothing gave the slightest hint of what was to come, when his name appeared on the "People's Ticket" in the general election running for Representative to the Legislative Assembly for Davis, Morgan, and Salt Lake Counties.[61]

In 1870, the Liberal Party was started in Utah by non-Mormons, with the help of a few apostate Mormons, to provide organized opposition to Mormon candidates. In response, church leaders found it expedient to form their own party, called the People's Party, and filled the People's Ticket with their handpicked candidates. Given a large Mormon majority, the outcome of the election was never in doubt: in Morgan County, for example, Stout and the other candidates for Representative on the People's Ticket polled 255 votes each, while the candidates from the Liberal Party each received only 9 votes.[62]

The legislative session was set to commence on Monday, January 9, 1882, but criticism of Stout poured in even before that date. On January 1, the *Salt Lake Tribune* wrote, "Hosea Stout was one of Bill Hickman's helpers, and is referred to in his book as a blood atoner of the worst kind; he has two wives."[63] Hickman, as a matter of fact, did not refer to Stout in his book as a "blood atoner," but that made little difference to the anti-Mormon press. On January 9, the opening day of the legislative session, the *Janesville* (Wisconsin) *Daily Gazette*, printed an article on the makeup of the Utah Territorial Legislature; echoing the Tribune report, the fifteenth Representative listed was "Hosea Stout, classed as one of the 'blood atoners,' a polygamist, with two wives."[64] The exact article subsequently appeared in many newspapers including the *New York Herald*, the *Galveston* (Texas) *Weekly News* and the New Jersey *Sentinel*.[65]

Despite his infamy across the nation, Stout proved to be an energetic and rational legislator who was an elder statesman in every sense, serving as a voice of reason though his wisdom frequently was ignored. He was a fiscal conservative, arguing against raising probate judge salaries because the counties couldn't afford "such an exorbitant sum"[66] and objected to "the adoption of Jefferson's manual as the guide for the house, on the ground of expense."[67] He argued against the language and amendments in a bill regarding "Licensing and regulating the manufacturing and sale of intoxicating liquors," stating, "The bill proposes that no man, except a man infinitely superior in character to the average of mankind, shall apply for a license, and being such a noble character, the bill doesn't do him justice."[68] Stout stood up for the common man, objecting to a bill to provide means for the collection of small debts, looking upon it "as a bill for the extinguishing of the poor man," the "most outrageous piece of legislation for its size he ever saw."[69] In each of the cases he was on the losing side.

Despite his setbacks, Stout maintained a sharp wit, prompting the *Salt Lake Herald* to write, "Judge Hosea Stout is coming to the front as the humorist of the House . . . During the brief remarks of Mr. Stout, he appeared unusually in earnest, and the laughter which greeted his points, or his references to lightning striking the statutes, did not move him in the least."[70] On another occasion, in seeking to modify a bill to "prevent bulls from running at large in Morgan County," Stout "moved the proviso that any bull residing in any other county, and traveling in Morgan on business, shall not be proscribed by this act. The amendment was greeted with laughter from members, and Mr. Stout supported the proposition in a cogent and irrefutable argument, and the amendment, when put was carried."[71]

The sixtieth and final day of the 1882 legislative session came on Friday, March 11. It was Stout's last hurrah in the political circle as he and many of his legislative associates soon were disenfranchised by the Edmunds Act, approved by the House on March 14 and soon signed into law by President Chester A. Arthur. Named for Senator George F. Edmunds of Vermont, the bill declared polygamy a felony punishable by five years imprisonment and a $500 fine. In addition, polygamists—who at the time constituted a majority of the Utah Territorial Legislature—could not hold political office, serve on a jury, or vote in elections.

Section Nine of the Edmunds Act declared all "registration and election offices in the Territory of Utah" vacant and provided that their duties were to be performed by the Utah Commission—a five person commission appointed by the President—until other provisions were made. Before the Commission arrived in Utah, a constitutional convention met in April to mount a statehood drive. On the third day of the convention, after Abram Hatch asked if rooms could be obtained for the uses of members of several committees, Stout wryly remarked that he "felt like leaving the chairmen of the several committees to their ingenuity to hunt their own woodpiles on which to deliberate."[72]

The convention framed a new constitution for Utah, for which J. C. Thoreson suggested that in article 3 the name "Deseret" be substituted for Utah. "A lively discussion ensued on the merits of both names," reported the *Ogden Standard Examiner*.[73] Arguing on behalf of the name

Utah, Stout stated, "we started out with the name of Deseret for our original organization; Congress had refused us that name, and it seems that we want them to take water." Thoreson's motion lost by a wide margin, and the name Deseret was abandoned.[74]

On May 22 the retooled constitution was ratified by a vote of the people in Utah, but the statehood bill was put on hold in the House and Senate and ultimately failed to pass. In the meantime, on August 18 the long awaited Utah Commission arrived in the Territory. Opposing factions of Mormons and non-Mormons, despite radically differing agendas, decided the best course of action in influencing the Commission would be in joining forces to make a pleasant and friendly initial contact. To that end, representatives of the two groups traveled together in a special railroad car to Ogden, as described in the *Salt Lake Tribune:*

> At last the long expected Commissioners for Utah, appointed under the Edmunds bill, have arrived in this city, to assume their duties under that act. It being known that they were on the road and would arrive by last evening's train, a party of gentlemen went to Ogden to greet and escort them to Zion. The Utah Central Company placed a special car on the regular train which left here at 3:40 p.m., and among those who went to Ogden to receive the Commissioners were Governor Murray, Secretary Thomas, General Bane, General Solomon, Messrs. Van Zile, W. H. Hooper, John Sharp, Dusenbury, Parley Williams, Mayor Jennings, ex-Mayor Little, Auditor Clayton, Treasurer Jack E. Sells, F. S. Richards, John T. Caine, G. M. Scott, Hosea Stout, Robert Walker and Mr. Billings.[75]

The Commission was swayed by neither faction but quickly moved to plan an election for November. Due to the Edmunds Act, all elective offices in Utah were vacated and polygamists and cohabitants were prevented from registering to vote or holding office. In 1882, all but five of the thirty-two committee chairmen in the legislature were polygamists and thus the ranks of the legislature were decimated.[76] In addition, the polygamists faced legal action, for under the Edmunds Act bigamy was a felony, carrying a maximum five-year imprisonment and a $500 fine, and unlawful cohabitation a misdemeanor, carrying a maximum $300 fine and six months imprisonment.

The first to be tried was Rudger Clawson, who appeared before recently appointed Utah Chief Justice Charles S. Zane in October 1884. Clawson was convicted by a jury of twelve non-Mormons of both polygamy and unlawful cohabitation and was sentenced to an $800 fine and four years in prison. When Salt Lake Stake President Angus Cannon was arrested in 1885, President John Taylor, George Q. Cannon, and other prominent church leaders went into hiding to escape prosecution. Under normal circumstances, Stout may well have been a prime target for arrest, but on May 27, 1885, his wife Sarah died from liver disease, and with her passing he had only one wife and therefore no longer could be charged either with bigamy or cohabitation.[77]

In the years preceding Sarah's death, Stout seemingly was in good physical and mental condition, particularly considering that, in the context of the times in which he lived, in his mid-seventies he was an old man. On January 30, 1883, an "Old Folk's social party" was held in the District Schoolhouse at Big Cottonwood. As reported in the *Deseret News,* "Among the veterans who tripped the light fantastic toe were Hosea Stout, Chas. A. Harper, Wm. H. Walker, Wm. Taylor, Edward Stevenson, John Holmes and many others too numerous to mention."[78] Several months later, in a handwritten letter of July 24 to Joseph F. Smith of the First Presidency, Stout displayed a steady hand and a sound mind while rendering an account of Joseph Smith revealing to the Nauvoo High Council the principle of plural marriage.[79] However, sometime in the months following Sarah's death he suffered a stroke that restricted his mobility and necessitated the use of a cane.[80] Then, at a special stake conference on May 7–8, 1887, in Salt Lake City, he was excused from the high council "because of failing health."[81]

On February 6, 1889, Dr. August Rauscher, one of the best-known physicians in the southern part of Salt Lake County, was summoned to Stout's home from the neighboring town of Murray.[82] The doctor examined his patient and left some medicine, but in reality there was no remedy, for Stout had suffered a severe paralytic stroke. Twenty-four days later he was dead.

One week following his death, a short article in the *Deseret Weekly* under the caption, "Demise of Hosea Stout," summarized his life:

> At 2:45 am, March 2nd, in Big Cottonwood Ward, Hosea Stout Esq. who has a figured prominently in the history of the Latter Day Saints for the past half century passed from life, the immediate cause of his death being paralysis with which he had been affected for the past four weeks. He was a native of Kentucky having been born in Mercer County September 18, 1810, but migrated when very young to [Clinton County, Ohio] and thence to Missouri where he embraced the gospel and from that time shared in the vicissitudes through which the church passed. He served in the Black Hawk war and

taught school in Illinois for a number of years. He was intimately associated with the Prophet Joseph Smith for a number of years prior to his death and for some time acted as his body guard as well as being an officer in the Nauvoo Legion and Chief of Police. He came to Utah in 1848 and located in Salt Lake City. He was a member of the Utah Legislature for a number of sessions, also of the City Council and practice at the bar when in the territory from the time the first court was established here until a few years since when his health became so impaired that he retired to his farm. He performed a mission to Hong Kong, China in 1853, was also one of the early settlers of St. George in Southern Utah where he remained about five years. He was a man of sterling integrity and excellent ability; and leaves a large family—a wife, nine sons and two daughters, besides a large number of grandchildren to revere his memory and emulate his virtues.[83]

Notes

1. *Millennial Star* 64:622.
2. *History of the Bench and Bar in Utah*, 28.
3. Cannon and Knapp, *Brigham Young and His Mormon Empire*, 357. Cannon was a son of George Q. Cannon, a counselor in the First Presidency to Brigham Young but later rejected Mormonism and spent the last two decades his life traveling around the United States lecturing against the religion.
4. *History of the Bench and Bar of Utah*, 30.
5. Stephen Cresswell, "The U.S. Department of Justice in Utah Territory, 1870–90," *Utah Historical Quarterly* 53 (1985): 207.
6. Baskin, *Reminiscences*, 36–7.
7. Ibid., 38.
8. Ibid., 54–5.
9. *Millennial Star*, March 26, 1872, 34:199; Baskin, *Reminiscence*, 39–44.
10. *Executive Documents printed by order of the House of Representatives during the Second Session of the Forty-Second Congress. 1871–72*; Executive Document No. 256, pp. 7–8.
11. *Millennial Star*, April 2, 1872, 34:210.
12. *Deseret News*, weekly, October 18, 1871.
13. Hickman, *Brigham's Destroying Angel*, 186–90.
14. Ibid., 191.
15. *Journal History*, April 18, 1870; Andrew Jenson, *The Historical Record*, 280. On May 9, 1873, Hosea was sustained as a regular member of the high council.
16. Baskin, *Reminiscences*, 36–38.
17. *Journal History*, September 26, 1871.

18. *New York World*, November 25, 1871, in MacKinnon, *At Sword's Point*, 304–7.
19. Ibid.
20. Brooks, *Mormon Frontier*, October 18, 1857, 643.
21. Hickman, *Brigham's Avenging Angel*, 125.
22. Ibid., 109.
23. *Louisville Commercial*, October 29, 1871.
24. *Journal History*, September 26, 1871; *The Executive Documents printed by order of the House of Representatives during the Second Session of the Forty-Second Congress, 1871–72*; Executive Document No. 256, 8.
25. *New York Observer*, November 2, 1871.
26. *New York Tribune*, November 9, 1871.
27. *Commercial* quoted in *Deseret News*, November 15, 1871.
28. *Indianapolis Journal* quoted in *Deseret News*, November 8, 1871.
29. Woodruff, "Journal," October 29, 1871.
30. Smith, "Journals," November 14, 1871, MS 1319, Church History Library.
31. *Deseret News*, November 1, 1871; *Salt Lake Herald*, October 29, 1871, in *Journal History* of the same date.
32. *New York Daily Tribune*, November 9, 1871 (article of November 1, 1871).
33. Ibid., October 30, 1871.
34. Ibid., November 2, 1871.
35. *Supreme Court of the United States. No. 478. Hosea Stout, Plaintiff in Error vs. The People of the United States in the Territory of Utah*, 1.
36. *San Francisco Chronicle*, January 6, 1872, reported in *Deseret News*, January 17, 1872.
37. *Supreme Court of the United States, No. 478. Hosea Stout, Plaintiff, vs. the People of the United States in the Territory of Utah.*
38. *Cases Argued and Decided in the Supreme Court of the United States, December Terms, 1870, 1871, Book 20*, 512–13.
39. *Deseret News*, January 10, 1872; Smith, "Journal," January 2, 1872.
40. *Salt Lake Herald*, January 27 and 31, 1872.
41. *New Chart for Marking Character*, by D. McDonald, Phrenologist and Lecturer, Chart of H. Stout, Salt Lake City, Utah, dated February 1, 1872, in Hosea Stout Papers, MS 16397, Church History Library.
42. Aird, Nichols, and Bagley, eds., *Playing with Shadows: Voices of Dissent in the Mormon West*, 364.
43. Ibid., March 6, 1872, 365.
44. *Millennial Star*, April 16, 1872, vol. 34:250.
45. *New Hampshire Sentinel*, March 28, 1872.
46. Aird, Nichols, and Bagley, eds., *Playing with Shadows*, 366.
47. *Millennial Star*, April 16, 1872, vol. 34:250.
48. *Cases Argued and Decided in the Supreme Court of the United States, December Terms, 1870, 1871, Book 20*, 659–63.
49. *New York Tribune*, quoted in *Millennial Star*, vol. 34:297–98.
50. *Deseret News*, May 8, 1872.
51. *Salt Lake Tribune*, April 24, 1872.
52. Alexander, *Utah: The Right Place*, 176.
53. *Salt Lake Tribune*, September 21, 1873.
54. Elias Smith, "Journals."

55. Letter from Hosea Stout to his daughter Elizabeth Ann Cox, November 30, 1875, Church History Library.
56. Brooks, *Mormon Frontier*, October 9, 1869, 734. A notice in the *Deseret News* on June 7, 1876, invited those with a claim against the estate of William Wilson to go to "the office of Hosea Stout, at his residence in Salt Lake City." On May 10, 1878, the *Deseret News* had another article of listing Hosea as a member of the farming community "on the north and south side of the Big Cottonwood Creek."
57. *Salt Lake Tribune*, July 21, 1877.
58. *Deseret News*, May 15, 1878.
59. Culmer, *Utah Directory and Gazetteer for 1879–80*, 52.
60. *Deseret News*, July 14, 1880. The appointment was for the fiscal year ending May 31, 1881.
61. Ibid., July 27, 1881.
62. Ibid., August 10, 1881.
63. *Salt Lake Tribune*, January 1, 1881.
64. *Janesville Daily Gazette*, January 9, 1882. The concept of blood atonement stemmed from a sermon given by Brigham Young in 1857 during the Mormon Reformation in which he stated that one who has committed certain grievous sins cannot be exalted "without the shedding his blood." Brigham continued, saying, "I could refer you to plenty of instances where men have been righteously slain, in order to atone for their sins." See *Journal of Discourses*, February 8, 1857, 4:219–20.
65. *New York Herald*, January 9, 1882; *Galveston* (Texas) *Weekly News*, January 26, 1882; New Jersey *Sentinel*, February 11, 1882.
66. *Ogden Standard Examiner*, February 18, 1882.
67. Ibid., January 12, 1882.
68. Ibid., February 17, 1882.
69. Ibid., February 28, 1882.
70. *Salt Lake Herald*, February 14, 1882.
71. Ibid., March 4, 1882.
72. *Ogden Standard Examiner*, April 11, 1882.
73. *Ogden Standard Examiner*, April 27, 1882.
74. *Deseret News*, May 3, 1882.
75. *Salt Lake Tribune*, August 19, 1882.
76. Coyner, *Handbook on Mormonism*, 61–63.
77. *Deseret News*, June 3, 1885.
78. *Deseret News*, January 31, 1883; Quinn, "Culture of Violence."
79. Letter from Hosea Stout to President Joseph F. Smith, July 24, 1883, Church History Library.
80. Interview with Mrs. Leslie S. Palmer, granddaughter of Hosea Stout, by Richard Grant Ellsworth, July 7, 1951, in Ellsworth, "A Study of the Literary Qualities in the Diary of Hosea Stout," Master's thesis, Brigham Young University, 21.
81. *The Historical Record*, 5–6:281.
82. Invoice of Dr. A. Rauscher, April 20, 1889, "Estate of Hosea Stout," in Salt Lake Probate Records, Mss B53, Utah State Historical Society.
83. *Deseret Weekly*, March 9, 1889.

Epilogue

Hosea Stout was not a man of great wealth despite being an attorney and having held many high-ranking public positions. Though his land and house together were valued at $4,000, at the time of his death he had cash on hand in the amount of $574, of which only $24 remained after paying creditors and Samuel Brinton's commission as executor of the estate. Renting the farm gave his widow Alvira an allowance of $20 per month for the year following his death. His most valuable possession was an organ with a stool, valued at $50, while his library of seventy-five volumes of "old books" was appraised at $15. His two "suits of Gentleman's cloth" were so badly worn that they had no value, and Alvira had to pay the undertaker, Joseph E. Taylor, $12 for a suit in which to bury him.[1]

Stout loved and cared deeply for his family. Eleven of his nineteen children survived him, as did his wife Alvira (who outlived him by twenty-one years), but he also experienced nearly unbearable tragedy as four of his wives and eight of his children preceded him to the grave.[2] He was in his seventy-ninth year at the time of his death, yet two teenage children (Edgar Walter, 17; and Charles Stephen, 13) still were living at home; three other sons (Brigham Hosea, 33; Alfred Lozene, 30; and William Hooper, 24) resided at Big Cottonwood and likely tended his farm, while the other six children were scattered across the Utah and Idaho Territories.

Stout was destined to be a religious man. As a young child, due to family financial misfortune, he and his older sisters were sent to live with the Shakers at Pleasant Hill, Kentucky. A few years after his father retrieved him from the Shakers and moved the family to Ohio, he found his best friends and examples among the Quakers, with whom he gradually identified, despite never joining their society. Nine days before his eighteenth birthday, he set out for Illinois, where a number of his Stout relatives had settled, and through his sister Anna he was introduced to Methodism, which he embraced on a six-month trial basis. Anna subsequently married a widower through whom she was converted to Mormonism. Stout at first considered her conversion to be a disgrace, but upon meeting her husband Benjamin Jones and befriending Charles C. Rich—both Mormons—he quickly altered his view and became a staunch supporter of the faith even before he became a member, defending the unpopular religion to others while professing not to believe what he advocated.

Ultimately, his life was defined by his commitment to Mormonism. He was officially a member of the Church of Jesus Christ of Latter-day Saints for fifty-one years, nearly all of his adult life, and his faith never waivered. At the general conference in April 1858, he said, "I always feel that it is my duty to look to myself, for I am in as much danger of apostatizing as any in the Church. If I ever do get led astray and depart from the principles of the gospel of salvation, it will be because I led myself off from the path; it was not my brethren who led me away, it was my own doing."[3] Still, even while nurturing and protecting his own faith, his greater concern was protecting the interest of the church and its leaders, for which he often was willing to use a heavy hand. Though his intent may have been noble, in many instances his violent methods were unacceptable; seemingly having learned their lesson, after reaching Utah, church leaders ceased placing him in positions where he could, in his own mind, justify the use of violence.

His mercurial temper was legendary and terrible to behold, gaining him a measure of widespread infamy, his steely gaze with his penetrating eyes could cause one to fear and tremble, and yet he cared deeply for his family and could be generous and kindhearted. Following the death of one plural wife and the desertion of another in 1846–1847, he lived as a monogamist for more than two decades before taking another plural wife, Sarah Cox Jones, whose husband David Hadlock Jones (the eldest son of Stout's old friend, Benjamin Jones), was killed by Indians three years earlier and whose brother, Isaiah Cox, was married to Stout's daughter Elizabeth Ann. At the time of her husband's death, Sarah was living in Sanpete County, nearly one hundred miles from Salt Lake City,[4] and it is likely that Stout learned of her plight either from his daughter or from his friend Benjamin Jones. That Sarah had been sealed "for time and eternity" to David Hadlock Jones and that, following her death on May 27, 1885, she was buried next to his grave in the Fairview City Cemetery in Sanpete County suggests that Stout may have taken her as a plural wife as an act of Christian charity in caring for a childless widow.

After reaching the Salt Lake Valley in 1848, a more mature Stout defended the interests of the Kingdom more with his mind than with his fists, likely in part due to his age (at thirty-eight he was one year shy of the life expectancy for those like him who were born in 1810),[5] and greatly due to his occupation, having shifted from being a lawman to a man of the law.⁶ Recorded accounts of his violent actions diminished greatly, with the only altercation an attack on opposing attorney Bradford Leonard on October 2, 1858, for which he was fined five dollars and made to pay the costs of the suit. He was accused by William Hickman of being present when Hickman in 1857 murdered Richard Yates, who had been suspected of being a spy as the Mormons prepared to confront the US Army, though he denied being complicit in the murder. Regardless, the consequence of earlier violence and terrible temper, coupled with his many hardships and personal tragedies, can be seen in photographic portraits in which, through the years, he appeared progressively hardened and even sinister.

Blessed with great intelligence, despite having no legal training or college education, Stout became an attorney in Utah, quickly developing a sharp legal acumen and being appointed the first attorney general of the new Territory of Utah. Brigham Young frequently counseled with him, relied on his advice and called on his services to defend the interests of the church (as well as Young's own personal interests) to the point that the *New York Times*, while reporting his appointment as interim US district attorney, labeled Stout "the attorney of the Mormon Church."⁷

Following the expulsion of the Mormons from Nauvoo, Stout wrote in his journal that the Saints were going "to the wilderness for safety and refuge."⁸ In the barren Utah desert, the Saints did find a refuge during some very crucial years. Primarily through legal and political maneuvering, in which Stout played a central role, the Mormon theocracy fought off efforts to destroy polygamy and perhaps the entire religion and thereby bought valuable time to settle Utah, construct a government, build an economy and establish a firm foothold from which the church prospered. The resistance was orchestrated by church leaders, but Stout was as loyal and important a soldier in the fight as any, undeterred by the deaths of four wives and eight children, by the loss of homes and property as the Mormons were driven from Missouri and Illinois, by the failed promises of a successful mission to China. Under similar circumstances, many others found reason to quit, but Hosea Stout always had the strength to carry on; despite his flaws (particularly his violent nature so evident in the years before arriving in Utah) and despite the many hardships and obstacles he encountered, whether as a lawman, a legislator, or a lawyer he always was ready and willing to be on the frontline in defending the spiritual and political "Kingdom of God."

Notes

1. "Estate of Hosea Stout," No. 1377, Salt Lake Probate Court Records, Utah State Archives.
2. After visiting the grave of his wife Louisa on December 14, 1853, Hosea wrote that seven of his children were buried. His young plural wife

Marinda had a stillborn child shortly before her death, and since five of Louisa's eight children died by that date, it is evident that another child died, quite possibly stillborn. See Brooks, *Mormon Frontier,* December 14, 1853, 499.
3. Powell, ed., *Utah History Encyclopedia,* 534.
4. US Bureau of the Census, 1860. At the time of the census, David and Sarah Jones were living in Mount Pleasant in Sanpete County.
5. According to a 2011 study by the National Institutions of Health, the average lifespan for a person born in the United States in 1810 was thirty-nine years, Hosea's age just one year after he entered the Salt Lake Valley. See http://www.ncbi.nlm.nih.gov/pmc/articles/PMC2885717/figure/F6/.
6. The vast majority of Stout's known violent incidents are found in his own journal; the possibility must be considered that perhaps many other violent incidents went unreported, both by him and others.
7. *New York Times,* September 28, 1859.
8. Brooks, *Mormon Frontier,* February 16, 1846, 123.

Appendix
Hosea Stout's Wives and Children

Samantha Peck

Born October 12, 1821, in Bainbridge, Chenango County, New York, to Benjamin Peck and Phoebe Crosby. Married Hosea Stout on January 7, 1838, in Caldwell County, Missouri. Died November 29, 1839, in Lee County, Iowa.

Samantha's father, Benjamin Peck, died on April 30, 1829, in New York; in June 1830 her mother Phoebe Crosby was baptized a member of the LDS church, along with a number of Benjamin's family members, becoming some of its earliest converts. Phoebe moved to Ohio with her children Hezekiah, Samantha, Henrietta, and Sarah in 1831 with a large group from the Colesville Branch of the church that became known simply as the Colesville Saints. After fourteen years of providing for her family alone, Phoebe married Joseph Knight, another of the Colesville Saints, following the death of his wife Polly Peck, who was Phoebe's sister-in-law.

No children.

Louisa Taylor

Born October 19, 1819, in Bowling Green, Warren County, Kentucky, to William Warren Taylor and Elizabeth Patrick. Married Hosea Stout on November 29, 1840, at Nauvoo, Hancock County, Illinois. Died on January 11, 1853, in Salt Lake City.

In November 1831, William Taylor followed two brothers-in-law, Ludson Green Patrick and Levi Turner, to Missouri and bought eighty acres of prime land in the Salt River Valley or northeastern Missouri near the Allred settlement of James and Isaac Allred. Several months earlier, while on their way to a religious conference in western Missouri, John Murdock and Hyrum Smith (older brother of the Mormon prophet) spent a week in the home of William Ivie, a nephew of Isaac Allred, while Murdock recovered from an illness. During that time, Murdock and

Smith preached about their new religion. Shortly after arriving at the settlement, William Taylor and his family as well as members of the Ivie and Allred families were baptized, becoming some of the earliest Mormon converts in Missouri.

Louisa was pregnant with her eighth child in 1852 when Hosea was called on a church mission to China. While Hosea was laid up in San Bernardino, California, awaiting passage from San Pedro to San Francisco and onto China, on December 30, 1852, their child Joseph Allen Stout was born in Salt Lake City. On January 9, 1953, the child died; two days later, while Hosea was on a ship laid up near San Luis Obispo due to heavy winds and rough seas, Louisa, most likely weakened by childbirth, passed away. In his journal Hosea displayed tender feelings towards Louisa that probably were matched only by his those directed to his sixth wife, Alvira.

Children

1. **Lydia Sarah Stout**, born December 20, 1841, in Nauvoo, Hancock, Illinois; died November 13, 1842, in Nauvoo.
2. **William Hosea Stout**, born April 16, 1843, in Nauvoo, Hancock, Illinois; died June 28, 1846, in Council Bluffs, Pottawattamie, Iowa.
3. **Hyrum Stout**, born July 4, 1844, in Nauvoo, Hancock, Illinois; died May 9, 1846, in Garden Grove, Decatur, Iowa.
4. **Louisa Stout**, born April 22, 1846, in Hog Creek, Decatur, Iowa; died August 5, 1847, in Winter Quarters, Douglas, Nebraska.
5. **Elizabeth Ann Stout**, born March 19 1848; died August 10, 1835, in Hinckley, Millard, Utah.
6. **Hosea Stout Jr.**, born April 5, 1850, in Salt Lake City, Utah; died March 1, 1918, in Glendale, Maricopa, Arizona.
7. **Eli Harvey Stout**, born September 17, 1851, in Salt Lake City, Utah; died November 22, 1925, in Alameda County, California.
8. **Joseph Allen Stout**, born December 30, 1852, in Salt Lake City, Utah; died January 9, 1853, in Salt Lake City, Utah.

Lucretia Fisher

Born March 13, 1830, in Dalton, Coos County, New Hampshire. Married Hosea Stout April 20, 1845, in Nauvoo, Hancock Illinois. Lucretia lived in the Stout household for two months, evidently on a trial basis, before she became Stout's first plural wife.

In a journal entry of August 5, 1847, Hosea stated that his family was "now but two"—namely his wife Louisa and himself, which was an indication that, in addition to the death of his plural wife Marinda

Bennett, sometime in the preceding eleven months Lucretia had left him. Moreover, in the 1850 census from Washington, Buchanan County, Missouri, a Lucretia Fisher, age twenty from New Hampshire, is listed as living in the household of Edward Freeman along with Freeman's wife Mary and four children, all of whom were born in Missouri. Washington is a present day suburb of St. Joseph, Missouri, about 120 miles south of the Iowa Mormon trail, and it would seem likely that Lucretia left Hosea somewhere along the trail across Iowa and traveled southward, taking up residence with another family.

Marinda Bennett

Born August 26, 1826, in Bedford County, Tennessee, to Richard Bennett and Mary Bell. Married Hosea Stout February 2, 1846. Died September 26, 1846, in Winter Quarters, Nebraska.

Marinda had experienced an extended illness when, on the evening of September 25, 1846, she had a stillborn child. Her extremely weakened state deteriorated the next day and in the early afternoon she died. In rapid succession in 1846, Hosea's sons William Hosea and Hyrum as well as Marinda had died, leaving a family of four (Hosea, his wife Louisa, their daughter Louisa, and Lucretia Fisher). On the day of Marinda's death Hosea wrote in his journal, "She had ever been true and faithful to me from the first of our acquaintance and had rendered her self by her sturdy true and subordinate habits, very near and dear to me which made this stroke of adversity more accutely felt by me and the rest of my family." In a few months after Marinda's death, Lucretia left Hosea, making one wonder whether his statement of Marinda being ever "true and faithful" might have inferred that Lucretia was not, particularly in light of the fact that Lucretia never again was mentioned by him.

No children.

Aseneth Harmon

Born November 12, 1823, in Fayette, Indiana, to Henry Harmon and Agnes Green. Married Hosea Stout January 9, 1854; divorced in early summer 1854. Died June 20, 1899, in Pleasant Grove, Utah.

Aseneth previously was married to William Gheen, a former member of the Nauvoo Legion in Illinois who died on August 19, 1852, while prospecting for gold Mormon Island near Sacramento, California. Her marriage to Hosea took place almost exactly one month following his return to Salt Lake City from a mission in China, suggesting that it was a whirlwind marriage with the intent on his part to have a new wife to care for his children. At the time of the marriage Aseneth had an eleven-year-old daughter (her two other children previously had died). Hosea was at Green River, Wyoming, at the time the divorce was finalized; upon his return he wrote simply, "All is well." A few months after the divorce, on October 29, 1854, Aseneth married Edward Thompson Mumford. Her gravestone in Pleasant Grove, Utah reads, "Aseneth Harmon Gheen Mumford," a clear indication that her marriage to Hosea Stout was one she wanted to forget.

No children (by Hosea Stout).

Alvira Wilson

Born April 21, 1834, in Green Township, Richland, Vermont, to Louis Dunbar Wilson and Nancy Ann Wagoner. Married Hosea Stout July 19, 1855, in Salt Lake City. Died March 20, 1910, in Holladay, Salt Lake, Utah.

Alvira's parents were early Mormon converts, baptized on May 23, 1836, in Green Township, Richland, Vermont. He moved the family to Far West, Missouri, in fall 1837 and then to Nauvoo after the Latter-day Saints were driven from Missouri. Going by his middle name Dunbar, Wilson served on the Nauvoo High Council from 1839 to 1846 and is mentioned in *Doctrine and Covenants 124:132* and would have been well acquainted with Hosea, whom for several years served as clerk of the council.

Children

1. **Lewis Wilson Stout**, born April 27, 1856, in Salt Lake City; died March 31, 1889, in Mammoth, Juab, Utah.
2. **Brigham Hosea Stout**, born September 5, 1857, in Salt Lake City, Utah; died September 24, 1925, in Salt Lake City.
3. **Alfred Lozene Stout**, born July 8, 1859, in Salt Lake City, Utah; died May 18, 1896, in Big Cottonwood, Salt Lake, Utah.
4. **Allen Edward Stout**, born February 18, 1861, in Salt Lake City, Utah; died October 5, 1938, in Hinckley, Millard, Utah.
5. **William Hooper Stout**, born October 10, 1863, in St. George, Utah; died March 1, 1940, in Salt Lake City.
6. **Alvira Stout**, born June 5, 1866, in St. George, Utah; died October 29, 1923, in Holladay, Salt Lake, Utah.
7. **Frank Henry Stout**, born June 9, 1869, in Salt Lake City, Utah; died July 9, 1869, in Salt Lake City.
8. **Edgar Walter Stout**, born August 2, 1870, in Salt Lake City, Utah; died October 19, 1933, in San Francisco, California.
9. **Arthur Stout** (twin), born February 9, 1875, in Salt Lake City, Utah; died February 9, 1875, in Salt Lake City.

10. **Ada Stout** (twin), born February 9, 1875, in Salt Lake City, Utah; died August 20, 1875, in Salt Lake City.
11. **Charles Stephen Stout,** born September 30, 1876, in Salt Lake City, Utah; died December 26, 1951, in Yountville, Napa, California.

Sarah Cox Jones

Born February 28, 1832, in Green Castle, Putnam, Indiana, to Jehu Cox Sr. and Sarah Riddle Pyle. Married Hosea Stout May 23, 1868, in Salt Lake City, Utah. Died May 27, 1885, in Salt Lake City.

Sarah Cox had strong connections to Hosea before they were married: her brother Isaiah Cox was married to Hosea daughter, Elizabeth Ann, and her late husband, David Hadlock Jones, was the son of Hosea's longtime friend, Benjamin Jones. In addition, Benjamin Jones's second wife, Anna Stout, was Hosea's sister, and his third wife, Rosanna Cox, was Sarah's older sister.

Sarah's husband David Hadlock Jones was killed by Indians in Fairview, Sanpete, Utah, on May 24, 1865, during what became known as the Black Hawk War. At the time of his death, Sarah was living in Sanpete County, nearly one hundred miles from Salt Lake City, and it is likely that Hosea learned of her plight either from his daughter Elizabeth Ann or from his friend Benjamin Jones (like Sarah a resident of Fairview). Sarah had been sealed "for time and eternity" to David Hadlock Jones and following her death on May 27, 1885, was buried next to his grave in the Fairview City Cemetery in Sanpete County.

No children.

Bibliography

Books

World's Fair Ecclesiastical History of Utah. Salt Lake City: George Q. Cannon and Sons, Printers, 1893.

Aird, Polly, Jeff Nichols, and Will Bagley, eds. *Playing with Shadows: Voices of Dissent in the Mormon West.* Norman, OK: The Arthur H. Clark Company, 2011.

Alexander, Thomas G. *Utah: The Right Place.* Salt Lake City: Gibbs-Smith Publisher, 1995.

Allen, James B. *No Toil nor Labor Fear: The Story of William Clayton.* Provo: Brigham Young University Press, 2002.

Allen, James B., and Glen M. Leonard. *The Story of the Latter-day Saints.* Salt Lake City: Deseret Book Co, 1976.

Allensworth, Ben C., ed. *Historical Encyclopedia of Illinois and History of Tazewell County.* Chicago: Munsell Publishing Company, 1905.

Alter, J. Cecil. *Jim Bridger.* Norman: University of Oklahoma Press, 1986.

Anderson, Devery S., and Gary James Bergera. *The Nauvoo Endowment Companies, 1845–1846, A Documentary History.* Salt Lake City: Signature Books, 2006.

Anderson, Maybelle Harmon, ed. *Appleton Milo Harmon Goes West.* Berkeley, CA: The Gillick Press, 1946.

Anderson, Nels. *Desert Saints: The Mormon Frontier in Utah.* Chicago: The University of Chicago Press, 1942.

Andrews, Edward Deming. *The People Called Shakers: A Search for the Perfect Society.* New York: Oxford University Press, 1953.

Arrington, Leonard. *Brigham Young: American Moses.* Urbana, Chicago: University of Illinois Press, 1985.

Arrington, Leonard. *Great Basin Kingdom: An Economic History of the Latter-day Saints, 1830–1900.* Salt Lake City: University of Utah Press, 1958.

Bagley, Will. *Blood of the Prophets: Brigham Young and the Massacre at Mountain Meadows.* Norman: University of Oklahoma Press, 2002.

Bancroft, Hubert Howe. *History of Utah, 1540–1886.* San Francisco: The History Company, 1889.

Barney, Ronald O., ed. *The Mormon Vanguard Brigade of 1847: Norton Jacob's Record.* Logan: Utah State University Press, 2005.

Bartholomew, Rebecca, and Leonard J. Arrington. *Rescue of the 1856 Handcart Companies.* Provo, UT: Brigham Young University, Charles Redd Center for Western Studies, 1992.

Baskin, Robert N. *Reminiscences of Early Utah.* Salt Lake City: Self-published, 1914.

Bateman, Newton, and Ezra Prince, eds. *Historical Encyclopedia of Illinois and History of McLean County*. Chicago: Munsell Pub. Co, 1908.

Baugh, Alexander L. *A Call to Arms: The 1838 Mormon Defense of Northern Missouri*. Provo: Brigham Young University Studies, 2000.

Bennett, Richard E. *Mormons at the Missouri, 1846–1854*. Norman: University of Oklahoma Press, 1987.

Bennett, Richard E. *We'll Find the Place: The Mormon Exodus 1846–1848*. Salt Lake City: Deseret Book Company, 1997.

Bennett, Richard E., Susan Easton Black, and Donald Q. Cannon. *The Nauvoo Legion in Illinois: A History of the Mormon Militia, 1841–1846*. Norman, OK: The Arthur H. Clark Company, 2010.

Bigler, David L., and Will Bagley. *The Mormon Rebellion: America's First Civil War 1857–1858*. Norman: University of Oklahoma, 2011.

Bigler, David L. *Forgotten Kingdom: The Mormon Theocracy in the American West, 1847–1896*. Spokane, WA: The Arthur H. Clark Company, 1998.

Bigler, David L., and Will Bagley. *Innocent Blood: Essential Narratives of the Mountain Meadows Massacre*. Norman, OK: The Arthur H. Clark Company, 2008.

Black, Susan Easton, and Harvey Bischoff Black. *Annotated Record of Baptisms for the Dead, 1840–1845, Nauvoo, Hancock County, Illinois*. Provo, UT: Brigham Young University Press, 2002.

Black, Susan Easton, Harvey B. Black, and Brandon Plewe. *Property Transactions in Nauvoo, Hancock County, Illinois and Surrounding Communities (1838–1859)*. Wilmington, DE: World Vital Records, 2006.

Bradley, Martha Sonntag. *A History of Kane County*. Salt Lake City: Utah State Historical Society, 1999.

Brodie, Fawn M. *No Man Knows My History: The Life of Joseph Smith the Mormon Prophet*. New York: Alfred A. Knopf, 1989.

Brooks, Juanita, ed. *On the Mormon Frontier: The Diary of Hosea Stout, 1844–1861*. Salt Lake City: University of Utah Press, 1964.

Brooks, Juanita. *The Mountain Meadows Massacre*. Norman: University of Oklahoma Press, 1960.

Brown, James S. *Life of a Pioneer, Being the Autobiography of James S. Brown*. Salt Lake City: George Q. Cannon and Sons, 1900.

Brooks, Juanita. *John Doyle Lee: Zealot – Pioneer Builder – Scapegoat*. Glendale, CA: The Arthur H. Clark Company, 1962.

Buchanan, James. *Utah Territory: Message from the President of the United States, communicating, in compliance with a resolution of the House, copies of correspondence relative to the condition of affairs in the Territory of Utah: May 2, 1860, laid upon the table and ordered to be printed by James Buchanan*. Washington, DC: Thomas H. Ford, 1860.

Burt, John Spencer, and W. E. Hawthorne. *Past and Present of Marshall and Putnam Counties, Illinois*. Chicago: The Pioneer Publishing Co., 1907.

Burton, Sir Richard Francis. *The City of the Saints, and Across the Rocky Mountains to California*. New York: Harper and Brothers, 1862.

Bushman, Richard Lyman. *Joseph Smith: Rough Stone Rolling*. New York: Alfred A. Knopf, 2005.

Campbell, Eugene. *Establishing Zion: The Mormon Church in the American West, 1847–1869*. Salt Lake City: Signature Books, 1988.

Cannon, Donald Q., and Lyndon W. Cook. *Far West Record: Minutes of the Church of Jesus Christ of Latter-day Saints, 1830–1844*. Salt Lake City: Deseret Books, 1983.

Cannon, Frank Jenne, and George Leonard Knapp. *Brigham Young and His Mormon Empire.* New York: Fleming H. Revell Company, 1913.
Cannon, Janath R. *Nauvoo Panorama.* Nauvoo, IL: Nauvoo Restoration, 1991.
Carroll, John Mark. *A Concise History of Hong Kong.* London: Rowman and Littlefield, 2007.
Carter, Kate B., ed. *Treasures of Pioneer History.* Salt Lake City: Daughters of the Utah Pioneers, 1952–1957.
Cases Argued and Decided in the Supreme Court of the United States, December Terms, 1870, 1871, Book 20. Rochester, NY: The Lawyers' Co-operative Publishing Company, n.d.
Caswall, Henry. *The City of the Mormons; Or, Three Days at Nauvoo in 1842.* London: J. G. F. &J. Rivington, 1842.
Clark, Thomas D. *The Kentucky.* Lexington: Henry Clay Press, 1969.
Clark, Thomas D., and F. Gerald Ham. *Pleasant Hill and Its Shakers.* Pleasant Hill, KY: Shakertown Press, 1968.
Cleland, Robert Glass, and Juanita Brooks. *A Mormon Chronicle: The Diaries of John D. Lee, 1848–1876.* 2 vols. Salt Lake City: University of Utah Press, 1983.
A Collection of Sacred Hymns for the Church of Jesus Christ of Latter-day Saints. Nauvoo: E. Robinson, 1841.
Collier, Fred C. *The Teachings of President Brigham Young.* Vol. 3., 1852–4. Salt Lake City: Collier's, 1987.
The Compiled Laws of the Territory of Utah, Containing all the General Statutes Now in Force. Salt Lake City: Deseret News, 1870.
Compton, Todd. *In Sacred Loneliness: The Plural Wives of Joseph Smith.* Salt Lake City: Signature Books, 2001.
Conrad, Howard Louis. *Encyclopedia of the History of Missouri.* New York: Southern History Co., 1901.
Corrill, John. *A Brief History of the Church of Christ of Latter Day Saints (Commonly Called Mormons) Including an Account of Their Doctrine and Discipline, with the Reasons of the Author for Leaving the Church.* St. Louis: Printed by the Author, 1839.
Coyner, John McCutchen. *Handbook Mormonism.* Salt Lake City: Hand-Book, 1882.
Cradlebaugh, John. *Utah and the Mormons.* Washington, DC: 1863.
Culmer, H. L. A. comp. and ed. *Utah Directory and Gazetteer for 1879–80.* Salt Lake City: J. C. Graham and Co., 1879.
Denton, Sally. *American Massacre: The Tragedy at Mountain Meadows, September 1857.* New York: Alfred A. Knopf, 2003.
De Voto, Bernard Augustine. *The Year of Decision 1846.* Boston: Little, Brown and Co, 1943.
Dinger, John S., ed. *The Nauvoo City and High Council Minutes.* Salt Lake City: Signature Books, 2011.
Doctrine and Covenants of the Church of Jesus Christ of Latter-day Saints. Salt Lake City: The Church of Jesus Christ of Latter-day Saints, 1981.
Duffield, Holley Gene. *Historical Dictionary of the Shakers.* Lanham, MD: Scarecrow Press, 2000.
Duis, E. *The Good Old Times in McLean County, Illinois: Containing Two Hundred and Sixty-one Sketches of Old Settlers, a Complete Historical Sketch of the Black Hawk War and All Matter of Interest Relating to McLean County.* Bloomington: Leader, 1874.

Dunlavy, John. *The Manifesto, or A Declaration of the Doctrine and Practice of the Church of Christ.* New York: Edward O. Jenkins, 1847.
Ekins, Roger Robin. *Defending Zion: George Q. Cannon and the California Mormon Newspaper Wars of 1856–1857.* Spokane, WA: The Arthur H. Clark Company, 2002.
Ellsworth, Spencer. *Records of the Olden Time; or Fifty Years on the Prairies.* Lacon, IL: Home Journal Seam, 1880.
Finger, John R. *Tennessee Frontiers: Three Regions in Transition.* Bloomington: Indiana University Press, 2001.
Firmage, Edwin Brown, and Richard Collin Mangrum. *Zion in the Courts: A Legal History of the Church of Jesus Christ of Latter-day Saints, 1830–1900.* Urbana: University of Illinois Press, 1988.
Flanders, Robert Bruce. *Nauvoo: Kingdom on the Mississippi.* Urbana: University of Illinois Press, 1965.
Ford, Thomas. *History of Illinois: From Its Commencement as a State in 1818 to 1847.* Chicago: S. C. Griggs, 1854.
Furniss, Norman F. *The Mormon Conflict, 1850–1859.* New Haven: Yale University Press, 1960.
Gavitt, Rev. *Elnathan Corrington. Crumbs from My Saddle Bags: Reminiscences of Pioneer Life and Biographical Sketches.* Toledo, OH: Blade, 1884.
Gentry, Leland Homer. *A History of the Latter-day Saints in Northern Missouri from 1836 to 1839.* Provo, UT: Brigham Young University Studies, 2000.
Gentry, Leland Homer, and Todd M. Compton. *Fire and Sword: A History of the Latter-day Saints in Northern Missouri, 1838–39.* Salt Lake City: Greg Kofford Books, 2011.
Gibbs, J.F. *Lights and Shadows of Mormonism.* Salt Lake City: Salt Lake Tribune, 1909.
Goodell, Jotham. *A Winter with the Mormons: The 1852 letters of Jotham Goodell.* Salt Lake City: Tanner Trust Fund, Marriott Library, University of Utah, 2001.
Graham, Hugh Davis, and Ted Robert Gurr, eds. *The History of Violence in America: Historical and Comparative Perspectives.* New York: Frederick A. Praeger, 1969.
Green, Nelson Winch. *Fifteen Years among the Mormons: Being the Narrative of Mrs. Mary Ettie V. Smith.* New York: Charles Scribner, 1858.
Gunnison, John Williams. *The Mormons, or, Latter-day Saints in the Valley of the Great Salt Lake: A History of Their Rise and Progress, Peculiar Doctrines, Present Condition, and Prospects, Derived from Personal Observation during a Residence among Them.* Philadelphia: J. B. Lippincott and Co, 1857.
Hafen, LeRoy R., and Ann W. Hafen. *Handcarts to Zion: The Story of a Unique Western Migration, 1856–1860.* Glendale, CA: The Arthur H. Clark Company, 1988.
Hafen, LeRoy R., and Ann W. Hafen. *Mormon Resistance: A Documentary Account of the Utah Expedition, 1857–1858.* Glendale, CA: The Arthur H. Clark Company, 1958.
Hagan, Albert. *Reports of Cases Determined in the Supreme Court of the Territory of Utah, from the Organization of the Territory, up to and including the June Term, 1876.* San Francisco: A. L. Bancroft and Company, 1877.
Hales, Brian C. *Joseph Smith's Polygamy.* 3 vols. Salt Lake City: Greg Kofford Books, 2013.
Hall, William. *The Abominations of Mormonism Exposed; Containing Many Facts and Doctrines Concerning that Singular People During Seven Years' Membership With Them from 1840 to 1847.* Cincinnati: I Hart and Co, 1852.

Hallwas, John E., and Roger D. Launius. *Cultures in Conflict: A Documentary History of the Mormon War in Illinois.* Logan: Utah State University Press, 1995.
Hallwas, John E., and Roger D. Launius. *Kingdom on the Mississippi Revisited: Nauvoo in Mormon History.* Urbana: University of Illinois Press, 1996.
Hamersly, Thomas H. S. *Regular Army Register of the United States, 1779–1879.* Washington: Thomas H. S. Hamersly, 1880.
Hamilton, Marshall. "From Assassination to Expulsion." In *Kingdom on the Mississippi Revisited: Nauvoo in Mormon History,* ed. Roger D. Launius and John E. Hallwas, 214–30. Urbana: University of Chicago Press, 1996.
Hammack, James Wallace Jr. *Kentucky and the Second American Revolution: The War of 1812.* Lexington: University Press of Kentucky, 1976.
Hartley, William G. *My Best for the Kingdom: History and Autobiography of John Lowe Butler, a Mormon Frontiersman.* Salt Lake City: Aspen Books, 1993.
Hartley, William G. *Stand by My Servant Joseph: the Story of the Joseph Knight Family and the Restoration.* Salt Lake City: Deseret Book, 2003.
Hasbrouck, Jacob L. *History of McLean County, Illinois.* Topeka: Historical Publishing Company, 1924.
Hickman, William. *Brigham's Avenging Angel: Being the Life, Confession, and Startling Disclosures of the Notorious Bill Hickman, the Danite Chief of Utah.* Bedford, MA: Applewood Books, 2009.
Hinshaw, Seth B. *The Carolina Quaker Experience, 1665–1985.* Greensboro: North Carolina Yearly Meeting, North Carolina Friends Historical Society, 1984.
Hinshaw, William Wade. *Encyclopedia of American Quaker Genealogy.* Baltimore: Genealogical Publishing Company, 1969.
History of the Bench and Bar in Utah. Salt Lake City: Interstate Press Association Publishers, 1913.
History of Tazewell County, Illinois: Together with Sketches of Its Cities, Villages and Townships; Educational, Religious, Civil, Military, and Political History; Portraits of Prominent Persons and Biographies of Representative Citizens. Chicago: Chas. C. Chapman and Co, 1879.
History of Warren County, Ohio. Chicago: W. H. Beers and Co, 1882.
Howard, Robert P. *Illinois: A History of the Prairie State.* Grand Rapids, MI: William B. Erdmans, 1972.
Hudson, John. *A Forty-Niner in Utah with the Stansbury Exploration of Great Salt Lake: Letters and Journal of John Hudson, 1848–1850.* Salt Lake City: Signature Books, 1981.
Huff, Emma. *Memories That Live: Utah County Centennial History.* Salt Lake City: Daughters of Utah Pioneers, 1947.
Hunter, Milton. *Brigham Young the Colonizer.* Santa Barbara: Peregrine Smith, 1973.
Hutton, Daniel M. *Old Shakertown and the Shakers.* Harrodsburg, KY: Harrodsburg Herald Press, 1936.
Hyde, Myrtle Stevens. *Orson Hyde: The Olive Branch of Israel.* Scottsdale, AZ: Agreka Books, 2000.
Jensen, Richard J. *Illinois: A History.* Champaign: University of Illinois Press, 2001.
Jenson, Andrew. *Encyclopedic History of the Church of Jesus Christ of Latter-day Saints.* Salt Lake City: Corporation of the President of the Church of Jesus Christ of Latter-day Saints, 1941.
Jenson, Andrew. *Latter-day Saint Biographical Encyclopedia: A Compilation of Biographical Sketches of Prominent Men and Women in the Church of Jesus Christ of Latter-day Saints.* 4 vols. Salt Lake City: Western Epics, 1971.

Johnson, Benjamin F. *My Life's Review*. Independence, MO: Zion's Print and Publishing Company, 1947.
Johnson, Clark V. *Mormon Redress Petitions: Documents of the 1833-1838 Missouri Conflict*. Provo: Religious Studies Center, Brigham Young University, 1992.
Jones, Daniel Webster. *Forty Years Among the Indians*. Salt Lake City: Juvenile Instructor's Office, 1890.
Kelly, Charles, ed. *Journals of John D. Lee, 1846–47 and 1859*. Salt Lake City: University of Utah Press, 1984.
Krakauer, Jon. *Under the Banner of Heaven: The Story of a Violent Faith*. New York: Doubleday, 2003.
Larson, Andrew Karl. *Erastus Snow: The Life of a Missionary and Pioneer for the Early Mormon Church*. Salt Lake City: University of Utah Press, 1971.
Launius, Roger D., and John E. Hallwas. *Kingdom on the Mississippi Revisited: Nauvoo in Mormon History*. Urbana: University of Chicago Press, 1996.
Lee, John D. *Mormonism Unveiled: or the Life and Confessions of the Late Mormon Bishop, John D. Lee*. St. Louis: Bryan, Brand and Co, 1877.
Leonard, Glen M. *Nauvoo: A Place of Peace, A People of Promise*. Salt Lake City: Deseret Book Company, 2002.
LeSueur, Stephen C. *The 1838 Mormon War in Missouri*. Columbia: University of Missouri Press, 1987.
Linn, William Alexander. *The Story of the Mormons: From the Date of Their Origin to the Year 1901*. New York: The MacMillan Company, 1902.
Ludlow, Daniel H., ed. *Encyclopedia of Mormonism*. New York: Macmillan Publishing Company, 1992.
Lyman, Edward Leo. *Amasa Mason Lyman: Mormon Apostle and Apostate, A Study in Dedication*. Salt Lake City: University of Utah Press, 2009.
Lyman, Edward Leo. *The Overland Journey from Utah to California*. Reno: University of Nevada Press, 2008.
MacKinnon, William P. *At Sword's Point, Part 1: A Documentary History of the Utah War to 1858*. Norman, OK: Arthur H. Clark Company, 2008.
MacLean, J.P. *Shakers of Ohio: Fugitive Papers Concerning the Shakers of Ohio, with Unpublished Manuscripts*. Philadelphia: Porcupine Press, 1975.
Madsen, Carol Cornwall. *Journey to Zion: Voices from the Mormon Trail*. Salt Lake City: Deseret Book Company, 1997.
Madsen, Brigham D. *Gold Rush Sojourners in Great Salt Lake City 1849 and 1850*. Salt Lake City: University of Utah Press, 1983.
Marquardt, H. Michael. "The Coming Storm: The Murder of Jesse Thompson Hartley." In *Playing with Shadows: Voices of Dissent in the Mormon West*, ed. Polly Aird, Jeff Nichols, and Will Bagley. Norman: The Arthur H. Clark Company, 2011. http://user.xmission.com/~research/mormonpdf/storm.pdf.
Maxwell, John Gary. *Gettysburg to Great Salt Lake: George R. Maxwell, Civil War Hero and Federal Marshal among the Mormons*. Norman, OK: The Arthur H. Clark Company, 2010.
Maxwell, John Gary. *Robert Newton Baskin and the Making of Modern Utah*. Norman, OK: The Arthur H. Clark Company, 2013.
Michaux, Francois Andre. *Travels to the Westward of the Allegany Mountains: In the States of Ohio, Kentucky, and Tennessee, and Return to Charlestown, through the Upper Carolinas; Containing Details on the Present State of Agriculture and the Natural Production of these Countries, as well as Information Relative to the Commercial Connections of these States with those Situated to the Eastward of the*

Mountains and with Lower Louisiana; Undertaken in the Year X, 1802, under the Auspices of His Excellency M. Chaptal, Minister of the Interior; with a Very Correct Map of the States in the Centre, West and South of the United States. London: J. Mawman, 1805.
Miller, Albert E. *The Immortal Pioneers.* St. George, Utah: Albert E. Miller, 1946.
Moore, Beth Shumway. *Bones in the Well: The Haun's Mill Massacre, 1838, A Documentary History.* Norman, OK: The Arthur H. Clark Company, 2006.
Moorman, Donald R. with Gene A. Sessions. *Camp Floyd and the Mormons: The Utah War.* Salt Lake City: University of Utah Press, 1992.
Morgan, Dale L. *The Great Salt Lake.* Indianapolis: Bobbs-Merrill Company, 1947.
Morgan, Dale L. *The State of Deseret.* Logan: Utah State University Press with the Utah Historical Society, 1987.
Munroe, John A. *History of Delaware.* Newark: University of Delaware Press, 2001.
Neal, Julia. *By Their Fruits: The Story of Shakerism in South Union, Kentucky.* Chapel Hill: University of North Carolina Press, 1947.
Neal, Julia. *The Kentucky Shakers.* Lexington: The University Press of Kentucky, 1977.
Neff, Alexander Love. *History of Utah, 1847 to 1869.* Salt Lake City: University of Utah Press, 1940.
Nevins, Allen, ed. *James K. Polk: The Diary of a President, 1845–1849.* London: Longmans, Green and Co, 1952.
Nissim, Roger. *Land Administration and Practice in Hong Kong.* Hong Kong: Hong Kong University Press, 2008.
Olsen, Andrew D. *The Price We Paid: The Extraordinary Story of the Willie and Martin Handcart Pioneers.* Salt Lake City: Deseret Book, 2006.
Owens, Kenneth N. *Gold Rush Saints: California Mormons and the Great Rush for Riches.* Spokane, WA: Arthur H. Clark Company, 2004.
Peck, J. M. *A Gazetteer of Illinois, in Three Parts: Containing a General View of the State, A General View of Each County, and a Particular Description of Each Town, Settlement, Stream, Prairie, Bottom, Bluff, etc.; Alphabetically Arranged.* Philadelphia: Grigg and Elliot, 1837.
Peterson, Paul. *The Mormon Reformation.* Provo: The Joseph Fielding Smith Institute for Latter-day Saint History and Brigham Young University Studies, 2002.
Powell, Allan Kent, ed. *Utah History Encyclopedia.* Salt Lake City: University of Utah Press, 1994.
Pratt, Parley P. *The Autobiography of Parley P. Pratt.* Salt Lake City: Deseret Book, 2000.
Quincy, Josiah. *Figures of the Past.* Boston: Roberts Brothers, 1888.
Quinn, D. Michael. *The Mormon Hierarchy: Origins of Power.* Salt Lake City: Signature Books, 1994.
Raitz, Karl, ed. *The National Road.* Baltimore: The Johns Hopkins University Press, 1996.
Ranck, George W. *Boonesborough, Its Founding, Pioneer Struggles, Indian Experiences, Transylvania Days and Revolutionary Annals.* New York: Arno Press, 1971.
Rawson, Glenn, and Dennis Lyman, eds. *The Mormon Wars.* American Fork, UT: Covenant Communications, 2014.
Reed, H. Clay. *Delaware: A History of the First State.* New York: Lewis Historical Publishing Company, 1947.
Remy, Jules, and Julius Licius Brenchley. *A Journey to the Great-Salt-Lake City, by Jules Remy and Julius Brenchley, with a Sketch of the History, Religion, and Customs*

of the Mormons, and an Introduction, on the Religious Movement in the United States. New York: AMS Press, 1972.

Roberts, Brigham H. *A Comprehensive History of the Church of Jesus Christ of Latter-day Saints*. 6 vols. Salt Lake City: Deseret News Press, 1930.

Roberts, Brigham H. *The Rise and Fall of Nauvoo*. Provo, UT: Maasai Publishing, 2001.

Rouse, Park Jr. *The Great Wagon Road from Philadelphia to the South*. New York: McGraw-Hill Book Company, 1973.

Rowell, Chester Harvey. *A Historical and Legal Digest of All the Contested Election Cases in the House of Representatives of the United States from the First to the Fifty-sixth Congress, 1789–1901*. Washington, DC: Government Printing Office, 1901.

Shepard, William, and H. Michael Marquardt. *Lost Apostles: Forgotten Members of Mormonism's Original Quorum of Twelve*. Salt Lake City: Signature Books, 2014.

Smart, Donna Toland, ed. *Mormon Midwife; The 1846–1848 Diaries of Patty Bartlett Sessions*. Logan: Utah State University Press, 1997.

Smith, George D., ed. *An Intimate Chronicle: The Journals of William Clayton*. Salt Lake City: Signature Books, 1995.

Smith, Joseph, II, Henry C. Smith, and F. Henry Edwards, eds. *The History of the Reorganized Church of Jesus Christ of Latter-day Saints*. 4 vols., 1896–903. IA: Lamoni.

Smith, Joseph. *History of the Church of Jesus Christ of Latter-day Saints*. 7 vols. Salt Lake City: Deseret News Press, 1902.

Snarr, D. Neil. *Claiming Our Past: Quakers in Southwest Ohio and Eastern Tennessee*. Sabina, Ohio: D. Neil Snarr, 1992.

Solter, Althea Jauch. *Tears and Tantrums: What to Do When Babies and Children Cry*. Goleta, California: Shining Star Press, 1998.

Stein, Stephen J. *The Shaker Experience in America: A History of the United Society of Believers*. New Haven: Yale University Press, 1992.

Stenhouse, Thomas B. H. *The Rocky Mountain Saints*. Salt Lake City: Shepard Book Company, 1904.

Stevens, Walter B. *Centennial History of Missouri (The Center State): One Hundred Years in the Union 1820–1921*. St. Louis: The S. J. Clarke Publishing Company, 1921.

Stott, Clifford L. *Search for Sanctuary: Brigham Young and the White Mountain Expedition*. Salt Lake City: University of Utah Press, 1984.

Stout, Hosea. *The Autobiography of Hosea Stout*. Salt Lake City: University of Utah Press, Utah State Historical Society, 2010.

Teague, Bobbie T. *Cane Creek, Mother of Meetings*. Snow Camp: North Carolina Friends Historical Society, 1995.

Tennessee Blue Book. Nashville: Secretary of State, 1976.

Thorp, Judge Joseph. *Early Days in the West*. Liberty, MO: I Gilmer, 1924.

Tullidge, Edward W. *Life of Brigham Young; or Utah and Her Founders*. New York: n.p., 1876.

Tullidge, Edward W. *History of Salt Lake City and Its founders*. Salt Lake City: E. W. Tullidge, 1886.

Turner, John G. *Brigham Young: Pioneer Prophet*. Cambridge, MA: Belknap Press, 2012. http://dx.doi.org/10.4159/harvard.9780674067318.

Van Wagoner, Richard S. *Mormon Polygamy: History*. Salt Lake City: Signature Books, 1986.

Walker, Ronald W., Richard E. Turley Jr., and Glen M. Leonard. *Massacre at Mountain Meadows: An American Tragedy*. New York: Oxford University Press, 2008.
Watson, Elden J. *Manuscript History of Brigham Young, 1846–1847*. Salt Lake City: Elden J. Watson, 1971.
Welsh, Frank. *A History of Hong Kong*. New York: Harper Collins, 1997.
White, Jean Bickmore. *Church, State, and Politics: The Diaries of John Henry Smith*. Salt Lake City: Signature Books, 1990.
Whitney, Orson F. *History of Utah: Comprising Preliminary Chapters on the Previous History of Her Founders, Accounts of Early Spanish and American Explorations in the Rocky Mountain Region, the Advent of the Mormon Pioneers, the Establishment and Dissolution of the Provisional Government of the State of Deseret, and the Subsequent Creation and Development of the Territory*. 4 vols. Salt Lake City: George Q. Cannon and Sons, 1892.
Wilcox, Pearl. *The Latter Day Saints on the Missouri Frontier*. Independence, MO: Herald House, 1972.
Wilson, Joseph H. *The Presbyterian Historical Almanac, and Annual Remembrance of the Church for 1863*. Philadelphia: Joseph M. Wilson, 1863.
Winn, Kenneth H. *Exiles in a Land of Liberty: Mormons in America, 1830–1846*. Chapel Hill: University of North Carolina Press, 1989.
Works Projects Administration. *Provo: Pioneer Mormon City*. Portland: Binsfords and Mort, 1942.
Young, Brigham. "Governor's Message: Deseret, December 2, 1850: To the Senators and Representatives of the State of Deseret." In *History of Utah, 1847 to 1869*, ed. Alexander Love Neff, 188–89. Salt Lake City: University of Utah Press, 1940.
Youngberg, Florence C. *Conquerors of the West: Stalwart Mormon Pioneers*. Scottsdale, AZ: Agreka Books, 1997.

Autobiographies, Diaries, and Journals

Allred, William Moore. "Autobiography." MS 1871. Church History Library.
Allred, William Moore. "Early History of William M. Allred." Daughters of the Utah Pioneers Museum, Salt Lake City.
Allred, Reddick N. "Journal." *Treasures of Pioneer History* 5 (1956): 301.
Ashby, Benjamin. "Autobiography." MS 2584. Church History Library.
Ballantyne, Richard. "Papers, 1848–1867, 1895." MS 7151. Church History Library.
Bean, George Washington. *Autobiography of George Washington Bean*. Salt Lake City: Utah Printing Company, 1945.
Beecher, Maureen Ursenbach, ed. "'All Things Move in Order in the City': The Nauvoo Diary of Zina Diantha Huntington Jacobs." *Brigham Young University Studies* 19, no. 3 (1979).
Bleak, James G. "Annals of the Southern Utah Mission." MSS B 171. Utah State Historical Society.
Brown, John. "John Brown Journal Extract, 1849 November–1850 January." MS 21607. Church History Library.
Brown, Lorenzo. "Journal." MS 270.1 B876b. Church History Library.
Bullock, Thomas. *"Journals, 1843–1849." M270.1 B9387tn*. Church History Library, 1994.
Church Historian's Office Journal. CR100 1. Church History Library.

Clark, Isaac. "Isaac Clark Record Book, 1846–1853." MS 794. Church History Library.
Crawley, Peter. "Two Rare Missouri Documents." *BYU Studies* 14, no. 4 (1974).
Crosby, Jesse W. "History and Biography of Jesse W. Crosby." mssHM 27975–27976. Huntington Library.
Farr, Winslow. "Diary, 1856 May–1899 September." MS 1743. Church History Library.
Foote, Warren. "Autobiography of Warren Foote." M270.1 F689f 1997. Church History Library.
Gardner, Robert. "Journal." *Heart Throbs of the West*. vol. 10. Salt Lake City: Daughters of the Utah Pioneers, 1949.
Haight, Isaac. "Journal." MS 20630. Church History Library.
Hancock, Mosiah. "Autobiography." MS 8175. Church History Library.
Haun, Catherine. "A Woman's Trip across the Plains in 1849." F593.W77 1992. Huntington Library, San Marino, CA.
Haven, Jesse. "Jesse Haven Journals, 1852–1892." MS 890. Church History Library.
Huntington, Oliver B. "Autobiography." http://www.boap.org/LDS/Early-Saints/OBHuntington.html.
Huntington, Oliver B. "Diary and Reminiscences." MS 1648. Church History Library.
Hyde, William. "Journal." M270.1 H996h. Church History Library.
Isom, George. "Autobiography." MSS SC 1851. L. Tom Perry Special Collections, Harold B. Lee Library, Brigham Young University.
Jessee, Dean C., ed. "The John Taylor Nauvoo Journal, January 1845–September 1845." *Brigham Young University Studies* 23, no. 3 (1983).
Jessee, Dean C., and David J. Whittaker, eds. "The Last Months of Mormonism in Missouri: The Albert Perry Rockwood Journal." *Brigham Young University Studies* 28 (Winter 1988).
Johnson, Luke. "The History of Luke Johnson." M270 J672h 197?. Church History Library.
Larson, A. Karl, and Katharine Miles Larson, eds. *Diary of Charles Lowell Walker*. Logan: Utah State University Press, 1980.
Lee, Lafayette C. Notebook. MS 964 n.d. Church History Library.
Lyman, Eliza Maria Partridge. "Journal of Eliza Maria Partridge Lyman." M270.07 L9865L. Church History Library.
Meeks, Priddy. "Journal." *Utah Historical Quarterly* 10 (1942).
Munson, Eliza. "Early Pioneer History." Brigham Young University Library Special Collections and Manuscripts.
Murdock, John. "Journal." MS 1194. Church History Library.
Neibaur, Alexander. "Journal, 1841–1862." MS 19986. Church History Library.
Peck, Reed. "Mormons So Called," also known as "The Reed Peck Manuscript." BX8645.P4. Henry Huntington Library, San Marino, CA.
Phelps, Morris. "Autobiography." MS 21298. Church History Library.
Pulsipher, John. "Journal and Autobiography." in *Joel Edward Ricks*, Cache Valley Historical Material, reel 4, item 88, 33–46.
Rich, Sarah. "Autobiography." MS 1543. Church History Library.
Rockwood, Albert P. "Journal Entries, 1838 October–1839 January." MS 2606. Church History Library.
Savage, Levi. "Journal." M270.1 W264h. Church History Library, 2011.
Shurtliff, Lyman. "Autobiography." http://www.boap.org/LDS/Early-Saints/LShurtliff.html.

Smith, Elias. "Journals." M270.1 S64595s. vol. 1–3. Church History Library, 1984.
Smith, George A. "Journal." MS 1465. Church History Library.
Smith, Job T. "Autobiography." MS 4809. Church History Library.
Snow, Eliza R. "Journal of Eliza R. Snow." MS 1439. Church History Library.
Stout, Allen Joseph. *"Journal of Allen Joseph Stout." M270.1 S889s.* Church History Library, 1889.
Stout, Allen Joseph. "Reminiscences and Journal." MS 17841. Church History Library.
Stout, Hosea. "Hosea Stout Papers." MSS B53. Utah State Historical Society.
Taylor, Pleasant Green. "Record of Pleasant Green Taylor." MS 13357. Church History Library.
Whitney, Helen Mar Kimball. "Reminiscences and Diary." MS 9670 38-39. Church History Library.
Wood, Daniel. "Journals." MS 1488. Church History Library.
Woodruff, Wilford. "Journal." M270.1 W89k. Church History Library, 1982.
Woolley, Catherine. "Journal." *Salt Lake Telegram*, 7–11 January 1935.

Documents

Executive Documents printed by order of the House of Representatives during the Second Session of the Forty-Second Congress, 1871–72.

Executive Documents, printed by the order of the Senate of the United States, First Session of the Thirty-Sixth Congress, 1859–1860.

Journal of the executive proceedings of the Senate of the United States of America, from December 2, 1861, to July 17, 1862, Inclusive, Vol. 12.

Supreme Court of the United States. No. 478. Hosea Stout, Plaintiff in Error vs. The People of the United States in the Territory of Utah. Transcript of Record, filed December 5, 1871.

Journal and Magazine Articles and Lectures

Aitchison, Clyde B. "The Mormon Settlements in the Missouri Valley." *The Quarterly of the Oregon Historical Society* 8 (March 1907–December 1907).

Alexander, Thomas G. "Brigham Young, The Quorum of the Twelve, and the Latter-day Saint Investigation of the Mountain Meadows Massacre." Leonard J. Arrington Mormon History Lecture Series no. 12. Logan: Utah State University Press, 2007.

Alexander, Thomas G. "Carpetbaggers, Reprobates, and Liars: Federal Judges and the Utah War (1857–58)." *Historian* 70, no. 2 (Summer 2008): 209–38. http://dx.doi.org/10.1111/j.1540-6563.2008.00209.x.

Alexander Thomas, G. "Federal Authority Versus Polygamic Theocracy: James B. McKean and the Mormons, 1870–1875." *Dialogue* 1, no. 3 (Autumn 1966).

Allaman, John Lee. "Policing in Mormon Nauvoo." *Illinois Historical Journal* 89, no. 2 (Summer 1996).

Allen, James B. "The Unusual Jurisdiction of County Probate Courts in the Territory of Utah." *Utah Historical Quarterly* (Spring 1968): 36.

Bigler, David L. "'A Lion in the Path': Genesis of the Utah War, 1857–1858." *Utah Historical Quarterly* 76, no. 1 (Winter 2008).

Britsch, R. Lanier. "Church Beginnings in China." *BYU Studies* 10, no. 2 (1970).

Brooks, Juanita. "The Cotton Mission." *Utah Historical Quarterly* 29, no. 3 (Summer 1961).
Brooks, Juanita. "The Southern Indian Mission and Its Effect upon the Settlement of Washington County." *Improvement Era* 48, no. 4 (April 1945).
Browne, A.G., Jr. "The Ward of the Three Guardians." *Atlantic Monthly* 39, no. 226 (June 1877).
Cresswell, Stephen. "The U.S. Department of Justice in Utah Territory, 1870–90." *Utah Historical Quarterly* 53 (1985).
Fleming, Robert. "Turning the Tide: *The Mountaineer* vs. the Valley Tan." *Utah Historical Quarterly* (Summer 1996): 54.
Gee, Elizabeth D. "Justice for All or for the 'Elect'?: The Utah County Probate Court, 1855–72." *Utah Historical Quarterly* (Spring 1980): 48.
Godfrey, Kenneth W. "Crime and Punishment in Mormon Nauvoo, 1839–1846." *Brigham Young University Studies* 32, nos. 1–2 (1991).
Godfrey, Kenneth W. "Telling the Nauvoo Story." *Mormon Historical Studies* 3, no. 1 (2002).
Hill, Marvin S. "Mormon Religion in Nauvoo: Some Reflections." *Utah Historical Quarterly* 44 (Spring 1976): 174–5.
Holmes, Gail Geo. "The LDS Legacy in Southwestern Iowa." *Ensign*, August 1988.
Homer, and W. Michael. "The Federal Bench and Priesthood Authority: The Rise and Fall of John Fitch Kinney's Early Relationship with the Mormons." *Journal of Mormon History* 13 (1986–87): 89–108.
Houchens, Mariam S. "Shakertown at Pleasant Hill, Kentucky." *Filson Club History Quarterly* 45, no. 3 (July 1971): 264–85.
Kimball, Stanley B. "Nauvoo West: Mormons of the Iowa Shore." *BYU Studies* 18, no. 2 (1978).
Kuhns, Frederick I. "Home Education and Missions in the Old Northwest." *Journal of the Presbyterian Historical Society* 32 (1954).
Journal of Discourses (London). Annual volumes, 1854–1866.
Little, James A. "Biography of Lorenzo Dow Young." *Utah Historical Quarterly* 14 (1946): 44–57.
"A Letter from William Smith, brother of Joseph, the Prophet." *Daily Illinois State Journal* (Springfield, Illinois), June 3, 1857.
Lund, Jennifer L. "'Pleasing to the Eyes of an Exile': The Latter-day Saint Sojourn at Winter Quarters 1846–1848." *BYU Studies* 39, no. 2 (2000).
MacKinnon, William P. "'Lonely Bones': Leadership and Utah War Violence." *Journal of Mormon History* 33, no. 1 (2007).
Manscill, Craig K. "'Journal of the Branch of the Church of Christ in Pontiac, . . . 1834': Hyrum Smith's Division of Zion's Camp." *BYU Studies* 39, no. 1 (2000).
Mills, H. W. "De Tal Palo Tal Astilla." *Historical Society of Southern California Annual Publications* 10 (1917).
Moody, Thurman Dean. "Nauvoo's Whistling and Whittling Brigade." *BYU Studies* 15, no. 4 (Winter 1975).
Morgan, Dale. "A Western Diary." *America West* 2 (1965).
Peterson, Paul H. "The Mormon Reformation of 1856–1857: The Rhetoric and the Reality." *Journal of Mormon History* 15 (1989): 59–87.
Poll, Richard D. "The Move South." *BYU Studies* 29 no. 4 (1989).
Poll, Richard D., and William P. MacKinnon. "Causes of the Utah War Reconsidered." *Journal of Mormon History* 20, no. 2 (Fall 1994).
Pooley, William Vipond. "The Settlement of Illinois from 1830–1850." *Bulletin of*

the University of Wisconsin, History Series 6 (1908).
Quinn, D. Michael. "The Council of Fifty and Its Members, 1844 to 1945." *BYU Studies* 20, no. 2 (1980).
Quinn, D. Michael. "The Culture of Violence in Joseph Smith's Mormonism." *Sunstone*, October 2011.
Rich, Charles C., "Extract from Charles C. Rich's History." *Millennial Star* 26 (1864).
Shepard, Bill. "The Notorious Hodges Brothers: Solving the Mystery of Their Destruction at Nauvoo." *John Whitmer Historical Association Journal* 26 (2006).
Smith, Joseph. Sermon, July 19, 1840, recorded by Martha Jane Knowlton. *Brigham Young University Studies* 19 (Spring 1979).
Spangler, Mrs. George. "Early Marriages in Tazewell County." *Journal of the Illinois State Historical Society* 14 (1922): 145.
Stapley, Jonathan A., and Kristine Wright. "'They Shall Be Made Whole': A History of Baptism for Health." *Journal of Mormon History* (Fall 2008).
Todd, Jay M. "More Members Now Outside U.S. Than In U.S." *Ensign* (March 1996).
Wyman, Walker D. "Council Bluffs and the Westward Movement." *Iowa Journal of History* 47 (1949).

Newspapers

Adams Sentinel (Gettysburg, PA)
Baltimore Sun (Baltimore)
Bangor Daily Whig and Courier (Bangor, ME)
Coshocton Age (Coshocton, OH)
Daily Alta California (San Francisco)
Davenport Daily (Davenport, IA)
Deseret News (Salt Lake City)
Deseret Weekly (Salt Lake City)
Galveston Daily News (Galveston, TX)
Galveston Weekly News (Galveston, TX)
Helena Independent (Helena, MT)
Idaho Tri-Weekly Statesman (Boise)
Janesville Gazette (Janesville, WI)
Louisville Commercial (Louisville)
Mountaineer (Salt Lake City)
Nauvoo Neighbor (Nauvoo, IL)
New Hampshire Sentinel (Keene, NH)
New Jersey Sentinel (Trenton)
New York Herald (New York City)
New York Observer (New York City)
New York Times (New York City)
New York Weekly Herald (New York City)
New York Tribune (New York City)

New York World (New York City)
Ogden Standard Examiner (Ogden, UT)
Sacramento Daily Union (Sacramento)
Salt Lake Herald (Salt Lake City)
Salt Lake Tribune (Salt Lake City)
San Francisco Chronicle (San Francisco)
San Francisco Herald (San Francisco)
Semi-Weekly Telegraph (Salt Lake City)
Syracuse Courier (Syracuse)
Territorial Gazette and Burlington Advertiser (Burlington, IA)
Times and Seasons (Nauvoo, IL)
Titusville Herald (Titusville, OH)
Union Vedette (Salt Lake City)
Valley Tan (Salt Lake City)
Voree Herald (Voree, WI)
Warsaw Signal (Warsaw, IL)
Western Standard (San Francisco)

Periodicals

Americana, vol. 9. New York: American Historical Society, 1914.
The Church Review (Salt Lake City)
The Contributor. Salt Lake City: Junius F. Wells, 1879–1896.
The Historical Record. Salt Lake City: Andrew Jenson, 1886–1889.
The Latter-day Saints Millennial Star (Liverpool, England)

Masters Theses and Dissertations

Brooks, Karl. "The Life of Amos Milton Musser." Master's thesis, Brigham Young University, BYU Library, 1961.

Ellsworth, Richard Grant. "A Study of the Literary Qualities in the Diary of Hosea Stout." Master's thesis, Brigham Young University, 1952.

Hansen, Klaus. "The Theory and Practice of the Political Kingdom of God in Mormon History, 1829–1890." Master's thesis, Brigham Young University, 1959.

Hansen, Ralph. "Administrative History of the Nauvoo Legion in Utah." Master's thesis, Brigham Young University, 1954.

Parkin, Jeremy S. "Police Work on the Mormon Trail, 1846–1848." Master's thesis, California State University, Long Beach, 2007.

Peterson, Charles S. "A Historical Analysis of Territorial Government in Utah under Alfred Cummings, 1857–1861." Master's thesis, Brigham Young University, 1958.

Pooley, William Vipond. "The Settlement of Illinois from 1830 to 1850." PhD diss., Philosophy, University of Wisconsin, 1905.

Bibliography

Collections
"Estate of Hosea Stout," No. 1377. Salt Lake Probate Court Records, Utah State Archives.

Historian's Office General Church Minutes, 1839–1877. CR 100 318. Church History Library.

Hosea Stout File, Church History Library.

Hosea Stout Papers, MS 16397, Church History Library.

Hosea Stout Papers, Mss B53, Utah State Historical Society.

The Joseph Smith Papers, http://josephsmithpapers.org/paperSummary/letter-to-the-church-and-edward-partridge-20-march-1839.

Nauvoo Legion Files, MS 3430, Church History Library.

Letters
Bogart, Samuel. Letter to the Postmaster, April 22, 1839. MS 5704. Church History Library.

Cummings, James, and Robert Burton. Report to Wells, September 27, 1857. Brigham Young Collection, Church History Library.

Wilson, Alexander. Letters of Alexander Wilson to Delano Eckels and Charles Sinclair, September 17, 1859. Condition of Affairs in Utah.

DVDs and CD-ROMs
Journal History of the Church of Jesus Christ of Latter-day Saints. Church History Library.

"Winter Quarters Municipal High Council Minutes." *Selected Collections from the Archives of the Church of Jesus Christ of Latter-day Saints.* DVD.

Rich, Charles C. DVD Library. BYU Studies. http://churchhistorycatalog.lds.org/primo_library/libweb/action/display.do?tabs=detailsTab&ct=display&fn=search&doc=ALEPH-PCHD000201754&renderMode=poppedOut&displayMode=full.

New Mormon Studies. CD-ROM.

Selected Collections from the Archives of the Church of Jesus Christ of Latter-day Saints. DVD.

Miscellaneous
"Acts, resolutions, and Memorials, Passed by the First Annual, and Special Sessions, of the Legislative Assembly, of the Territory of Utah, begun and held at Great Salt Lake City, on the 22nd day of September, A.D., 1851." 345.12 U891 1851. Church History Library.

Constitution of the State of Deseret. 342.792 D451c 1850. Church History Library.

George R. Maxwell v. George Q. Cannon. Papers in the case of Maxwell v. Cannon, for a seat as delegate from Utah. *Serial set Vol. 1617, Session Vol. No. 1, 43rd Congress, 1st Session.*

Proclamation of the Twelve Apostles of the Church of Jesus Christ of Latter-day Saints. To All Kings of the World, the President of the United States of America; to the Governors of the Several States, and to the People of All Nations. Liverpool: F. D. Richards, 1845.

Missouri House Journal. 1836.
Nauvoo City Records. MS 16800. Church History Library.
New Harmony Ward Record. LDS Family History.
"Resolution of the Legislature of Maine," relating to *The assassination of John King Robinson, at Salt Lake City.* House of Representatives Miscellaneous Document No. 4, February 28, 1867. Fortieth Congress, Second Session, 1867–68.
Salt Lake County Probate Court Records. October 2, 1858. Utah Historical Society.
US Bureau of the Census. 1820. https://www.census.gov/population/www/documentation/twps0027/tab05.txt.
US Bureau of the Census. 1860. http://www.censusrecords.com/Search?FirstName=sarah&LastName=jones&State=Utah&CensusYear=1860.
Warrant (issued by Judge Elias Smith). MS 17213, May 1859. Church History Library.
Washington County Probate Court Records. LDS Family History Library.

About the Author

STEPHEN L. PRINCE is an independent historian who practiced dentistry in the shadow of his alma mater, UCLA. His previous book, *Gathering in Harmony*, published by the Arthur H. Clark Company, won the Evans Handcart Award, presented at Utah State University, and the Thomas Rice King Award from the Mormon History Association.

Index

Abrams, Levi, 230–31, 233–34
Adam-ondi-Ahman, 62–63, 87
Adams, Azra, 143
Alexander, E.B., 267–68
Alexander, Robert, 226
Alger, Fanny, 89
Alger, John, 166
Allen, Charles, 124, 151
Allen, Henry, 199, 202, 219, 233; adopted by H.S., 189–90
Allred, Isaac, 226, 347
Allred, James, 96, 127, 347
Allred, Reddick, 3, 58, 122, 247, 250
Allred, William Moore, 62, 99
Anderson, Kirk, 284, 292
Andrus, Milo, 336
Appleby, William, 226, 305
Arnold, Josiah, 169, 293
Arthur, Chester A., 337
Atchison, David R., 59
Avard, Sampson, 58, 153

Babbitt, Almon, 178, 234
Backenstos, Jacob, 111–13
Baker, Samuel G., 232, 235, 240, 256–58
Baldwin, Caleb, 65
Ballantyne, Richard, 166–67
Barlow, Israel, 76
Bartholomew, Joseph, 288–89
Baskin, Robert N., 314, 318–19, 322, 326–28, 330–34
Bates, Edward, 307
Bates, George C., 332
Battle of Crooked River, 59–61
Beadle, John Hanson, 225, 328
Beaman, Louisa, 89
Bennett, John C., 85, 91
Benson, Ezra T., 309

Bernhisel, John, 209, 266
Bevan, William F., 209, 212
Big Elk, 144
Billings, Titus, 85
Bills, John, 157
Black, Adam, 153
Black, Jeremiah S., 258, 290–91, 294
Black Hawk War, 41
Blair, Seth M., 184–88, 248, 284–86, 290, 292–93, 309, 316
Blazzard, John, 142
Bogart, Samuel, 59–60, 62–63, 68
Boggs, Lilburn, 64, 66, 71, 86–87; issues "extermination order," 61
Book of Mormon, 45–46, 51, 142
Boyd, George, 224
Bragg, Benjamin, 60
Brandenberry, Lemuel, 186
Bridger, Jim, 223, 246
Brig Fremont, 214
Brinton, Samuel, 343
Bristow, B.H., 334
Brocchus, Perry, 184–86
Brown, Homer, 273
Brown, James S., 187, 226
Brown, Lorenzo, 260
Browne, Albert G., 280
Brunson, Seymour, 78, 89
Buchanan, James, 255–56, 260, 265 271–74, 283, 291, 309
Buffington, Joseph, 184, 186
Bullock, Benjamin K., 286
Bullock, Isaac, 225, 250
Bullock, Mary Ann, 225
Bullock, Thomas, 124, 162, 164, 197
Bunker, Edward, 245
Burfett, Daniel, 21
Burmester, Theodore, 334–35

371

372 Index

Burr, David, 237, 251–53, 255, 257–60, 282–83, 285
Burt, William, 40
Burton, Richard Francis, 267, 276
Burton, Robert, 266
Butler, John L., 157

Cahoon, Reynolds, 92, 169
Calhoun, John C., 93
Call, Anson, 225, 230–31
Cannon, Angus, 339
Cannon, Frank J., 325
Cannon, George Q., 236, 251, 259, 326, 339
Capps, Daniel, 77–79
Carlin, Thomas, 87
Carn, Daniel, 157, 164–65, 168
Caroll, Ada, 229
Carpenter, Alex, 293
Carter, George, 32
Carter, Gideon, 60
Cass, Lewis, 280, 311
Caswall, Henry, 88–89
Cathcart, Daniel, 47
Caw, Capt, 143–44
Charles, John F., 109
Chase, Salmon P., 332
Clark, Horace, 200
Clark, Isaac, 156–57
Clark, John B., 61
Clawson, Rudger, 338
Clay, Henry, 93
Clayton, William, 99, 116, 161–63
Clinton, Jeter, 316, 333–34
Clinton vs. Englebrecht, 333–34
Commerce, Illinois. *See* Nauvoo, Illinois
Cooke, Philip St. George, 294
Cooley, Joe, 22
Corrill, John, 46, 64, 151
Cotton Mission, 296, 301–3
Council of Fifty, 176–77
Cowdery, Oliver, 56–57
Cowles, Austin, 90, 94, 109–10
Cox, Isaiah, 344
Cradlebaugh, John, 275, 284–90, 294–95, 308–10, 312
Crosby, Jesse, 76
Crosby, Mrs. S., 315
Cullom Bill, 318–19, 325–26, 330
Cullom, Shelby M., 318
Cumming, Alfred, 271–74, 284, 286, 291, 296, 309–11
Cummings, James, 252, 266
Curtis, Dorr, 249
Curtis, Hiram, 215

Daley, John, 289
Dalton, Simon C., 157
Danites, 57–58, 153–54
Deming, Minor, 111
Dent, Louis, 325–26, 329–34
DeWolfe, Stephen, 291, 293, 310–11
Dixson, Andrew Scott, 208, 212
Doniphan, Alexander W., 55, 59, 65
Dotson, Peter K., 252, 255, 286–87, 295
Douglas, Stephen A., 88
Drown, Charles, 293
Drummond, William W., 229–36, 256–60, 263–64
Duddell, George, 206
Duncan, Chapman, 189, 197, 199, 206–8
Dunham, Jonathan, 92, 94–98, 113
Dunlavy, Anthony, 13, 18
Durfee, Abraham, 288–90
Durphee, James, 60

Earl, Wilbur, 157
Eckels, Delano R., 275, 280, 284, 290–91, 293–95, 309–10
Edmonds, Lawyer, 121
Edmunds, George F., 337
Edmunds Act, 337
Egan, Howard, 4, 186–87
Eldredge, Horace S., 139–40, 259, 303
Ellsworth, Edmund, 244
Emmett, James, 46–47, 66

Fallis, John, 23
Farr, Winslow, 161, 285
Ferguson, James, 185, 223, 246, 248, 252–53, 257, 260, 270, 272–73, 282–83, 292, 295
Ferguson, Thomas, 293
Fielding, Mary, 90
Fillmore, Millard, 186
Fishback, William Pinkney, 330
Fitch, Thomas, 331, 334
Floyd, John B., 275
Foote, Timothy B., 179, 183
Ford, Thomas, 91–92, 95–98, 100, 111, 114, 121
Forney, Jacob, 310
Fort Bridger, 170, 187, 223–25, 246–48, 267, 269, 272
Fort Supply, 224–25, 246, 269
Foster, Robert D., 93–94, 179
Fox, John D., 214
Fullmer, David, 186
Fulmer, Almon, 165, 173

Galland, Isaac, 76, 83
Garden Grove, Iowa, 127
Gardner, Elias, 173
Gardner, Robert, 301
Garr, Abel, 246
Gee, Solomon, 335
Gheen, Aseneth Harmon. *See* Stout, Aseneth Harmon Gheen
Gibbs, Horace, 280
Gillett, Truman, 124
Gilson, H., 326
Gold Rush, 180–81
Grant, George, 72, 121, 179, 245–46
Grant, Jedediah, 179, 198, 249–50, 259
Grant, Ulysses S., 325, 332
Greely, Horace, 280
Green, Moroni, 234–36, 257
Green Addison, 60
Greene, John, 95
Green River Mission, 218–19, 223–26
Groves, Elisha, 169–70
Grow, Almerin, 238
Gunnison, John W., 231
Guthrie, John, 129

Haight, Isaac, 250, 310
Hall, Job, 128
Hall, William, 111
Hambleton, Madison, 183–84, 187, 272
Hamblin, Jacob, 309
Hampton, Brigham Young, 332
Hancock, Mosiah, 109
Hanks, Ephraim, 245–47
Hannum, Ashael, 41
Harmon, Appleton, 161
Harmon, Elmeda, 168
Harmon, J.P., 106
Harney, William S., 265, 267, 269
Harper, Charles A., 339
Harris, Broughton D., 184, 186
Harris, Moses, 306
Hartley, Jesse, 225
Harvey, Eli, 23, 30–32, 150, 184
Harvey, Jesse, 31–32
Hatch, Abram, 337
Haun, Catherine, 168
Hawk, Nathan, 180
Hawkins, Thomas, 326, 329
Hawley, Benjamin, 226
Hawn's Mill Massacre, 61–62, 64, 71
Hempstead, Charles, 316, 318, 325–26
Hendricks, Thomas A., 251, 253
Herring, George, 142
Herring, Joseph, 142–43

Heywood, Joseph L., 184, 229, 237, 304
Hibbard, William, 116, 155
Hickman, William (Bill), 224–26, 233, 239, 293–94, 336; implicates Daniel Wells, Joseph Young, and H.S. in Yates murder, 326–29; Jesse Hartley murder, 225; Yates murder, 267
Higbee, Elias, 60
Higbee, John, 310
Hill, Alexander, 301
Hill, C.H., 334
Hill, Isaac, 157–58
Hillyer, Curtis J., 331, 333
Hinkle, George, 47, 59–60, 64
Hittle, Jonas, 38
Hoagland, Abraham, 92, 169–70
Hodges, Ervine, 63, 110–11
Hodges, Stephen, 110–11
Hodges, William, 110–11
Holland, William, 40
Holman, Joseph, 230
Homes, John, 339
Hong Kong, 206–9, 211, 213, 340
Hooper, William, 259, 338
Hornaday, Ezekiel, 31
Horner, John, 202
Hously, John, 189
Howell, Benjamin, 22–23, 30
Hunter, Jesse, 116, 128
Huntington, Lott, 294
Huntington, Oliver, 57, 166
Huntington, William, 111
Hurt, Garland, 235
Hyde, John, 280
Hyde, Orson, 115–16, 124, 141, 145, 157, 224–25, 230, 296, 311

Isom, George, 307
Ivie, James, 214

Jan Van Hoorn, 203, 205
Jasper, Thomas, 87
Johnson, Archibald, 38–39
Johnson, Benjamin, 77, 177
Johnson, Lyman, 56–57
Johnson, Neil, 38
Johnston, Albert Sidney, 269–70, 272, 274–75, 280, 286–87, 294–95
Jones, Benjamin, 42, 50, 52, 60, 65–66, 72, 84, 88, 127, 344, 351; baptized a Mormon, 48; divorced Anna Stout, 219; joint business with Hosea Stout, 51; married Anna Stout, 47
Jones, Daniel, 246

Jones, David Hadlock, 344, 351
Jones, John, 315
Jones, Nathaniel, 199, 265–67, 328
Jones, Sarah Cox. *See* Stout, Sarah Cox Jones

Kane, Thomas, 271–72
Kay, John, 249, 284, 310, 314
Kay, Nellie, 314
Kearnes, Hamilton H., 289
Kearns, Hamilton, 286
Kearny, Stephen W., 136
Keel, Alexander, 214
Kelsey, Eli, 198
Kelting, Joseph, 232
Kimball, Heber C., 108, 116, 123–24, 161, 163–65, 168, 177, 183, 246, 251, 255, 311, 329
Kimball, William, 245–47, 267, 329–30, 332
King, Austin, 65, 71,74
King, Thomas, 87
Kingdom of God, 114, 158, 176–77, 180, 191, 204, 314, 325, 344–45
Kinney, John, 228–29, 234–37, 258
Kirtland Safety Anti-banking Company, 56
Klingensmith, Philip, 310
Knight, Joseph, 56, 357
Knight, Phoebe Crosby Peck, 55, 347

Larkey, John, 72
Las Vegas, 199
Law, Jane, 93
Law, William, 90, 93–94
Law, Wilson, 93–94, 179
Lee, Ann, 8–9
Lee, John D., 79, 123–24, 130, 137, 145, 165, 175, 177, 306, 310–11
Leonard, Bradford, 236, 280–81, 345
Lewis, James, 189, 197, 199, 203, 206–7, 211, 214–15, 306
Liesi, Henry, 110
Lincoln, Abraham, x, 41, 88, 304, 307
Lish, Peter, 178
Little, Jessee C., 135, 252, 260, 282–83
Lockhart, John, 60
Long, John, 284
Loomis, Washington, 183
Lord Malmesbury, 280
Lord Napier, 280
Lord Palmerston (Henry John Temple), 205
Lott, Cornelius, 144
Lucas, General Samuel, 62, 64
Lunt, Henry, 304

Lyman, Amasa, 64, 199–200, 310
Lyman, Eliza Maria Partridge, 124
Lytle, Andrew, 179
Lytle, John, 158

Major, William, 92, 169
Manning, Peter, 130
Markham, Stephen, 94–95, 108, 113, 136
Marshall, James, 180
Marshall, Samuel, 111
Martin, Edward, 245
Martin Handcart Company, 245–47, 249, 265
Mason, Charles, 111
Mayer, Jane, 280
McArthur, Daniel D., 244
McBride, Squire Thomas, 62
McCabe, James, 183
McClellin, William, 56
McClure, Robert, 40
McCulloch, Ben, 273
McCurdy, Solomon, 316
McDonald, A.C., 286, 289
McDonald, D., 332
McDonald, Randolph, 60
McKean, James B., 325–26, 329, 330, 331–32, 333–34
McKenzie, David, 290–92
McLeod, Norman, 314
McMurdy, Samuel, 310
McRae, Alexander, 65, 76, 237, 252
Michaux, Francois-Andre, 8
Miller, D.F., 111
Miller, George, 3–4, 106, 122–23, 125
Miller, Henry W., 143
Miller, John, 110
Miller, Reuben, 301
Miller, William, 121
Millikan, Elihu, 24
Miner, Aurelius, 233, 282, 307–8, 318
Mitchel, R.B., 145
Mogo, Charles, 259
Monroe, James, 186–87
Moody, J.M., 304
Morley, Isaac, 45–46, 140, 169
Mormon Battalion, 136, 180
Mormon Reformation, 249–51, 255, 284–85
Morris, Elias, 310
Morris, Isaiah, 24–25, 29–30, 32, 150
Morris, John, 310
Mott, John, 227
Mountaineer, The, 292–93
Mount Pisgah, Iowa, 128
Mountain Meadows Massacre, 284, 308–12

Murdock, Hiram, 156
Murdock, John, 46. 52, 59, 347

National Road, 32–33
Nauvoo, Illinois, 76–77, 83, 88, 109
Nauvoo Charter, 85, 94, 100–101, 107–8, 112
Nauvoo Expositor, 94–95
Nauvoo Legion (Illinois), 85–88, 91–94, 96–97, 101, 105–7, 112–14, 136, 154, 183, 186, 340, 349
Nauvoo Legion (Utah), 177–79, 253–54, 266–67, 270–71, 288
Nauvoo Temple, 87, 105
Nebeker, John, 312–13
Nelson, David, 74
Noble, Joseph Bates, 89

O'Banion, Patrick, 60
Old Elk, 144

Pack, John, 162, 175, 177
Parrish, Beatson (Beason), 284–85
Parrish, Orrin, 284–85
Parrish, William R., 284–85
Parrish-Potter murders, 284–87, 289–91, 295, 308
Partridge, Edward, 45–46, 76, 151
Patrick, Matthewson, 325
Patten, Charles W, 156
Patten, David, 60–61
Payton, John L., 230
Pea, John, 72
Peck, Benjamin, 347
Peck, George, 74
Peck, Henrietta, 84
Peck, Phoebe Crosby, 347
Peck, Reed, 61
Pedigrew, David, 173
Perkins, Andrew, 113
Perkins, William, 165
Perpetual Emigrating Fund, 232, 243–44
Phelps, Henry, 156
Phelps, Morris, 37–38, 45–47, 52
Phelps, William W., 57, 91–92, 156, 226
Pierce, Franklin, 208, 228–29
Pinkham, Nathan, 60
Pleasant Hill Shaker Village, 9–10, 13–14; discipline and punishment at, 11–12
plural marriage, 89–91, 107, 208–9; policy announced publicly, 189
Polidori, Frances, 279
Polk, James K., 135–36
Polydore, Henrietta, 279–80, 290

Polydore, Henry, 280
Polygamy. *See* plural marriage
Porter, Lyman, 38–39
Porter, Robert, 179
Porter, Sanford, 37, 45–47
Potter, Gardner "Duff," 284–85
Powell, Lazarus W., 273
Pratt, Orson, 125, 161, 189, 208–9, 306, 313, 319
Pratt, Parley P., 50, 64
Pulsipher, Charles, 226
Pulsipher, John, 167, 226
Pulsipher, Zera, 165

Quakers, 8, 18–19, 30–32, 34–35

Rau, Henry, 230
Rauscher, August, 339
Redden, Return Jackson, 111
Redding, Jack, 157
Reed, Lazarus H., 229
Rees, Amos, 61
Reynolds, John, 41
Reynolds, William, 62
Rich, Charles C., 37, 46, 50, 52, 73, 76, 84, 100, 112–13, 153; commander in Battle of Crooked River, 60–63; delegate to Michigan, 94; establishes Rich Branch, 55; established San Bernardino, 199–200; falling out with H.S., 128–30; flees Far West with Hosea Stout, 63–66; Nauvoo Legion, 85–86, 90; Nauvoo police, 92
Rich, Minerva, 47
Rich, Sarah Pea, 62–63, 72–73
Rich, Thomas, 52, 65–66, 73, 79, 84
Richards, Franklin D., 231, 233, 244–45, 251
Richards, Phineas, 186
Richards, Samuel, 231, 233
Richards, Willard, 95–99, 108, 113, 123, 143, 163–64. 177
Rigdon, Sidney, 56, 58, 65, 74, 99, 151, 153
Rio Virgin, 199, 215
Robb, Squire, 35
Roberts, B.H., 83
Robinson, George W., 64
Robinson, John King, 314–18, 322, 324
Robinson, Nellie, 318
Rockwell, Orrin Porter, 95, 112
Rockwood, Albert, 60, 71–72, 86, 250–51
Rose of Sharon, 210, 212
Rossetti, Christina, 279–80
Rossetti, Dante Gabriel, 279
Rossetti, Gabriele, 279

San Bernardino, California, 199–200, 202, 214–15, 271, 348
Savage, Levi, 245
Savage, Samuel, 31, 150
Schussler, Leonard, 114
Scott, John, 110, 116, 140, 179
Scott, Mary Pugh, 166
Scott, Winfield, 256, 265
Sea Bird, 201–2
Seeley, William, 60
Sessions, Patty, 123
Sessions, Peregrine, 180
Shain, John, 11
Shakers, 7–14, 17–18, 20–21, 26, 47, 53, 149, 150, 343
Sharp, Thomas, 94, 111, 113
Shaver, Leonidas, 229
Sherwood, H.G., 199
Shumway, Charles, 122
Shurtliff, Lyman, 71
Simmons, Joseph M., 246
Sinclair, Charles E., 275, 282–84, 290–91, 293–95, 310
Smith, Alvin, 99
Smith, Charles F., 294
Smith, Charles Maurice, 282
Smith, Elias, 219, 225, 280, 309, 330, 335
Smith, Emma, 95
Smith, George A., 164, 187–88, 193, 211, 237, 252, 284–85, 290, 301, 305, 308–12
Smith, Howard, 93
Smith, Hyrum, x, 46, 49, 54, 62, 64–65, 79, 90–91; murdered, 96
Smith, Joseph F., 339
Smith, Joseph, x, 3–4, 49–50, 52, 64–66; arrested at Far West, 64–65; bank failure in Ohio, 56; beaten, tarred and feathered, 151; escape from Liberty Jail, 74; establishes Nauvoo, Illinois as new gathering place, 75–78; establishing Nauvoo, 83; Lieutenant General in Nauvoo Legion, 85–86; murdered, 96–97; Nauvoo Temple construction, 87; organizes Council of Fifty, 176; organizes Mormon Church, 46; plural marriage, 89–90; presidential candidate, 93–94
Smith, Lot, 266
Smith, Pleasant, 7
Smith, Samuel, 98–99
Smith, Sardius, 62
Smith, William, 99, 111
Smoot, Abraham, 140
Snow, Eliza R., 124–25

Snow, Erastus, 306, 313
Snow, Gardiner, 63
Snow, Lorenzo, 165, 250
Snow, Zerubbabel, 184, 186–87, 229, 236
Sparks, Quartus S.,202
Spencer, C.N., 246
Spencer, Daniel, 107, 113, 177
Steptoe, Edward, 229
Stevenson, Edward, 339
Stiles, George P., 228–29, 234–36, 251–53, 255, 257–58, 260, 272, 282–83
Stillman, Isaiah, 41
Stout, Ada, 351
Stout, Alfred Lozene, 228, 343, 350
Stout, Allen Edward, 228, 350
Stout, Allen, 13, 17, 22, 25, 36, 65, 72, 97–98, 127, 156, 193, 216; called to Cotton Mission, 302–4; converted to Mormonism, 52; Danite member, 57–58; Ervine Hodges murder, 110–11; moved to H.S. house to take care of family, 202; ordained an elder, 79; punished by H.S., 20; returns with father to Illinois, 51; takes H.S. family to Harrisburg
Stout, Alvira, 228, 350
Stout, Alvira Wilson, 227, 230, 232–33, 265, 272–73, 284, 305, 335, 343, 348, 350; married H.S., 228
Stout, Amasa, 34
Stout, Anna, 8, 20, 25, 34, 38–39, 217, 272, 343; becomes a Methodist, 35; caring for H.S. family, 228; divorce from Benjamin Jones, 219; H.S. letter to sister, 40; leaves Pleasant Hill, 21; married Benjamin Jones, 41–42, 47
Stout, Anna Smith, 12–13, 18; death from tuberculosis, 22; marriage to Joseph Stout, 7; moves to Tennessee and Kentucky, 8; severely ill, 20–21
Stout, Arthur, 350
Stout, Aseneth Harmon Gheen, 217, 219, 227–28, 349–50
Stout, Brigham Hosea, 228, 265, 343, 350
Stout, Charles, 127
Stout, Charles Stephen, 228, 335, 343, 350
Stout, Cynthia, 9, 15
Stout, Daniel, 8
Stout, David, 36
Stout, Edgar Walter, 228, 343, 351
Stout, Eli Harvey, 184, 296, 307, 348
Stout, Elizabeth, 21; death, 22
Stout, Elizabeth Ann, 164, 307, 335, 344, 348
Stout, Ephraim, 18, 33–36

Stout, Hosea: abandoned by family, 25; accused by William Smith as co-conspirator in death of Samuel Smith, 99; admitted to bar, 186; appointed deputy U.S. district attorney, 293; appointed special district attorney for U.S., 230; appointed to Utah House of Representatives, 177–78; appointed U.S. Attorney for Utah by Abraham Lincoln, 304; attorney for Gold Rush emigrants, 181; attorney general for Territory of Utah, 178, 181, 183–84; Battle of Crooked River, 59–61; becomes a Methodist, 35–36; becomes committed to Quaker life, 29–30; birth, 8; birth of son Eli Harvey, 184; birth of son Hosea Jr., 181; birth of son Lewis Wilson, 237; Brigadier General in Nauvoo Legion, 96–97; called to Cotton Mission, 296, 302–4; called to go on mission to China, 189; call for vengeance, 98; captain of company of missionaries, 198–200; captain of "old police," 107–8; captain of police at Winter Quarters, 139–40; city attorney for St. George, 306; clerk of Nauvoo High Council, 84–85; conflict with and contempt for William Clayton, 161–63; conversion to Mormonism, 51–53; crossing the plains, 164–71; dealings with Judge Drummond, 230–36; dealings with Judge John Cradlebaugh, 284–90; death of wife Marinda, 137–38; death of wife Samantha, 79–80; death of son Hosea, 131; death of son Hyrum, 127; debilitated by malaria, 38–39; declined to be captain of guard for pioneer company, 141; declining health, obituary, 339–40; defender of the faith, 345; defense against U.S. Army, 267–70; delegate to Kentucky, 94; destitute, given help by B.Y., 136–37; divorce from Aseneth finalized, 227; elected to legislature, 184–85; Ervine Hodges murder, 110–11; estate, 343; expedition to rescue Joseph Smith, 87–88; falling out with Charles C. Rich, 128–30; flees Far West with Charles C. Rich, 62–64; gains education, tries to form school, 40–41; goes into hiding, 114–15; Green River Mission, 224–27; in Hong Kong, 206–12; *Hosea Stout v. People of the U.S.*, 331–32; illness, made captain of guard, 126–27; in charge of early exodus from Nauvoo, 121–24; introduction to Mormonism, 41–42, 45–48; jesting threats against George Miller, 3–4; Judge Advocate of Nauvoo Legion, 179; 253–54; keeping the peace in Nauvoo, 112–14; learns of death of wife Louisa, 213–15; learns of plural marriage, 90; learns reward of physical force, 24–25; lectures police on liquor usage, 114; life at Pleasant Hill Shaker Village, 9–14; marries and divorces Aseneth Gheen, 217–19; marries Louisa Taylor, 84; marries Samantha Peck, 55–56; marries Sarah Cox Jones, 319; mayhem in Judge Stiles' court, 252–53, 257–58; meets Zion's Camp Mormons, 49–50; mission blessing from Wilford Woodruff, 190–92; moves to Illinois, 32–34; moves to Lee County, Iowa, 77–78; myriad duties in Nauvoo, 105–6; Nauvoo Legion in Utah formed, 177; Nauvoo police, 92–93; no investigation of Mountain Meadows Massacre, 308–12; non-functioning U.S. Attorney, 307–8; officer in Nauvoo Legion, 85–86, 90–91; ordained an elder, 78–79; plural marriages to Lucretia Fisher and Marinda Bennett, 106–7; possible mission to England, 115–16; practices revenge on younger brother Allen, 20; prepares to defend Nauvoo, 95; promoted to police captain, 100; publishes *The Mountaineer* with S. Blair and J. Ferguson, 292–93; punishment from father, 19; rebuttal in Robinson murder case, 317–18; relations with Native Americans, 142–45; representative in Utah legislature at age 72, 326–27; rescuing Martin Handcart Company, 246–49; response to Cullom Bill, 319; return to Salt Lake City, 215; return voyage to San Francisco, 212–13; reunion with family, 17–18; reunion with wife Samantha, 73; reverses attitude towards Shakers, 17–18; Richard Yates murder, 267; seeks redress for property loss in Missouri, 75; sent to live with and work for others, 22–24; skirmish with Indians, 175–76; Speaker of the House, 250–51; temper, 280–82; violence in guarding the temple, 116–17; violent nature, 149–59; voyage to China, 203–5; voyage to San Francisco, 200–202; Yates murder case, 328–31
Stout, Hosea Jr., 181, 296, 307, 348
Stout, Hyrum, 115, 348–49, death, 127
Stout, Isaac, 18–19, 29

378   Index

Stout, Isaac Jr., 19, 30
Stout, Isaiah, 19
Stout, Jesse, 30,35
Stout, John, 19, 34
Stout, Joseph, 17, 21–24, 72; dies of consumption, 77; disperses family, 29; marriage to Anna Smith, 7; moves family to Ohio, 18; moves family while abandoning Hosea, 25; moves to Tennessee and Kentucky, 8; removes son Hosea from Pleasant Hill, 13–14; returns with son Allen to Illinois, 51; strict with son Hosea, 19–20
Stout, Joseph Allen, 202, 348
Stout, Lewis Wilson, 228, 237, 250
Stout, Louisa (H.S. daughter), 126, 348, death, 156
Stout, Louisa Taylor, 106–7, 122, 169; death, 202; gave birth to daughter Louisa, 125–126; H.S. learns of her death, 213–14; married H.S., 84
Stout, Lucretia Fisher, 106–7, 156, 348
Stout, Lydia, 21–22, 25, 36, 39, 41, 51–52; married John Larkey, 72
Stout, Lydia Sarah (H.S. daughter), 115, 348
Stout, Margaret, 8–9, 21, 32–34; death, 35
Stout, Marinda Bennett, 106, 130, 156, 346; death, 137–38
Stout, Mary, 8–9, 25; death, 31; leaves Pleasant Hill, 21
Stout, Mathew, 34
Stout, Peter, 7
Stout, Rachel, 7, 89
Stout, Rachel (Ephraim Stout's mother), 34
Stout, Rebecca, 8, 89; joins Shakers, 9
Stout, Samantha Peck, 61–63, 72–73, 77, 153; died at age eighteen, 79; marries Hosea Stout, 55–56
Stout, Samuel (H.S. brother), 8
Stout, Samuel (H.S. grandfather), 7, 89
Stout, Samuel (H.S. uncle), 34
Stout, Sarah, 8, 36; dies of consumption, 77; first pauper of Tazewell County, Illinois, 49; leaves Shakers, 13
Stout, Sarah Cox Jones, 319, 335, 339, 344, 351
Stout, Stephen, 32–33
Stout, William (Bill), 21
Stout, William (cousin), 200
Stout, William Hooper, 228, 343, 350
Stout, William Hosea, 115, 348–49; death, 131
Stout's Grove, 33–35, 39–41, 48

Strawn, John, 41
Stringham, Bryant, 265
Strode, J.M., 157
Sutter's Mill, 180

Tanner, Nathan, 234
Tarwater, Samuel, 61
Taylor, Allen, 84, 122, 164–69, 218, 249–50
Taylor, Elizabeth, 182, 202, 216–17, 347
Taylor, Hawkins, 4, 109
Taylor, John, 96, 98, 105, 110, 113, 124, 140–41, 144, 179, 259, 339
Taylor, Joseph, 182, 184, 190, 218, 267, 343
Taylor, Levi, 190
Taylor, Pleasant Green, 99, 127, 182
Taylor, William, 128, 190, 339
Taylor, William Warren, 347
Thomas, Elisha, 9
Thompson, Jacob, 237
Thoreson, J.C., 337
Titus, John, 314–16, 318
Tracy, Albert, 274
Troskolawski, Joseph, 237
Tufts, Elbridge, 111

Valley Tan, 283, 292–93, 310
Van Buren, Martin, 75, 93, 106, 109
Vance, John, 304
Van Cott, John, 246–47
Van Vliet, Stewart, 265–66
Vasquez, Louis, 223
Vaughn, John, 183, 187

Walkara, 214
Walker, Charles Lowell, 274
Walker, Felix, 8
Walker, William H., 339
Walker War, 214–15, 223
Wall, William, 235
Watson, James, 35
Weatherby, Jacob, 145
Webster, John, 273
Weeks, Allen, 106, 114
Weller, John B., 316–18
Wells, Daniel H., 178–79, 190, 193, 253, 259, 266–69, 273, 288, 309, 313, 315, 326–27, 329–31
Wheelock, Cyrus, 245
Whistling and Whittling Brigade, 108–9
White, David N., 83
White, Hugh, 83
Whitehouse, Isaac, 232
Whitmer, David, 56–57
Whitmer, John, 56–57

Wight, Lyman, 46, 49–50, 52, 55, 59, 64–65, 74, 152
Wiliams, George H., 334
Williams, Alexander, 176
Williams, Levi, 112
Williams, Thomas S., 236, 251, 293
Williams, Wily C., 61
Willie, James, 245
Willie Handcart Company, 245–47, 265
Wilson, Alexander, 282, 286, 291, 293, 295, 309–10
Wilson, Alvira. *See* Stout, Alvira Wilson
Wilson, Lewis Dunbar, 107, 228, 350
Winchester, Stephen, 85
Winter Quarters, 135, 138–39
Wixom, Nathan, 48
Woodruff, Wilford, 130, 142, 190, 211
Woolley, Edwin, 258
Worrell, Franklin, 112

Yates, Richard, 267–68, 327–30, 334, 345
Young Elk, 144
Young, Brigham, x, 3–4, 62–63, 66, 108, 123, 140, 173–74, 180, 182, 223, 229, 269, 291; accused of counterfeiting in Nauvoo 121; appeared to some transfigured as Joseph Smith, 99–100; appointed governor, 184; arrested, 326; authorizes Mormon Battalion, 136; chastises H.S. and police, 158–59; decision to leave Nauvoo, 113–14; 1848 pioneer companies, 165–71; First Presidency organized, 163–64; gave sermon at funeral of Louisa Stout, 202; handcart company rescue, 244–45; in Judge Sinclair's court, 283; Mountain Meadows Massacre, 309; "Move South," 272–73; never again hold back H.S., 92; presidential pardon, 274; proposed sending H.S. on mission to England, 115–16; railed against judges and legal system, 235–36; rebuke of lawyers, 187, 197; reorganized camp in Iowa, 125–26; replaced as governor, 255–56; resists U.S. Army incursion, 266; "Sebastopol policy," 270; Yates murder case, 328–31
Young, John, 250
Young, Joseph (B.Y. brother), 164, 245–46
Young, Joseph (B.Y. son), 249
Young, Lorenzo, 62–64
Young, Phineas, 63–64

Zane, Charles S., 338
Zion's Camp, 49–50, 152

www.ingramcontent.com/pod-product-compliance
Lightning Source LLC
Chambersburg PA
CBHW070125080526
44586CB00015B/1562